Praise for *Social Media Marketing: The Next Generation of Business Engagement*

"*Social media has become a primary tool for higher levels of fan engagement, directly driving lead generation through interaction and content sharing that is especially relevant to media companies.* Social Media Marketing: The Next Generation of Business Engagement *deconstructs the tools and techniques, showing you how to apply social technology to your business.*"
— JOHNI FISHER, CEO, Looppa, Buenos Aires

"*Innovation is not a one-way street where you walk alone! Take your customers on the journey, and see the difference. Social technologies, clearly explained in Dave's book, enable you and your customers to work as a team.*"
— KAUSHAL SARDA, Founder, Uhuroo, Bangalore

"*Rigorous, measurable quality improvement is critical for getting social media and word-of-mouth working for your business. Dave's book highlights quality programs that work, and shows you how to implement them in your business.*"
— JEFF TURK, CEO, Formaspace, Austin, TX

"*What's so appealing about social media is its power to reach not just one consumer at a time, but a huge network of friends through the open graph. Businesses must learn to do this or risk losing their connection with consumers altogether.* Social Media Marketing: The Next Generation of Business Engagement *shows you how.*"
— ROGER KATZ, CEO, Friend2Friend, Palo Alto, CA, and Barcelona

"*Dave provides a practical approach for leaders who want to harness the power of social media to cost-effectively transform their business and catapult themselves ahead of the competition. At the same time,* Social Media Marketing: The Next Generation of Business Engagement *is extraordinary because it is a fun, genuine, and inspiring resource that sets a new standard for social media insights.*"
— IAN GILES, Vice President, Strategic Services, Thindata 1:1, Toronto

"*Dave takes social media from concepts and theory to concrete, simple steps that make it easy to implement social technology in your business.*"
— MARCO RONCAGLIO, Director of Online Marketing, Personal Care, Philips Consumer Lifestyle, Amsterdam

"*Purchase decisions are now influenced by complex networks of friends, family, and peers. The new market winners will be the companies that excel at identifying and engaging with their customers' influencers across the Social Web.*"
— PAUL MAY, Founder and CEO, BuzzStream, Austin, TX

Social Media Marketing

The Next Generation of Business Engagement

Dave Evans

with Jake McKee

Wiley Publishing, Inc.

Senior Acquisitions Editor: WILLEM KNIBBE
Development Editor: HILARY POWERS
Technical Editor: JAKE McKEE
Production Editor: DASSI ZEIDEL
Copy Editor: KATHY GRIDER-CARLYLE
Editorial Manager: PETE GAUGHAN
Production Manager: TIM TATE
Vice President and Executive Group Publisher: RICHARD SWADLEY
Vice President and Publisher: NEIL EDDE
Book Designer: FRANZ BAUMHACKL
Compositor: MAUREEN FORYS, HAPPENSTANCE TYPE-O-RAMA
Proofreader: JOSH CHASE, WORD ONE NEW YORK
Indexer: ROBERT SWANSON
Project Coordinator, Cover: LYNSEY STANFORD
Cover Designer: RYAN SNEED
Cover Image: © IMAGE SOURCE / GettyImages

Dear Reader,

Thank you for choosing *Social Media Marketing: The Next Generation of Business Engagement*. This book is part of a family of premium-quality Sybex books, all of which are written by outstanding authors who combine practical experience with a gift for teaching.

Sybex was founded in 1976. More than 30 years later, we're still committed to producing consistently exceptional books. With each of our titles, we're working hard to set a new standard for the industry. From the paper we print on, to the authors we work with, our goal is to bring you the best books available.

I hope you see all that reflected in these pages. I'd be very interested to hear your comments and get your feedback on how we're doing. Feel free to let me know what you think about this or any other Sybex book by sending me an email at nedde@wiley.com. If you think you've found a technical error in this book, please visit http://sybex.custhelp.com. Customer feedback is critical to our efforts at Sybex.

Best regards,

Neil Edde
Vice President and Publisher
Sybex, an Imprint of Wiley

For my family and friends, and the business executives and organizational leaders I've had the pleasure to work with. I've learned from all of you. Thank you.

Acknowledgments

This book is, first and foremost, an acknowledgement to the collective contributions of professionals, business executives, organizational leaders and an entire "social media" industry that has dedicated itself to delivering on the opportunities that the Social Web offers: the opportunity to understand, first-hand, what markets are saying, the opportunity to identify specific influencers and to quantify the impact that social media has as a result on markets and the businesses and organizations that serve them, and the opportunity to learn faster, to adapt more quickly, and to build and bring to market the next generation of globally acceptable, sustainable goods and services.

Following the founding principles of the Web, I've built on shared knowledge: There is barely a page that is 100 percent "mine." Instead, this book is my point of view and my insights—shaped by my experiences largely in business—in the context of a growing, collective body of knowledge that is itself available to all via the Social Web. For the professionals whose names appear inside I am indebted: It is my hope that I have likewise contributed.

In particular, I'd like to acknowledge Starbucks and Dell, both of whom I am passionate about and whose products I buy. Their work in redefining their own business processes—driven by marketplace realities that emerged through the Social Web—which they have then shared openly so that others may benefit stands as testament to what can be accomplished when customers and their points-of-view and willingness to collaborate toward the betterment of the brands they love are fully recognized. As well, an acknowledgement to my friends at SAS Institute, Lithium Technologies, Alterian, and each of the professional services and consulting firms I often work with.

On that note, a special acknowledgement for the people I have had the pleasure of working with around the world: For Sunil Agarwal, Gaurav Mishra and my colleagues at 2020Media and 2020Social in New Delhi and across India, for the experiences gained with Austin's Z3 Partners, FG SQUARED and Social Web Strategies, Marco Roncaglio and the Philips' Consumer Business Units in Amsterdam, John Fisher and the Looppa team in Buenos Aires, Ian Giles and Thindata in Toronto, and Clara Nelson with the American Marketing Association my sincere appreciation: You have shaped my understanding of social media as it applies to business and cause-related marketing on a global scale. And of course, Austin, Texas—to Jim Butler, Gary Kissiah, John Harms, Hugh Forrest and the staff of SXSW Interactive, and to Hal Josephson and San Francisco's Multimedia Development Group, who inspired me in 1994 to have Austin declared—by charter—as friendly to the emerging Internet technologies that would come to define both cites.

For the book itself, I'd like to acknowledge technical editor Jake McKee and the team at Ant's Eye View for their effort in reviewing, correcting, suggesting and extending my initial drafts, and Susan Bratton, who upon return from Africa provided the Foreword along with a lot of inspiration and industry connections— starting in 2003— through ad:tech. As well, to Hilary Powers, an outstanding developmental editor who agreed to work with me a second time! Finally, to the entire team at Wiley | Sybex: Willem Knibbe, Pete Gaughan, Liz Britten and Dassi Zeidel, and Connor O'Brien. I am thankful and appreciative for each of you.

Social technology has been, for me, a truly collaborative learning experience. As you read this book you'll find dozens of references to the people who are helping to take the founding concepts of the Web and bring them to strategically sound, quantitatively expressed tactical implementations that create genuine, long-term competitive advantage. Take the time to explore their work and their points of view as you strengthen your own understanding of Web 2.0. For they are the experts: I am simply the narrator.

About the Author

The author of *Social Media Marketing: An Hour a Day* (Wiley, 2008), Dave is involved with the development of products and services that extend social technologies to business. Dave consults with firms and professional services organizations through Digital Voodoo, a consultancy he cofounded in 1994. Dave is currently working with Social Dynamx, a technology firm based in Austin that is focused on the development of tools to measure the value of social media and quantitatively tie insights from the Social Web to what actually drives business.

Dave has extensive social media marketing and advertising experience, having worked with public relations agency 2020 Social and its clients including the Bengaluru International Airport, Pepsi, Dell, United Brands and Intel in India, with Social Web Strategies and Philips in The Netherlands, and advertising agency GSD&M | Ideacity in Austin, Texas, and its clients including Southwest Airlines, AARP, Walmart, and the PGA TOUR. Dave served as well as a Product Manager with Progressive Insurance, and as a Telecom Systems Analyst on the console in Mission Control with NASA/JPL for the Voyager I and II deep space programs.

Dave holds a B.S. in physics and mathematics from the State University of New York/ College at Brockport and has served on the Advisory Board with ad:tech and the Measurement and Metrics Council with WOMMA.

You can connect with Dave on Twitter (@evansdave) and follow his business blog at ReadThis.com.

Contents

Chapter 6   Social Analytics, Metrics, and Measurement   139

Chapter 7   Five Essential Tips   165

Foreword

My phone rings on a sunny January morning.

A friendly voice—the chief content officer from ad:tech, the world's largest digital marketing conference, has an offer I can't refuse.

He asks me to run a Marketing Masters double session at the next event to review the state of the industry for social technologies, all current trends and data, and to present case studies and best practices from smart brands—all in *two hours*.

I say, "Sure!" (I know I have an ace in my pocket.)

The ace in my pocket is Dave Evans.

Dave has a "catalogic" perspective of social media. *Catalogic* is a word I've made up to describe Dave. He's that unique. Catalog + Logic = Dave Evans. He has indexed and organized social technologies and strategic approaches. He has dissected exactly how to measure this world, from ROI to KPIs to quantifying the Intangible Value of social marketing. His experience working with brands and at an enterprise level to integrate social strategies results in straightforward, no-fluff processes you can use to get your social business plans confidently organized.

With the help of speakers from Toyota, Levi's, and New Belgium Brewing, and especially from Dave, we satisfied the hundreds of eager social strategy seekers in the audience at ad:tech that day.

Think about this social networking phenomenon as a big, black stallion that used to be owned by marketing. Now it's kicked down the fence—and HR, Ops, Customer Care, and the CEO are out there in the field, all trying to get Social Stallion back in the marketing paddock.

Social Stallion ain't gonna go back: Instead it's taking over your entire business.

The Internet and search engines have fundamentally altered biz ops, and now social networking is the next gale force to blow us forward. As football moms in Australia and tribal chiefs in Tanzania get on Facebook, or one of hundreds of thousands of other niche social networks, and bring their opinions and their contacts with them, the way we connect with customers hits a whole new dimension of complexity, yes, but more importantly, opportunity.

Social media marketing seeks to engage customers where they naturally spend their time. As Dave says in this book, "Social business picks up on what customers are talking about and connects this back into business where it can be processed to create the next round of customer experiences and hence, the next round of customer conversations."

Yet social business goes beyond listening to your socially distributed customer feedback loop that's spread across Twitter, a zillion blog posts and social network profiles. There's a larger change afoot, the concept of applying social technologies to your *whole business*.

No more sweeping consumer's problems under the rug in your Customer Care department—active social listening, understanding consumer sentiment, and having a social policy are baseline smart business practices in the twenty-first century. This book will teach you how to create internal applications with social technologies so you can transform customer insights (and complaints) into useful ideas and practical business processes.

That's "social business."

Suddenly, by using social platforms internally, Ops, HR, Customer Care, the CEO, and Product Development are networking cross-organizationally, and vendors and customers are an integral part of your business conversations. Now business decisions take into account customer intelligence to generate customer-driven and collaboratively designed products that are simply more successful and profitable.

This book will reveal to you the tools, platforms, and technologies to operationalize and capture collaborative activities. That's the whole notion of social business. Simply put, use social platforms internally and with vendors and customers to listen, collaborate, and then measure the effectiveness for growing revenue, cutting costs, or both.

Dave says, "The Social Web is, in a sense, the great equalizer between large brands with big budgets and small brands that simply "do it better." No matter what your size, social business tools are affordable and mandatory to stay competitive in today's global market.

You are the Social Stallion, kicking down the walls in your organization, the walls between you and your vendors, the walls separating you from your customers. It's time to do the internal schmoozing and get the buy-in to rework the very way you do business. It's up to you. You have chosen to read this book. You have nominated yourself to be the social business vanguard. It's an imperative.

There's bigger work to be done here. It's not just about kicking down the walls around our own organizations, it's about creating social technologies that unite business and people to light the way for the challenges ahead of us.

We must become skillful with these social platforms so we can leverage our collective global input, to create better solutions for humanity. People need access to information, water, medicine, and sources of income. Camfed, oDesk, Kiva.org, and Care2 are philanthropic organizations making tremendous headway because of their use of social business technologies. Make your business a social business, and then apply your talent and experience to humanitarianism.

Start to work on things that matter.

Ring…Ring…

It's for you.

It's Social Stallion saying, "Let's go kick down a few walls."

—SUSAN BRATTON
  CEO, Personal Life Media, Inc.

Introduction

"If you have questions, go to the store. Your customers have the answers."

SAM WALTON, founder, Walmart

The challenges facing global businesses and the people who lead them are now, more than ever, intertwined in the direct empowerment and involvement of customers and stakeholders. The World Wide Web— described by Sir Tim Berners-Lee as "an interactive sea of shared knowledge…made of the things we and our friends have seen, heard, believe or have figured out"—has dramatically accelerated the shift to consumer-driven markets. For millennia, power has rested with those resources: first with land, then capital, and most recently, information. In a socially connected marketplace, shared knowledge is now emerging as the ultimate resource. Information wants to be free, and in these new markets it is: free of constraints on place, free of control on content, and free of restrictive access on consumption.

Social technologies, on a mass scale, connect people in ways that facilitate sharing information, thereby reducing the opportunities for marketplace exploitation—whether by charging more than a competing supplier for otherwise identical goods and services or charging anything at all for products that simply don't work. Sunlight is a powerful disinfectant, and the collective knowledge that powers the Social Web is the sunlight that shines in these new connected marketplaces. The Social Web dramatically levels the playing field by making information plentiful, just as it also levels businesses and organizations that operate on the principles of making information scarce.

The Social Web exposes the good, the bad, and the ugly, simultaneously raising up what works and putting down what doesn't without regard for the interests of any specific party. Web 2.0 technologies—expressed through social CRM, vendor relationship management, collective ideation, customer-driven support forums, and communities where participants engage in all forms of social discourse—act together to equalize the market positions of suppliers, manufacturers, business and organizational leaders, customers and stakeholders. To again quote Sir Tim Berners-Lee, "If misunderstandings are the cause of many of the world's woes, then (we can) work them out in cyberspace. And, having worked them out, we leave for those who follow a trail of our reasoning and assumptions for them to adopt, or correct."

So whether supporting Unilever, P&G, and Nestlé, all working *with* Greenpeace to ensure supplier compliance in the use of sustainable palm oil and thereby reducing environmental damage in no-longer "far away" places like Malaysia, or just making someone's day run a little more smoothly by preventing a coffee stain through a simple innovation like Starbucks' "no splash" stirring stick, the businesses and organizations embracing social technologies are delivering better solutions—developed through direct collaboration with customers and stakeholders—to the world's woes however large or small they may be. Contemporary businesses, cause-based organizations, and governing authorities are increasingly meeting the challenge of "opening up" and *operating with their customers and stakeholders*—often through a similarly empowered and connected workforce—to deliver self-evident value *that gets talked about*. For these entities, their customers, suppliers, and stakeholders are the new source of future innovations and "marketing," and therefore also the drivers of long-term growth and success. This is what social business is all about.

How to Use This Book

This book has three parts: Taking a tip from one of the reviewers of my prior book, I've written this one so that *you don't have to read the whole book!* I recognize that you were already busy *before* you purchased this book, and that the true cost of any social media program—at least at the outset—very much includes the opportunity cost of your time. So, here's how the book works:

Part I: Social Business Fundamentals

At just over 100 pages, Part I will get you up-to-speed quickly on the primary aspects of social technology and how it applies to business. Its four chapters include plenty of examples and references to experts and thought leaders freely accessible via the Web, along with a set of "hands-on" exercises that will provide you with a firm grasp of social technology, applied to business.

Part II: Run a Social Business

Part II takes you deeper into the application of social technology to your business or organization, showing you how business decisions are informed through collaborative software and surrounding processes. Part II provides a starting point for measurement and, like Part I, includes references and pointers that quickly take you further as you develop your specific social business programs and initiatives. Part II concludes with a set of tips and best practices, along with a couple of things not to do—and what to do instead.

Part III: Social Business Building Blocks

Part III takes social technology as it is applied to business down to its basic elements. More abstract than Parts I and II, Part III includes cases and examples that bring the essential core social concepts to life. Engagement and Customer Advocacy, Social CRM, social objects, and the social graph are all covered (and defined) to give a you a solid understanding of the principles of social business and the use of social technology. Each of the five chapters in Part III presents one key concept, in depth and again with hands-on exercises and additional pointers to online references and thought leaders.

Appendices

Appendix A (key definitions), Appendix B (thought leaders and resources), and Appendix C (hands-on exercises) *are applicable to anyone reading this book*. They provide a handy way to quickly locate key terms, find thought leaders, and revisit the hands-on exercises presented at the end of each of the individual chapters.

What This Means

- If you read Part I, you'll understand the basic concepts well enough to participate on a team that is suggesting, planning, or otherwise requesting your involvement in a social business initiative for or within your organization. If that's you, you can stop at the end of Part I. Of course, you may not want to, but then that's your choice.

- If you read Part II, you'll be informed well enough to question or guide a specific implementation of social business practices. If you are a business or organization executive, or a process leader within one that is championing a social business initiative, you should consider reading at least through Part II, and especially "What Not to Do" in Chapter 7.

- If you read Part III, you'll have a solid handle on the underlying concepts along with the resources and pointers to actually plan and implement social technologies. You'll be prepared to actively participate in the design of social-technology-based solutions for your business or organization. If you are responsible for such an implementation, or if you are planning to undertake a project like this yourself, you should read through Part III.

Above all, enjoy this book. Use it as a starting point and reference as you define and specify the way in which your firm or organization will adopt social technologies, and to then use them to *engage* your customers and stakeholders. Social media is the next generation of business engagement.

Social Business Fundamentals

I

Arriving at Bengaluru International Airport in India in June 2009, I found my checked bags on the luggage carousel within seven minutes. Wow! I tweeted that. Leaving Seattle in April 2010 I discovered that I'd mistakenly requested a flight on Wednesday, but showed up on Tuesday expecting to fly home to my son's Little League game in Austin that evening. Continental Airlines made it happen, without charge, in less than 30 seconds. Wow! I wrote a blog post about that. This is social business in action: Running your organization in a way that generates the conversations you want. Read on to find out how these businesses did it, and how you can too.

Social Media and Customer Engagement

Given the visible impact of Web 2.0 in market-places around the globe—or more correctly, the marketplace of the globe—social technology is now considered a "given" in business. So many have assumed that social media and a presence on the Social Web are "must haves" that a sort of land rush to build communities and create brand outposts in places like Facebook and Twitter has resulted, too often without fully understanding the long-term organizational impact and the business opportunity that these efforts—done in a systematic manner—actually offer. This chapter tackles the basics of what makes social business work.

1

Chapter Contents

The Social Feedback Cycle

For a lot of organizations—including business, nonprofits, and governmental agencies—use of social media very often begins in Marketing, public communications, or a similar office or department with a direct connection to customers and stakeholders. This makes sense given that a typical driver for getting involved with social media is a slew of negative comments, a need for "virality," or a boost to overall awareness in the marketplace and especially in the minds and hearts of those customers increasingly out of reach of interruptive (aka "traditional") media. In a word, many organizations are looking for "engagement," and they see social media as the way to get it.

The advent of Web 2.0 and the Social Web is clearly a game-changer, on numerous fronts. Given the rush to implement, and the opening focus on marketing specifically versus the business more holistically, many "social media projects" end up being treated more like traditional marketing campaigns than the truly revolutionary ways in which a savvy business can now connect with and prosper through collaborative association with its customers. As a result, the very objective—engagement, redefined in a larger social context—is missed as too many "social media campaigns" run their course and then fizzle out.

Whether that's right or wrong is another matter, and the truth is that a lot of great ideas have given rise to innovative, effective, and measurable social business programs. But these are still the exceptions, which is unfortunate as social technology is within the reach of nearly everyone. The collaborative technologies that now define contemporary marketplaces—technologies commonly called "social media," the "Social Web," or "Web 2.0"—offer a viable approach to driving changes in deeper business processes across a wide range of applications. There is something here for most organizations, something that extends very much beyond marketing and communications.

This chapter, beginning with the Social Feedback Cycle, provides the link between the basics of social media marketing and the larger idea of social technologies applied at a "whole-business" level. As a sort of simple, early definition, you can think of this deeper, customer-driven connection between operations and marketing as "social business."

Beginning with the emergence of Web 2.0 technologies—the set of tools that make it easy for people to create and publish content, to share ideas, to vote on them, and to recommend things to others—the well-established norms of business marketing have been undergoing a forced change. No longer satisfied with advertising and promotional information as a sole source for learning about new products and services, consumers have taken to the Social Web in an effort to share among themselves their own direct experiences with brands, products, and services to provide a more "real" view of their research experience. At the same time, consumers are leveraging the experiences of others, *before* they actually make a purchase themselves. The impact on marketing has been significant, to say the least.

Figure 1.1 shows the classic purchase funnel, connected to the Social Web through "digital word-of-mouth" (aka social media). This loop—from expectation to trial to rating to sharing the actual experience—is now a part of most every purchase or conversion process. Whether consumer-facing, B2B, for-profit or nonprofit, people are turning to people like themselves for the information they need to make smart choices. These new sources of information are looked to by consumers for guidance alongside traditional media; advertising and traditional communications are still very much a part of the overall marketing mix. The result is a new vetting that is impacting—sometimes positively, sometimes negatively—the efforts of businesses and organizations to grow their markets.

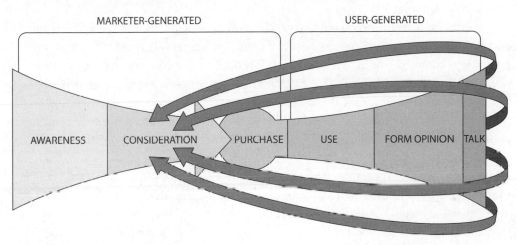

Figure 1.1 The Social Feedback Cycle

Open Access to Information

The Social Feedback Cycle is important to understand because it forms the basis of social business. What the social feedback loop really represents is the way in which Internet-based publishing and social technology has connected people around business or business-like activities. This new social connectivity applies between a business and its customers (B2C), between other businesses (B2B), between customers themselves, as is the case in support communities and similar social applications, and just as well between employees.

As such, this more widespread sharing has exposed information more broadly. Information that previously was available to only a selected or privileged class of individuals is now open to all. Say you wanted information about a hotel or vacation rental property: Unless you were lucky enough to have a friend within your personal social circle with specific knowledge applicable to your planned vacation, you had to consult a travel agent and basically accept whatever it was that you were told. Otherwise, you faced a mountain of work doing research yourself rather than hoping blindly for a good experience in some place you'd never been before. Prior to visible ratings systems—think Yelp.com here—you could "ask around" but that was about it, and "around" generally meant "nearby," friends, family and perhaps colleagues

The travel agent, to continue with this example, may have had only limited domain expertise, lacking a detailed knowledge of rental versus hotel properties, for example. This knowledge, or lack of it, would be critical to properly advising you on a choice between renting a vacation property and booking a hotel. Austin's Homeaway, which brings tens of thousands of rated and reviewed vacation properties within a click of booking, has built an entire business around empowering consumers looking for vacation rentals as an alternative to hotels and resorts, a market that itself only blossomed post–Internet 1.0.

Even more to the point and beyond the issue of specific knowledge, an intermediary in a transaction may or may not have *your* best interests in mind when making purchase recommendations. The same certainly applies to a company or organization wanting to sell you something. This has long been an issue—correctly or incorrectly—that has dogged pharmaceutical and insurance sales: Is the recommendation based on the needs of the customer, the incentive offered by the drug's manufacturer or insurance underwriter, or some combination? From the consumer's perspective, the difference is everything.

At Progressive Insurance, where I worked for a number of years as a Product Manager, we implemented a direct-to-consumer insurance product as an alternative to policies sold through agents. We created this product specifically for customers who wanted to take personal control of their purchases. This made sense from Progressive's business perspective because the degree of trust that a customer has in the sales process is critical to building a long-term *trusted* relationship with its insured customers. While many insurance customers have solid and long-standing relationships with their agents, it is also the case that many are seeking additional information, second opinions, and outright self-empowered alternatives. This reality is now commonplace across a range of businesses, and it is driven by the choice that easily accessible, web-based information brings.

Where information beyond what was provided to you at or around the point of sale was relatively difficult to access only 10 years ago, it is now easy. Look no further than the auto sales process for an indication of just how significant the impact of scalable, connected self-publishing—ratings, blog posts, photo and video uploads—really is. It is this access to information and the opinions and experiences of others, along with the outright creation of new information by consumers who are inclined to rate, review, and publish their own experiences that is driving the impact of social media deeper into the organization.

Social Business: The Logical Extension

Social business follows right on the heels of the wave of interest and activity around social media and its direct application to marketing: Social business is the logical extension of social technology throughout and across the business. Social business takes social concepts—sharing, rating, reviewing, connecting, and collaborating—to *all* parts of the business. From Customer Service to product design to the promotions team, social behaviors and the development of internal knowledge communities that connect people and their ideas can give rise to smoother and more efficient business processes. Social business—viewed in this way—becomes more about change management than marketing. That's a big thought.

Take a step back: Social media marketing—properly practiced—seeks to engage customers in the online social locations where they naturally spend time. By comparison, social business picks up on what they are talking about and what they are interested in and connects this back into the business where it can be processed and used to create the next round of customer experiences and hence the next round of conversations.

It's important to understand the role of the customer—taken here to include anyone "on the other side" of a business transaction: It might be a retail consumer, a business customer, a donor for a nonprofit organization, or a voter in an election. What's common across all of these archetypes—and what matters in the context of social business—is that each of them has access to information, in addition to whatever information you put into the marketplace, that can support or refute the messages you've spent time and money creating.

But, as we say, "Wait. There's more." Beyond the marketing messages, think as well about suggestions for improvements or innovation that may originate with your customers: As a result of an actual experience or interaction with your brand, product, or service, your customers have specific information about your business processes and probably an idea or two on how your business might serve them better in the future.

Consider the following, all of which are typical of the kinds of "outputs" a customer or business partner may have formed after a transaction, and will quietly walk away with unless you take specific steps to collect this information and feedback:

- Ideas for product or service innovation
- Early warning of problems or opportunities
- Awareness aids (testimonials)
- Market expansions (ideas for new product applications)
- Customer service tips that flow from users to users
- Public sentiment around legislative action, or lack of action
- Competitive threats or exposed weaknesses

This list, hardly exhaustive, is typical of the kinds of information that customers have and often share amongst themselves—and would readily share with you if asked. Ironically, this information rarely makes it all the way back to the product and service policy designers where it would do some real good. Importantly, this may be information that you don't have, information that precisely because you are so close to your business you may never see. Collecting this information and systematically applying it is in your best interest.

For example, someone may find that your software product doesn't integrate smoothly with a particular software application that this customer may also have installed. How would you know? This information—and the ensuing pleas for help expressed in online forums—is something you can collect through social analytics (tools and processes). It can then be combined with the experiences of other customers, as well as your own process and domain knowledge, to improve a particular customer experience and then offered generally as a new solution. This new solution could then be shared—through the same community and collaborative technologies—with your wider customer base, raising your firm's relative value to your customers in the process and *strengthening your relationship* with the customers who initially experienced the problem.

The resultant sharing of information—publishing a video, or writing a review—and its use *inside the organization* forms the stepping-off point from social media marketing and social analytics into social business. From a purely marketing perspective—as used here, meaning the MarCom/advertising/PR domain—this shared consumer information can be very helpful in encouraging others to make a similar purchase. It can enlighten a marketer as to which advertising claims are accepted and which are rejected, helping that marketer tune the message. It can also create a bridge to dialog with the customer—think about onsite product reviews or support forums—so that marketers can understand in greater detail what is helping and what is not.

Prior to actually making process changes, this listening and information gathering—treated in depth in Chapter 6, "Social Analytics, Metrics and Measurement"—falls under the heading of "more information" and so drives a need for enhanced social analytics tools to help make sense of it. It's worth pursuing. Access to customer-provided information means your product or service adapts faster. By sharing the resulting improvement and innovations while giving your customers credit, your business gains positive recognition.

Although customers can provide an invaluable source of information, you should be aware of the impact anonymous—and often negative—comments can have. It is imperative to understand the role of your customer as both a recipient and publisher of the content that circulates on the Social Web. Is a specific voice within a conversation that is relevant to you coming from an evangelist, a "neutral," or a detractor? It is important that you know. Is it coming from a competitor or disgruntled ex-employee? The same holds true: You need to know, so that you can plan your response. While the overall trend on the Social Web is away from anonymity and toward identity, it's not a given—at least not yet—that any specific identity has been verified. This means you need to dig deeper.

This persistent anonymity opens the door for "comment and rating abuse," but social media also provides for a general raising of the bar when it comes to establishing actual identity. More and more, people write comments *in the hopes that they will be recognized*. With this growing interest and importance of actual identity, in addition to marketplace knowledge, social business and the analytical tools that help you sort through the identity issues are important to making sense of what is happening around you on the Social Web. Later sections tie the topics of influencer identification and the use of the "social graph," the inner working of the linkages that connect people and the status updates that tell you what they are doing now, into business formally. For now, accept that identity isn't always what it appears, but at the same time the majority of customer comments left are done so for the dual purpose of letting you know what happened—good or bad—and at the same time letting you know that it happened to someone in particular. They signed their name because they want you (as a business) to recognize them.

> *"As people take control over their data while spreading their Web presence, they are not looking for privacy, but for recognition as individuals. This will eventually change the whole world of advertising."*
>
> ESTHER DYSON, 2008

Social Business Is Holistic

When you combine identity, ease of publishing, and the penchant to publish and to use shared information in purchase-related decision-making processes, the larger role of the Social Feedback Cycle and the practice of social business emerges: Larger than the loop that connects sales with marketing—one of the areas considered as part of traditional Customer Relationship Management (CRM)—the Social Feedback Cycle literally wraps the entire business.

Consider an organization like Freescale, a spin-off of Motorola. Freescale uses YouTube for a variety of sanctioned purposes, including as a place for current employees to publish videos about their jobs as engineers: The purpose is the encouragement of prospective employees—given the chance to see "inside Freescale"—to more strongly consider working for Freescale. Or, look at an organization like Coca-Cola: Coke is reducing its dependence on branded microsites in favor of consumer-driven social sites like Facebook for building connections with customers. Coke is also directly tapping customer tastes through its Coca Cola Freestyle vending machines that let consumers mix their own Coke flavors. Comcast and may other firms now use Twitter as a customer-support channel. The list of examples of the direct integration of collaborative and shared publishing applications in business—beyond marketing—is growing rapidly.

I explore all these applications of social technology in business in greater detail in subsequent chapters. For now, the simple question is, "What do all of these applications have in common?" The answer is, *"Each of them has a larger footprint than marketing.*" Each directly involves multiple disciplines within the organization to create an experience that is shared and talked about favorably. These are examples not of social media marketing, but of social business practices.

Importantly, these are also examples of a reversed message flow: The participation and hence marketplace information is coming *from* the consumers and is heading *toward* the business. Traditionally, over mass media it's been the other way around. In each of the previous examples of social business thinking and applications, it is the business that is listening to the customer. What is being learned as a result of this listening and participation is then tapped internally to change, sustain, or improve specific customer experiences. When subsequently tied to business objectives, the practice of social business becomes holistic indeed.

The Connected Customer

The upshot is that the customer is now in a primary role as an innovator, as a source of forward-pointing information around taste and preference, and as such is *potentially* the basis for competitive advantage. I say "potentially" because customers having opinions or ideas and actually getting useful information from them and then using it are two different things. Here again, social business and the related technologies step in: Where social media marketing very often stops at the listening stage, perhaps also responding to directly raised issues in the process, social business takes two added steps.

First, social business practices provide formal, visible, and transparent connections that link customers and the business, and internally link employees to each other and back to customers. This is a central aspect of social business: The "social" in "social business" refers to the development of connections between people, connections that are used to facilitate business, product design, service enhancement, market understanding, and more. Second, because employees are connected and able to collaborate—social business and Web 2.0 technology applies internally just as it does externally—the firm is able to respond to what its customers are saying through the social media channels in an efficient, credible manner.

Before jumping too far, a point about fear: fear of the unknown, the unsaid, the unidentified, and even the uninformed saying bad things about your brand, product, or service that aren't even correct! Fear not, or at least fear less. By engaging, understanding, and participating, you can actually take big steps in bringing some comfort to your team around you that is maybe more than a bit nervous about social media. Jake McKee, a colleague of mine and the technical editor for this book, attended one of Andy Sernovitz's way cool social media events. The group toured an aircraft carrier *while it operated in the Pacific.* One of the things Jake noted was that even though the deck of an active aircraft carrier—considered among the most dangerous workplaces on earth—was to the untrained eye chaotic and therefore scary—it was surprisingly fear-free. Everyone knew their place and everyone watched out for each other (and especially for Andy's tour group). F-18s were launching 100 feet away: Average age of the crew? 19. Fear? Nope. The point is this: You can overcome fear with structure and discipline—on the deck of an active aircraft carrier or in business on the Social Web. Chapter 5, "Social Technology and Business Decisions," Chapter 6, "Social Analytics, Metrics and Measurement," and Chapter 7, "Five Essential Tips When Starting Out," provide insights into the organizational adoption of social technology along with the best practices and essential quick-start tips to put you at ease.

The Social Web and Engagement

This next section provides a conceptual starting point in understanding how the critical activities of engagement and response are enabled through the adoption of social technology and supporting processes. Beware: It's a different viewpoint than that which applies to "engagement" in traditional media. Engagement is redefined by consumers when acting in an open, participative social environment. This is a very different context than the "read-only" setting in which traditional media defines "engagement," so take the time here to understand the four stages of engagement.

Engagement on the Social Web means customers or stakeholders become *participants* rather than viewers. It's the difference between *seeing* a movie and participating in a screening of "The Rocky Horror Picture Show." *The difference is participation.* Engagement, in a social business sense, means your customers are willing to take their time and energy and talk *to you*—as well as *about you*—in conversation and through processes that impact your business. They are willing to participate, and it is this participation that defines engagement in the context of the Social Web.

The engagement process is, therefore, fundamental to successful social marketing and to the establishment of successful social business practices. Engagement in a social context implies that customers have taken a personal interest in what you are bringing to the market. In an expanded sense, this applies to *any* stakeholder and carries the same notion: A personal interest in your business *outcome* has been established. This applies to customers, to partners, to employees, to anyone and everyone who can express and share an opinion or idea somewhere along your path to market.

Consider the purchase funnel shown in Figure 1.1. As customer conversations enter the purchase cycle in the consideration phase of the sales process, there is a larger implication: Your customer is now a part of your marketing department. In fact, your customers and what they think and share with each other form the foundation of your business or organization.

The impact is both subtle and profound: Subtle in the sense that on the surface much of "social business" amounts to running a business the way a business ought to be run. Businesses exist—ultimately—to serve customers through whose patronage the founders, employees, shareholders, and others derive (generally) an economic benefit as they are ensured a future in running that business. At times, however, it seems the customer gets dropped from that set. The result can be seen on Twitter most any day by searching for the hashtag #FAIL.

It's also a profound change, however, in the sense that the stakes in pleasing the customer are now much higher. Customers are more knowledgeable and more vocal about they want, and they are better prepared to let others know about it in cases of over-delivery or under-delivery. On top of that, not only are customers seeing what the business and the industry are doing, they are building their own expectations for *your* business based on what *every other* business they work with is doing. If Walmart can quickly tap Bazaarvoice and put ratings and reviews on any product it sells, the expectation is that American Airlines will prominently place customer ratings on every flight it flies. Think about it: If flight attendants, by flight, were rated according to service and demeanor by past fliers and that information was used to make future flight choices in the same way as on-time performance, how would the flying experience overall change? It happens in restaurants: We all have a favorite waitperson. If this seems a stretch, consider that Southwest, Alaska Airlines, and Continental have all placed emphasis on exactly this service point, and they enjoy higher than average Net Promoter scores partly as a result.

Social business, therefore, is about equipping your entire organization to listen, engage, understand, and respond directly through conversation and by extension in the design of products and services in a manner that not only satisfies customers but also encourages them to share their delight with others. If social media is the vehicle for success, social business is the interstate system on which it rides into your organization.

Share their *delight*? What scares a lot of otherwise willing marketers is the exact opposite: sharing dismay, or worse. The fact is, negative conversations—to the extent they exist, and they do—are happening right now. Your participation doesn't change that. What does change is that those same naysayers have company—you. You can engage, understand, correct factual errors, and apologize as you address and correct the real issues. Watch out for what Paul Rand has labeled "Determined Detractors." See the sidebar "Respond to Social Media Mentions" for a response flow chart. It's simple, and it works. Be confident, Grasshopper.

Respond to Social Media Mentions

Wondering how to handle a negative mention or whether or not to say "Thank You" for a nice compliment? The United States Air Force developed a flow chart that formed the basis of Altimeter's recommended responses in various social media scenarios. You'll find the chart here:

http://www.web-strategist.com/blog/2008/12/31/diagram-how-the-air-force-response-to-blogs

In Chapter 8, "Engagement on the Social Web," and Chapter 9, "Social CRM," I show how the basic principle of incorporating the customer directly into the marketing process extends throughout the product lifecycle. In this opening chapter, I focus only on the supporting concepts and techniques by which you can build these principles—now—into your business processes. For example, encouraging participation in discussion forums, or helping your customers publish *and rate* product or service reviews can help you build business, and it can put in place the best practices you'll need to succeed in the future. Social business includes product design, pricing, options, customer service, warranty, and the renewal/re-subscription process and more. All told, social business is an organization-wide look at the interactions and dependencies between customers and businesses connected by information-rich and very much discoverable conversations.

So what is it that gets talked about, and why does it matter? Simply put, anything that catches a consumer or prospective customer's attention is fair game for conversation. It may happen between three people or three million. This includes expectations exceeded as well as expectations not met, and runs the gamut from what appears to be minutiae ("My bus seems really slow today…") to what is more obviously significant ("My laptop is literally on fire…right now!").

How do these relate to business? The bus company, monitoring Twitter, might tweet back "Which bus are you riding on right now?" and at the least let its rider know that it noticed the issue. At most, it might discover a routing problem and improve its service generally. As for the laptop on fire, if I were the brand manager and it were my product line, I'd want to know about this as soon as possible and by whatever means. That most certainly includes Twitter.

News travels fast, and nowhere does it travel faster than the Social Web. In his 2009 *Wired* article "Twitter-Yahoo Mashup Yields Better Breaking News Search," writer Scott Gilbertson put it this way: "Whenever there's breaking news, savvy web users turn to Twitter for the first hints of what might be going on." What's important in a business context is this: In both the bus schedule and laptop fire examples, the person offering the information is probably carrying a social-technology-capable, Internet-connected mobile phone. It is very likely that Twitter or a similar mobile service *is also this person's first line of communication about any particular product or service experience!* The respective service and brand managers could easily track this using real-time social media analytics tools and thereby become immediate, relevant participants in these conversations. This kind of participation is both welcomed and expected to be present by customers. The great part of all of this is that by connecting, engaging, and participating, as a business manager you tap into a steady stream of useful ideas. See Chapter 12, "Social Applications," for more on idea-generation platforms and their application in business.

The Social Web (aka Web 2.0) revolves around conversations, social interactions, and the formation of groups that in some way advance or act on collective knowledge. Social media analytics is focused on understanding and managing specific attributes of the conversation: sentiment, source, and polarity, for example. Social business takes it a step further and asks "How or why did this conversation arise in the first place?" For example, is the conversation rooted in a warranty process failure? The practice of social business is helpful in determining how to fix it. Is a stream of stand-out comments being driven by a specific, exceptional employee? Social-business-based processes will help your organization create more employees like that one. From the business perspective—and Marketing and Operations are both a part of this—understanding how conversations come to exist and how to tap the information they contain is key to understanding how to leverage the Social Web and to move from "So what?" to "I get it!"

Social business processes and technologies share insights generated by customers, suppliers, partners, or employees through collaborative applications in ways that actually transform a conversation into useful ideas and practical business processes. Social business is built around a composite of technologies, processes, and behaviors that facilitate the spread of experiences (not just facts) and engender collaborative behavior.

An easy way to think about social technology and its application to business is in its conveyance of *meaning* and not just attributes such as "polarity" or "source" or "sentiment," and in what a business can do in response to this information. Social business is built around collaborative processes that link customers to the brand by engaging them as a part of the Product Development Cycle. Consider the social business framework now in place at Dell.

Dell, hit hard by Jeff Jarvis's August 2005 "Dell Hell" reference in his Buzz Machine blog posts, needed to become a brand that listened and engaged with customers, employees, and suppliers across the Web. Dell employees like Bob Pearson, now CEO of The Social Media Business Council and Sean McDonald, now a principal with Ant's Eye View, believes that people spent a lot of time on the Web, but not necessarily on *your* domain buying *your* product. So, the engagement strategy has to begin with going out onto the Web and meeting them on their terms and on their turf. In other words, it's better to fish where the fish are, not where you wish the fish were.

The team at Dell built on the strength it found in its customers: There were 750,000 registered users in the Dell Community at the time, with a good portion "highly engaged." *These customers wanted Dell to participate.* Dell quickly realized that engaged users were stronger contributors and more vocal advocates of the brand. This realization was the breakthrough for the wide range of social media programs that Dell offers today. Dell's programs are built around its customers (not just the brand), and they actively pull customers and their ideas into Dell where Dell employees collaborate and advance the product line, completing the customer-business information cycle.

Social business includes the design of an external engagement process in which participants are systematically brought into the social processes surrounding and supporting the business. This is achieved within the communities frequented by stakeholders through the implementation of the community and associated software services presented throughout this book. These social applications include the internal business processes that link across the organization and connect consumers and employees with the business as a whole and facilitate the process of customer engagement.

The Engagement Process

Engagement is central to the effective use of social technology and the creation of social business. Unlike traditional media and the business processes of selling based on it, social technologies push toward *collaboration* rather than *exposure and impression*. In the first wave of social technology—social media and the rise of personal activities (e.g., friending) that occurred on the Social Web, collaboration between consumers took off as they recognized that by sharing experiences they could (collectively) make better purchase decisions.

In the context of social business, the process of engagement is expanded to include not only the collaborative activity that occurs between customers, but also the activities that connect the business with its customers as well as those that connect the employees inside the business, where this connectivity fosters sharing and collaboration so that employees may more effectively respond to customers' needs. The social engagement process moves customers and similar participants in brand, product, or service-related conversations beyond the act of consumption (reading an article about a product, for example) and toward the shared act of working together (customers alongside employees) to collaborate and produce an experience that improves over time.

Following a methodology practiced at 2020 Social, a firm I am associated with in New Delhi, the upcoming sections present a set of fundamental "social action" building blocks (shown in Figure 1.2) that make it easy to step through the *engagement* process of tapping customer conversations and turning them into useful insights. These insights give rise to a systematic process for moving customers to increasingly engaged states. These foundational blocks lead to and support a ladder-type engagement model with customer collaboration—not simply content consumption—as the end point. As such, they are useful in understanding the various ways in which technologies and strategies can be combined to drive smart tactical, business-building processes in both marketing and operations.

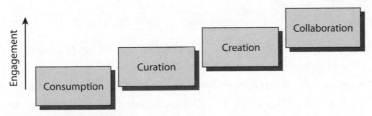

Figure 1.2 Structured Engagement

Consumption

The first of the foundational blocks in the process of building strong customer engagement is *consumption*. Consumption, as used in the context of social media, means downloading, reading, watching, or listening to digital content. Consumption is the basic starting point for nearly any online activity, and especially so for social activities. It's essentially impossible (or at least unwise) to share, for example, without consuming first: habitually retweeting without first reading and determining applicability to your audience, for example, will generally turn out badly.. More practically, if no one reads (or "consumes") a particular piece of content, why would anyone share it? Further, because humans filter information, what we share is only a subset of what we consume. As a result, consumption far outweighs any other process on the Social Web: It's that cliché that holds the majority of the people on the Web are *taking* (consuming) rather than *putting back* (creating). It's often said that the Web makes everyone a publisher: I guess a lot of people are just too busy consuming to create!

You can take a tip from this reality: If you want your audience or your community members to move beyond consumption and into activities like content creation, then short of irritating them (which works, but not in the way you want it to and certainly not in the way that sand in an oyster shell produces a pearl), you've got to encourage them and empower them to create. It's really important to help move participants beyond consumption and into creation: The remaining social action building blocks are keys to getting beyond the "media property/page view" model of monetization of interactive web applications, which really isn't "social" at all.

Interactive Versus Social: What's the Difference?

A simple distinction between interactive and social was drawn by Gaurav Mishra, CEO, 2020 Social: "Interactive websites connect customers with software applications: Social sites connect customers with each other." As an example, compare social listings from CitySearch in the United States or India's Burrp with the more socially connected Eventful. Although all have great listings, the latter offers significantly more opportunity for social interaction between visitors.

You can follow Gaurav on Twitter (@Gauravonomics) and read more from him at his blog:

http://www.gauravonomics.com

The move beyond consumption is an important realization in the development of your social business: Content consumption without a direct consumer/audience role in creation—think TV, radio, print—is an interactive but not necessarily social approach to building a successful business. In a content-driven interactive media site, the content is the draw and the consumption of it is the primary activity. In a social application, the content still matters—no one wants to hang out in a vacuum—but the interactions and conversations that the content enables between members take center stage.

Curation

Curation is the act of sorting and filtering, rating, reviewing, commenting on, tagging, or otherwise describing content. Curation makes content more useful to others. For example, when someone *creates* a book review, the hope is that the review will become the basis for a subsequent purchase decision. However, the review itself is only as good as the person who wrote it, and only as useful as it is relevant to the person reading it. Reviews become truly valuable when they can be placed into the context, interests, and values of the person reading them.

This is what curation enables. By seeing not only the review but also the "reviews of the reviewers" or other information about the person who created the review, the prospective buyer is in a much better position to evaluate the applicability of that review given specific personal interests or needs. Hence, the review is likely to be more useful (even if this means a particular review is rejected) in a specific purchase situation. The result is a better-informed consumer and a better future review for whatever is ultimately purchased, an insight that follows from the fact that better informed consumers make better choices, increasing their own future satisfaction in the process.

Curation also happens more broadly, at a general content level. Curation is an important social action in that it helps shape, prune, and generally increase the signal-to-noise ratio within the community. Note as well that curation happens not only with content, but also between members themselves. Consider a contributor who is rewarded for consistently excellent posts in a support forum through member-driven quality ratings. This is an essential control point for the community and one that all other things being equal is best left to the members themselves: Curation "of the members and by the members," so to speak.

Of note, the process of curation is the first point at which a participant in the social process is actually *creating* something. Consumption, as defined here, is a one directional action: You read, you download, you listen, etc. Consumption, by itself, does not drive social interaction.

Curation is, therefore, a very important action to encourage. *Curation teaches people to participate, to create, in small, low-risk steps that are easy to grasp.* It's a lot like learning to dance: Fear, concern of self-image, and feelings of awkwardness all act as inhibitors of what is generally considered an enjoyable form of self expression and social interaction. Introducing your audience to curation makes it easy for them to become active members of the community and to participate in the later creative and collaborative processes that drive it over the long term. That's how you build a community.

Creation

Beyond curation is what is more generally recognized as "content creation." Unlike curation, a great first step that requires little more than a response to an event—you indicate your like or dislike for a photo, for example—content creation requires that community members actually offer up something that they have made themselves. This is a significantly higher hurdle, so it's something for which you'll want to have a very specific plan. "You can upload your photos!" by itself is generally not enough.

How do you encourage creation? Step 1 is providing tools, support, help, templates, samples, and more. The less work your members have to do the better. Does your application require a file of a specific format, sized within a given range? You can count on a significant drop in participation because of that. When someone has taken a photo on a now-common 6- or 8-megapixel phone camera, stating "uploads are limited to 100 Kbytes is tantamount to "Sorry, we're closed." Instead, build an application that takes *any* photo and then resizes it according to your content needs and technology constraints. Hang a big "All Welcome" sign out and watch your audience create.

When MTV's Argentinean business unit sought to extend its consumer presence in the social spaces, it teamed up with Looppa, a firm I work with in Buenos Aires, to create online communities that encouraged content creation and sharing. Using the content tools, participants created in excess of 300,000 photos and 200,000 comments. Over 30,000 videos were uploaded and shared by members within the community. It is this sort of active content creation that marks the shift from the read-only traditional brand community—come and play our games, read our announcements, and buy our product—to the socially participative Web 2.0 community.

Driving this content creation is a simple underlying theme: People like to share what they are doing, talk (post) about the things that interest them, and generally be recognized for their own contributions within the larger community. Reputation management—a key element in encouraging social interaction—is based directly on the quantity *and quality* of the content created and shared by individual participants. The combination of easy content publishing, curation, and visible reputation management are the cornerstones of a strong community.

Looppa: A Connected Community Platform

Based in Buenos Aires, Looppa provides a set of social technologies that enable the creation of branded social communities built around passions, lifestyles, and causes. You can find out more about Looppa on the Web. (In the interest of full disclosure, I should mention I'm associated with Looppa as a shareholder and an Advisory Board Member.)

http://www.looppa.com

Collaboration

Finally, at the top of the set of the core social-business building blocks is collaboration. Collaboration is a key inflection point in the realization of a vibrant community and the port of entry for true social business. Here's why.

The collective use of ratings aside, consumption, curation, and creation can be largely individual activities. Someone watches a few videos, rates one or two, and then uploads something. That can build traffic, can build a content library (hey, it built YouTube, right?), and can drive page views, all important aspects of a media property. But they aren't necessarily strong *social* actions. Collaboration is.

Collaboration occurs naturally between members of the community when given the chance. Blogging is a good example. Take a look at a typical blog that you subscribe to, and you'll find numerous examples of posts, reinterpreted by readers through comments—that flow off to new conversations between the blogger and the readers. Bloggers often adapt their "product" on-the-fly based on the inputs of the audience.

Blogging and the way in which participant input shapes the actual product is a deceptively simple example of what is actually a difficult process: Taking *direct input* from a customer and *using it* in the design of your product. Many effective bloggers take direction from readers' comments and then build a new thought based on the reader's interests and thoughts. This is actually a window into what social business is all about: Directly involving your customers in the design and delivery of what you make. How so? Read on.

Consider a typical newspaper, online or off. A journalist writes an article, and the subscribers read it. The primary feedback mechanism— Letters to the Editor—may feature selected responses, but that's generally the end of the line. The original journalist may never again come back to these individual responses much less visibly build on them in future stories. Traditional media is "one way."

Now move to a blog or a blog-style online paper, something like the Huffington Post, Pluggd.in, or Mashable. With the online publications of these businesses, audience participation is actually part of the production process. The comments become part of the product and directly build on the overall value of the online media property. The product—news and related editorial and *reader* commentary—is created collaboratively. As news content in particular moves to increasingly capable hand-held and Internet-connected devices like the iPad, news will increasingly find its way back to the living room where it may again be discussed socially—even if in the "online living room"—with the (also digital) social commentary continuing to become an increasingly important part of the content.

Back on the business context, taking collaboration into the internal workings of the organization is at the heart of social business. This is equally applicable to the design of physical products, long-lived (multiyear) services, and customer relationship and maintenance cycles. By connecting customers with employees—connecting parents with packaging designers for kids' toys—your business can literally leapfrog the competition and earn favorable social press in the process.

The Engagement Process and Social Business

Taken together, the combined acts of consumption, curation, creation, and collaboration carry participants in the conversations around your business from readers to talkers to co-creators. Two fundamentally important considerations that are directly applicable to your business or organization come out of this.

First, your audience is more inclined to engage in collaborative activities—sharing thoughts, ideas, concerns—that include you. It may be a "negative" process: your audience may be including you in a conversation whose end-goal is a change in your business process that improves a particular (negative) experience they've had. Or, it may be simply "We love you…here's what else we'd like to see." The actual topics matter less than the fact that your customers are now actively sharing with you their view of the ways in which what you offer affects them. By building in social behaviors and inviting customers into these processes, your business or organization is in a much better position to identify and tap the evangelists that form around your brand, product, or service.

Second, because your customers or other stakeholders have moved from reading to creating and collaborating, they are significantly closer to the steps that follow collaboration as it leads to engagement: trial, purchase, and advocacy. The engagement process provides your customers with the information and experiences needed to become effective advocates, and to carry your message further into their own personal networks.

As examples of the value customers and organizational participants will bring as they gather 'round and talk, consider the following:

- You don't get to the really good results until you go through the necessary venting of people you've previously ignored: Opening up a dialog gives you a natural way to enable venting and healing.

- The way you deal with negative issues is an exhibition of your true character: become a master and reap the rewards.

- It's your job to understand what was really meant, given whatever it was that was actually said. "I hate you" isn't always as simple as it sounds: This kind of seemingly intense negativity may arise because the customer involved *likes you enough* to actually *feel* this way when things go wrong.

- Ultimately, your customers *want* to see you do well: They want your product or service to please them.

Looking ahead at the engagement end goal—advocacy—note that the benefits of advocacy apply beyond the immediate customers involved. Advocates gather around your brand, product, or service to spread their experiences for the purpose of influencing others. For you, it's a double payoff: Not only does it make more likely the creation of advocates through collaborative social applications, but because these and other social applications exist, the advocates that emerge are actually *more able* to spread their stories.

In the end, the engagement process as applied to social business is about connecting your customers and stakeholders with your brand, product, or service, and then tapping their collective knowledge and connecting into your organization to drive innovation and beneficial change. With this linkage in place, the larger social feedback loop is available to you for use in ways that can—and do—lead to long-term competitive advantage.

The Operations and Marketing Connection

So far this chapter has covered two primary topics: The importance of understanding the mechanics of the Social Web and the Social Feedback Cycle, and the *collaborative* inflection-point within the larger *social* engagement process. Engagement has been redefined for social business as a more active (participative) notion compared with the decidedly more passive definition of engagement—reading an ad or mechanically interacting with a microsite—typically applied in traditional media, where terms like "Engagement Ad" literally means "an ad you can click on to see more promo copy." That's not what participants on the Social Web think of as "engaging," as the Social Web is a distinctly participation-centric place.

The final section ties the mechanical processes of the social technologies together with the acts of participation and collaboration, and establishes the foundational role of the *entire business or organization* in setting up for success on the Social Web. The Social Feedback Cycle—the loop that connects the published experiences of current customers or other stakeholders with potential customers or other stakeholders—is powered by the organization and what it produces. This is a very different proposition from a traditional view of marketing where the message is controlled by an agency and the experience is controlled—in isolation—by the product or services teams and others.

Figure 1.3 shows the alignment that needs to occur between what can be loosely be called "Operations" and the Marketing team in support of Customers. Included in "operations" are the functional areas that control product design and manufacturing, customer service and support policies, warranty services and similar. In other words, if Marketing is the discipline or function within an organization that defines and shapes the customer's expectation, then Operations is the combined functional team that shapes and delivers the actual customer experience.

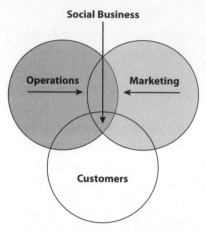

Figure 1.3 The Marketing-Operations Connection

The connection between the disciplines of marketing and operations and social media—and in particular the conversations, ratings, photos, and more that circulate on the Social Web—is this: The majority of conversations that involve a brand, product, or service are those that arise out of a difference between what was expected and what was delivered or experienced. After all, we tend to talk more about what was *not* expected than what was expected. In this simple relationship between expectation and actual experience, the folly of trying to control conversations on the Social Web becomes clear: Conversations on the Social Web are the artifacts of the work product of someone else—a blogger, a customer, a voter, etc.—who typically doesn't report to the organization desiring to gain control! You can't control something that isn't yours to control.

Instead, it is by changing the product design, the service policy or similar in order to align the experience with the expectation or to ensure the replicable delivery of "delight," for example, as Zappos does when it upgrades shipping to "Next Day" for no other reason than to delightfully surprise a customer. At Zappos, it's not just a story of an occasional surprise upgrade that got blown out of proportion in the blogosphere. When bloggers—and customers—rave about Zappos, it's for good reason: Zappos creates sufficient moments of delight that many people have experienced them and gone on to create and share content about them It's expensive—and Zappos isn't always the lowest cost shoe retailer. But in the end, delight wins. Zappos set out to build a billion-dollar business in 10 years. As a team, they did it in eight. Ultimately, it is the subsequent customer experiences—built or reshaped with direct customer input—which will drive future conversations and set your business or organization on the path to success.

Connect Your Team

Social media marketing is in many ways a precursor to social business. Social media marketing is most effective when the entire business is responsible for the experiences and everyone within the organization is visibly responsible for the overall product or service. When engagement, for example, is considered from a customer's perspective— when the measure for engagement is the number of new ideas submitted rather than the time spent reading a web page—the business operates as a holistic entity rather than a collection of insulated silos. The result is a consistent, replicable delivery experience that can be further tuned and improved over time.

When it comes to rallying the troops to support your organization-wide effort, there is no doubt that you'll face some push back. Very likely, you'll hear things like this:

- We don't have the internal resources and time.
- We lack knowledge and expertise.
- Not till you show me the value and ROI.
- We don't have guidelines or policies.
- It's for young kids—not for our business.
- Our customers will start saying bad things.

You'll hear all of this, and more. Of the first tasks you are likely to face when implementing a social media marketing program and then pushing it in the direction of social business is the organizational challenge of connecting the resources that you will need. The good news is that it can be done. The not-so-good news is that it *has to be* done.

When you're a marketer, one of the immediate benefits of a social media program is gaining an understanding of what people are saying about your brand, product, or service (listening); analyzing what you find to extract meaning (social media analytics) that is relevant to your work; and then developing a response program (active listening). This information can be presented internally, and done so in a way that is inclusive and draws a team around you. Listening is a great way to start: As you move toward social business, it will become clear rather quickly that this is best done through an effort that reaches across departments and pulls on the strengths of the entire organization. Anything you can do to get others within your business or organization interested is a plus. As a starting point, listening is the low-hanging fruit.

Each of the above—listening, analyzing, and some aspects of responding—can be done without any direct connection to your customers or visible presence with regard to your business or organization on the Social Web: In others words, it's very low risk. While it may not be optimal, the activities around listening and analyzing, for example, can be managed within the marketing function. With workflow-enabled analytics tools—for example, using a listening platform that automatically routes tweets about warranty issues to customer service—you can certainly make it easier to oversee all of this.

Building on this approach, when you move to the next step—responding to a policy question or product feature request—you'll be glad you pulled a larger team together and built some internal support. Otherwise, you'll quickly discover how limited your capabilities inside the marketing department *to respond directly and meaningfully to customers* actually are, and this will threaten your success. How so?

Suppose, for example, that you see negative reviews regarding the gas mileage of a new model car you've introduced, or you see those posts about an exceptional customer service person. In the former case, you can always play the defensive role—"True, but the mileage our car delivers is still an improvement over...." Or, you can ignore the conversation in hopes that it will die out or at least not grow. In the case of the exceptional employee, you can praise that particular person but beyond the benefit of rewarding an individual—which is important, no doubt about it—what does it really do for your business? What would help you is delivering more miles per gallon, or knowing how to scale exceptional employees, or how to create *more* exceptional employees from the start.

Ignoring, defending, and tactically responding in a one-off manner doesn't produce sustainable gain over the long term. Instead, the information underlying these types of events needs to get to the product teams, to Customer Support or Human Resource (HR) managers or whomever it is that is responsible for the experience that is being talked about. In the case of the mileage, someone needs to determine whether there is a design problem: Does hot weather cause mileage dips, and are your Texas auto dealers leading in sales? Or, is it an application mismatch (such as buying a Hummer to run back and forth to the gym or tanning salon) or simply an unrealistic customer expectation (set by, gee, I don't know...maybe those EPA estimates that appear in bold type in automobile advertisements?). All of these are real examples.

To address these kinds of issues, action is required, and the action has to connect the source of the experience to the actual solution. This generally means involving a team beyond marketing. Otherwise—if the root cause is not addressed, the current conversations will continue.

What you are really after—and where social business practices can actually deliver—is in understanding, validating, and implementing the processes or process changes needed to move the conversation in the direction that supports your business objectives. In the case of the exceptional employee, what is this person's history? To whom does this person report? How can your organization encourage more people to adopt the specific behaviors that drove the positive comments? These are the types of issues that a holistic approach to social business can impact.

In all of these cases, the take-away is this: Faced with an issue of interest coming off of the Social Web, your next step—armed with the conversational data and some analysis—is likely going to take you outside of marketing. You'll want to have a larger team in place, so the activity of encouraging support among colleagues and internal influencers and decisions makers must begin early.

Who is that larger team, and how do you build it? The answers may surprise you: Your best allies may be in unlikely or prior unconsidered places. Consider, for example, the following:

- Your legal team can help you draft social media and social computing policies for distribution within the organization. This is great starting point for team-building because you are asking your legal team to do what it does best: Keep everyone else out of trouble.

- You can connect your customer service team through social analytics tools so that they can easily track Twitter and similar Social Web conversations, and using low-cost listening tools and the USAF response matrix you can enlist your corporate training department to teach service representatives what to do.

- You can outsource the development of a relevant business application for your Facebook business page or other community site to a qualified technology partner (and not your cousin or an intern who will be gone in 6 weeks).

- Enlist your own customers. Most business managers are amazed at how much assistance customers will provide when asked to do so.

Your Customers Want to Help

While it may surprise you, your own customers are part of the solution. They are often the biggest source of assistance you've got. Flip back to the engagement process: Consumption, curation, creation, collaboration. At the point that your customers are collaborating with each other, it is very likely that they are also more than willing to provide direct inputs for the next generation of your product or service, or offer tips on what they think you can quickly implement now. Starbucks' customers have been busy using the Salesforce.com-based "My Starbucks Idea" platform. Since implementation in 2008, about 80,000 ideas have been submitted with over 200 direct innovations as a result. Based on direct customer input, Starbucks has been averaging two innovations introduced per week. That's impressive, and it pays off in business results.

Ideation and support applications are discussed in Chapters 9 and 12. They are among the tools that you'll want to look at, along with social media analytics and influencer identification tools covered in Part II of this book. However you do it, whether planning your social business program as an extension of an in-place marketing program or as your first entry into social technology and its application to business take the time to connect your customers (engagement) to your entire team (collaboration).

Review and Hands-On

This chapter connects the current practice of social-media-based marketing—a reality in many business and service organizations now—with the more fundamental application of the same technologies at a "whole-organization" level. In other words, social business is the next generation of customer engagement: it connects customers to employees, links unstructured conversational data to structured business data, and recognizes that the same desire to collaborate in the pursuit of better decisions exists both inside and outside your firm.

Review of the Main Points

This chapter focused on social media and social technology applied at a deeper business level for the purpose of driving higher levels of customer engagement. In particular, this chapter established the following fundamentals:

- There is a distinct social "engagement" process: Beginning with content consumption, it continues through curation, creation, and collaboration. The final stage—collaboration—can be used to form an active link between you, your colleagues, and your customers.

- Operations and Marketing teams must work together to create the experiences that drive conversations. The Social Feedback Cycle is the articulation of the relationship that connects all of the disciplines within your organization around the customer experience.

- Collaboration—used to connect customers to your business—is a powerful force in effecting change and driving innovation. Collaboration is, in this sense, one of the fundamental objectives of a social *business* strategy.

Now that you've gotten the basics of the engagement process and understand the usefullness of social applications along with the ways in which you can connect your audience, employees, and business, spend some time looking at the following real-world applications. As you do, think about how the engagement process is applied, and about how the resultant interactions leverage the larger social networks and relevant communities frequented by those who would be using these applications.

Hands-On: Review These Resources

Review each of the following, taking note of the main points covered in the chapter and the ways in which the following resources demonstrate or expand on these points:

- Starbucks' "My Starbucks Idea" ideation application:
  `http://mystarbucksidea.com`

- The blog of Gaurav Mishra, on the topic of social business:
  `http://www.gauravonomics.com`

- The blog of Peter Kim, on the topic of social business:
  `http://www.beingpeterkim.com`

Hands-On: Apply What You've Learned

Apply what you've learned in this chapter through the following exercises:

1. Define the basic properties, objectives, and outcomes of a collaborative application that connects your customers to your business and to your employees.

2. Define an internal application that connects employees and enables efficient resolution of customer-generated ideas.

3. Map out your own customer engagement process and compare it with the engagement process defined in this chapter.

The New Role
of the Customer

The Social Web visibly connects your business or organization and its stakeholders—customers, suppliers and influencers, each of whom have defined new roles for themselves very much in control of the information they share as they evaluate competing options. This chapter explains these new roles in business terms, showing you how to determine who is influencing whom and where the next great ideas are likely to originate.

2

Chapter Contents

The New Role: Social Interactions

The "social" in "Social Web" implies more than technology, more than the networks where people post photos and review books: It's less about the "what" and more about "how, why, and among whom" that distinguishes the Social Web from earlier, transactional online technologies. The term "social" refers to the ways in which people connect—friends, requiring a two-way acknowledgement of a relationship are different than more casually associated followers, for example. The term "social" also provides insight into why they are connecting—perhaps to learn something, to share an experience, or to collaborate on a project. As such, a great place to start learning about the Social Web and its connection to business is with the basic relationships that are created between participants in social networks and social applications, and to then look at the types of interactions between them that follow.

It is the relationships and interactions between participants that connect community members and define the social graph, a term of art that means simply who you are (e.g., your profile), who you are connected to (e.g., your friends or followers), and what you are doing (e.g., status updates). The social graph is to building relationships what ordinary links between websites are to building an information network: They define the social connections. Without the social graph—without the profiles and friends, followers, and similar relations that form between them—online social communities are reduced to task-oriented, self-serve utilities much as a basic website or shopping catalog might present itself.

A quick way to see this is to think about a site like Yelp. Yelp provides review, ratings, venue, and schedule information...all of the things needed to plan an evening or other outing. This is the kind of activity that an individual might do or an individual might do on behalf of a small, known group of friends with a specific personal goal in mind: Find a good restaurant and then see a show, etc. That's the basic utility that Yelp provides, and by itself it isn't particularly social with the allowance of the shared ratings and reviews that Yelp offers.

Go one step further, though, and Yelp becomes a social site as well. When someone builds a Yelp profile and connects with other Yelpers—that's what people using Yelp call each other—the transactional service becomes a relationship-driven community. Rather than "*What* would I like to do this evening?" the question becomes "*With whom* would I like to do something this evening?" This is a distinctly social motive, and it is the combination of utility value (information and ratings) along with the other Yelper's own profile and messages (the social elements) together with whom they are connected that makes the social aspects of Yelp work. It is the social—not transactional—tools that power Yelp.

By encouraging the development of relationships within a collaborative community—or across functional lines within an organization or between customers and employees of a business—the likelihood of meaningful interaction, of collaboration, is significantly increased. This kind of collaborative, shared experience drives the production and exchange of information (experiences) within a customer community and just as well within an organization. It works for Yelp, and it works in business networks connecting manufacturers with suppliers and employees with each other. The key to all of these is building relationships and providing relevant, meaningful opportunity for personal interaction.

> ## The Social Graph
>
> The *social graph* is the collection of links, relationships, interactions and other connections that comprise a social network. Wikipedia has more on social graphs here:
>
> http://en.wikipedia.org/wiki/Social_Graph

Relationships and interactions are typically built around a set of primary participant activities. This section covers three of the primary actions: friending and following, reputation management, and moderation along with the development of conduct and use policies (aka Terms of Use) that are essential to maintaining a healthy, collaborative environment. Each of these plays a fundamental role in developing purpose-driven communities—think support sites, supplier networks, and employee knowledge sharing—and, therefore, in implementing a successful social business strategy.

People Want to Make Friends

Friending—the mutually acknowledged linking of profiles within or across defined communities—is the cornerstone of collaborative social interaction. Just as in real life, the various relationships that exist between profiles (people) often imply certain aspects of both the nature of the expected interactions and the context for them. Relationships at a club or church are different in context—and therefore in expectation —from relationships in a workplace, for example: When someone elects to follow another on Twitter, or inside an employee network built on a platform like SocialText, there is likewise an expectation of value received in exchange for the follower relationship, all within the context of the network in which this relationship has been established. People create relationships to exchange value, at some level, with the others in and through that relationship.

Compared with a website—where navigating a self-service library of content is a typical interaction path—the extension of a link between profiles and the formation of a relationship between the people they represent is a fundamental requirement for value exchange between community members. Without these links, people can post content, rate submissions, and similar—but to what end? YouTube is a great example of exactly this sort of content creation and sharing. The result is a highly trafficked site and lots of buzz, but the "social interaction" still occurs for the most part at the individual, content-consumption level rather than as truly shared or collaborative experiences. Compared with Facebook, for example, YouTube participants share and consume content in a decidedly less social manner: The interaction on YouTube revolves around a sharing or referral of content that each may feel the other will find interesting. Compare this to Facebook, where the majority of sharing involves thoughts, ideas, and conversations and occurs between members that have a true (albeit virtual in many cases) friendship link in place.

Moving from a personal to a business context, "friending" drives the creation and refinement of knowledge because it connects people and facilitates their working together. Collaborative behaviors emerge in environments of linked friends as the recognition of a joint stake or shared outcome becomes evident between participants. Working together—versus alone—almost always produces a better end-product. Think about the corporate training exercises that begin with a survival scenario: The group nearly always develops a better solution given the stated scenario (meaning, the group members are more likely to survive!) than do individuals acting alone.

In communities built around shared content, the process of *curation* (touched on in Chapter 1, "Social Media and Customer Engagement") and its associated activities such as rating and recommending a photo improve the overall body of content within the community and thereby improve the experience and raise the value of membership. This type of public refinement and informal collaboration results in a stronger shared outcome. These acts of curation additionally manifest themselves in the context of the social graph through the practice of reputation among friends or colleagues in that network. Just as a photo is rated, so are the contributions of a specific community member, giving rise to the reputation of that member. It is this sense of "shared outcome" that you are after when implementing social technologies within the enterprise or when creating an active, lasting customer or stakeholder community that wraps around it.

Ultimately, it is the acts of friending, following, and similar formally declared forms of online social connections that support and encourage the relationships that bond the community and transform it into an organically evolving social entity. As these relationships are put in place, it is important that the participants in the community become more committed to the care and well-being of the community. Plenty of social networking services have failed even though lots of members had lots of friends. There needs to be an activity or core purpose for participants that encourage peer-to-peer interaction. Chapter 10, "Social Objects," Chpater 11, "The Social Graph," and Chapter 12, "Social Applications," offer in-depth discussions on how to ensure that these essential relationships form.

Club Membership Brings Expectations

In the preceding discussion of relationships and interactions and their importance in the development of a strong sense of shared purpose within a community, left aside was the question of how the social norms or rules of etiquette are established and maintained within a community. Cyberbullying, flame wars, and the general bashing of newbies clearly work at cross-purposes with most any online community development effort. In the design of any social interaction—be it as simple as posting on Twitter or as complex as driving innovation in an expert community—the policies that define and govern the conduct of participants are of utmost importance.

To maintain order and a defined sense of decorum, the practices of moderation along with the implementation of policies—also known as *Terms of Use*—are fundamentally important. While there are entire texts on these topics, there are some core concepts that should be part of any community effort within a social business program. Effective *moderation*—the guiding of participants and conversations within the bounds set by the Terms of Use—is likewise key to the successful implementation of a community or collaborative workspace.

Typically, the Terms of Use will provide for the following, each of which contributes directly to the overall health of a collaborative community:

- Expectation of participation, perhaps managed through a reputation system that rewards more frequent and higher quality contributions
- Ensuring that participants stay on topic within any specific discussion, so that the discussion remains valuable to the larger community, *and so that the topics covered are easily found again at a later date*
- Curtailing any form of bullying, use of hate speech, posting of spam, and similar that are obviously counter-productive within a typical business (or related) community

Beyond these core practices, the function of moderation is to watch for issues that surface or problems that require some sort of escalation. At a basic level, moderation enforces the Terms of Service by warning members about inappropriate posting, language, or behavior. Moderation provides a sense of comfort for newer members who may be unfamiliar with more subtle rules or expectations that exist within the community. Moderation practices, Terms of Use (governing external communities—for example, a customer or supplier community), and social computing policies (governing internal use of social technology—for example, by company employees) together provide an organizational safeguard when implementing social media and social technology programs. Understanding who can participate, what is and isn't appropriate for social channels, disclosure practices, and more are all part of an effective social computing and community moderation policy.

Social Computing Policies

A clear policy for organizational adoption of social computing is essential. You can think of social computing policies as the "Terms of Use" governing the use of social media within a business. IBM offers its social computing policies for review. Some time spent with these is highly recommended.

http://www.ibm.com/blogs/zz/en/guidelines.html

Before leaving moderation—and do visit Jake McKee's resources (see sidebar feature on Community Moderation) for further discussion on moderation best practices—one last point with regard to ensuring community health: Moderation provides an important relief valve for seasoned members. By guiding conversations in the proper course and keeping discussions on track, skilled moderators actually make it easier (and more pleasant) for the experts in a community to stay engaged and to continue contributing in ways that benefit everyone. This too contributes to the overall development of effective social community programs.

Community Moderation: Best Practices

Jake McKee, Chief Strategy Officer at Ant's Eye View (as well as the Technical Editor for this book) offers a great interview with community moderation experts Joe Cotrell and Jay Bryant. Check out this interview, and consider following Jake (@jakemckee) on Twitter.

http://www.communityguy.com/1626/ocrn-online-moderation-best-practices-interview

In addition to Jake's blog, The Community Roundtable is a great resource for community managers: the link below leads to a solid discussion of community management considerations and best practices. You can follow Community Report principals Rachel Happe (@rhappe) and Jim Storer (@jstorer) on Twitter.

http://community-roundtable.com/2010/01/the-value-of-community-management

You Are What You Post

Curation, which was touched on previously, is often presented in the context of *content*, rating a photo or commenting on or scoring an article. As briefly noted, curation also occurs between community participants: In the context of the community participants, curation occurs between members with regard to contributions and behavior. Members are voted up and down or otherwise ranked according to the relative value of the quality of their contributions and impact or value of their participation as individual community members. This is directly analogous to the way personal reputations are built (and sometimes destroyed) in real life.

Reputation systems—formalized manifestations of the curation process when applied to profiles and the acts of the people represented by them—are essential components of any business community. Without them, all sorts of negative behaviors emerge, ranging from unreliable posts being taken as fact (bad enough) to rampant bullying and abuse (which will kill the community outright).

Recall from social media basics that you cannot directly control a conversation on the Social Web. Unlike your ad or public relations (PR) campaign that you can start, stop, and change at will, on the Social Web it's generally not your conversation in the first place, though you may well be a part of it. Rather, the conversation belongs to the collective, *which includes you but is typically not yours alone.* On the Social Web it is the actual customer experiences, combined with your participation and response to it, that drive the conversations. Here's the connection to customers, communities, and reputation: *Authority*—manifested through *reputation*—has to be earned rather than assumed. *Reputation,* which applies at the individual level just as it does to the brand or organization, accrues over time in direct response to the contributions of specific members associated with that brand or organization. A declaration of "guru" means relatively little without the collective nod of the community as a whole.

Reputation management works on the simple premise of elevating participants who behave in ways that strengthen the community and by discouraging the behaviors that work against community interests. Posting, replying, offering answers or tips, completing a personal profile, and similar are all behaviors that typically result in elevated reputations. Intel's Developers program, shown in Figure 2.1, has an excellent reputation management system based on the martial arts belt levels. It's an easily understood systems of points earned for specific actions, and the achievement of elevated levels is truly of badge of honor among the community members. Taking specific steps when designing a community program that encourage profile completion are referenced in Chapter 4, "The Social Business Ecosystem," and then covered in detail in Chapter 11, "The Social Graph."

The importance of the reputation system in a social community cannot be overstated. Absent reputation management, individual participants are essentially left on their own to assess their own value and that of the participants around them, which rarely leads to a satisfying experience. Beyond the work of a skilled moderator and a well-designed reputation system, tips and guidelines should be presented clearly. Helping your community members do the right thing on their own—rather than simply telling them to do it—is a direct benefit of a reputation management system. Rather than prescriptive rules, a dynamic reputation management system provides feedback that guides members—in the moment and in the context of specific activities— in the direction that supports the collective need of the community. *When implementing any collaborative social program, pay specific attention to the design of the reputation management system.* Developer communities such as Intel's Black Belt program are well worth study. Look too at support communities such as Dell's or Best Buy's—both built on the Lithium Technologies platform, known for its specific capabilities supporting reputation management and expert identification. All of these are great "best practice" applications to study and compare as you go about creating the design specifications for your own community or other social application.

Figure 2.1 Intel's Black Belt Program

Customer Relationships: CRM Gets Social

In the traditional sales cycle, CRM (customer relationship management) forms a data-driven understructure that powers an overall customer life cycle. Based on historical transactions, the insights into what a customer may need next, or when a particular customer may be ready for an *upsell,* offers are generated based on past transactional data and the larger purchase or use patterns that exist across the entire customer base.

On the Social Web, where the customer is now becoming an integral part of the sales process, CRM is being adapted to support this new role of the customer. Think here specifically about the Social Feedback Cycle and the role of a brand ambassador, or an advocacy program that plays out in social media. In each of these, there is a specific development process—from tire kicker to car owner to loyal customer to brand advocate—that can be understood in terms of available behavioral data. Posts on social sites, collected through social analytics tools, for example, can provide real clues as to where in the ascension to brand advocate (or descension to detractor) a particular individual is at any given moment.

This new role of the customer, based in relationships and shared activities that play out on the Social Web, can be effectively understood and managed by borrowing some of the ideas and practices of traditional CRM and then weaving into them the essential social concepts of shared outcomes, influencer and expert identification, and general treatment of the marketplace as a social community.

On the Social Web, participants form relationships for specific purposes: fun, discovery, or other uses of collective knowledge to better accomplish their own goals. In the context of social business, the motivations include becoming smarter about a product or service as a customer or innovating and extending the value of personal contributions as employees. The changing nature of the overall relationship between a business and its customers can be understood by following the conversations along with the participants and the relationships between them: From the design of the products and services and their delivery into the marketplace to the conversations that form about them on the Social Web the telltale indicators are available. This provides a highly valuable window of insight into what your customers or stakeholders are really thinking, and what they are likely to do next. Social CRM, as it is being defined now, gives you a potential competitive advantage in both strategic planning and tactical response with regard to what is happening on and around the Social Web.

The New Role of Influence

Consider a typical conversation on the Social Web, say a potential customer who is reading a review and talking with a friend over Twitter about it. That review was written by someone, and it was written for a reason. Who that person is—think profile plus connections—provides a clue as to the motivation behind the review. Further, that review is the result of an experience that is itself driven by a business process.

Looked at in a macro sense, a potential customer reading a review is actually looking at the net result of a business process through the eyes of someone with an identifiable motive or point of view. If that motive or point of view can be understood, you can sort out the real business impact of the review (if any) and then apply this knowledge to your business and adjust as necessary your own business processes that are creating the experiences that drove that review. In other words, knowing who is talking about you (and not just what they are saying) is fundamental to understanding and then optimizing your processes to produce the conversations you want, and addressing and correcting the processes that drive the conversations you'd rather not see.

Social CRM—treated in depth in Chapter 9, "Social CRM"—is the emerging discipline that does just this. Social CRM joins up a couple of existing business technologies and associated practices. The "social" component draws on the interactions between people, on relationship management, and on the study of the life cycle of that relationship and its various trigger points. More traditional customer relationship management (CRM) has to do with *customers* and the prior *transactions* between your customers and your business or organization. What was purchased, what was sent back under warranty, which services were renewed or upgraded, and by whom—all of the interactions and the data around customer transactions are captured in the systems that power the typical CRM installation. Taken together, it's an incredible source of sales insight based directly on past behaviors. CRM is a core best practice in most leading businesses and organizations as a result.

As a step into *Social CRM,* think about customer relationship management as it's practiced currently in many leading firms, where prior sales data is used to improve the next pitch and extend the customer life cycle on into the future. Social CRM is conceptually similar—data driven and operating on a feedback loop—but is extended across your entire business and wraps the entire customer experience, *including external influencers.* An understanding of the present role of the customer in your business, *along with the role of influencers and a resulting ability to connect with them just as with customers*, is what makes Social CRM so potentially powerful.

Very importantly—and a big insight into what separates social business from social media marketing—is taking note that customer relationship management systems are often used by Operations in addition to informing Marketing in regard to customer trends and business issues. The same holistic application of data and processes applies to Social CRM. As used here, "Operations" refers to the departments and functions inside your organization that deliver the actual customer experiences. Beyond product promotion, CRM data and related analytical tools are often used to estimate phone unit staffing levels, to spot warranty-driven design or product use/misuse issues, to identify potential innovations, and more. Much of this occurs outside of the marketing department, and especially so in those organizations where marketing is more closely tied to advertising and communications than to product development and business strategy.

Given these factors, what then really is Social CRM? Simply put, it's an approach to business that *formally* recognizes the role of the customer and external influencers as a key in understanding and managing conversations around the brand, product, or service. If the reference to "conversations" seems to narrow the definition, consider this: The conversation in the contemporary business context is nothing short of a holistic, digital artifact that captures and conveys the sum total of what your firm or organization has delivered. Markets *are* conversations, right?

Think back to Chapter 1 and the engagement building blocks: consumption, curation, creation, and collaboration. These are decidedly social activities, with the level of participation increasing as one moves through the engagement process. Traditional CRM manages a customer relationship in a passive sense from the *customer's* point of view.

The attributes defining the relationship are all based on past transactional data—purchases, calls, and other past-tense events. From the customer's point of view, the events have happened and are done: there is no ongoing role for the individual as a customer.

By comparison, Social CRM invites the customer into your business or organization through the *future-oriented* process of collaboration. It recognizes what has happened, just as traditional CRM does, but then takes the added step of inviting the customer into the processes that govern *what is about to happen* or *may potentially happen* or *should never happen again* by asking "How can this product or service be made better?" This kind of forward-looking collaboration involves the entire set of stakeholders in the business or organization, including its employees, partners, and suppliers. It is a whole-business, future-oriented process, and it is core to an overall methodology and strategy that is designed and implemented to delight customers.

Social CRM and Engagement

I highly recommend downloading and studying Paul Greenberg's whitepaper on Social CRM, "Social CRM Comes of Age." You can also follow Paul, a thought leader around Social CRM and its application, on Twitter (@pgreenbe).

`http://www.oracle.com/ocom/groups/public/@ocompublic/documents/`
`webcontent/036062.pdf`

Ant's Eye View's Kira Wampler, formerly of Intuit, provides great insight into the new role of the customer: She points out that most organizations know ahead of time where their next "Dell Hell" (the online forum where consumers vent frustrations with the computer maker) or "United Breaks Guitars" (the video that reportedly resulted in an estimated 10 percent market cap loss for the airline) is going to come from, so why not be proactive and fix things ahead of time? An example of a well-publicized social media nightmare that turned out well, Dell is now a model of what to do right, and United wound up being merged with Continental partly because its stock price made it attractive. Kira lays out a set of steps that are worth noting, steps that clearly place the customer and the conversations they are having at the center of the Social CRM effort:

- Audit existing "voice of customer" channels: How many are in use, what is being said, and what is the process for analyzing, responding, addressing, and closing the loop with a solution?

- Map the customers' end-to-end experiences: Understand in detail each step that a customer undertakes when doing specific tasks that relate to your product or service. Create cross-functional teams to relate what you learn to each point in your process that impacts the customer experience at that point.

- Overlay the moments of truth with a feedback channel audit: Where are the gaps? Where do the channels overlap? What feedback do you have that shows how you are performing at these points?

- Establish a baseline of customer experience and priorities to improve: Based on the above, align efforts with your business objectives and set out a plan.

- Establish a regular process for reporting: Use the associated metrics for each step in the process along with your plan to keep your larger (cross functional) team updated. "No surprises" is the best surprise.

Put these ideas together and you have the basic value proposition for Social CRM, in the context of a new role for the customer, in a participant-driven business: By understanding *who* among your customers is influential, by noting who is at the center of a specific conversation, and by developing relationships with these people, you create the opportunity to more deeply understand why they feel—positively or negatively—the way they do. You can use this information in a forward-looking (proactive) rather than reactive manner to drive innovation and to ultimately shape the conversations in ways that benefit rather than hinder your business.

Looking at Figure 2.2, you can see that the product or service experience creates a conversation, one that is often directed or intended for a specific audience and which often exposes or suggests an opportunity for innovation. This is the new role of the customer, expressed through its impact via the traditional CRM process, integrated now with a social component.

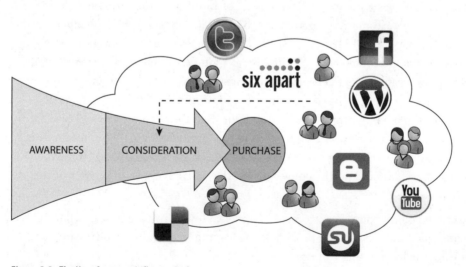

Figure 2.2 The New Customer Influence Path

The Social Graph

Just as you are able to track your communication with an existing customer through the relationship life cycle, you can track customers and other influencers through that same relationship as they create content and converse on the Social Web. This can be very enlightening and is really useful when pulled into the product design process.

Social CRM helps you understand and apply the significant points in the conversations happening around you. It helps you tie this information into your business, where you can use it to build relationships with influential customers and with influential bloggers, critics, and others who follow your firm or track your business or industry.

You can apply this same discipline internally, too, and connect customers and external influencers to your employees, to the Customer Service manager, to brand managers, and to others. Once connected in this way, your customers and employees can bond further, moving toward collaboration. It's collaboration that drives customer-centric product and service innovation, and collaboration that leads to the highest forms of engagement with your customers.

If you now add to this your data around customer registration or similar information that you may have collected separately—remember, like any other form of CRM, Social CRM tracks specific profiles and contacts, so it can be synched with existing customer data sets—you can begin to track what the people who matter to you, your current and prior customers, are saying about your product or service, or about your brand, firm, or organization in the context of actual purchases and experiences. You can use this same process to bring other influencers—bloggers, for example, who may not be customers—into the Social CRM pool as well. All of this adds up to information you can use to drive change and innovation, just as Starbucks, Dell, IBM, and others are doing.

How do you do it? Consider a tool like BuzzStream, a representative tool with basic Social CRM and social graph capabilities centered on influencer identification and contact management. Figure 2.3 shows the BuzzStream console and the social linkages identified for a typical discovered influencer and the corresponding profile of interest.

BuzzStream and similar tools include "influencer" dashboards that allow the easy monitoring of conversations based on keywords and the conversion of source data in much the same way as basic social web listening tools works. With the influencer monitoring tools like Buzzstream, the profiles and links of people directly contributing to the conversation you are following are converted into contacts in an influencers database that can be managed alongside your other customer data. Note that BuzzStream provides one component of a larger Social CRM effort: Combined with your business data, deeper social analytics and an internal collaboration platform, BuzzStream's contact information provides an easy way to manage subsequent conversations with the influencers around your brand, product or service as you track issues, look for opportunities and introduce innovations driven in part by these same conversations.

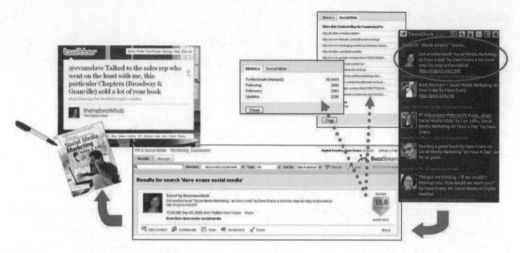

Figure 2.3 BuzzStream and the Social Graph

At the heart of tools like BuzzStream is the social graph, a map of who is connected to whom. Social influence and Social CRM tools work by "crawling" the personal and profile links in your online conversations to find information about the source of the conversation in much the same way as a searchbot crawls page links to find related or supporting content. Starting with a comment or a blog post, BuzzStream looks for a reference to a website or email or Twitter handle that may be present in or near that post. As it finds contact information, the social graph crawler will organize and return potential or contact points.

As these contact points are discovered, a list of potential links and identities are grouped together and presented through the dashboard. As a human (Yes, we are still needed!) you can review this information and pick out the bits that actually seem related. Then, click a button and create your influencer contact. A typical contact may have a profile name, a Twitter handle, and perhaps an email address or phone number. Over time you'll add to it, as your *actual* relationships with these influencers develop. Once created, any tweets, emails, or similar will be logged, just as with a traditional CRM system. You can then build and manage your relationship with these influencers just as you would any other contacts.

Google's Social Graph API

Google publishes an API—a way to access existing functionality within Google's open code-base—that supports the development of applications that can crawl the public pages on social sites and present the related links, providing the social graph of a specific person. Check it out: Even if you're not a programmer understanding what it is and how it works is useful.

http://code.google.com/apis/socialgraph/

Social CRM: Two Cases

Enough theory! It's time to take a quick look at two cases in order to understand where and how Social CRM and similar concepts can be applied in business.

The Women's Fund of Miami-Dade County

The Women's Fund of Miami-Dade County serves women and girls in the Miami area. The purpose of the organization is supporting and working with women and girls through programs that stress self image, pride, self reliance, a sense of belonging, and purpose in their community that result in their reaching full potential as individuals. Facing the issues common to many local nonprofit organizations, The Women's Fund of Miami-Dade County sought to improve its website, connect in a more efficient manner online with donors, and in general develop a more functional online presence built around staff and member participation. This included Social CRM efforts.

Working with local agency The Cunningham Group, the social business strategy included a combination of basic online blocking and tackling, Social CRM, social-media-based promotion, and plain old, traditional "feet-on-the-street" marketing, as social media and its various incarnations, like any other form of media, are best applied *in addition to* the other forms of marketing and communications that remain important to businesses and organizations.

Although many of the "social makeover" goals were related to the use of social media and/or basic business objectives—the use of member's content and the provision of up-to-date information about the organization and its programs—there was also a deeper effort aimed at engaging visitors with the donor program. For nonprofits, the donor program is the engine of the organization: Without donors, the mission and very existence of many of these types of business is threatened.

Because it leverages traditional CRM and then extends it to the Social Web, Social CRM is an ideal approach to building a robust donor program. Through Social CRM, not only can the relationships with current or past donors be maintained, but the relationships with potential donors or those influential in the donor identification and activation process can be identified and built.

Working with Tasha Cunningham, the Women's Fund did the following:

1. Created content in easy-to-consume formats. Recall that consumption is the first building block in social engagement. Podcasts, YouTube-embedded videos, and similar forms of content were used.

2. Leveraged this new content as conversation starters. Participants were invited to rate, review, comment—to curate—and thereby to move themselves up the social engagement ladder. The Women's Fund's "Real Women, Real Voices" campaign resulted.

3. Connected this content to the actual, real-world impact of the organizations' grants and donors programs. Participants are now able to see directly what

happens as a result of their participation whether through time, financial contribution, or the investment of personal social capital—recommending to a friend that he or she consider supporting The Women's Fund, for example—thereby completing the engagement cycle.

4. Internally, The Women's Fund undertook a web-based extension of its Social CRM system to connect its staff with donors, board members and supporters, completing the collaborative cycle.

Taken together, The Women's Fund of Miami-Dade County is tapping Social CRM in a straightforward and sensible, strategically sound manner. Their work is a solid example of how Social CRM can be applied by local nonprofit organizations.

For more information on the The Women's Fund of Miami-Dade County and The Cunningham Group, see the following:

```
http://www.womensfundmiami.org
http://www.thecunninghamgroup.com
```

SoHo Publishing

Soho Publishing, LLC, a local B2B publishing firm, began business in May of 2005. The main product was the Milwaukee-based *Magazine Soho*. In March of 2009, Soho launched Sohobiztube.com, a multimedia delivery platform for marketing, promoting, and positioning small entrepreneurial businesses.

Rather than the personal brands of small business founders, which typically form the story in small business write-ups, the focus of the companies featured in *Magazine Soho* is on the brand, products, services, and employees—everything *but* the founder. After all, in keeping with the social aspects of customer and employee ownership, these companies need to focus on why they are in business and what they are promising to their clients and customers. In May of 2009, Soho Publishing, LLC held Milwaukee's first, one-day social media seminar to further drive home the ideas of a true customer focus and where it could take a small business with a great idea and solid, customer-backed execution.

Cd Vann, Publisher of *Magazine Soho*, doesn't consider herself a social media advocate, thought leader, or guru. She is a business owner who wants to take advantage of new media strategies and apply them to her work. Sohobiztube.com, a related site, gives customers—*Magazine Soho* clients—a way to easily contribute content that highlights products and services. The result is a strong B2B connection linking these businesses to their marketers through social channels.

It was in this spirit that Cd created Sohobiztube, a Social CRM and publishing platform that pulled customers into the consumption and curation stages of engagement, and in doing so enabled small business owners to recognize and tap into their customers as a source of direction for their respective businesses, just as Cd had done with hers.

For more information on Sohobiztube, see the following:

http://sohobiztube.com

Vendor Relationship Management

Given the rise of the Social Web, the new role of the customer and the concepts of Social CRM have a counterpart in business supply-chain processes: Vendor Relationship Management (VRM). Beyond employee-customer interactions and Operations-led production and delivery processes, what are the additional points of impact in the creation of the customer experience? What about businesses with a more complex supply chain, or whose control over the delivery experience depends on the direct or indirect contributions of other firms and organizations? Think about vacation and destination travel services, where a holiday package offered through American Express may involve multiple customer-facing partners. How do the concepts of Social CRM transform?

The Cluetrain Manifesto holds that the best marketing is conversational, built around interaction between the business and its customer, and between customers themselves. This philosophy underlies Social CRM in that it ties the conversation—not just the transaction—into the business processes. Vendor Relationship Management is about the application of the social tools that create and support collaborative conversations throughout the supply chain and delivery channels. To the extent that the Social Web is the evidence of pushback by consumers against traditional marketing in favor of a more collaborative experience with brands, products, and services, VRM is about extending the sought-after collaborative experiences to the entire supply chain.

Jon Lebkowsky, a cofounder of Austin, TX–based Social Web Strategies, along with Doc Searls, a leading proponent of VRM, and others are advancing this issue. You'll find more about Jon Lebkowsky, Doc Searls, and VRM here:

http://en.wikipedia.org/wiki/Vendor_Relationship_Management

http://cyber.law.harvard.edu/research/projectvrm

http://en.wikipedia.org/wiki/Jon_Lebkowsky

http://en.wikipedia.org/wiki/Doc_Searls

Outreach and Influencer Relations

In the prior sections, I presented the new role of the customer and the impact of this new role on business disciplines like CRM and the identification of influencers. I've shown how Social CRM fits into an organization's intelligence and relationship management program, and how it ties the response-driven foundation of traditional CRM to the Social Web's customer-driven engagement process. Social CRM literally ties your business into the influence path that is guiding the development of your markets by connecting you with the conversation makers.

In this next section, the focus is on very specific conversation makers: the bloggers who cover your particular market or "speak" to your customers and stakeholders along with the more general group of influencers who play a nontrivial role in the way in which your product or service finds its way into your customers' shopping carts.

Social CRM and Blogger Outreach

In referencing bloggers and blogger outreach, I'm *not* talking exclusively about A-list bloggers. These individuals are certainly factors and have most definitely earned their reputations by consistently delivering value to their subscribers. However, the idea that "reaching them" and asking them to do your bidding is somehow a sufficient social marketing effort is misplaced at best, and it will land you in trouble at worst.

Like celebrities, A-list bloggers are few in number and easy to spot. There are lists of them, making them easy to connect with. As a part of your blogger outreach program you'll want to connect with the A-listers that matter to you, but a word of caution: Holding to their own professional standards—their personal brands depend on it, after all—the A-listers will write as they please. Develop a relationship with them when your product or service is up to snuff. Prior to that, or when first establishing your relationship with them, look for ways to help them out but don't do it out of expectation for a favor. Simply pay it forward, as the saying goes, and focus on delivering a great product or service. The rest will follow.

A-list bloggers write to satisfy a passion and not (primarily) for a paycheck, though many do earn a living or contribute significantly toward one through their writing. Their passion is their chosen topic and the process of sharing the information related to it with others. You want these people in your camp, no doubt about it. But there are others that you need as well.

Far more important at the outset is to identify, reach, and build solid relationships with the B, C, and as comedienne Kathy Griffin puts it, the D list. You are looking for the people who have a reach of 10, 100, or 1,000, maybe even 10,000 who write for *your* market. *These bloggers are looking for the information that you have.* They would love to write about you—again assuming that what you offer is worth writing about—if only they knew about you.

This is where tools such as BuzzStream, Sysomos, Scout Labs, and Alterian's SM2 platform really shine. They'll help you find the sources of conversations that relate to your business, and then through their own decoding of the social graph, they will connect enough information together (in most cases—no system is ever perfect) that you can initiate a relationship and then develop it through a managed Social CRM and influencer program.

Social CRM and Influencer Relations

Influencer relations extend the basics of blogger outreach one more level, taking your outreach and relationship management efforts to the individual level. In an AdWeek post covering the release of Accenture's 2010 Global Content Study, columnist Marco Vernocchi summarized one of the key findings this way:

> "Target individuals, not audiences. The days of thinking about audiences in broadly defined demographic buckets are over. As consumers abandon analog and consume more and more content on digital, connected platforms, media companies have been handed an opportunity—an obligation, even—to engage with customers as never before."

This is again where the power tools come in. You don't have to "meet and greet" every single customer: Instead, you need a way to identify them individually when they need or want your attention—a capability of a traditional CRM program—*and* you need a way to engage these people and connect them into your business so that the collaborative processes they'll engage in have a chance of taking root. This is the *Social* CRM component on your overall social business program, and this is what you are after.

The Social Web is open to all comers: there is a place for everyone in your program. Today's one-off customer interaction may just turn someone into tomorrow's evangelist. In addition to known customers, bloggers, and enthusiast influencers, your Social CRM program will identify and help solidify relationships at a near-grassroots level with large numbers of local or small-network influencers. Added up this can be significant, and it is well worth your effort.

Here's why: Aside from reaching and building relationships with people who may be influential to large groups of people important to you—a blogger with a following, a journalist, an industry expert, or similar—consumers are increasingly making their purchase decisions based on information, tips, and recommendations from "people like themselves." Take a look at the sidebar on the Edleman Trust Barometer and go and download that free report (a PDF file). The Trust Barometer, itself from a trusted source, makes a very convincing case for both the need for social media listening programs and for extracting from these conversation the information and insight you need to position your business for long-term success.

The Edelman Trust Barometer

The Edelman Trust Barometer is a measure of the relative trustworthiness of various sources of information. Over the past 10 years there has been a significant shift, corresponding first with the mainstream adoption of the Internet and more recently with the use of social tools. In short, traditional sources of trust—people like CEOs, analysts, and news reporters—have been replaced with "people like me," with word-of-mouth and curated social media. It is a significant shift that you cannot ignore.

You will find the complete 2009 report here:

http://www.edelman.com/trust/2009

Influencer Relations: A Representative Case

Following is a quick case on the use of Social CRM tools for influencer outreach. In this case the primary challenge was assembling a cross section of influencers from a very large and distributed set of individuals who are influencers of relatively small numbers of people. It's a great example of the "influencers" challenge described previously.

Grasshopper

As a B2B virtual phone services company, Grasshopper's motivation in adopting a Social CRM program for its business grew out of its need to understand and internalize the influencer process and customer renewal cycle. The business objective for the company's use of social media was simple enough: According to Jonathan Kay, Grasshopper's Ambassador of Buzz, "Everywhere you look, someone should be talking about Grasshopper." We should all want for as much.

Strong believers in social media and "PR 2.0," the firm doesn't have an agency, and they're not focused on pumping out press releases. Instead, they're focused on building relationships with influencers. Pay it forward, right? This includes traditional media small business stalwarts such as *Inc. Magazine* and *BusinessWeek,* along with high influence blogs such as *TechCrunch* and niche bloggers in both the mid- and long-tail that are focused on entrepreneurship and business (hardware) communications.

Grasshopper's marketing strategy depends heavily for intelligence on its Social CRM program. Jonathan routinely engages with people on Twitter and other brand outposts where they talk about Grasshopper, entrepreneurship, and similarly related topics. Based on the content of these conversations, Grasshopper's Social CRM program connects people who are looking for information with those who have it: the firm's brand evangelists.

Having looked at a number of platforms, Jonathan concluded that most important to him was a Social CRM toolset that fit the *workflow* of a marketer, and one that automated the capture of the conversational information. His starting point in influencer discovery is typically a blog post, a tweet, or a forum post, which he finds based on specific key words that appear in the conversations. From that starting point, Jonathan needs to turn this raw data—the conversations and possible contact links—into an actual contact. Going forward, he also needs to keep track of their subsequently published content and the associated metrics underlying his developing relationship with this person.

BuzzStream, the tool Jonathan uses, manages the process for him, automatically bringing back the information that he scans before creating an actual contact. Once done, supporting metrics and outreach tracking built into the platform complete the picture. Social CRM platforms like BuzzStream increase outreach efficiency, which in turn allows the development of more and stronger relationships with the influencers that matter to Grasshopper.

For more information on Grasshopper, see the following:

`http://grasshopper.com`

Review and Hands-On

This chapter defines the new role of customers and stakeholders—the recipients of the experiences associated with the product or service you are providing—and then connects those customers and stakeholders into your business. Social CRM is the larger analytical process that wraps all of this and helps you understand how to respond in a dynamic, conversation-driven marketplace.

Review of the Main Points

This chapter explored the more participative role of the customer and the tools that support the new expectation of an opportunity to talk back to the brand, so to speak, and shape future experiences and interactions. In particular, this chapter covered the following:

- Social CRM is a business philosophy. It refers to the tools and technologies used to connect your customers and influencers into the forward looking, collaborative processes that will shape your business or organization as you move forward.

- Where your traditional CRM system is transaction-centric—defining customers in terms of behaviors related to past purchases or interactions—Social CRM is about tapping "what's next" from their point of view. Like traditional CRM, Social CRM is most useful when applied at the business (operational) level.

- Influencer identification programs—whether targeting bloggers specifically or consumer/enthusiasts and similar influencers—can be automated, with the resultant conversations routed directly into your organization and to the people where it can be most effective. Look for automation, workflow, and contact management when selecting social media analytics and influencer identification tools.

- Your employees are an integral component of your social business program. Implementing a knowledge-assimilation-and-sharing platform can beneficially impact the ability of your organization to respond to customer-generated innovation.

In summary, social business involves the entire organization and the complete management team in response to the newly defined role of the customer *as a participant* in your business. Some of the concepts and technologies may have grown out of or been most recently associated with marketing. Unlike the adoption of social-media-based marketing initiatives, however, picking up on and implementing ideas generated through social business inputs requires the participation of the *entire* organization.

Hands-On: Review These Resources

Review each of the following, combining the main points covered in the chapter and the ways in which the following resources expand on these points. Then tie each into your business or organization:

Paul Greenberg's "Social CRM Comes of Age"

http://www.oracle.com/ocom/groups/public/@ocompublic/documents/
webcontent/036062.pdf

Jeremiah Owyang's listing of Social CRM tools

http://www.web-strategist.com/blog/2009/12/08/list-of-companies-providing-
social-crm

The 2009 Edelman Trust Barometer

http://www.edelman.com/trust/2009

Hands-On: Apply What You've Learned

Apply what you've learned in this chapter through the following exercises:

1. Define your ideal Social CRM platform: What are your business objectives, and who are you looking to create relationships with? How would your current customers fit into this, and how might they participate in your business or organization?

2. Integrate step 1 into your current CRM and product design programs. Who will participate in the various initiatives that define your plan? What is the role that you see customers playing?

3. Identify the key stakeholders in the departments you will need to work with in order to address and resolve the *broad types* of issues you are likely to encounter.

Build a Social Business

Creating a social business—that is to say, a business that is connected through deliberately collaborative processes with both its customers and its employees—is the task now facing many C-level and other business executives with similar responsibilities. Web 2.0 is challenging business leadership not only in the marketplace but now as well across business fronts ranging from corporate reputation and the attraction and retention of key employees to the design of new products and services. This chapter looks into the fundamental concepts of what makes a business "social."

3

What Is Social Business?

Social business—the application of social technologies as a formal component of business processes—revolves around understanding how your customers or stakeholders connect to your business and how you reshape your business to understand, accept, and innovate based on their involvement. Social business is about integrating all of your business functions: customer support, marketing, the executive team, and more. It means doing this for the purpose of creating collaborative innovation and engagement at meaningful, measurable levels tied clearly and directly to your company's business objectives.

Social Businesses Are Participative

Ultimately, social business is about participation with and by your customers and stakeholders in pursuit of an organization that is strongly connected to them through participative and collaborative processes. As a result, a social business is often better able to respond to marketplace dynamics and competitive opportunities than a traditionally organized and managed firm. This may occur through participation in a social community, a support or discussion forum, or any of a variety of other social applications and contexts. The efforts leading to the creation of a social business often begin with identifying or creating an opportunity for participation with (or between) customers, employees, or stakeholders within community or similar social applications.

An important point to note here is that when social business practices are approached and implemented correctly, everyone wins. By bringing customers into the business, or directly involving stakeholders in the design and operation of the organizations with which they are associated, a steady flow of ultimately constructive ideas emerges. One of the biggest misconceptions about social media and the Social Web as regards business commentary is that it's all negative, that the participants are all complainers and whiners. Not so.

In a 2007 Zenith Optimedia study, of the 3 billion or so word of mouth conversations that occur worldwide, every day, about 2/3 of them involve or reference a product, brand, or piece of media. Moreover, positive mentions significantly outweighed negatives. The fact is, unless your business strategy is to generate negative comments—I can think of a few outfits for whom that might actually be the case—the Social Web very likely presents significant opportunity for building your business and improving it over time.

Building a social business starts with establishing a community or other social presence around or in which your brand fits naturally—whether through a casual presence on Twitter, a more involved Facebook business presence, or your own community built for suppliers, partners, or customers. Element 14, an Indian electronics components supplier, offers engineers using its catalog a community that facilitates idea sharing, shared ratings, and collaboration around hardware solutions. The community is now a core component of Element 14's B2B go-to-market strategy: The engineer's community drives new applications, more timely information shared between engineers, and a stronger connection between Element 14 and its business customers.

Build Around Customer Participation

Regardless of who the community is intended to serve, strong communities are best built around the things that matter deeply to the members of the community: passions, lifestyles, causes, and similar fundamentally aligned needs. This applies whether the audience is primarily business—B2B communities like Element 14's engineering community or Dell's "Take Your Path" small business owners community form around very specific shared needs common to small business owners—or a personal-interest B2C or nonprofit or cause related community.

The core elements powering a social business in any case need to be something to which the community members (customers or potential customers, for example) will spontaneously bond, and that as a result will encourage them to invite others to join. In the case of Dell's "Take Your Own Path," the common element is the unique set of challenges faced by small businesses. If you've ever met a small business owner, you know how passionate they are about what they do. Dell has found a very effective way through the practices of social business to tap this by identifying and serving the needs of the small business owner—for example, by encouraging discussion about finance and investments in business hardware.

Similarly, smaller communities—think here about the need to reach highly defined groups of customers, where personal interests drive strong relationships—are prime opportunities for social business initiatives: Again, take for example Dell and their "Digital Nomads" program, aimed at a specific segment of Dell's customer base that literally thrives on the availability of an online connection. Digital nomads are productive in the office or outside of it, staying in touch with friends and updating colleagues on work in progress through social applications as close as the nearest WiFi enabled coffee shop or hotel. One of the common factors identifying "Digital Nomads" is the combination of lifestyle and digital tools, along with the wherewithal to get connected in just about any situation. Dell hardware powers this and thereby taps into the nomadic lifestyle of these on-the-go professionals. It's important here to recognize that communities like "Digital Nomads" and "Take Your Own Path" are not defined by a business or consumer or nonprofit motive—call this *your* point of view or need—but rather by the needs and desires of the *participants* within these communities.

Participation Is Driven by Passion

Getting the activity focused on something larger than your brand, product, or service is critical to the successful development of social behavior within the customer or stakeholder base and as well within the firm or organization itself. After all, if narrowly defined business interests take center stage, if the social interaction is built purely around business objectives, then what will the customers of that business find useful? What's in it for them?

Further, how will the employees of that business rally around the needs of your customers? At Southwest Airlines, employees are bound together in service of the customer, through a passionate belief for the freedom to fly being a reality for anyone. So much so that when times are tough or situations demand it, the employees don the personas of "Freedom Fighters" and literally go to work on behalf of preserving the "right to fly" for their customers. As Freedom Fighters, they keep the characteristic Southwest energy up: This translates directly into the positive conversations about this aspect of Southwest Airlines found on the Social Web. Being a Freedom Fighter is the kind of powerful ideal that unites businesses and customers and the kind of passion— for travel, exploration, or the ability to go out and conquer new markets as a business executive—that powers Southwest. It's the kind of passion around which a business traveler's community can be built.

Build a Purpose-Driven Business

If you're interested in how Southwest Airlines built its legendary service teams, you'll find the complete story in "It's Not What You Sell, It's What You Stand For," by GSD&M's Roy Spence and Haley Rushing. If a business fails to connect to its customers through their passions and points of interest, it cannot hope to engage them in ways that lead to collaboration.

While the preceding section used community formation as an example, the social business summary point is this: By understanding the passions, lifestyles, and causes that are relevant to your customers, you can identify the best social pathways through which to build connections to your product, brand, or service. This is where a number of otherwise well-intentioned efforts go wrong: Attempting to build a community around a brand or product will often fail as participation is driven primarily by advertising expenditure and (costly) promotions rather than by organic interest generated by and between the participants themselves.

In Search of a Higher Calling

The surest way to avoid this trap is to appeal to passion, lifestyle, or cause—in other words, to anchor your initiatives in something larger than your brand, product, or service: Appeal to a "higher calling," in a manner of speaking, one that is carefully selected to both attract the people you want to associate with and to provide a natural home or connection to your brand, product, or service.

Figure 3.1 shows the traditional business model: You make it, you tell your customers about it, and they (hopefully) buy it. This works well enough provided your product or service delivers as promised with little or no need for further dialog. It helps too if it is marketed in a context where traditional media is useful and covers the majority of your market. Traditional media has wide reach, and it is interruptible: This provides a ready pathway to attentive customers and potential markets. The downside is that traditional media is also getting more and more expensive—TV advertising costs have increased over 250 percent in the past decade—and it's harder to reach your entire audience: What took three spots to achieve in 1965 now takes, by current estimates and measures, in excess of 100. Figure 3.1 is largely representative of this basic approach that has defined business for the past fifty years.

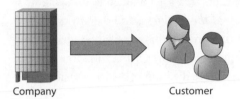

Company   Customer

Figure 3.1 Traditional Business

Figure 3.2 shows an evolved view of business and the beginning of a move away from a purely transactional view of the customer: The customer receives (or consumes) marketing messages, for example, buys the product or service, or enrolls in your organization, but then also goes on to provide feedback, whether directly through a survey card, via CRM or similar or through a listening program that collects and analyzes conversations. The difference is that there is a feedback mechanism: As such, compliments can flow your way, and concerns, because they can be expressed, don't turn into frustrated rants provided of course that something is done about them. Recall that this opportunity to listen and understand, and thereby craft a response, is a direct benefit of participation with customers, whether through traditional methods or as now, on the Social Web.

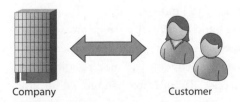

Company   Customer

Figure 3.2 Evolved Business

Finally, Figure 3.3 shows the business-customer relationship when the idea of a higher calling is introduced. The higher calling forms a common bonding point for both the business or organization and customers and stakeholders, and in particular in the context of social participation with a business. To be sure, savvy marketers have tapped this best practice even through their traditional campaigns: At GSD&M | Idea City, where I worked with clients ranging from the Air Force to Chili's to Land Rover, Walmart and AARP, we connected the brand with the customer through a shared value and purpose, something larger than the brand itself and to which both the brand and customer simultaneously aspired. This created a very powerful linkage that transcended the basic brand-consumer relationship. This same type of appeal to a common purpose or value that is larger than the brand itself can be applied in an analogous manner on the Social Web.

Social media takes this practice to the next level. Social media inherently revolves around passions, lifestyles, and causes—the higher calling that defines larger social objects to which participants relate. The social media programs that are intended to link customers to communities and shared social activities *around the business*, and thereby around the brand, product, or service must themselves be anchored in this same larger ideal. Compare Figure 3.3 with Figures 3.1 and 3.2: Simple in concept, getting this larger social object identified and in place is critical to the successful realization of a social business.

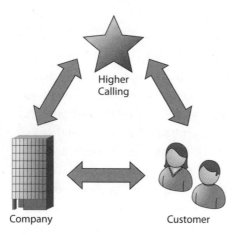

Figure 3.3 The Higher Calling

Here is a down-to-earth example: Tupperware, and more specifically Tupperware parties. Having seen more than a few of these first-hand as a child, a Tupperware party seemed to me to be little more than a dozen or so women getting together to spend a couple of hours laughing and talking about plastic tubs. Obviously, I didn't get it: There was a higher purpose involved, a much higher purpose: Tupperware had tapped into the basic human need for socialization, and a Tupperware party provided the perfect occasion to link this need with its product line. The combination of great products, meeting its customers' human needs (social interchange) as well as their practical needs (efficient, organized food, and related item storage) has helped Tupperware build a business as timeless and durable as the products it sells.

Pepsico's "The Juice" campaign is another example of how this higher calling and shared purpose (in the traditional marketing context, extended to social media) works. The strategy behind this campaign shows how effective social media programs—and the savvy businesses with the skills to correctly execute in this medium—really work. Built on BlogHer, The Juice was a core element of the promotional platform for Pepsico's low-cal Trop50 brand orange juice. BlogHer co-founder and COO Elisa Camahort Page shared the following insight—consistent with the idea of a higher purpose. The campaign anchor—the social motive—for BlogHer and The Juice *is not* the sponsoring brand. Instead, it is something larger: The anchor is found in the common interest of *all* women around seeking ways to find more balance, more health, and more helpful tips for use in their lives. PepsiCo's value proposition to its customers and the larger BlogHer community as both sponsor and purveyor of Trop50 fits naturally within this.

The Juice benefits from the natural alignment between brands, interests, passions, lifestyles, and causes along with the specific tasks, questions, and the things people want to know more about. It's the questions they want answered, the moments they want to share, and the problems that they want solved that drive this effective social program.

$pend Your Way to a Social Presence

The appeal to a higher calling—to a lifestyle, passion, or cause—is what drives organic participation and growth in online social communities. The payoffs are lower ongoing expenses and a higher degree of "stickiness" and participation and advocacy for the community. Given the central role established for the higher social object, a question arises here: What is it that powers social marketing applications, communities, and sites *which lack a cause, passion, or lifestyle connection* as seen in programs like Pepsi's "The Juice"?

The answer is typically spending. This is not to overlook the great creative work that goes into promotional campaigns, but rather to note that spend-driven programs versus purpose or values-aligned programs will often lag in the organic growth that truly powers social media and the waves of activity that occur on the Social Web.

To understand why this is so, compare the social appeal of the Old Spice Deodorant social media campaign shown in Figure 3.4 with the basic social appeal of Facebook, Orkut or other social networking sites, where participation is driven largely out of a desire to interact with other members of these networks. People join them to meet other people as well as to share experiences around the brands they love (along with a whole lot of other things).

Great social sites grow organically based on an individual's realization of a reason to be there: Facebook and Orkut, for example, both deliver on the basic desires of people to meet other people and socialize. Members see the value in "more members" so they actively encourage their friends to join. The obvious purpose and basic appeal of these sites combine to drive organic growth.

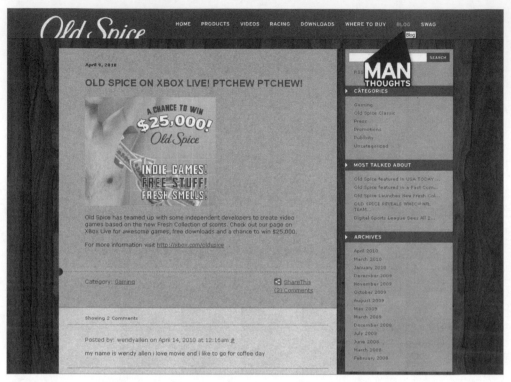

Figure 3.4 Old Spice "Swaggerize" Campaign

As a result, participation and organic growth occur naturally, without the need for costly promotions: People will join social networks like Facebook and Orkut and use these services on their own, for hours at a time, without paid incentives.

By comparison, the participation in the Old Spice deodorant campaign—which includes many of the same basic social elements like a blog, send-to-friend and similar—is driven by awareness advertising and a continuous series of promotions and contests, all of which come at a direct cost to Old Spice. This is not necessarily a negative. From a marketing perspective, this may be a very effective campaign. That said, lacking a genuine lifestyle, passion, or cause at the root of the social motivation it's clear that when the promotional spending supporting the Old Spice social site stops, the activity in the campaign will likely subside as well. Compared with the ongoing organic (free!) growth of a passion- or lifestyle-driven community, this is likely to be a more expensive and less engaging route, and not as likely to result in the types of collaborative behaviors that are associated with solid social business initiatives.

In the case of the social business, the collaboration occurs in two venues: customers between other customers, and customers between employees. In the latter, collaboration generally occurs *only* when your customers develop sufficient trust—and your employees develop sufficient visibility—such that the two begin a conversation about how the business may be changed for the better. When charting your course in social business, be sure that you distinguish between social media *marketing* efforts—like the Swaggerize campaign—and social business programs that more tightly link the personal lifestyles, passions, and causes of customers with the business and its products and services as was done with Pepsi's "The Juice." Social-media-based marketing efforts like Swaggerize can drive awareness—and there is value in that. That said, The Juice builds on the organic growth and participation in the underlying BlogHer community by naturally placing its product into this context. There is a compelling (and measurable) value to the brand in that, too.

Three Levels of Social Activities

Jake Mckee has created a nice articulation of the views on building a social presence advanced by Chris Brogan and others. Following this view, the activities that surround social media and social business can be thought of in three layers:

A Home Base

Your home "brand" or organizational home base consists of your website, related properties, and associated microsites.

Outposts

The outposts are the properties or sites that you do not own or control, but in which you participate and create connections. Twitter, Facebook, and Orkut are examples of outposts. Importantly, brands can have an "official" presence in these outposts, which can be managed as a part of a larger, integrated marketing and business effort.

Passports

Passports are the places where you are invited or otherwise welcomed to participate: A guest blogging program or a blogger outreach program, for example. Note that if your participation is not overt in its connection to your business, you should take the steps needed to ensure such disclosure.

You can read more about the concepts and best practices around the use of a home base, brand outposts, and passports here:

http://www.presenceframework.com

http://www.chrisbrogan.com/a-simple-presence-framework

62

Build Your Social Presence

Campaign-centric communities are *not* the focus of a social business program. If you find yourself thinking "campaign," you are either heading for social-media-based marketing or traditional/digital marketing that is made to "look like" social media. Beware: The focus of social business—distinct from social media marketing—is around the application of the Social Web to business in ways that are driven fundamentally through organic versus paid processes and which are intended to benefit your business generally versus sell products specifically.

Organic communities and Social Web activities built around a business are designed to exist independently of direct spending in marketing, with the possible caveat of initial seeding. They are intended to inform the business, to connect it to its audience, and to encourage collaboration between customers and employees toward the objective of improving the business, and to sustain this over time for the purpose of driving superior business results. It is equally likely that the software and related infrastructure expenses of a social business program will be paid for through Operations or IT as through Marketing.

Again, this is not to say that there is no value in spend-driven communities. There is potentially significant promotional value that arises out of measured fulfillment against marketing and advertising goals. It is to say that in addition to these types of marketing campaigns, social business programs are centered on core business objectives and expressed through an appeal to the lifestyles, passion, and causes of customers. These types of programs are specifically put in place to encourage collaborative participation. The collaboration that occurs between customers and between employees is the root focus of social business.

The Elements of Social Business

The following are helpful when considering a social business strategy. Taken together, and built around a central alignment between Marketing and Operations, these core elements support an organic approach to the application of the Social Web to business. The later chapters that focus on each are also indicated.

Customers, Stakeholders, and Employees

Beginning with the conversations occurring on the Social Web, actively listening, responding, facilitating collaboration, and retaining customers are among the primary objectives of a successful social business implementation. Chapter 5, "Social Technology and Business Decisions," Chapter 6, "Social Analytics, Metrics and Measurement," and Chapter 7, "Five Essential Tips When Starting Out" in Part II along with Chapter 8, "Engagement on the Social Web," and Chapter 9 "Social CRM," in Part III provide tips, best practices, and examples of how this is accomplished.

The Elements of Social Business *(Continued)*

Communities and Forums

Built around a cause, lifestyle, passion, or similar attraction, communities and forums encourage social interaction between participants. These community and similar platforms create natural conversational space—controlled by the community participants—that can be simultaneously useful to a business or organization. Chapter 10, "Social Objects," and Chapter 11, "The Social Graph," provide insights and cases supporting the development of strong online communities and forums.

Social Applications

Social applications are the components of a social business implementation that connect participants within existing communities—think Twitter, Facebook or Orkut—to which they belong. Social applications deliver on a specific need or utility that exists within the community but is not directly provided by it—for example, a Facebook application such as Super Wall or the SocialVibe cause-supportive application delivered through Facebook. Social applications can be used to express the brand and/or deliver a brand-related value—like being able to trigger or direct a contribution to a selected cause—without leaving the larger community in which the application is deployed. Chapter 12, "Social Applications," provides a deeper dive into social applications and how to plan your use of them.

So what is it that drives organic growth and sets the social technology-powered business on a road of its own? It comes back to the initial assertion that organic growth occurs around lifestyles, passions, causes, specific task-based utilities, and similar participant-centric activities and interests rather than brand-, product-, or service-centered attributes. The primary challenge is therefore to align or connect the firm or organization to an existing community or to build one around an existing lifestyle, passion, or cause that connects to the core business.

In Figure 3.5, the fundamental relationship between experiences that are talked about (word of mouth), community participation, and the function of the brand outpost is shown. Unlike social media marketing, the application of the Social Web to the business itself views the participants as an integral component of the business, rather than simply participants in a campaign. In this context, the naturally occurring (non-paid) activities of participants are the most valuable. The design of the social business components is powered by the activities that are sustained through participant-driven interest.

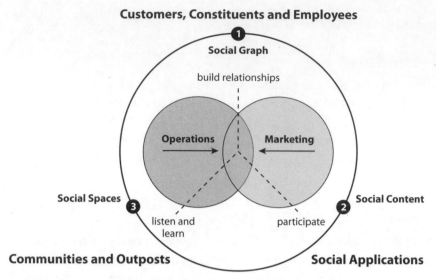

Customers, Constituents and Employees

Figure 3.5 The Social Business

Business as a Social Participant

People gather around a shared interest, cause, or lifestyle in pursuit of a sense of collective experience. Important to understand is that they are often motivated by an apparent desire to talk about a brand, product, or service experience with each other, relating this to what they have in common. What they have in common may in part be that brand, product, or service, but it is generally also something deeper. Apple products—and the following they have created—are a great example of this: Apple owners are seemingly connected by Apple products, but in a deeper sense they are connected by the ethos of Apple and the smart, independent lifestyle associated with the brand.

For LEGO enthusiasts—and in particular adult LEGO enthusiasts— there is a gathering that occurs on LUGNET.com along with a variety of other fan-created websites, forums, and blogs. Conversations appear to revolve around LEGO products, but in reality the higher calling is the shared passion for creation, which LEGO (as a product) facilitates. While LEGO creation may bring members to the community, and while it may be the common thread that unites a seemingly disparate group, the camaraderie is what keeps members together years upon years. A business or organization is itself in many respects a social place. In much the same way, the social business is a place where employees and customers gather together around a common purpose of creating the products and services that define—and are often subsequently defined by—the brand and its higher purpose. Employees and customers, together through collaboration, create the experiences they want: Together they are responsible for the business. When the conversations that result are a reflection of this shared interest of both customers and employees, the conversations themselves are very likely to be powerful expressions that carry the business or organization forward.

This kind of end result—an expressed passion around a brand, product, or service—is associated with the higher stages of engagement. Beyond consumption of content, engagement in the form of curation of community interaction, creation of content and collaboration between participants are the activities leading to advocacy. Consider the role that collaboration plays in contributing to the sense of ownership as a result of the combined efforts of employees and customers, participating together in the creation of a shared outcome. This sense of joint ownership, however subtly it may be expressed, is in fact a reasonable and even required customer sentiment that once and for all "cuts through the clutter."

Brand Outposts

As a result of the growth in social activities on the Web, there is a natural expectation on the part of consumers to find the brands they love in the social sites they frequent. As a matter of course, customers expect this kind of presence and participation. In addition to the branded community efforts described prior, an alternative (or complementary) approach to connecting a brand or organization with an *existing* community also exists: The creation of *brand presence*—known as a brand outpost—within an established social network or online community—a Facebook Business Page, a Twitter presence or a YouTube channel to list just a few. In creating a brand outpost—in comparison to a self-standing community—there need not be any reason other than the expectation for the brand to be present and a tie back to business objectives that are served by such a presence. There does, of course, need to be a relevant contribution by the brand, product, or service *to the community it wishes to join.* Simply posting TV commercials to YouTube, for example, is in most cases not going to produce engagement beyond the firm's own employees and perhaps their families watching these commercials. New content created for YouTube—Freescale's allowance of employee videos—is the kind of content that is both welcomed and appreciated, since it is created specifically for this venue.

In particular, Facebook members expect to find their favorite brands on Facebook. So Aircel, an Indian Telecom provider, created a Facebook application that embeds Aircel voicemail services within Facebook, providing both a link to customers in an important new media channel and a point of competitive differentiation. Aircel Customers present on Facebook, who as a group tend to be younger and savvier when it comes to their use of the social web use this application to stay up with voicemail without ever leaving Facebook. The Aircel voicemail application is shown in Figure 3.6.

Citing its own business objectives around customer service, Australia's Telstra created its Twitter presence (@telstra) partly out of recognition that Twitter is a burgeoning customer service portal and that—as is the case with Facebook, Orkut, and other leading social networks—its own customers expect it to be there.

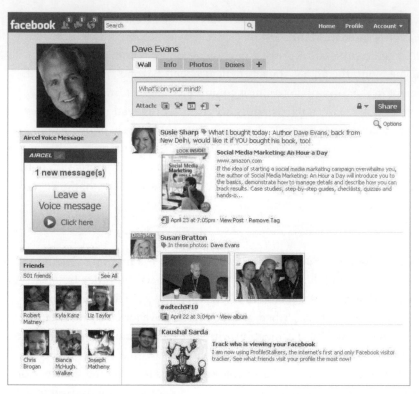

Figure 3.6 Aircel: Facebook voicemail

This kind of presence in existing social networks is welcomed as it makes sense from the perspective of consumers. Most brands are present in all of the other places where people spend time: on TV, on the radio, in movies (before the show and integrated into it), in all forms of outdoor advertising, and at sports events and more. Social sites—the new gathering place—are no exceptions. Movie studios, soft drink brands, auto manufacturers, and more are all building "brand outposts" on Facebook, Orkut, and other social sites because their audience spends significant time on those sites. Many of the brands and organizations participating in the social web are coincidentally skipping the development of dedicated product microsites and even major TV brand campaigns in favor of a stronger presence in these social sites. As a part of your overall social business strategy, don't overlook the obvious: Orkut, Facebook, Twitter, LinkedIn, Slideshare, Delicious…all offer places where your business or organization can add value to the larger social communities that naturally form around these social applications.

Social Business and Measurement

Before diving into the use of social media in business, consider the basic measurement methods as they apply to the business use of social technology. Chapter 6 explores measurement and metrics in-depth. As an initial step into the integration of metrics within your social programs, however—and to get you thinking about this aspect of undertaking a social business effort—consider the assessment of participation, applied knowledge transfer, and the measurement of social activity in general as a starting point to a quantitative guide in building and running your social business.

Collaborate

Collaboration—sitting atop the engagement process—is the defining expression of measurable engagement. Marketers often speak of engagement: For example, one might focus on time spent on a page, or the number of retries a customer is willing to undergo before meeting with success. Measures such as "returning visitors," connected to concepts such as "loyalty" are also used as surrogates for engagement. While all of these have value within the discipline of marketing—and most certainly have a role in establishing efficacy of brand and promotional communications over a period of time—they do not in and of themselves provide a quantitative basis for the stronger notions of engagement as defined in the social business context. The direct observation of collaboration does.

Collaboration between community members, between employees, or between a firm and its representatives comes about when both parties in the transaction see a value in completing the transaction, often repeatedly. The output of collaborative processes—the number of jointly developed solutions advanced in an expert's community, for example—is directly measurable. Think about counting the number of collaborative processes that lead to a solution, or the number of shared results. Each is an indicator of the respective participant's willingness to put effort into such processes. In this sense, the quantitative assessment of collaboration becomes a very robust indicator for the relative strength of the engagement process.

Participation

Participation is likely one of the easiest metrics to capture and track. Indicators of participation can be gathered from existing measures—content creation, curation, and the number of reviews, comments, and posts—and can then be used to assess the overall levels of interest and activity within online communities.

Foursquare—Gaming Drives Participation

Foursquare is a location-based service that provides users with tips left by others when they check in at a specific location. To help spur participation, Foursquare uses a gaming-like point system—which itself is a useful metric for the Foursquare development team—that directly rewards participants for checking in, adding new venues, and leaving tips—exactly the activities that increase value for the Foursquare community.

http://foursquare.com

At the most basic level, as with any online interaction, the activity itself can be tracked. Accessing a page, submitting a form, downloading a file and similar content measures provide a well-understood framework for measurement. However, given the existence of *profiles* (explored more in the next section) and the behaviors associated with *curation*—rating, ranking, etc.—much more interesting and useful metrics can be established and used to create very robust measures of participation.

As another aspect of participation and its direct measurement, consider "point-based" social community reputation systems. Participants in a support community are very often rewarded through increasing social rank based on contribution to the community. Upon joining, you may be assigned the rank of "newbie" and then over time earn your way to "expert" status as you contribute and gain the votes of others in the community as they curate your contributions. At some level, there is a basic point system that is translating individual actions within the community into personal reputations: it may be visible, or it may be buried in the inner working of the community's reputation management system. Either way, it's there and can tapped as a source of metrics. When participants do something beneficial, they earn a point. When they do something that offends the community they might lose a point. Track both and you've got a solid assessment of participation.

In a thoughtful analysis using tested techniques applied in a novel manner, social media strategist Bud Caddell points out a very straightforward method for calculating the relative distribution for participation and thereby gaining quantitative insight into the role of community influencers. Bud's method—simplified—is based on a statistical approach to tracking the spread in variance based on ratings points over time. Communities that have high variance are being influenced by a relatively small number of people compared with those with lesser variance. This is important because over time what is generally desirable is a more equitable distribution of participative effort—lower variance—across the community.

Measure Relative Participation

Bud Caddell's insightful measurement technique for assessing the degree to which a community is influenced versus peer led is not only useful, but also shows the ways in which existing, well-understood statistical techniques can be applied to behavioral analysis when setting up measures of participation for your online community. You can follow Bud on Twitter: @Bud_Caddell.

http://www.seomoz.org/ugc/measuring-participation-inequality-in-social-networks

As a practical example of the ways in which measurement can be brought to social computing, consider the ongoing investment and attention to social computing at IBM. Literally for decades, IBM employees have been building, studying, and improving its implementation of social computing both internally connecting employees—and externally—connecting customers.

Social Networking for Business

For more on the direct application of social networking and social computing for business, consider reading Rawn Shah's "Social Networking for Business," published in 2010. Follow Rawn on Twitter: @Rawn.

`http://www.onlinecommunityreport.com/archives/599-Online-Community-Expert-Interview-Rawn-Shaw,-IBM.html`

In a 2010 interview, Bill Johnston, now with Dell, talks with Rawn Shah, Practice Lead for IBM's Social Software Adoption effort, about assessing internal versus external participation:

Internally we have a closed population of users where we know all the individuals involved. Therefore our internal metrics can be focused down to the activities of specific groups and populations of individuals—we avoid getting down to specific individuals to protect privacy—so we can assess participation based on organizational role: regional versus global sales, for example. Externally however, the population is much more mixed and rarely do we have data per specifically identified people. This leads us to very different types of behavioral information: internally we can categorize users by their level of participation (zero, low, medium, high, elite) in our social environments, and then examine the actions or distribution of these members across the geographies. With the external environment, social media monitoring tools and services from other companies allow us to take the pulse of activity along different topics. We then have to infer behavior based on the level of interest in topics across the Web.

Applied Knowledge Transfer

Understanding and tracking participation is obviously important in managing the growth and development of a collaborative community. However, participation is only half the challenge. Participation speaks to action but not necessarily value. The key to measuring the *value* of participation is simultaneously ensuring that something useful—as defined within the community and then connected to your business objectives—is also happening. It's a lot like the general notion that "having momentum" is good. True enough, but ensuring that it is not primarily the angular variety is also important.

How do we keep from spinning in circles? By tying levels of participation and collaboration to an ultimate end point: the accumulation of applied knowledge—for example, a wiki of customer solutions that have been tested and are known to work—in the context of specific business objectives.

Whether your social business application is internal, external, or a combination of the two, the ingredients for success are high levels of participation and the realization of useful applied knowledge—the "value" component that defines many communities. Platforms like Salesforce.com's "Ideas" are particularly good in this regard because they encourage participation and in the process create a useable body of collaboratively amassed knowledge that can be directly applied to a business or organizational challenge or opportunity.

Assessing the sharing of solutions, for example, is surprisingly easy. Combining two best practices taken from the business uses of social computing points the way. First, track the overall accumulation of content and ideas. Then, encourage the community to curate and refine this content, pushing the most valuable content to the top and improving it over time. Establish a "cutoff" based on the norms of your community and measure the applied knowledge or resultant solutions created that are ranked at or above that threshold.

As a further basis for the evaluation of knowledge and solution transfer, weight the amount of content produced by the curation scores—in other words, develop a weighted scoring that emphasizes the value of more useful content—and then track that over time. Tie the profile data into this, and you'll spot the sources of high-demand expertise, both within and external to your organization. You can then study the internal sources and extract the best practices associated with these relatively higher knowledge sources and apply these resources across other teams. Externally, you can use tools such as BuzzStream (covered in Chapter 2, "The New Role of the Customer") to build relationships with the leading holders of external knowledge.

Frank Leistner

Frank Leistner is SAS Institutes' Chief Knowledge Officer. Frank's book, *Mastering Organizational Knowledge Flow*, published by Wiley and SAS Business Series, guides you through the process and considerations useful when developing collaborative teams inside your organization.

You can find the book at leading booksellers, and you can follow Frank (@kmjuggler) on Twitter.

Social Activity

In addition to the measures of *what* is happening within the community, brand outpost or the internal online workspace, *where* the activities are occurring also lends itself to measurement.

Starting with social profiles, one of the easiest (and as it turns out most important) metrics to keep track of is profile completeness. Long ago, LinkedIn implemented an easy-to-understand indicator of profile completeness: Does a specific profile include a picture, an address, and contact information, for example? Because this information is often central to creating a relationship, the average state of completion is worth knowing. Profile data, actual content production, and community reputation are the primary visible attributes on which a decision to accept a connection request are based. Be sure that you have a way to assess these.

Relationships themselves are also worth tracking. To what extent is a community driving the creation of relationships? How many are being formed, and between whom? This can be understood by tracking the number of unidirectional (think "following" in Twitter) relationships as well the number of mutually affirmed friendships or other similar connections that exist. Add to this the relative number of communications that flow between mutually connected profiles to create a measure of the importance of relationships in day-to-day activities.

Outposts and communities—the places where social activity happens—are a final source of quantitative data that leads to an assessment of value. Within these social spaces, tracking the number of member versus nonmember interactions (if the latter are permitted), the number of times members log in, membership abandonment (for example, members who have not logged in for 90 days or more) all provide a basis to understand—quantitatively—what is happening inside social communities and by extension with the organizations that implement social media-based business programs.

Chapter 6 provides an in-depth treatment of these and additional metrics: As you work through the next sections, keep these initial measurement techniques and sources of data in mind. Rest assured that when you're implementing social computing and social media techniques as a part of a business strategy, the outcomes can most certainly be held to quantitative performance standards.

Employees as Change Agents

Getting social business right depends on more than understanding what your customers or stakeholders are talking about and how that relates to your firm. Social business depends as well on connecting your employees into the social processes. For example, the learning vis-à-vis the social data collected may be routed to and applied in marketing, to operations areas like customer support or to other departments *within* the organization where it can be acted on.

The final link in the chain is therefore to connect employees (organizational participants in the more general sense) to each other and into the flow of customer information. This last section of the chapter introduces the internal applications of social technologies that lead to an effective response mechanism. This completes the customer collaboration cycle, shown in Figure 3.7, and enables the business to capitalize on the implementation and use of social technologies.

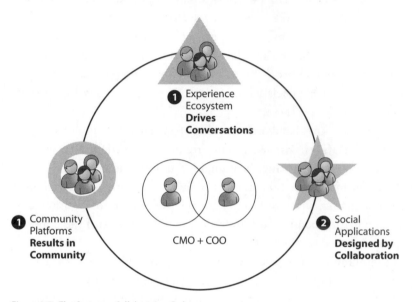

Figure 3.7 The Customer Collaboration Cycle

Empower an Organization

Consider the following scenario: Imagine that your employer is a major hospital chain. Clearly, this is a complex business, and one that customers readily talk about. Health care in a sense is one of the "this was made for social" business verticals: It cries out for the application of social technology.

Taking off on social media marketing, imagine that you are in the marketing group—perhaps you are a CMO, a VP of Marketing, Director of Communications, or PR, or advertising for a community hospital. You're reading through social media listening reports and you find conversations from a new mother that reflects a genuine appreciation for the care and attention during the birth of her child. You also find some pictures uploaded by the people who attended the opening of your newest community health care center. Along with that you find other conversations, some expressing dissatisfaction with high costs, unexplained charges, a feeling of disempowerment...in short, all of those things outside of the actual delivery of quality health care that make patients and their families nuts.

In health care or any other business vertical for that matter, what you're discovering is the routine mix of conversations that typify social media. So you get interested, and you begin monitoring Twitter in real time, using a free tool like Tweetdeck. One day you notice that a patient and her husband have checked in: They seem to like your hospital, as you note in the tweets you see in real time via Tweetdeck as they enter your hospital. By the way, this is an entirely reasonable scenario (and in fact actually happens). When I fly on Kingfisher or Continental, I routinely post to them via Twitter and very often hear back soon after. People do exactly the same thing when they enter a hospital and many other business establishments: Remember that if a mobile phone works on the premises, so do Twitter and Foursquare.

A few more tweets from your newly arrived patient and spouse pop through as they head from your hospital check-in to the waiting area and finally to pre-op. And then you see the following actual tweet, posted from inside your hospital, shown in Figure 3.8.

Figure 3.8 An Actual Hospital Tweet: What Would *You* Do?

Looking at Figure 3.8, if you saw this tweet, in real time, what would you do? By clicking into the profile data on Twitter and then searching your current admittance records, you could probably locate the person who sent it inside your hospital in minutes. Would you do that, or would you let the opportunity to make a difference in someone's life, right now, just slip away?

It's these kinds of postings that take social business to a new level. Beyond outbound or social presence marketing, social business demands that you think through the process changes required within your organization to respond to the actual tweet shown in Figure 3.8. It's an incredible opportunity that is literally calling out to you. Don't let it slip away, which in this case is exactly what happened. That is not only an opportunity lost, but a negative story of its own that now circulates on the Social Web.

The conversations that form and circulate on the Social Web matter to your business, obviously through the external circulation they enjoy and the impact they have on customers and potential customers as a result. But they also have a potential impact inside your organization: Each of these conversations potentially carries an idea that you may consider for application within your organization, to an existing business process or a training program or the development of "delight" oriented KPIs. You are discovering the things that drive your customers in significant numbers to the Social Web where they engage others in conversations around the experiences they have with you brand, product or service. As such, these would be the things considered "talk worthy," and if you were to tap the ideas directly and incorporate them in to your business you'd be onto something. You are exploring the conversations that indicate a path to improvement and to competitive advantage, if you can only see the way to get there.

Too often, though, instead of taking notes, marketers sit there, frozen in panic. As a marketer, *what are you going to do* in response to posts like that of Figure 3.8? Your hospital Facebook page, your "New Parents" discussion forum and your connection to the community through Twitter are of basically no help in this situation. Marketing outreach through social channels is designed to connect customers to your business and to give you a voice alongside theirs, a point of participation, in the conversations on the Social Web. All great benefits, they are certainly the core of a social media marketing program. Problem is, you've already done this. Yet the challenging conversations—and opportunities lost—continue.

Distinctly separate from social media marketing, the challenge facing marketers in health care and near any other consumer-facing business, B2B firm, or nonprofit is not one of understanding or being part of the conversations—something already covered through your adoption of social media analytics to follow conversations as they occur. Instead, the challenge is *taking action* based on what customers are saying and then bringing a solution to them to close the loop. The challenge here is getting to the root cause of the conversation and rallying the entire organization around addressing it. That's why the panic sets in, and that's what makes social business so hard.

It's at this point that social media marketing stops and social business begins. Going back to the health care example, billing systems, in-room care standards, access to personal health care records all require *policy changes*, not a marketing program. Hospital marketers are certainly part of the solution, but only a *part*. Social business extends across the entire organization, and typically requires the involvement of the C-suite or equivalent senior management team. Connecting employees, tapping knowledge across departments, and conceiving and implementing holistic solutions to systemic challenges is difficult. What is needed is a methodology that can be consistently applied. Touchpoint analysis—referenced in more detail in Chapter 5, "Social Technology and Business Decisions" is extremely useful in this regard. Touchpoint analysis helps pinpoint the root causes of customer satisfaction as well as dissatisfaction. Social business takes off from this.

In short, connecting employees in ways that encourage knowledge sharing converts whole teams from "I can't do this in my department" paralysis into "As a collaborative business, we can solve this." It allows employees to more fully leverage learning, by being aware of what is going on all around them in the business and in the marketplace. Customers are often more than willing to share their ideas, needs, suggestions, and even to put forth effort. The problem is, as the "Knowledge Assimilation" sidebar shows, most organizations aren't set up to hear it. Some are actually built—or so it seems—to outright *suppress* it.

If the degree to which businesses fail to assimilate knowledge is even close to what Socialtext CEO Ross Mayfield has noted in his blog—that only about 1% of all customer conversations result in new organizational knowledge while 90% of the conversations never even reach the business—the actual loss through missed opportunities to innovate and address customer issues is huge. Turned around, if only a small gain in knowledge sharing and assimilation were made—if every tenth rather than every hundredth customer (the current assessment of typical practices) who offered up an idea was actually heard and understood and welcomed into the organization as a contributing member—the change in workplace and marketplace dynamics would be profound. In a practical sense, you'd have uncovered a source of real competitive advantage. As noted, Starbucks is implementing, on average, 2 customer driven innovations per week since 2008. Take a look at its stock price over that period and ask yourself if these are perhaps related.

This is exactly what is happening with the "ideation" tools used not only by Starbucks and Dell, but by an increasing number of businesses and nonprofit organizations. Tapping customers directly, and visibly involving them in the collaborative process of improving and evolving products and services is taking hold. Chapter 12 treats ideation and its use in business in detail.

Connect Employees to Employees

If knowledge assimilation throughout an organization is the goal, what's the path that leads there? Enterprise applied-knowledge sharing applications are *part* of the answer. Lotus Notes was one of the earliest providers of peer-to-peer shared workplace communications tools. Newer enterprise platforms include Basecamp, DeskAway, Lotus Connections, SharePoint, and Socialtext. Regardless, they all provide straightforward whole-organization implementations that can be adapted for nearly any application. For those with very specific needs, or simply a sense of adventure, programming frameworks like Drupal can be used to create solid internal (and external) infrastructures from the ground up. However you choose to build your organizational applied knowledge sharing platform, the essential objectives are covered in the following section.

Clear Policies

The first element of any social or collaborative undertaking is setting out clear policies. Applicable to any social technology application, establishing up front who can post, what they can and cannot say, what the rules of conduct are, etc. Most organizations will quickly recognize the need for such policies on *external* efforts: If not, the in-house legal team will quickly step in. The same considerations apply internally. Employee lawsuits and the issues that cause them are avoidable: Too many out-of-the-box intranet and knowledge-sharing applications are still launched without an adequate policy review. That's a roadmap to trouble. You can use Google to search for Intel's, IBM's, or similar organizations' policies on social computing: They will provide a great starting point.

Specific Business Objectives

Business objectives are next: Why are you doing this? When we first rolled out IBM's PROFS and later Lotus Notes at Progressive in the late '80s and early '90s, there was an overall business objective along the lines of "connecting people and tapping synergies" but not a lot else in the way of a definition or expectation. It was as much an experiment in innovation processes as a defined strategy for communication. To this point—I was part of it and loved every day of it—the idea of connecting employees in ways that broke existing hierarchies was new and the concept appealing.

Progressive has always been a dynamic, innovative company, and so a certain amount of pure experimentation fit into its culture. At the same time, not too long after rollout it became apparent that a lot of unstructured conversation was taking place, at least partly because the 1,000 (give or take) employees at the time realized—for the first time—they could talk to anyone else in the organization *instantly*. Because there were no specifically articulated and measurable objectives, it was hard to push back against it, to channel the energy where it would do some (business) good. Over time, business goals, policies, and expectations evolved and the platform became an integral part of work. So, outside of experiments, start with business objectives: By setting expectations, policies, and objectives in advance, you can get where you want to go much more quickly than you would otherwise.

An Inclusive Rollout Program

The rollout and launch program should accommodate everyone. There is an important insight here: Your customers will self-select: They will choose the technology they are comfortable with. Because they have a choice, they generally won't feel left out if they choose not to use some particular channel. Beware: When it comes to employees, there is a real "digital divide" issue. When implementing any internal workflow, sharing or similar application, it is essential that everyone be included.

Just *how* individuals are included is specific to the organization: The point to get right is to ensure inclusiveness. If the new enterprise platform is seen as being "for *those* people," then not only will it fail to deliver on the core goals of cross-functional knowledge transfer, it may actually force the organization *backward* as it reinforces rather than breaks the walls that stymie collaboration. Penn State's "Outreach" enterprise platform rollout (see sidebar) is a particularly nice example of the deployment done right.

Review and Hands-On

This chapter covered the concepts of building or reshaping a business or service organization to take advantage of Web 2.0 technologies. This chapter served to set a foundation for the processes, cases and specific solutions covered in detail in upcoming chapters in Part III, "Social Business Building Blocks." For now, focus on the attraction to social media by customers and how they use it to improve decisions and then ask yourself, "What if my organization could behave this way and tap this collective knowledge directly?" Digging into that question will lead right into the remaining chapters.

Review of the Main Points

This chapter provided an overview of the considerations when moving toward social business practices. In particular, this chapter covered the following:

- A social business uses the same Web 2.0 technologies that power the broader use of social media to connect itself (externally) to its customers and to connect (internally) its employees to each other.

- Social media marketing and the activities associated with social business are fundamentally measurable. Because the activities are expressed digitally, integrating social media analytics with internal business metrics produces useful, valuable insights that can guide product and service development efforts.

- Your employees can be connected via social technology just as customers already are: Using a platform like Socialtext, for example, results in an internal, social-profile based linkage that encourages and facilitates collaborative problem solving.

With the basics of social business defined, you're ready to begin thinking through what this might look like in your own organization, and how connecting your own working team together with customers through collaborative technologies can speed and refine your business processes that support innovation, product and service delivery, and similar talk-worthy programs.

Hands-On: Review These Resources

Review each of the following, taking note of the main points covered in the chapter and the ways in which the following activities demonstrate these points:

- Arrange a meeting with your CIO or IT leadership to review the social capabilities of your current intranet or similar internal information sharing tools.

- Create an inventory of your current social media programs. List out home bases, outposts, and passports (see sidebar earlier in this chapter for definitions of each) and then define the metrics and success measures for each.

- Meet with the leadership of your customer service and product design teams, and meet with legal and HR to review the requirements or concerns with regard to connecting employees in a more collaborative manner, or engaging more fully on the Social Web.

Hands-On: Apply What You've Learned

Apply what you've learned in this chapter through the following exercises:

1. Define the basic properties, objectives, and outcomes of a collaborative application that connects your customers to your business and to your employees.

2. Explore the available internal (enterprise) applications that connect employees with each other and with customers and thereby enable efficient response and resolution with regard to customer-generated ideas or challenges.

3. Draw a map of how external information about a selected product or service currently flows through your business or organization and how it might (better) flow if internal collaboration were the norm or more fully developed and practiced.

The Social Business
Ecosystem

4

This chapter concludes Part I and the introduction to social technology applied to business: it pulls together the elements of the social business ecosystem—profiles, applications, communities and forums, and more—and thereby provides the basis for understanding how to connect current and potential customers with the inner workings of your business or organization, where collaborative processes can take hold and drive long-term benefits.

Chapter Contents

Social Profiles

At the center of the Social Web and the shared activities that define it are the online personas of participants: More than with prior anonymous discussion boards or cloaked personas, it's an actual identity that is of value in a business context, since it is generally the motivation of an individual to be noticed as such that drives social participation in the first place. Though detailed personal information is (still) generally not available except to "trusted friends" or colleagues, the use of a real name or photo in one's social profile is becoming common. Along with any optionally provided information, the result is a a basis for understanding who it is that is actually participating.

The profile is therefore the starting point of *social* interaction, because without it the interaction that would otherwise occur is purely transactional, between the participant and the online application or other unknown party. The existence of a profile or equivalent is, in this sense, what differentiates social platforms and applications from (online) interactive applications. In an interactive application—consider a typical website—the interaction is between the application and the user: navigate to a help file, download a PDF, or place an item in a shopping cart. In each of these, the primary activity occurs between a user and an application designed to facilitate a specific task. Identity—beyond basic security or commerce validation requirements—in this context is of relatively little importance. Because the individual participant is steering the entire process, and because this is typically a task-oriented transaction, the identity of the participant matters little beyond the requirements of the task at hand.

In a social context, by comparison, the interaction occurs between the participants as much or more than it does (overtly) between a specific participant and the application or platform. It's not just that someone is doing something as with a transaction site: On the social web, that person wants to be noticed (talked about) or joined with while doing it. Basic tasks aside—uploading a photo, for example—the majority of the interactions involve profile-based connections or exchanges: curating a photo, extending and confirming a friend request, modifying a wiki document, or sharing a review. Each of these requires a certain degree of assurance that the identity of the other person(s) involved is reasonably well understood, and at least partly so that the person committing the action will be noticed by someone for having done that particular thing.

So it follows that in an online network, *without* a robust profile—the central carrier of visible identity—the act of sharing is relatively shallow. Participants in older forums and discussion boards, often lacking a more formal or detailed description of who was who, based identity on little more than a signature and then augmented that by studying writing style or specific interests of various members, and by doing so slowly pieced together an understanding of who the other participants were. People are social, and they will seek to sort out social order in nearly any situation. Ultimately, it is the relationships and the interactions they facilitate that drive successful social business applications.

By fundamentally enabling relationships, profiles dramatically speed the process of social bonding within a network and so are very important elements of modern forums, discussion boards, support communities, or other online social spaces. Profiles provide human starting points for bonding with other participants, including the profile(s) associated with a brand, business, or organization.

Readily identifiable participants are beneficial on the social web: Consider what happens when identity is introduced into an otherwise anonymous online application. Among other things, with identity comes an increase in the overall sense of individual accountability: If participants know who the others around them are, and understand as well that their own identity (as least as far as it exists via their profile) is equally known, there is a more tempered behavior than exists absent this sense of identity and individual accountability. Flame wars, for example, are less likely—all other things being equal—in communities with a strong implementation of identity. It's a lot like driving in traffic: In the relative anonymity of a sound proof, air-conditioned cabin, it's not uncommon for one driver to become visibly frustrated with other drivers. When that same driver realizes that the object of such frustration happens to be a friend, co-worker, or neighbor in the car ahead, that knowledge often alters that driver's attitude, for the better. Visible identity makes a difference within an online social community for exactly the same reason.

J. D. Lasica

Writer J.D Lasica offers as an e-book his work on the impact of *identity* on society and the application of cloud computing. This book, developed in conjunction with the Aspen Institute, is highly recommended as a starting point in understanding how identity and the role of the social profile impact the business applications of social technology. You can follow J. D Lasica on Twitter: @jdlasica.

```
http://www.socialmedia.biz/2009/05/08/free-ebook-identity-in-the-age-of-
cloud-computing
```

The Profile as a Social Connector

The role of the social profile as a *connector* cannot be understated in business applications of social media. Following on the prior discussion, the social profile provides two central social elements, both of which are essential:

- A tangible personal identifier around which a relationship can be formed
- A framework for accountability for one's actions, postings, and roles taken in the relationship that forms

Taken together, the significance of the profile is its central role in establishing *who* is participating. When people have that basic information, they will more readily enter into functional relationships and share or transfer useful knowledge. This is, of course, the primary objective in building a social business or supporting application. By connecting the organization with its stakeholders—whether a business and its customers or a nonprofit and its members—social profiles form the basis for an accountable, productive relationship.

Corporate Blogs and Identity

Understanding the importance of the social profile makes clear why social media experts will generally recommend that corporate blogs are written within the company and not by an outside agency. Challenges of time pressure and writing skill aside, the issue worth noting is the relationship between identity and trust.

At the center of the relationship with a reader is the identity of the writer: When humans read something, they imagine that some*one*—not some*thing*—wrote it. They connect with that person, so it's important that the personality and voice be both genuine and consistent.

Ask yourself: Who would you rather build a relationship with around a product or service: The CEO or head of customer service or a project engineer…or someone at the firm's public relations agency? Understanding what the firm is doing—the kinds of things you can learn by reading the PR communications, for example, is worthwhile. At the same time, if you want to engage the business when suggesting an alternative product or service policy, it is more satisfying to do it through a direct link to the company rather than through its agent.

When weighing the cost of direct participation against the value of the relationships created, consideration of the corporate identity is worth more than passing thought.

Premiere Global: A Practical Example of Profiles

In my experience working with Atlanta-based Premiere Global (PGi) on the implementation of a community, the role of the social profile in activating and sustaining the community is particularly instructive as regards the role of the profile in a community application. This particular project—a developer's community built around PGi's communications API—was intended to bring independent developers and internal PGi experts together in a collaborative venue that would spur the development of new and innovative communications applications.

The PGiConnect Developers Community, shown in Figure 4.1, was built on the Jive Software community platform. When communities and social applications using ready-made platforms such as Jive are being created, it is important to recognize that while the core elements needed to get a solid program up and running quickly are present, there are often opportunities to extend these platforms through the platform's API, a programming feature that allows a development team to quickly build additional capability—based on specific business needs—and extend the functionality of the core platform.

Figure 4.1 PGiConnect: Profile Completeness

Implemented for PGi by Austin's FG SQUARED, Jive's toolset worked very well out of the box. One of the advantages of building on a white-label platform is the speed with which a fully functional community can be launched. Missing, however, was a direct feedback indicator to members with regard to not only current profile completion but what steps were needed on the part of a specific member to move toward 100 percent completion of a personal profile. Taking a page from LinkedIn, a profile component was developed that provided an indication of profile completeness and a simple "what to do next" prompt to move completeness to the next stage.

When designing a collaborative application, provide the means for people to quickly identify each other and establish common interests and goals. The social profile really does sit at the center of a strong community, and specific effort in encouraging that these profiles be sufficiently completed to encourage and support the formation of relationships is a best practice.

The Profile and the Social Graph

Recall the discussion of the social graph in Chapter 2, "The New Role of the Customer." Looking ahead, Chapter 11, "The Social Graph", will provide an in-depth treatment. For now, understand that the social graph includes the set of profiles that describe the members of a social network and the interactions, activities, and relationships that connect specific profiles on the Social Web. In perhaps the simplest view, the social graph defines the way in which one profile is connected to another, through a friendship relationship perhaps. Because the profile itself is tied to a person—however vaguely that profile may have been defined—there is a sense of accountability and belonging that translates into shared responsibility between those so connected. This relationship might be highly asymmetric: Robert Scoble's individual fans may get more from him than he gets from any *one* of them. Nonetheless, there is a set of rules and expectations that define these relationships, and in doing so set up the value-based transaction and knowledge exchange that ultimately occurs between participants on the Social Web.

Understanding the construction of the social graph in the context of the profiles (people) collecting around your brand is essential in creating an organic social presence. Go back to the core challenge of effective participation on the Social Web: How do you participate without being branded as a "self interested *only*." Your firm or organization needs to assert its relevance and then deliver through utility, emotion, or gained knowledge some sort of tangible value if it is to develop a strong bond with your customers that outlast contests, advertising spending, and other direct incentives aimed at driving early involvement with the online social presence of the brand, product, or service.

What are the first steps in developing a social presence where this can happen? You go where your customers are: Look to the existing communities such as LinkedIn, Orkut, or Facebook and create *an appropriate* place within them for your business or organization. As you work your way into these communities you'll discover (or confirm) what or where you can add value. By participating, actively listening, and understanding and tracking influencers, you'll see the relationships, interactions, and needs that exist within the community, and which intersect with the value proposition of your business or organization. That is your entry point, and one on which you can build your presence.

Social Applications

Taking the four basic building blocks together—consumption, curation, creation, and collaboration—one possible model (there are many) for driving engagement emerges. Engagement can be tapped for marketing purposes by anchoring it within the context of the basic social structures—communities, social applications, and similar—and then connecting these back to your brand, product, or service. In this section, *social applications* are the focus.

The basic process of engagement begins with content consumption and builds up to collaboration between participants in the creative process. This is the kind of activity that binds community members together. Taking off on this, there are specific social applications—forums, collaborative tools, contests, and games among them—that you can implement under your own brand to lead your participants through the steps of engagement that drive your business.

Importantly, the social applications are not necessarily communities per se, though some amount to as much: they are more generally enablers of an activity or outcome that is useful to the members of a community with which an application is associated. Simply put, and critical to understanding how to build an effective social presence, is recognizing that most brands, products, or services will *not* support a "community" by themselves. Why not? Think about the products that you use, the organizations you support, and the real-world community around you. What among them constitute the things you think about daily, regularly, that you obsess over? These—and only these—are the things that are candidates for long-lived, organically developed "communities."

Despite a lot of time and effort spent to the contrary, most brands, products, and services do not command sufficient daily mindshare to sustain a community of their own. To see why this is so, make a quick mental list for yourself of the real-world organizations of which you are a member. The typical individual has one, three, perhaps five or even a few more organizations. After that, most people literally run out of bandwidth, the combination of an individual's time, and attention. There are only so many social organizations one person can effectively participate in. Online it's no different: How many social communities can you really belong to? More importantly, how many will you actively participate in? For most, the answer is surprisingly similar (or perhaps not surprising at all) to the capacity for participation in real life.

Against that, ask yourself: "How likely are you to join a deodorant, toothpaste, or laundry soap community?" Yet, more than a few CPG/FMCG brand managers have undertaken to build just these types of communities. Make no mistake: As long as the advertising spending is happening, people join, take advantage of offers, and maybe even engage in light social activities. But understand that membership is being driven by ad spending and not organic social interaction. Organic growth—versus ad spending and incentive driven growth—is what you need to build long-term participation in a community.

This is not to knock "awareness" communities or the application of social media channels in awareness plays: These communities may well be important parts of overall marketing programs and often do deliver on some of the surface promises of the Social Web. Content consumption certainly happens, and to an extent curation—people voting or ranking what they see or do in these communities—may also be happening. But above that, in the more important behaviors of content creation and collaboration, activity generally starts to drop off. And as noted, when the ad spending stops, the community generally stops growing as well.

Now, consider social applications. Social applications are designed to facilitate *accomplishing something in the context of a shared or collaborative goal*— "Look at us!" —and thereby to provide a specific value to a given group of participants. Social applications are rooted in the task-orientation of many Internet activities, but then extend beyond that, into social activities. By delivering a service and then encouraging the sharing of results, interpersonal relationships are created. In this way social applications drive their own longevity and usefulness. This is a very beneficial attribute when you are trying to encourage repeat visits and you don't have an unlimited supply of funds to make up for organic interest and participation.

There is another aspect of social business and social application design that warrants attention. *A utility-oriented application by itself is not social.* This means that unless you design your social application to be a part of the larger social framework— the ecosystem—in which your audience spends time, you'll end up with an island. What makes the "social application" social is its connectedness to the communities in which participants are also members. For example, if someone is a member of Facebook, Orkut, or LinkedIn, or uses Twitter regularly and has built up 100, 1,000, or more real connections, the larger value of your social application comes when the application itself, or whatever it is that it produces or does, is *shared and pushed out through that person's social graph.*

Think back to the laundry soap site, and set aside the media-driven *awareness* uses of the site. How might this site look if it were to be built as a social application?

The typical laundry site probably has a stain removal chart, right? There is clear utility value in knowing what types of pretreatments are effective on what types of stains. To this end, there are literally dozens of these types of sites. The problem is, specific products can be "recommended" for all sorts of reasons, and among them is "because someone paid for the recommendation." This is of course the underlying issue with traditional and marketer-driven communications versus social or collective/consumer-driven communications. As a consumer, the only thing you *know* is that the marketer is trying to sell you something. The rest is based on the combination of brand reputation, your experience, and the shared experience of those you trust.

Enter social media, part one. The first element of the social application—and the first use of the engagement processes associated with it—is curation. Consumers are often more candid (issues of transparency and disclosure noted) in their reviews than marketers. Reviews are part of the solution, and the reviews of reviews go further and help others interested in the specific product or service to sort out and make sense of specific reviews by identifying those considered most helpful.

The contemporary social application takes it one step further: Building on the connectivity afforded by Web 2.0 technologies, the social application makes its results available to others, outside of the social application itself. In the context of the present example, where the basic consumer-driven reviews on the laundry site makes relevant information available to people who visit the site, the well-connected social application makes the results of trying a specific solution available to everyone to whom the person posting that specific solution is connected. This can dramatically impact the spread of useful information (and sometimes not-so-useful information from the brand's point of view).

Here's an example of how this might work: Suppose someone discovers a particular stain removal technique to be useful and posts this onto the stain-fighting social application. The application then sends a message to Twitter—with the contributor's explicit permission—alerting the contributor's followers that an effective stain-removal technique has been found. The member's social graph takes over from there, spreading and amplifying the underlying consumer-generated content.

In this example, not only has the social application shown the customer how to better use a cleaning product, it has encouraged the customer to post a new review and then facilitated its sharing through that customer's larger (online) social community. Now those "friends of friends" have this information, and if confronted with a similar stain, or queried by someone they know, they can point back to the original source and benefit from it. This is how information traverses the social graph and adds value to participants.

Central to social business is the act of sharing, facilitated by the connectedness of the application to the communities around it. This is what creates the real value to a marketer. Sharing has a significant impact on the spread of positive (or negative—watch out!) information that amplifies and drives marketing at no cost beyond the construction of the application and its maintenance. Miss out on this aspect of social applications—build a social application that is more like an island than a shared space—and you will surely decrease the potential return on your investment.

The "Good Guide," shown in Figure 4.2, is a customer driven, shared, and socially connected shopping application, available in Apple's app store for installation on the iPhone. (It is coming as well for other smartphones.) The Good Guide is a great example of how the Social Web is beginning to exert an impact on business units within the enterprise *outside of the marketing department*. The Good Guide is a social business application. Read on to see how it works.

Figure 4.2 The Good Guide

Mobile applications for smartphones that scan a barcode and present pricing data and customer reviews are common. When I was looking for a portable spin-style toothbrush in Target, I was confronted with over two dozen competing models of semi-disposable, single-user (versus family applications) brushes in the under-$5 category. Standing there, I had zero information other than "Buy Me!" to go on. So, I used my Android-based G1 phone to scan the barcodes, right there in the aisle. Sure, I got a few odd stares (normal for me...) but I also got access to independent product reviews, instantly through Google's shopping guides. Based on the combination of independent reviews and manufacturer's information, I made my decision. This was a classic use of social media in a business (commerce) context: For the most part, as a consumer I was working with the marketing data, evaluating things like price, promoted feature set, and then extending this with a mix of company and *consumer-generated product reviews*.

The Good Guide moves beyond this core review data, which is now largely considered "cost-of-entry" for consumers nearing the point of actual purchase. It also moves *well beyond the marketing department* and into the core values and purpose of the business itself. The Good Guide serves up health, environment, and societal impact ratings: A score of "10" on "society," for example, means the product in consideration is offered by a *manufacturer* with responsible investment policies, equitable hiring practices, an appropriate commitment to philanthropy and a firm policy toward workplace diversity. As noted, this goes way beyond the purview of the Marketing and Communications department.

Compare the above with ratings, reviews, prices, and features. Investment policy, hiring practices, and environmental impact are decidedly outside the marketing domain in most businesses, although social business certainly suggests that this is likely to change. Customers are now armed with a much more holistic view of the countries of origin, manufacturers, suppliers, retailers, and even taxing entities that make up the entire purchase chain. This is all part of the decision-making process now.

Social applications such as The Good Guide bring visibility to the larger business process and with it an entirely new set of considerations that reach across departments and functions. This is the dawn of the social business. If you are looking to enable more of your organization in the creation of favorable conversations, this is the starting point.

Support Forums

Accepting that social applications are an adjunct to social networks and online communities, the starting set of applications—support forums— are built around the white-label social technology platforms offered by more than a few software providers. As used here, "white label" means "software application that can be branded to your specification" but is otherwise ready to use. The platforms may be delivered for internal use on an enterprise appliance, as an SaaS (Software as a Service) delivery, or as licensed software from providers like Lithium Technologies, Cyn.in, or Jive among many others.

White-Label or Custom-Built?

In this section, I'm covering white-label social platforms in order to quickly bring clarity of the role that support and similar communities play in the development of social applications. In addition to the white-label platforms, you have the option of building from scratch using Drupal, Joomla, .NET, and more. Google any of these for more information and business examples built on these platforms.

Table 4.1 shows a representative set of these platform providers, with a more complete listing appearing in the Appendix. By far, the most up-to-date and complete listing is maintained…you guessed it, through a social wiki application, hosted by the Dachis Group in Austin, TX.

▶ **Table 4.1** Social Software—Selected Examples

Provider	Core Strength	Examples
Lithium Technologies	Influencer Identification	Dell Support Forums
Broadband Mechanics	Participant Connections	Times of India's "iTimes.com"
Jive Software	Community Workflow	Premier Global's "PGiConnect"
Looppa	Media Publishing	SONY/MTV "Gaurida Azul"
Powered	Customer Communities	Radio Shack Learning Community; HP's "Learning Center"
Salesforce.com	Ideation	My Starbucks Idea, Dell IdeaStorm
SharePoint	Enterprise Workflow	KraftFoods.com. content management
Small World Labs	Niche Communities	American Cancer Society, employee collaboration
SocialText	Enterprise Collaboration	TransUnion, *internal* social networking

The Dachis Group's Software Service Wiki

Headquartered in Austin, TX, the Dachis Group maintains a wiki-based listing of social software. It's a great resource. You'll find it here:

http://softwarewiki.dachisgroup.com/

The trick to using a white-label platform solution in the development of your social business program is being clear about how "social" fits into the larger social ecosystem and supports the very specific behaviors that you want to encourage. By "ecosystem," I am referring to the larger set of online services, tools, communities and more that your audience is participating in and using. It's rare, for example, that a long-lived support community operates in a vacuum: More likely, the support forum is connected to one or more membership communities whose participants are interested or dependent on some aspect of the support they receive in the forum.

Dell's "Take Your Own Path,' the community built for entrepreneurs referenced in Chapter 3, is part of one such ecosystem. The entrepreneur's community itself acts as the central hub of the ecosystem: It can do this because being an entrepreneur is a lifestyle, a passion. Surrounding it are the Dell support forums, Dell's IdeaStorm and a host of external social networks including Orkut, Facebook, Twitter, and LinkedIn. All of these work together to provide a complete environment for entrepreneurs. In so doing, they ensure that awareness of—and support for—Dell small- and medium-sized business products is readily available (good for marketing) and more importantly that the community's participants remain engaged based on their own needs and passions (which is good for the entrepreneur's and good for Dell since their success is dependent on the the success of their customers.)

Looking deeper into the platforms and social applications, beyond community and support forums, there is the growing area as application of "Social CRM.' Not surprisingly, CRM is the newest connection between social media and the Social Web: I'll cover this extensively in Chapter 9, "Social CRM," so for now just recognize that who the influencers are, and how they relate to your potential customers, can be tracked and managed in the same way that you'd manage relationships with your existing customers. In other words, you can grow your business leads and influencer base—discovered on the Social Web—in a manner analogous to traditional enterprise CRM.

The combination of support applications, CRM, social networking, and sharing mechanisms like Twitter, along with the activity streams in Facebook and Orkut can be quite powerful. When compared with building a stand-alone community around a brand, product or service—go back to the toothpaste or deodorant community examples—these highly integrated social applications result in much more widespread and more free-flowing interchange of information between consumers. This, of course, brings up one of the aspects of the Social Web and its use by consumers that causes some marketers sleepless nights: The prospect of negative conversations circulating, outside of their control but very much visible to potential customers.

Unfortunately, there is no easy answer when negative conversations arise, unless you consider "fixing the problem at its source" as being easy. Do reference the "Responding to Social Media Mentions" sidebar in Chapter 1, though, as you develop your basic response process.

Here too, however, social business concepts provide relief: Support forums—properly managed—can go a long way toward improving the customer service experience (lowering the incidence of negative conversations in the process) and reducing the costs of customer service delivery in the process. At the very least, support forums can be used to quickly spot common problems. Once identified, the issues can be addressed and corrected, often by involving the very customers raising the objections and creating a more favorable relationship in the process.

Here again you see the larger connection between the Social Web and *business*: Beyond social media marketing and the monitoring of conversations, the integration of social applications that connect your business to the larger (customer) ecosystem provide you with the data, solutions, and basis for relationships that can help you fix what needs fixing and preserve what's presently working.

Much of what was just covered sounds simple—and in theory it is—but beware: Stepping up and actually doing "social business," exposing your engineers to your customers through an authentic blogging program, for example, so that they might learn first-hand the pain-points of customers is likely to be challenging if not outright difficult within your organization. That said, getting it right creates both a barrier to entry and a competitive differentiator that is difficult for slower-off-the-mark competitors to counter. If you move first, you get the advantage, and that can pay measurable benefits down the road.

Content Sharing

If support forums and similar social applications provide the connections between communities and your business, what is it that is actually shared? This is where the content creation and sharing tools come in. Recall the engagement building blocks— consumption, curation, creation, and collaboration. Sharing first emerges in the curation phase of engagement as people rate the works of others in a public setting. Content creation is almost universally undertaken specifically for the purpose of sharing.

Given this, social applications as well as social communities are typically built with the idea of members creating and sharing something. "Something" might be a rating, a photo, a solution, or any number of other things. Expert communities are examples of "sharing," wherein the content being shared relates to a specific problem posed by the community. On a different scale—and typically serving many times the number of people— support forums operate in this same way.

Where the challenge in building a compelling social application is identifying the *purpose* of the application, the challenge in driving shared content is encouraging participation in the first place. The degree to which content is created and shared is almost purely a function of how easy it is to do, and in the rewards for having done it. By rewards, I don't mean cash: I mean social recognition. If someone is contributing *quality* content, ensure (as a moderator or through moderation policies or your reputation management system) that this person is recognized. Identifying and developing experts/ influencers by watching content production and sharing is one the keys to building a powerful social application.

Purpose-Built Applications

Purpose-built applications—including so-called "widgets"—can provide a very easy way to quickly implement social behavior. Like communities and social applications in general, these small, purpose-built applications are designed to facilitate specific interactions between community or stakeholders. In contrast to communities and larger social applications—which often have more than modest building costs and longer development cycles—purpose-built applications can be created that literally "snap in" and can be fitted and ready for use in days or even hours.

So, what's a widget? Widgets are small pieces of ready-to-use software designed to do very specific things: Contests, gifting, and content-sharing applications are examples of the kinds of things that you can add to your overall social presence to increase visitor participation. Further examples include advertising modules or "Share This with Friends" blocks of code that you drop into a page template on your site to enable some external sharing or publishing service. The advantage of widgets is that you can quickly implement them, without a lot worry over scale and other issues. The big assumption here—so do check it—is that the *widget provider* has worried about these things for you. Drop a chunk of clever-looking but alpha code onto your high traffic application and you may well be surprised—as in "Oops!"—with the results.

Table 4.2 lists a set of leading, proven, purpose-built social tools that can be implemented quickly on Facebook and Twitter. The tools range from the simple—photo or video sharing—to the complex. Providers such as Friend2Friend and BuddyMedia offer a range of full-featured marketing tools that support contests, gifting, sharing, and more. *Disclosure: I am a board advisor with Friend2Friend.*

▶ **Table 4.2** Easy Social Solutions on Facebook and Twitter

Provider	Core Strength	Examples
BuddyMedia	Ready-to-Use Facebook Applications	Budweiser and Samsung Facebook tabs
Context Optional	Custom Social Applications	Microsoft's "Bing-Thon"; Target's "Bullseye Gives" corporate social responsibility feature
Step Change Group	Facebook applications and widgets	Southwest Airlines' Facebook sweepstakes ; Gold's Gym - Facebook presence
Friend2Friend	Social Amplification	New Belgium's "What's your Folly"; Atari's "Tweet in Klingon"

One of the more popular Friend2Friend-based solutions was Tweet in Klingon. Start Trek fans used this application to generate tweets—Twitter posts—in the Klingon language. Certainly a lot of fun, the application was also serious business. Built for Atari by SocialTyze to support the release of Cryptic Studio's Star Trek video game, the social application generated awareness and participation as it connected an existing community—the Trekkies—through an established social channel—Twitter. Figure 4.3 Shows the Tweet in Klingon application.

Figure 4.3 jaH DaqtlhIngan (Tweet in Klingon)

What I like about the Tweet in Klingon application is how easy it is to build a compelling social program *without* building a complete community. Rather than trying to compete with the likes of Facebook, Orkut, or Twitter, Tweet in Klingon leverages the participant base that is already there by providing a small, well-defined activity that has meaning and relevance to a precise audience. The additional solutions shown in Table 4.2 from BuddyMedia, ContextOptional and Step Change Group are all great examples of promotional programs with a decidedly social element: Take the time to visit the providers listed in Table 4.2—all have extensive client lists and all are top-notch.

It is exactly this kind of smart approach to social media marketing and the larger area of social technology applied to business that makes obvious the way in which the Social Web is maturing. While Web 1.0 was typically implemented as "competing islands"—large portals going for traffic dominance in the hopes of selling ad space—Web 2.0 brought shared experiences and mashups to the table. Savvy marketers picked up on this by building applications that connected their brands to the existing communities where their target audience spent time. The Social Web, the subject of this book, continues the shift toward *shared* versus *competing* experiences by integrating the audience and the business through a set of applications that facilitate collaboration, knowledge exchange, and consumer-led design.

Using Brand Outposts and Communities

It's time to connect the basics, to put in place the beginning of a framework for a social business. Chapter 1 covered the basics of engagement, Chapter 2 covered the new role of the customer as a potential participant in your business. Chapter 2 also touched on the social graph and social CRM, highlighting tools like BuzzStream that help you identify and build relationships with people who are talking about your brand, product, or service and influencing others in the process.

Chapter 3, "Building a Social Business," framed social CRM and social applications in the context of a social business, a firm or organization that is being run based on the direct collaboration between itself and its customers. The basic interactions—creating relationships between community members and creating shared knowledge—come about through specific, replicable actions that can be designed into the organization itself.

In this section of Chapter 4, the social behaviors described so far are applied in specific social spaces—think online communities here—where the actual interactions, discussions, and conversations take place.

Recall from Chapter 3 that communities are built around things like passions, lifestyles, and causes, the *big things* that people choose to spend their time with. Very often, a brand, product, or service by itself does not warrant a community of its own: Even when it does, that particular community is typically only participated in by a fraction of the total potential audience. For most businesses and organizations, the places where customers willingly spend time—often engaged in conversation about the business or organization—is a social network or online community that is dedicated not to brands, products, or services, but rather to other people like themselves, with interests like their own.

So how do you participate as a business? Even more pressing, how do you get your customers to spend time doing real work with your team, contributing ideas and insights that will help you better define products or innovate in ways that will lower costs or differentiate you from your competitors? In short, how do you become part of the communities your customers or members belong to and begin to realize the promised benefits of social computing? You participate in the activities they are involved in—with full disclosure and transparency—in order to build the levels of trust that that will elicit their contributions of knowledge back to you.

This is the purpose of the brand outpost, a place you create for your brand within the context of an existing social network. Offering useful applications to your audience *at the location of their choosing* rather than requiring that they come to your website (or simply assuming they will) is the final element in setting up for social business.

In an interview with *BusinessWeek,* author and blogger Jeff Jarvis noted three common mistakes that many companies make when adding social-media-based marketing programs to their overall communications mix. Of the three mistakes (see sidebar for complete reference), one in particular applies to brand outposts: The mistake is expecting your audience to come to you, to visit your website for example, for information. Jeff points out that it is essential for you to go to them instead. Look at the following list of the typical places where brand outposts are established: In each of these cases, *you* are going to *them.* The following are examples of common brand outposts:

Twitter

Second Life Islands

Facebook Business Pages

YouTube Channels

What defines a successful brand outpost, one that enjoys organic (aka "viral") growth? Most likely, it's an application, a tool, or an articulated purpose that meets a clear need for an important subset of the community participants around the outpost who are themselves part of your target market or are the influencers for it. This isn't as self-serving as it sounds: When you cut away the fluff, it's all about providing something useful for someone you'd like to do business with, and doing it on their terms and in "their part of town." That's pretty simple.

Fundamental to the brand outpost and its role in social business is that it is *part of* the larger community. Outposts exist to *serve the needs* of community members that are not met directly elsewhere. Effective brand outposts are created where a target audience already exists: Your outpost should include a useful application or compelling activity related to your brand, product, or service that connects with your customers frequenting that outpost.

Coca-Cola: Facebook

At about 10 million fans, Coke's original outpost—its Facebook page—was one of the most successful examples of a brand outpost. Even more remarkable, it wasn't created by Coke: it was built by Dusty Sorg and Michael Jedrzejewsk, two passionate Coke Fans. When confronted with a site built on Facebook, but outside of Coke's control, Coke chose to empower the fans that created the site and embraced the work they'd done. The result? Under the continued stewardship of its creators, Coke's Facebook page now has over 4 million fans.

Coke's Facebook brand outpost, shown in Figure 4.4, is now a valued element of its online marketing program, so much so that in January, 2010, Coke announced that it would deemphasize one-off online campaigns in favor of extended social-media-based efforts, in part built around its brand outposts at Facebook and YouTube. In an interview at the time of the announcement, Prinz Pinakatt, Coke's interactive marketing manager for Europe, said "We would like to place our activities and brands where people are, rather than dragging them to our platform." Look back at Jeff Jarvis's list of common mistakes and the steps he advises taking to avoid them: Coke clearly gets it.

Coke Zero: Department of Fannovation

If a Facebook Business Page is an obvious first step in a brand outpost strategy, what else can be done? A lot, and surprisingly it's not rocket science but is instead savvy thinking combined with a deep-seated commitment to understanding the Social Web and how it really works.

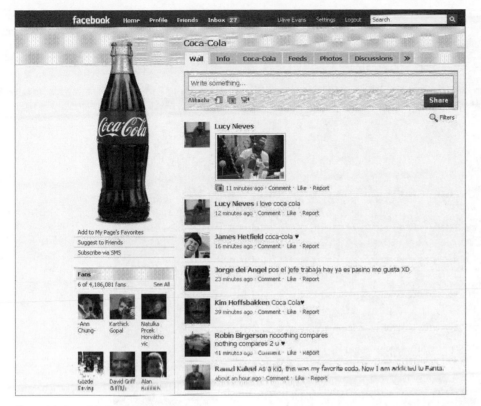

Figure 4.4 Coca-Cola: Facebook Brand Outpost

Consider Coke's "Department of Fannovation" shown in Figure 4.5, a campaign that ran in 2010 during the run-up to March Madness. Created on the Posterous blogging platform, this is a combination outpost—Posterous has developed a community of its own—and a social application. Built around fan participation and a contest theme, the purpose of the site is simple: Ask NCAA fans (followers of the various sanctioned U.S. collegiate athletic programs) to offer ideas for improving the experience of being an NCAA Fan. As you might expect, the ideas flowed forth.

Drawing on the activities common in ideation platforms to encourage idea sharing, Coke has used a blogging platform and its content ratings tools to create a shared space where members participate socially with each other. Consider the fundamental engagement building blocks as they apply to the Coke Fannovation site.

Consumption clearly occurs as fans read through each others ideas about the things that might improve the experience of being a fan. Some ideas are obvious— create chat rooms for rival fans—or a stretch at best: "Let the fans vote on the starting lineup for the upcoming game," for example. Participants read these and then vote them up or down.

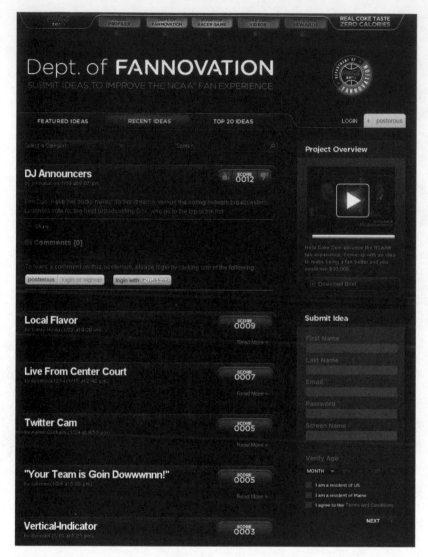

Figure 4.5 The Department of Fannovation

Curation occurs through a simple voting process. See an idea you like? Vote it up. See one you don't? Vote it down. Over time the best ideas—from the perspective of the fans—rise to the top. Bringing fans into the *formal* content creation process is always intriguing in settings like NCAA athletics. Mitsubishi tapped this in the release of "The Great Driving Challenge," a automotive launch program that let people choose bloggers/photographers to drive around India and document their passion for driving and exploration. The Royal Challengers Bangalore—a leading India cricket club—tapped the same technique in creating its fan bloggers, photographers and club historians. (Disclosure: 2020 Social, the firm I work with in India, is associated with the Royal Challengers project.)

Curation drives creation. As noted in Chapter 1, curation—voting, rating, or reviewing—is a great way to introduce an audience to actual content creation. For The Department of Fannovation, the audience creates the ideas that power the central site activities.

Collaboration occurs as fans work together to evolve the best ideas, creating new options around the experience of being a fan. Most important, Fannovation wasn't about a trivia contest or contrived "invent a flavor" contest: It was about pure, simple fan interest, and the related role that Coke products play in enjoyment, including the enjoyment of being a fan. Figure 4.6 shows a typical take-off on this campaign, by fans. This is the kind of thing that brand managers live for, and it is exactly the kind of thing that smart social applications like Coke's Fannovation deliver.

Figure 4.6 Fannovation: Your Mascot Sucks

The NCAA audience is obviously part of Coke's target, and the experience of being a fan is relevant to that audience segment. Rather than serving its own immediate goals—advertising and selling Coca-Cola products—the Department of Fannovation exists for the benefit of fans. This goes a long way toward demonstrating Coke's preference for participation in social sites rather than one-off "come to us" branded microsites.

One final note on Coke's Department of Fannovation campaign: It ended properly, because it was set up properly. One of the mistakes that social media marketers make is viewing "communities" as "campaigns." They aren't. Communities encourage relationships, and in matters of relationships no one likes to get dumped. When a community is created, there is an expectation that the community, if it becomes active, will be supported into the future. In the case of Fannovation, it was a time-bound idea: NCAA and March Madness. This was clearly set up front, so that when the campaign ran its course the "end" was expected. It's important to spend as much time thinking about how a social effort will end as it is in planning how it will get started.

Take a tip from Coke, Starbucks, Dell, and dozens of other brands: Approach the Social Web as a *consumer* and understand how you relate to it in that context. What do you find useful? Why are you using Facebook? What do you like about your business blog or internal company intranet? What utility do these provide and why are they useful to you? Apply the answers to these questions to the design of your social programs, and let them guide your participation in the online communities that the people you are interested in choose to spend their time.

The Social Ecosystem

The social ecosystem, taken as a whole, provides three fundamental opportunities for understanding and leveraging the behaviors associated with collaborative interaction. These opportunities—the social graph, social applications, and social platforms—are shown in Figure 4.7.

The *social graph*—the connective elements that link profiles and indicate activities through status updates and the like—provide a framework for understanding who is related to whom, who is influential, where to look for potential advocates, and what is happening right now. This is important for participants: The social graph and the applications that rely on it facilitate friending, for example, and the sharing of content and experiences throughout a social network.

Behind the scenes, the social graph supports the programming techniques that allow social applications to discover relationships and to navigate the links that define them, suggesting potential friends or helping to spot influencers and generally providing an indication as to how participants in a social network are connected to each other and what they are sharing between themselves.

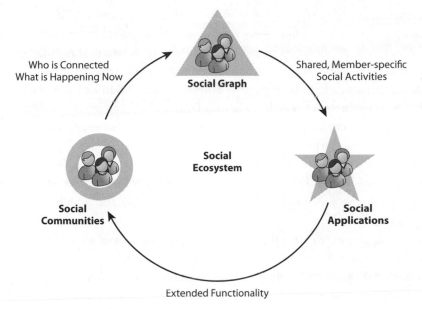

Who is Connected
What is Happening Now

Shared, Member-specific
Social Activities

Social Graph

**Social
Ecosystem**

**Social
Communities**

**Social
Applications**

Extended Functionality

Figure 4.7 The Social Ecosystem

Social applications—extensions to the core capabilities of the social platforms and software services that support social networks—provide the additional, specific functionality that makes the larger community and platforms useful to *individual* participants. The Aircel voicemail application and Slide's Top Friends application that extend the functionality of Facebook are examples of social applications.

Social applications enable the extension of relationships between a brand, product, or service to the individual level by providing very specific, member-selected functionality. Interested in supporting cause-related organizations through the traffic to your Facebook? Install the SocialVibe application. No need for voicemail in Facebook? Don't install the Aircel application. This flexibility allows members to create a functional environment that efficiently delivers the specific services they want: Imagine if Facebook had to provide all of the applications available itself? It's not a hypothetical question: this was Facebook prior to the opening of its API. As evidence of the value of social applications, consider that if there was a defining event that ramped up Facebook's growth, it was the opening of its API in May of 2007 and the proliferation of applications—some 12,000 created in the first six months alone—that resulted.

Social applications are also important in that they facilitate the overall growth of the network: By incorporating specific applications in a larger social network, that network becomes more useful to the members taking advantage of that application, increasing the value of the network itself to those members in the process.

Finally, communities and other social platforms—built around passions, lifestyles, and causes or similar higher callings—provide the gathering points for individuals interested in socializing and collaboration in pursuit of the specific activities they enjoy together. These communities, support forums, and related social platforms are all places where your business or organization can participate and add value (including by direct sponsorship of the social space itself) as is the case with Powered's customer communities built for Kodak, HP, Radio Shack, and iVillage or any of the developer's communities built on the Jive or Lithium platforms.

By building a community around a passion, lifestyle, or cause and then fostering and strengthening the relationships between the brand, product, or service and customers and influencers, the progression to collaborative participation and higher-level engagement is enabled.

Importantly, these three—the social graph, social application, and social platform (community)—drive each other. Take any one of them away and the value of business or organizational participation drops. This follows from the interconnection between these three: Without the social graph, for example, relationships between participants do not form and the "community" becomes transactional and self-oriented rather than social and collectively oriented. Without the communities and larger social objects (passions, lifestyles, and causes), the participants lack a sufficient motive to drive organic social growth. And without the social applications that extend the functionality of the core social platform, the activities within the community are limited to the broad activities of larger demographic groups, missing the highly engaging and very specific activities of small groups or even individuals. As a result, the social graph fails to develop in the way it would otherwise.

Review and Hands-On

This chapter connects the audience and the tools and utility applications into the communities where they naturally congregate. By using these tools to properly position your business as a value-added member of a community and then participating from that perspective you can establish a basis for trust. You'll have to deliver, or course: Where fine print and high-speed voice-over can legally disclaim whatever expectations an advertisement may have set, in a social setting walking the talk is required. If you say it, you have to do it.

The benefits are significant: The combination of trust and relevance drives engagement, and encourages people to share the information that leads to long term success through the delivery of a superior experience. This applies within your organization—where the goal is instilling in everyone an attitude and empowered commitment to customer satisfaction—as well as outside, in the store, where as Sam Walton said, "Your customer has the answer."

Review of the Main Points

Implementing social business initiatives challenges many of the accepted norms in traditional top-down management systems. It requires rethinking some aspects of running a business, and in many ways involves the not-so-obvious discipline of running your business as if you were a customer.

The main points covered in this chapter pull together the connection points between an organization and its stakeholders, and in particular accomplish this in a way that facilitates knowledge sharing.

- Businesses connect socially to customers through visible relationships and useful, collaborative applications.
- Participation, knowledge transfer, and social activity can be measured.
- Friending and reputation management are important aspects of social behavior that lead to strong communities.
- Effective moderation and clear policies spur community growth.
- Brand outposts created within communities popular with your audience are ideal places to "connect" your social business.

By recognizing the components of the Social Web and the ways that your customers or stakeholders use them, you can adapt your business or organization to a more participative, collaboration-oriented audience. This closer connection comes at a cost: Accepting customers as collaborative partners imposes an obligation to consider what they offer and to act on it. Not all businesses can do this, and even fewer can do it easily. That said, there is a clear process for accomplishing this; and there are plenty of cases and best practices from globally recognized firms that have been successfully building their own businesses using social computing and related techniques.

Hands-On: Review These Resources

Review each of the following, ensuring that you have a solid understanding of the concept being shown in the example:

- Brand outposts like Coca-Cola's Facebook page are viable alternatives to one-off microsites and branded communities:

  http://www.facebook.com/cocacola

- Atari's Tweet in Klingon is an example of a social application that taps an existing audience and its passion: You don't have to reinvent wheels to create great social media points of presence:

  http://tweetinklingon.com/

- Clearly articulated policies create a strong platform for collaboration and the adoption of social computing:

  http://www.ibm.com/blogs/zz/en/guidelines.html

Hands-On: Apply What You've Learned

Apply what you've learned in this chapter through the following exercises:

1. If you use Twitter or LinkedIn, bring your personal profile up to 100 percent completion.

2. If your office or organization has a profile-driven knowledge-sharing application, repeat exercise 1 for your profile on that network. Then, get three colleagues to do the same.

3. List your favorite social communities, and describe an application that your business or organization might offer within that community. *Connect it to your business objectives.*

Run a Social Business

Ready to see how the basic building blocks and concepts fit together? Part II pulls together the concepts in Part I and provides a framework for social business that you can use to get started quickly. Throughout Part II, "best practices" are highlighted through examples that show you how to create and run collaborative organizations and how to connect them with customers and stakeholders.

II

Social Technology and Business Decisions

The real business challenge with the Social Web isn't social media itself, but rather its relationship to the business or organizational processes that create the experiences that are talked about in the first place. Understanding how your internal processes drive the conversations that circulate on the Social Web—and how social analytics can be used to inform business decisions and potential process changes that relates to them—is the hinge point in moving to a social business.

5

Chapter Contents

Create a Social Business
Understand the Conversations That Matter
Social CRM and Decision Support

Create a Social Business

Part I of this book started with the engagement processes and the ways in which interaction and participation with social content can connect your audience with your brand (for better or for worse!). Built into the engagement process is a recognition of the new role of the customer, now much more of a participant in the marketplace and increasingly in the businesses and organizations that serve it. The final foundational element of Part I—the social business ecosystem and its collaborative processes—exposed the collective knowledge of the Social Web and showed you how to use it in building, running, and evolving your business or organization. Collaboration between the business as a whole and its customers is the hallmark of a social business.

Social Media Marketing: An Hour a Day

If some of the core social media marketing concepts are unfamiliar to you as you head into Part II, you may find my earlier book helpful. *Social Media Marketing: An Hour a Day* (Sybex, 2008) covers the basics of social media marketing and provides a nice introduction to the fundamental connection between the purchase funnel and the Social Web.

Collaboration in the context of social business means several things. First, it means working together, which is pretty obvious. Less obvious is *who* is working together. Social business implies a collaborative process not only between the business and its customers, which is tough enough, but also within the business itself—across "silos"—and between individual customers. Using the combination of conversations and active listening to guide your business planning process is a logical—but deceptively simple—approach to social business. More often, the processes of organizational change, of breaking down silos, and of appropriately sharing and exposing information quickly and widely present the real challenges. It is critically important not to repeat the business mantra that goes "Our customers are at the center of everything we do" *while operating largely without their input* and without formally integrating your customer's experiences, thoughts, and ideas into your internal business processes. Only when this occurs—when customer ideas and inputs are brought into the business or organization in a visible, meaningful way—is it a "social business."

The key to combining listening data, obtained via support forums and similar applications, and other information gathered through direct connection with your customers is that this needs to be connected to your business strategy and the processes that surround it. In other words, traditional marketing is largely focused on market study (both pre and post) that informs a *message*. Listening—in the simple sense—conveys back to you the degree to which that message was consistent with the actual experience of customers and stakeholders, including in venues that you may not have originally envisioned.

For example, an outbound marketing message may claim to be "Created for working mothers like you!" If it also turns out that the firm does not equitably promote women within the workplace, this contradiction will inevitably become known, very likely being spread through social channels. This raises the requirements for *active listening* and the incorporation of customer feedback into your business processes: Without a strategic basis for participation, any involvement in the Social Web will be limited to listening (but not responding) and using platforms such as Twitter or Facebook for talking (as opposed to participating). Neither of these is optimal, and neither will result in the desired outcomes.

The Innovation Cycle

The combination of social-media-based marketing and the application of Social CRM is powerful. Connecting customer intelligence and what is learned through active listening deeply into your business results in a customer-driven innovation cycle.

Driving your business or organization according to your business objectives is always your end goal. In combination with an understanding of your audience, your business objectives are what dictate the specific actions you need to take. The use of social technologies to create a presence for your brand on the Social Web—whether though a smart application that a community finds useful or a space of your own built around your customer's lifestyles—creates a durable, relevant connection to the Social Web. Social CRM is the complementary connection for your business: Social CRM tools like ideation platforms and support communities encourage customers to provide insights, thoughts, and ideas on how you can better serve them. This is precisely the information you need to succeed over the long term.

What all of this adds up to is a new view of the customer in the context of engagement. Figure 5.1 offers a view of the innovation cycle, codeveloped with Uhuroo cofounder and 2020 Social colleague Kaushal Sarda, that combines the engagement processes of a social business. The primary loop—Learn, Abstract, Do, Offer—provides a framework for engagement that is based on an understanding of the endpoint use or application of the product, service, or cause-related program that you deliver. By closing the loop—by iterating—a continuous cycle that drives long-term innovation through listening and collaboration is set up.

Kaushal Sarda

Kaushal Sarda leads the enterprise applications and products practice at 2020 Social in New Delhi. You can follow Kaushal on Twitter (@ksarda) and read his blog here:

http://kaushalsarda.com/

Social CRM sits at the core of this cycle—see for example the work of Esteban Kolsky. It is *repeated innovation*—not one-off hits—that drives success. The Apple iPod is a great example. The first models launched in the early 2000s bear only passing resemblance to the wide range of devices comprising the iPod family and to the ultra-sleek, button-free iPod Video models available in the market now. The iPod's market-share stands at around 75 percent: What other proof of the value of innovation does one need?

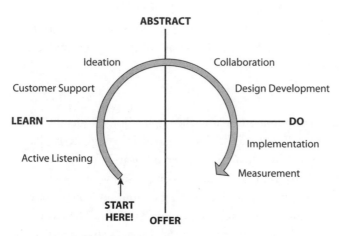

Figure 5.1 Innovation and Social Engagement

The connection between innovation and social engagement is directly applicable to social business and its attendant processes, including Social CRM. This relationship spans the stages of learning, applying the ideas gained to design, and then iterating to steadily improve (sometimes in radical steps) what is offered to customers or cause-related constituents in the marketplace. This is what makes Social CRM different from traditional sales-cycle-oriented CRM: It's the addition of customer-powered *collaborative* participation that powers Social CRM and the realization of a social business. Without collaborative processes, Social CRM quickly devolves to a more standard company-driven marketing and business development effort.

It is important to understand the requirement for collaboration in creating a social business: Otherwise, it's easy to fall into the trap of "this (Social CRM) is the same as what we've been doing…only now our customers are a formal part of it." The problem with this kind of thinking is not that there aren't analogies to existing processes—there are, just as there would be in any business process evolution. Rather, it's because the "same as…" is exactly the excuse used to avoid substantive change inside your firm or organization, an excuse that inertial forces within will desperately seek. Does this sound like an overstatement? It's not. As with any other aspect of business transformation, moving toward a social business mindset involves fundamental process change and recognition of the need for collaboration across many fronts. This *is different*, and it is important to set these expectations early on.

Getting Social CRM right—and successfully applying it to your business to create a genuinely collaborative relationship that leverages customer insight—depends *more* on creating an internal culture around change, around collaborative workflow, and around processes like ideation than on the implementation of any particular toolset. In my social media marketing workshops, for example, the workshops and exercises do not begin with social media tools: they *end* with them. The workshops begin with an explanation of business objectives and customers and the dynamics of the Social Web. With such an understanding in place, it's easy to choose the particular tools that are most likely to produce the desired results. Starting instead from the point of view of tools, the result would be an endless chasing of me-too ideas. Sometimes this approach works, fair enough, but more often this copy-cat approach doesn't.

Adoption of Social CRM follows the same rules: Without an underlying, business-driven framework, your efforts to redefine your innovation process will quickly die out. Social CRM directly impacts the management and decision-making processes within an organization by connecting the experiences that form around the products and services delivered to the marketplace with the business processes that create and sustain them. Product and service innovation, where ideas become reality, is certainly part of it. So are customer-support processes, where the post-purchase issues that inevitably occur are sorted out. So too are your HR department, your supply chain, and your delivery network. You get the idea.

When choosing a Social CRM toolset, start with your business, your culture, and your internal processes to create the overall platform that provides the connections to your customers, that supports the formal processes of active listening, and that encourages your customers to share their ideas on how they'd like to see your business evolve based on their own experience with your product or service.

Understand the Conversations That Matter

Listening to the conversations in your marketplace is the starting point in becoming a business that deeply integrates customer input. The application of more rigorous analytics to these conversations yields clues as to how an organization might use this input to improve a product or service. It also reveals *why* the highly recommended cross-functional work team approach to managing the Social Web is so essential.

Listening is an intuitively sensible starting point in a social business program and is largely risk-free. Unless you make it known otherwise, no one knows you're listening except you! As a further motivator, your customers and stakeholders will almost surely recognize when you are *not* listening. If you've ever hollered for help in an empty room, you know how obvious it is—and what it feels like—when no one is listening. Even worse, customers who are nearby—in the social sense, meaning part of the conversation or closely connected to the person(s) at the center or it —will also notice any lack of response. Given a comment that warranted attention, they will likely join in and amplify it, and will themselves draw a similarly negative conclusion if there is no response to the comment from an appropriate person within the firm or organization cited in the comment.

Listening is also generally noncontroversial within your organization. Listening does not *itself* oblige you to do anything with what is heard. This can play to your advantage when first starting out. A great use of listening, especially at the start of your social media and social business programs, is to bring your organization up to speed on what people are saying about your brand, product, or service *before* you actively engage your customers through social technologies. Like *not* listening, however, *not* responding also sends a message to your audience. Plan to participate not-too-long after you've started listening; prioritize and address the conversations that you can respond to most easily.

Taken together, *listening* is by far the easiest entry into understanding what the Social Web is all about. By listening—and in particular when using a dashboard-style monitoring tool—you can quickly see what is being said about your brand, product, or service. Moreover, you can do the same for your industry and competition—all of which is great intelligence, even if it's qualitative. From that base, you can gain solid insights into how your audience perceives you, in the context of your industry.

Based on this kind of upfront work and analysis, and with an understanding as to where these conversations are taking place, you can introduce the rest of your organization to the Social Web in a way that makes the connection to the business obvious. *This will help you build the internal constituency that you'll ultimately need.*

Consider the Workload

If you've ever looked at conversational data pulled from the Social Web—perhaps you've tried Google Alerts, for example—you're no doubt thinking "Sounds great, but who's going to filter through all of this?" If you've got a small brand, or you're in an industry that isn't talked about a lot, or you are a professional services consultant, realtor, or similar; you may have relatively few conversations that are of interest to you or require your attention. If you're Coke or Boeing or Bank of America, and in particular if your industry is in the news currently or is otherwise talkworthy, you may find yourself facing hundreds (or orders of magnitude more) of conversations daily. To get an idea of just how seriously businesses are taking social analytics, use Google to search for "Gatorade social media mission control." It's an amazing installation (myself having worked in Mission Control with NASA/JPL) from a technological perspective and a solid testament to just how important social analytics and understanding what is happening on the Social Web has become.

That's the catch (Yes, there is a catch!) to all of this "free data." For well-known brands or cause-related groups, and increasingly for many smaller brands and organizations, the amount of data can be overwhelming. Someone has to filter through it. Hopefully, that someone is not you. If it is, and in all seriousness, even it's not, there are tools available that make this work much easier.

Just as a social analytics dashboard, for example, will save you work by automatically displaying selected KPIs (Key Performance Indicators) around conversations in an organized and revealing manner, and as well automatically routing conversations and discovered issues to the departments where they can be acted on is an essential efficiency in making effective use of conversational data. This is where workflow enters the picture, and where you begin to transition from "listening" to "active listening" and from generally "free" to generally "paid" social analytics tools.

Workflow, which you reviewed briefly in Chapter 2, "The New Role of the Customer," includes the processes by which the filtering, routing, and tracking of listening results are automated so that you can manage large amounts of data (and often filter out larger amounts of noise). Active listening, which is described in the upcoming section, is all about doing something with the information you gather, and doing it in a structured, replicable manner that ties the conversations about your brand, product, or service to your business. Figure 5.2 shows schematically how all of this fits together, around a typical conversation.

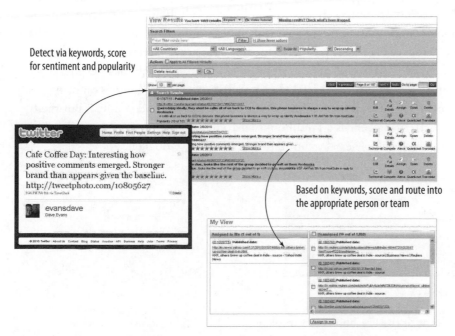

Figure 5.2 Workflow and Automation

Active Listening

Active listening, a term coined by Rohit Bhargava, implies integrating what is being talked about *outside* of your organization with the processes *inside* your organization that are driving those conversations. In other words, it means listening intently enough that you actually understand not only what is being said, but how and why it came about, and formulating at least a basic idea as to what you will do next because of it. The implication here is deeper than what social media marketing would typically consider: The ensuing analysis and response will more often than not involve the entire organization, or the better part of it.

> ### Rohit Bhargava
>
> Rohit is a founding member of Ogilvy's 360 Digital Influence and the author of *Personality Not Included* (McGraw-Hill, 2008). Rohit blogs actively and also teaches marketing at Georgetown University.
>
> You can follow Rohit on Twitter (@rohitbhargava) and read his blog, aptly named the "Influential Marketing Blog," here:
>
> http://rohitbhargava.typepad.com/

Consider the case of Freshbooks, a small business billing and time tracking service. Freshbooks makes a practice of paying attention to its customers, including what they are saying on Twitter. One post in particular caught their attention: Freshbooks customer Michelle Wolverton had been stood up on a date. Freshbooks' response, shown in Figure 5.3, taken from social media pro Erica O'Grady's series on using Twitter in business, got right to the point: "*We* would never stand you up." But then they did one better: Michelle is a Freshbooks customer, so Freshbooks sent Michelle fresh flowers. The result is near-legend status on the Web. Google it.

Figure 5.3   Freshbooks would never stand her up.

The point of the Freshbooks example is this: Listening alone didn't win Freshbooks praise. Instead, there was a process inside Freshbooks—at an operational level—that flexibly provided for an appropriate response to customer conversations. It is the combination of listening, understanding customers, and enabling the organization to respond effectively and in a talkworthy manner that is really at the heart of the Freshbooks' example.

One may argue that "Freshbooks is a small business" or "If Freshbooks sent flowers to everyone, they'd be out of business." To the first objection, the counter is that plenty of small businesses could not have done this *even if they had wanted to*. Freshbooks actually did it, and in a timely manner. Freshbooks' internal process—not their marketing campaigns—facilitated their talkworthy response. To the second point, the counter is *they only have to do it once in a while* to advance in the eyes (and hearts) of many of their customers. There is no expectation that every Freshbooks customer will get flowers. Instead, there is an expectation that Freshbooks consistently recognizes and cares about its customers. Freshbooks is free to express this in any way it wants, whenever it chooses. Consider the similar practices at Zappos: They've built a billion-dollar business by doing things that were sometimes more expensive—free shipping, *both* directions and occasionally even overnight shipping upgrades—"just because." Creating customer delight is a proven business builder.

Touchpoint Analysis

Touchpoints are my passion. As a product manager, I was immediately drawn to the simple reality that everything I did in terms of product design came down to one customer moment. That moment is, of course, the point in time when a customer uses and experiences some aspect of the product I'd designed or brought to market. That moment, and only that moment, is the single truth that exists from the customer's perspective. *What happens* when your customer plugs it in, turns it on, calls with a question, or shifts it into drive.

These points of intersection between the customer's world and the brand, product, or service are what I refer to as *touchpoints*. They include marketing touchpoints—a commercial that someone sees on TV that elicits an emotional response (as a dad, I still get happy tears when I see the "Sea World" spots we created at GSD&M) —as well as operational touchpoints, such as the feeling you get walking into a Whole Foods Market.

Touchpoint analysis is often presented from a marketing perspective but is applicable nonetheless across the organization. The key to applying this analytical methodology lies in understanding your firm or business—how it operates—and in knowing what your customers consider important and talkworthy.

The combination of talkworthiness and importance comes about because conversations don't happen when no one cares to start them. Recognize here that some aspects of any product or service may not be talkworthy (customers may not recognize or attribute significance to them) but they are still required—by law or regulatory rule for example—or in some way essential to the actual delivery of the service or the functioning of the product. For the aspects of your product or service that are both important *and* talkworthy, touchpoint analysis provides a method to analyze and prioritize how you go about applying what you learn on the Social Web to building your business.

Look more deeply into touchpoint analysis. The experience I opened the book with involving Continental Airlines and separately the Bengaluru International Airport are great examples of touchpoints done right. Add to that the Freshbooks' example and the general "customer delight" practices at Zappos. It's important to understand that across these very different businesses—of very different sizes and operating environments—the same basic practice exists: an emphasis on creating specific, tangible moments of delight that customers are very likely to talk about.

In the discipline of touchpoint analysis, I encourage plotting these two specific measures—performance and talkworthiness—against each other, prioritizing focus and action on the correction of *lowest* performance, highest talk-value touchpoints while ensuring the preservation of the high performance, high talk-value touchpoints. Figure 5.4 visualizes this concept.

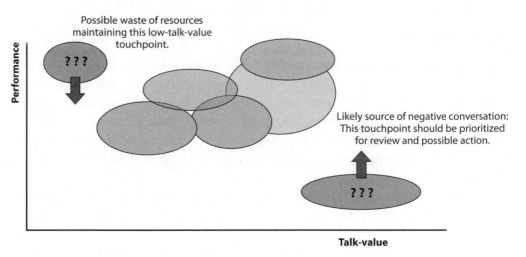

Figure 5.4 Touchpoint Analysis and Response Prioritization

In the case of Freshbooks, they sent flowers—$50 and change—to a customer who may spend $500 on Freshbooks services. In the case of Zappos, they provide free shipping—maybe $10 plus an occasional upgrade (at a cost of perhaps $20) for customers with an average purchase of $100 to $200. In the case of Continental, change fees and fare differences were waived that may have totaled $1,000 or more, given a customer who has spent something like 20 times that *with Continental* in six months. None of these are trivial decisions, and all require an understanding of business fundamentals: objectives, capabilities, constraints, and similar. Yet each drives—measurably—favorable brand sentiment and purchase consideration.

Consider the "return on effort" at Freshbooks: even a conservative valuation of the positive, unpaid media coverage around its "We would never stand you up" response greatly exceeds what it spent. Zappos clearly runs a profitable business, all the while providing their own branded moments of delight. In return for Continental's *demonstrated* acts of consideration, I have personally spent—from my own pocket, and *not* the reimbursed charges paid by my clients—more than $1,000 in that same six months simply because I choose first to fly with Continental even in cases where it is *not* the lowest cost option.

Active listening combined with a formal discipline like touchpoint analysis inevitably leads to insights into the business processes that drive marketplace conversations. The difficulty that is exposed, first with social media marketing and then with social business, is that it becomes quickly apparent that controlling the message (aka, "conversation" in the traditional media view, where "we" talked and "they" listened) necessarily gives way to the more informed strategy of controlling *the business processes that drive the conversations*. Unfortunately, most businesses and organizations—with a number of notable exceptions including those previously mentioned—are better at controlling what they *say* they do as compared with what they *actually* do.

The bottom line is that businesses and customers, together, both play a role in providing, demanding, and proving out the business case for creating great conversations. Creating brand ambassadors—at the heart of methodologies like the Net Promoter Score—is a powerful strategy that is greatly advanced by smart use of social technology.

This is the challenge of social business. It is not something that can be faked, and it not something that is undertaken lightly. It requires a specific, whole-business strategy and is rooted in active listening and the rigorous analysis of conversations.

Touchpoint Analysis: Bengaluru International Airport

In the course of traveling, I had a remarkable experience at Bengaluru International Airport: My checked bags were waiting for me on the baggage carousel less than 10 minutes after my plane landed. Coincidentally, I met Anjana Kher Murray, the airport's Director of Public Relations, the next day in one of my workshops in Bengaluru where, to her delight, I used the baggage example in my discussion of touchpoint analysis.

Naturally, I was interested in how the airport had created this experience, and I was invited to tour the airport. In Figure 5.5, Airport CEO Marcel Hungerbuehler (right) explains the baggage process to me (center) as Anjana (left) also listens. I came away with a detailed understanding of just how my baggage experience happened. As you read through this interview with Anjana, think about how each specific design consideration translates into a specific customer experience. Whether you do this upfront or you use this type of process in remediation efforts, one thing is clear: The experience of your customers at a given touchpoint is the experience you designed into the process (or failed to design) supporting that touchpoint.

Figure 5.5 My behind-the-scenes tour of Bengaluru International Airport with Anjana Kher Murray (left) and Marcel Hungerbuehler (right)

When I first asked Anjana about the overall design of the airport, she replied:

"We are committed to establishing the Bengaluru International Airport as India's leading airport in terms of quality and efficiency, to set a benchmark for the future commercial development of Indian airports. One of the pioneering concepts that were kept at the forefront while designing the Bengaluru International Airport was short walkways. This simple, functional terminal building is designed to ensure passengers don't have to walk till they drop. Short walkways take the passenger quickly from the entrance to the check in counters and into the aircraft and the reverse for arriving passengers."

Compare that with the endless walks (or runs) as you change planes in some of the airports you frequent. Having been through the Bengaluru International Airport a number of times, I now expect to be through security and comfortably seated within about 10 minutes of having stepped out of the taxicab when leaving from the airport, and about the same when arriving.

Next, I asked Anjana specifically about my baggage experience. What were the design goals, and how were they measured? Here is her reply:

"The following elements are critical in maintaining the baggage delivery standards: people, processes, and systems. The prompt delivery of arriving passengers' baggage is an important element of an enjoyable travel process and the aim is to provide high standards of efficiency in this area on a consistent basis. While the passenger reaches the baggage carrousel faster due to the short walkways, a long wait for the baggage could be disappointing. Upon arrival, it has been observed that passengers take about 6–10 minutes to reach the baggage claim area. Hence, it has been determined that the ideal time for baggage delivery should be between 7–10 minutes."

Important in Anjana's response is this: Each process is designed in the context of the processes that surround it. Baggage delivery standards are not set in a vacuum but rather in the context of precisely when the bags would be expected to be available by the disembarking passenger. This would naturally be the point at which this person first approaches the baggage carousel. For some arriving flights—for example, with international flights where passengers must clear customs *before* retrieving bags—the first bags are not placed onto the carousel until those passengers are likely to be heading for the carousel. Recall the touchpoint diagram (Figure 5.4). There is no sense in expending resources to have bags on the carousel *before* passengers get to it: That incremental money and human effort can be better applied at some other passenger touchpoint.

Finally, I got into the Operations issues. Designing a process that is supposed to delight customers and actually delighting them are two different things. So, how does the airport actually do it? Again, Anjana's reply:

"A total of seven baggage carousels have been installed at Bengaluru International Airport, three for domestic and two for international arrivals; in addition, two carousels can be used for either domestic or international, depending on the peak hour requirement. Also known as a 'swing area,' it enables flexibility and maximizes utilization of available infrastructure. The baggage delivery time is applicable to arriving passengers and is tracked on a first bag–last bag basis. 'First bag' is defined as the time taken for the first baggage to be placed on the baggage belt. The same goes for the last baggage dropped on the conveyer belt and is defined as 'last bag.'"

As with the maintenance of any customer experience, measurement is a key aspect:

"In order to ensure prompt baggage delivery on passenger arrival, we follow strict tracking methods: Ground handlers use radio communications,

our Trunk Mobile Radio System (TMRS), to alert the airline ground staff on delivery of the first and last bags. This information is then sent to the Airport Operation Command Centre (AOCC) and recorded to monitor the time taken between the aircraft chalk-on time (time when the chalks are placed under the aircraft wheels) to baggage delivery.

"Periodic verification is done by the terminal team to confirm the baggage drop time for the first and last bag. We have also deployed special technology solutions such as Universal Flight Information Systems (UFIS) that help gather status information for the first and last bag. This system provides an alert if the first bag is not dropped on the conveyer belt within the specified minutes of flight arrival."

By this point it should be obvious that my bags being ready when I arrived was no accident, and that the multiple processes that contributed to this experience were all operating in parallel, under control of the AOCC. Just how important is the AOCC's role? Critical, as it turns out. Bengaluru International Airport's Operation Command Centre is the collaborative nerve center for the airport. When an airplane is delayed, for example, or when two flights are departing at the same time, the AOCC—which has airline representatives, ground staff, and other critical control personnel *physically* seated in the same room—calls for a quick conversation between affected parties. As a result, decisions are made in seconds rather than tens of minutes, and bottlenecks that would otherwise flare into actual flight delays are avoided. Anjana describes the AOCC and its purpose like this:

"Our belief is that successful airport operations can only be achieved when all partners of the airport work closely together. This includes the processes and functions that ensure the baggage arrives on the correct belts within the set time frame. Hence, representatives of the Bengaluru International Airport's partners come together at the country's first 24/7 Airport Operation Command Centre (AOCC). This is where crucial daily operations are streamlined for smooth, efficient, and well coordinated airport functioning. As the nerve center of the entire airport, real-time data is being fed into it from diverse departments and collaborative decision making process is facilitated."

As you consider your own business or organizational processes that drive customer experiences—and hence the conversations around your brand, product, or service—consider the practices of the Bengaluru International Airport in designing and measuring customer experiences with its facility. It should be clear that they are not simple, that they require a collaborative, cross-functional team to deliver, and that they do in fact produce very favorable conversations as a result.

There is another take-away from cases like the Bengaluru International Airport: Operations and infrastructure projects may not be as glamorous as a splashy Super Bowl ad. However, from your customer's or stakeholder's perspective, how your business or organization actually runs is much more important. The Social Web is, in a sense, the great equalizer between large brands with big budgets and small brands that simply *do it better*. As a case in point, consider the new Dyson bladeless fans: If someone *needs* a fan, a standard 3-blade model can be purchased for under $20. But someone wants a bladeless fan that is quieter, works better, and looks better, it's a short step to $300 Dyson bladeless. On top of that, the new owner will actually talk about the Dyson because it simply a better fan, just as I have talked to anyone who will listen about the Bengaluru International Airport: It is simply a better airport, and its *operations* staff and infrastructure are big parts of what makes that so.

Social CRM and Decision Support

Tracking and measuring the dynamics of a marketplace conversation to understand sources of influence, spot problems, and create loyal advocates is largely what drives the current interest in social analytics. Beyond this, connecting the impact—or more correctly, the *underlying cause*—of these conversations deeply into business processes defines the emerging discipline of Social CRM.

Just what is Social CRM and how do you apply it in a decision making context? In Chapter 3, "Building a Social Business," you saw a quick overview and simple definition: "Social CRM is an approach to business that formally recognizes the role of the customer as a key in understanding and managing conversations around the brand, product and service." In this section, building on the practices that place the customer solidly at the center of the product or service experience, the basic definition of Social CRM will become operational.

Esteban Kolsky

Esteban Kolsky is a social strategist and consultant, and he is widely regarded as a thought leader in Social CRM. You can follow Esteban on Twitter (@ekolsky) and read his blog here:

`http://www.estebankolsky.com/`

Social CRM includes the following five elements:

- A genuine effort on the part of the firm or organization to understand and consider the point of view of its customers and/or stakeholders, for whom the business or organization exists.
- An understanding and mapping of the social graphs, communities, and the social applications that connect individuals within your overall audience to *each*

other (rather than to you) and thereby gaining an insight as to *how you fit into their world*.

- The identification of the *specific* difference between the activities your customers want to take ownership for versus those in which they look to you for guidance, relief, assistance, and similar contributions from you that improve their quality of life.

- The optimization of your commerce or conversion processes given the role of customers and stakeholders in the conversations that impact conversion.

- The connections—*touchpoints*—between your activities and those of your customers with the internal business processes that drive the experience that occurs at those touchpoints.

The first column in Table 5.1 shows the basic decisional-support elements associated with Social CRM. Take these five elements together and you have the basis for an enterprise-wide implementation of a feedback process based on customer insights gathered through active listening that be harnessed and used to drive your business. This is what Social CRM is all about.

▶ **Table 5.1** Social CRM and Decisional Building Blocks

Social CRM Element	Applicable Technique	Example Platform
Understanding the Customer Point of View	Social Analytics and Rigorous Assessment of Conversations	Alterian SM2, Nielsen | Buzzmetrics, Oxyme, Radian6, SAS Institute, Scout Labs, Sysomos, TNS | Cymfony
Mapping Social Graphs	Source Identification and Social Status	BuzzStream, Sysomos, Gephi
Differentiating Control versus Leadership	Support Communities and Expert Identification	Lithium Technologies, Jive Software
Commerce Optimization	Quantifying and Tracking Ratings and Reviews	Bazaarvoice, SAS Institute, IBM WebSphere
Quantification of Customer Touchpoints	Touchpoint Analysis and Prioritization of Business Activities	Create this yourself: See Chapter 6 of *Social Media Marketing: An Hour a Day* for more.

Table 5.1 provides a starting point in understanding and investigating some of the best-in-class tools that can be used to create the quantitative framework for a Social CRM program. By linking social analytics (conversation analysis) and source identification (social graph analysis) together with commerce feedback (ratings and reviews) an end-to-end view of your commerce pipeline emerges. Taking the further step—through touchpoint analysis or an equivalent process—of tying sources, conversations, and commerce data to the internal business or organizational processes that

drive the experiences that your customers and stakeholders talk about provides the business insights you need to evolve your business in alignment with your customers.

The Customer Point of View (POV)

Social analytics, even in their purely qualitative form, provide powerful insights into the personal views of your customers. Because the analytics platforms collect large amounts of data, you can get beyond the anecdotes of focus groups. Because the tools are real time (or near real time) and ongoing, you can also move beyond one-off surveys. Going further, in exchange for your time spent configuring these tools, they'll organize the relatively unstructured qualitative data into themes or categories so that you can make sense of the conversations. Figure 5.6 shows a typical social analytics dashboard and the way in which its data can be used to understand a conversation.

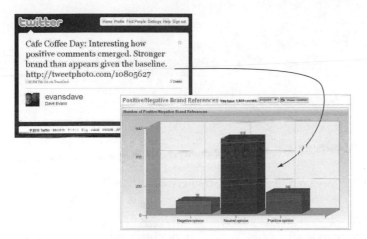

Figure 5.6 Social Analytics

The insight gained into what customers are talking about—and hence how your product or service experience is perceived in the marketplace by your customers—is useful beyond marketing. This is an important point to note, as I mentioned in Chapter 4, "The Social Business Ecosystem," in that many organizations adopting social-media-based programs place the marketing department at the focal point for this work.

Here's why this happens and why it's important to see beyond marketing. Connecting social media with marketing makes sense if one considers the impact of a positive or negative post on sales. Clearly, these outside-of-brand-control comments, helpful or otherwise, keep sales managers and marketers up at night precisely because they cannot be controlled. However, when a business as a whole steps past marketing in its collective view of "social business," the conversations become more predictable and as such the ability to manage these conversations (in the direction of "more favorable") becomes possible.

Looked at across the business or organization, social media extends far beyond marketing. Looking at the purchase funnel, shown in Figure 5.7, you can see that it's actually a better bet that social media has relatively little to do with marketing. Beyond creating a platform in which marketers—certain caveats respected—are welcome to participate along with everyone else in appropriate conversations, the origin of the conversations themselves has more to do with Operations, HR, and Customer Care—all of whom contribute in a tangible manner to what is talked about on the Social Web—and relatively less to do with marketing per se.

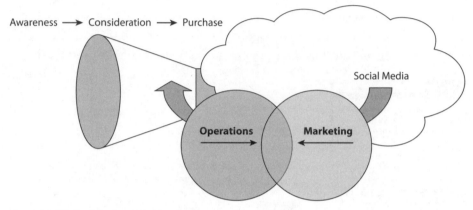

Figure 5.7 The Purchase Funnel and Operations

Social CRM picks up on this and formally recognizes that the conversations circulating on the Social Web *started* in, for example, Operations but then exerted themselves upon Marketing (by encouraging or dissuading sales). Again, this is a very different process than the more or less unidirectional flow of outbound messages associated with traditional campaigns.

This is why Social CRM is so powerful and so timely. Connecting customers into the business, and understanding their perspective and what attracts or repels them from your brand, product, or service is a path to long-term success. Social CRM combines the insights of Fred Reichheld's Net Promoter —itself a benchmark metric for long-term success—with quantitative tools and a flexible methodology for defining and evolving your business.

Map the Social Graph

Once you've got a handle on *what* is being said, the next step in implementing a Social CRM program is understanding *who* said it. By "who said it" I'm not referencing the personal details of a specific individual, though you may in some cases be able to discern this information from actual customer data or a similar source.

Rather, I'm referring to profile and social graph data, understanding who is talking about you by also understanding the other places where this same person publishes content and with whom it is shared. By seeing a profile in the context of that individual's social graph, you get a much more complete picture of individual motivation, influence, reach, and connectedness that allows you to prioritize your next steps in reaching out and responding (or not) to that specific individual.

The social graph itself—first covered in Chapter 2 and explored in detail later in Chapter 11, "The Social Graph,"—defines the social links that exist between people within social networks. As well, the social graph includes pointers to the various other places where this individual publishes or otherwise participates. Social CRM and the more focused source identification tools navigate this social graph to create a map so that these relationships and linkage can be understood in a business context. Understanding where someone publishes and participates on the Social Web leads you to the additional relationships that can provide real insight into the conversations you've located that specifically reference your brand, product, or service. Figure 5.8 shows a typical map, generated by BuzzStream, for a potential contact based on an initial keyword search.

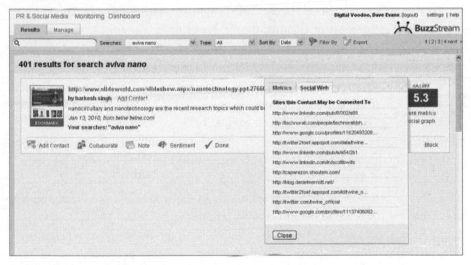

Figure 5.8 Mapping the Social Graph

As an example of how social analytics can be put to use in combination with an understanding of the social graph, consider what happens when you find a post that is favorable to your brand, product, or service, on Twitter, for example. Figure 5.9 shows a different example of social graph mapping, this time with the original tweet related to the map of the social graph. Using a combination of basic search tools—Alterian's SM2 and Tweetdeck (as a real-time search tool)—along with BuzzStream, I was able to connect with the person who posted the original comment. The result is a new friend and business connection at The Hub Network in Vancouver. What if you could do this with everyone who mattered to your business? You can, and Social CRM is the way you do it.

Figure 5.9 Connecting Source and Social Graph

Tools like Alterian's SM2, BuzzStream and Tweetdeck—none of which are break-the-bank expensive—provide simple and straightforward ways to implement these practices in your business or organization. For example, using the combination of Tweetdeck (available free of charge) and BuzzStream (under $100/month) enables you to actively monitor Twitter for mentions of your brand or a competitor's and ascertain the social influence of those talking about your products and services. This gives you precisely the data you need to prioritize your actual response effort (which is decidedly *not* free) given what is being said and who is saying it. This data translates directly into meaningful key performance indicators (KPIs), too: The number of mentions on Twitter, positives versus negatives, average influencer rankings, and mean response time are all examples of KPIs that you can add into your existing dashboards.

Being able to prioritize your responses allows you to connect more deeply with individual customers, be it a one-off interaction around a particularly delightful or upsetting experience, or the development of a longer-term relationship with a significantly influential individual within your customer base. If you've ever posted a favorable comment—or any comment, for that matter—about a brand, product or service, think about what it would feel like if you were personally acknowledged by the brand manager, for example, as a result. In general, people post because they have something to say—and because they want to be recognized for having said it. In particular, when people post positive comments they are expressions of appreciation for the experience that led to the post. While a compliment to the person standing next to you is typically answered with a response like "Thank You," the sad fact is that most brand compliments go unanswered. These are lost opportunities to understand what drove the compliments and create a solid fan based on them.

Integration of Listening

In the previous section, "Social CRM/ Mapping of Social Graphs," I illustrated how using a simple listening platform (for example, using Tweetdeck as a real-time monitor for Twitter in combination with BuzzStream for social graph mapping) can yield valuable KPIs. The step-up in business value from listening/monitoring to actively listening and responding along with measuring is seen in the usefulness of the KPIs as drivers of business processes that connect what is learned on the Social Web with the way in which the business operates.

This combination, whether through use of a set of tools like Alterian's SM2 and Tweetdeck along with BuzzStream or an integrated tool like the Sysomos Heartbeat platform or Radian6 with Salesforce.com's social graph add-ons ought to be a formal part of your business toolset. And why not? Where else do you find customer conversations, served up and categorized, labeled by level of potential influence, all presented in the context of an historical baseline?

The active listening process is depicted in Figure 5.10. The integration with your business or organization occurs first in the "routing" processes and then in "tracking." Of course, the act of responding itself is a business process: That, however, is really a function of having or not having a listening program and does not in itself imply a "social business" orientation. To be sure, listening is better than not listening, and listening combined with responding is a solid idea. But to really see the benefit of a social business program within your organization, you've got to take a further step.

Monitor and Detect

Route and Respond

Review and Track

Figure 5.10 The Active Listening Process

Susan Abbott

President and senior consultant and researcher at Abbott Research and Consulting, Susan Abbott helps clients discover insights and develop response strategies that support their business. Susan's down-to-earth take on the Social Web and Social CRM is refreshing. You can follow Susan on Twitter (@SusanAbbott) and read her blog here:

http://www.customercrossroads.com/customercrossroads/

That further step is reviewing what you discover, tracking the issues—the positives and negatives—and then using this information to inform, change, and innovate inside your organization. This information can be used to develop a response strategy that includes elements of both customer response and internal business response and adaptation.

Here's a great example, from Abbott Research and Consulting principal Susan Abbott:

> *"I was mixing up some dip yesterday, and observed (for the hundredth time) that when you open the package, you rip off half the instructions."*
>
> —Susan Abbott, Customer Crossroads

Susan goes on to note that this is probably an "avoidable accident"—the barcode, she notes, is safely tucked out of the way. As we say in New York, "I'm not sayin'…I'm just sayin.'" There is clearly an insight here, and trivial as it may seem—or not, depending on how critical those instructions were to successfully making whatever is in the package—these are the kinds of things that are within your control, that impact the customer experience, and that result in conversations.

Looking at Susan's packaging comment, what would you do if it was your dip and you had control over (or could influence) the packaging design? First, you could create a specific strategy, either as you discovered those comments for the first time (good) or before you began listening at all (better). An effective listening strategy considers several elements, including who will respond, how the associated workflow rules will be set up, and the threshold for response, set by the seriousness of the issue—"tore the instructions" versus "hate tiny print" versus "found something growing inside the sealed package." Your response strategy should be built around an assessment of timeliness standards—backed up with timely KPIs—and should also include an assessment of the effort required so that appropriate staffing plans can be created.

Digging into Susan's packaging comment further, by responding *and tracking,* you can tell the difference between a one-off case and an opportunity for process change that leads to better conversations on the Social Web. Maybe Susan—like more than a few of the professionals now tasked with social media responsibilities in addition to whatever was expected of them previously—is time-pressured, resulting in this mishap. Or maybe, just maybe, the actual packaging process places the chip dip mix envelopes in the larger box that Susan bought at Costco *upside down* so that when Susan takes it out, she's actually holding the envelope in a way that guarantees ripping the bottom every time—and thereby destroying the instructions—instead of ripping across the top where you had intended.

This may seem like a trivial example, but scale it up across your own processes and the actual expectations you have of your customers: How many seemingly small, but crazy, things do you place into the marketplace every day? For example, how many times have you sprayed yourself with (pressurized) salad dressing when opening the little container on an airplane? Someone designed that package, someone oversaw the filling of it, and someone else sold cases of it to airlines catering firms with *at least the opportunity* to understand what was likely to happen when it was opened inside an airplane. If you don't listen and track, you'll never know, and without an effective strategy and planned response, you won't be able to do anything about it.

These seemingly small things are actually important to identify and fix. Each, in its own way, contributes to a conversation, a parody, or a joke—or something far more serious that plays out on the Social Web. Rarely do any of these help you. The other great thing is that as you find these on your own or with help from customers— and you can announce in channels like Twitter that you have fixed them. Not only does it send a nice message to customers like Susan, it also says to anyone else listening that your business or organization actually pays attention to what is happening on the Social Web. At the least, this gives you an image bump; at most, it will help you spot a problem early as customers realize that *because you are present and listening,* it is worth their time to let you know about some particular service or product issue.

Here's the take-away: Active listening combined with the strategic integration of what you learn into your business processes form a solid pathway to better customer experiences and thereby to the conversations that you really want. The program can be lightweight—basic listening combined with a triage process that picks off the big issues and makes sure they don't escalate—or it can be a deeply embedded and formalized source of continuous feedback that provides a customer-feedback "heartbeat." Either way, by building strategically sound active listening into your *internal* processes, you've successfully connected your business to your customers. Further, you've done it in a way that they are sure to notice and appreciate. That will not only further solidify your relationship with your customers but will also result in them spreading your good word.

> ## Nathan Gilliatt, Workflow and Social Media
>
> Nathan Gilliatt, Principal, Social Target, provides analysis and services supporting the implementation of active listening and supporting business strategy. You can read Nathan's blog here:
>
> http://net-savvy.com/executive/

Customer Support and Social CRM

Salesmanship begins when the customer says "no." Support begins when the customer says "yes." In a sort of basic truth about business, this view of customer support clarifies one of the biggest opportunities a firm or organization will ever have: The opportunity to make those who were happy to buy from you even happier that they did. I point this out because in too many businesses, whether by accident or actual design, customer support feels to customers like an obligation whose cost is to be minimized.

A different orientation—viewing a call from a customer as an opportunity to create a moment of delight—is what defines firms like Zappos, though they are hardly alone. Beth Thomases-Kim, Director of Consumer Services at Nestlé, took exactly this view when she transformed a cost center—Customer Service—into a brand-building touchpoint. By viewing each call as an opportunity and measuring the outcomes of the calls, the customer service objectives morphed from optimizing call time (i.e., reducing call time) to creating happier customers who are more likely to make subsequent purchases as a result.

Beyond the support tools themselves, the essential practices that connect the conversations occurring within them have to do with tracking and quantifying the specific themes that recur. Issues in design, production, clarity of instructions, and a lot more can be identified and corrected by examining these themes in detail. Tracking service issues through associated tools like Jira is an easy way to identify candidate activities for process improvement, just as looking at delivery or inventory issues leads to improvement in supply chain processes.

Beyond directly addressing support and related issues, what else can you do with a support forum? Along with product or service-related findings, support forums can also yield valuable insights into the "hidden experts" that exist within your customer base.

This is precisely what Dell discovered as it acted on its own belief that the discussions in and around its prior support structure indicated the presence of brand advocates and subject matter experts within its customer base. By first turning controlled degrees of support over to its customers—and increasing this over time—while additionally making use of the reputation management tools that are available in best-of-class support platforms, Dell was able to not only reduce its support costs while improving the overall levels of customer satisfaction with its support services, Dell was also able to identify the customer experts who existed in the support networks. This recognition drove higher levels of engagement from these experts, in support of Dell's overall efforts to respond to the issues that Jeff Jarvis had called out.

When evaluating a support platform, pay particular attention to its reputation management and expert identification tools. Support platforms from Lithium Technologies (providing the support platform for Dell referenced in the prior section) are particularly good in this regard: Expert identification is the core strength of this particular platform. When considering the use of a branded support community, look for ways to identify and reward members who are providing above-average value.

Activate Your Customers: Control vs. Leadership

Consider customer/product interactions like those described in the case of Dell, and in particular the roles played by the customer versus the business or organization. The people creating and posting the content (for example, customers uploading pictures) have *immediate* control of the content and hence control over their side of the conversation. It's "immediate" because it applies to this particular interaction: they get to define what is being said right now and to influence others who are listening right now.

By comparison, brand teams, product managers, organization fundraisers, and similar have control only as far as the design of the experiences that led to the conversations. In this sense, understanding the specifics that surround a conversation—who said it, what was said, and who (else) this conversation is likely to influence—provides the "proof points" for the business decisions and processes that gave rise to the conversations observed. These conversations close the loop—beyond the *immediate* sale—with regard to efficacy of business programs intended to drive *long-term* sales and profits.

The net impact is that the position the product manager is in, for example, is more a leadership role (as in "leadership of the conversation") than a control role. This is worth noting, as again this transition from "control" to participant that is part of social media and hence social business, is evident. By shifting from control to leadership, the now-proper orientation toward the role of marketing and business design is clear. The end objective is, of course, to create the experiences that lead to the conversations you want and in turn drive the sales (or other conversions) that matter to you.

Filberto Selvas

Filberto Selvas, Product Director at Crowd Factory, a provider of SaaS-based social networking tools, provides practical insights into Social CRM through his blog and related posts. You can follow Filberto on Twitter (@filbertosilvas) and read his blog here:

http://www.socialcrm.net/

Collaborative Processes

With the audience connected to the business, and employees and customers connected to each other, knowledge begins to flow along pathways that prior to the widespread adoption of social technologies were not always seen as primary to the operation of a business. The high degree of connectivity and the ease with which consumers, business partners, and other stakeholders can talk about brands, products, and services is (overall) a beneficial thing—long term, it leads to better products and services. But it also raises a challenge: What does the head of a marketing group—or for that matter a lone operations manager—do with the sometimes massive amounts of information and ideas that customers willingly offer?

Connecting the new flows of consumer-generated information with the units inside the business that might benefit from it is, to put it simply, hard to do, for a number of reasons beginning with the required changes to the internal modes (regimented channels) of communication that exist in many businesses. Add to that the additional workload of managing customer input gathered through social technologies: It's that old cliché that goes "My day was going great until the customers started showing up." It's hard to accept input when you're already fully loaded, yet (and especially in lean times) that's exactly where most businesses really want to operate: smaller numbers of employees, each of whom is fully tasked.

The successful adoption of social technologies in business is, therefore, as much about strategy and results as it is about process and efficiency: getting a smaller number of people to produce better products, faster, for example. Not coincidentally, it is by collaboration—internally— and by working in cross-functional teams and accepting customers as a key part of the business that a solution emerges. Collaboration has the *potential* to bring better solutions to the market faster, partly by the enhanced synergies and partly by the efficiency of avoided missteps resulting when customers are brought into the design process earlier. A big part of what is driving the adoption of social technologies across businesses, therefore, has to do first with knowledge extraction and collaboration, and second with putting it to use inside the organization.

Of these, getting *customers* to work together is often the easiest. After all, it is generally in their collective self-interest to do so, and the Social Web, with or without your participation, provides the tools needed. The allure of better products, better prices, and the satisfaction of venting…all ensure that customers will readily self-organize. Customers will do this spontaneously any time they sense that joining forces will produce a desired result more quickly than acting alone, and their attraction to the Social Web is proof positive of their desire to do just this.

Importantly, your primary desire is to encourage customers to work with your firm or organization. For example, rather than venting to other customers, or suggesting ideas that are as equally visible to competitors as they are to you, wouldn't it be better if they were shared with you directly? This is where toolsets like support forums and ideation platforms come in: They provide customers with a sanctioned forum that you can monitor, wherein exactly these types of conversations take place.

By comparison, getting *employees* to work together can be another matter entirely. But this is exactly what must happen. Fortunately, "there's an app for that." The opportunities for collaboration exist within the organization: between product managers and Customer Service, between Legal and Operations, and between HR and everyone else. Effectively resolving challenges exposed on the Social Web is a multidisciplinary task, as is maintaining a great reputation for those more fortunate brands. The best product in the world combined with poor customer service delivered by employees who are less than passionate about their jobs will not result in the kinds of customer conversations that drive long-term success. Facilitating collaboration between these disparate groups and between customers is the key to the long-term health of the business.

Look back at Table 4.1, in Chapter 4. Social platform providers such as Jive Software and Socialtext provide tools and technology that are aimed at making it easier for cross-functional teams—inside or outside the organization—to form and accomplish real work. If there is one thing that will drive the rapid adoption of best practices, it's making those best practices easier to adopt than to ignore. Collaboration is often seen—rightly or wrongly—as harder, or slower, than working alone. The smart use of appropriate technology can go a long way toward addressing—and correcting if needed—this condition.

Consider Socialtext as an example of a tool that makes it easier for people to work together across an organization. Socialtext provides a basic "community" framework built around a familiar profile model. The community is typically the organization itself, and the profiles are those of the people who work within it. Each participant has a basic set of social tools—a shared workspace, the ability to share basic forms of content, and utility/functional applications including things like shared calendars. The result is a complete set of identity and content production tools that facilitate the collaborative and creative processes.

Ross Mayfield

Ross Mayfield is the founder and Chairman of Socialtext, a workplace collaboration platform. You can follow Ross on Twitter (@ross) and read his blog here:

http://ross.typepad.com/

In summary, the relationship between your listening program, social applications, and your business processes is critical. Managing your business with the inclusion of social technologies opens up the opportunity for collaboration with customers through both the response steps and the final disposition of reviewed and tracked issues. Both of these open the possibility of collaboration between customers or stakeholders and the (employees of) the firm or organization. Collaboration occurs between customers themselves as well as between the people within your firm or organization. The connected nature of the collaborative process again underscores the cross-functional impact of social media and the rationale for moving toward a social business framework.

Review and Hands-On

This chapter covered the integration of active listening and formalized Social CRM into the business decision-making processes that drive an organization. Most important is to recognize that the source of customer or constituent conversations—the specific things that people will convey to others through social media that relate to your brand, product, service, or cause—are driven more by your organizational processes acting in concert than by marketing acting alone. This is a departure from traditional PR and advertising. While traditional channels remain vitally important in anchoring and promoting what you offer, it is the actual experience—created deep inside your organization—that drives the conversation that can significantly amplify your message and more fundamentally drive long-term success.

Review of the Main Points

The main points covered in this chapter are summarized below: now more than ever, social technology brings a significant capability to the decision-making activities inside your organization.

- Active listening is the core mechanism for tapping the Social Web as a decision-making tool, powered by the quantitative application of formalized Social CRM.

- Social CRM is built around fundamental components, all of which must be present: direct customer input, influencer and expert identification, ideation and feedback gathered through organized customer support services, and process-driven internal culture of collaboration.

- Decision making benefits directly from the integration of social technologies, applied at the levels of customers (social media), the organization (internal collaboration), and the connection between the two (Social CRM).

The main points in this chapter set out a framework for applying what can be learned and applied to business through the use of social technologies to the processes of business decision making. This has an impact in tactical issues—responding to a localized negative event—as well as long-term strategic planning and product innovation.

Hands-On: Review These Resources

Review each of the following and connect them to your business.

1. Spend time reading Esteban Kolsky's blog (http://www.estebankolsky.com/), and in particular search for and read the entries on "analytics engines." As a hands-on exercise, create a plan for integrating social analytics into your *operational* (not marketing) processes.

2. Review Kaushal Sarda's 2010 InterOp Mumbai presentation on slideshare. The easiest way to find this is to visit slideshare (http://www.slideshare.com) and search for "Kaushal Sarda." In the InterOp presentation, look at the product innovation cycle and map this onto your business and identify the specific areas or functions within your business that contribute to innovation. Think about the Bengaluru International Airport example as you do this. How can you "design in" the experiences you want your customers or stakeholders to talk about?

3. Visit Socialtext (http://www.socialtext.com) and watch the short videos that show you how this product is used inside an organization. As a hands-on exercise, use that information combined with your reviews of additional collaboration tools to create and present to your team a survey of enterprise collaboration tools, tying them to your business.

Hands-On: Apply What You've Learned

Apply what you've learned in this chapter through the following exercises:

1. Visit with the IT, Marketing, or Operations teams that use your existing CRM data. Explore ways of incorporating social data into these processes, and connecting that information to your business or organization.

2. Building on your exercises in Chapter 1, define one or more internal collaboration points based on what you discovered in exercise 1, above.

3. Building on your exercises in Chapters 2 and 3, create a workflow path for social data (e.g., conversations) that carries this information to the points inside your organization that can act on it. Include a method for tracking results.

Social Analytics, Metrics, and Measurement

Chapter 6 hits my personal passion point with regard to social media and business: measurement. This is the chapter that covers the aspect of "social anything" that keeps most decision makers and change/process champions up at night. Many sleepless nights have been spent wondering "How do I measure this and make sense of it?" This chapter takes a hard look at the rationale for establishing the specific metrics required to make sense of the Social Web and track success, along with the tools and platforms that provide and analyze these metrics in the context of your objectives.

6

Chapter Contents
Social Analytics
Know Your Influencers
Web Analytics
Business Analytics

Social Analytics

The previous chapters have provided a basis for understanding how social media and Web 2.0 technologies are reshaping the relationship between Marketing, where the promise is created, and Operations, where the promise is kept. Building on the basics of managing conversations through decided behavior rather than attempts at control, this chapter presents the fundamentals of actual measurement.

Measurement is critical to building social media acceptance within an organization beyond the marketing department. Facebook pages and Twitter profiles are useful as marketing extensions, no doubt about it. However, at this point in the book it is my hope that the really big levers of social technology (reshaping products and services; creating a robust, two-way, collaborative relationship with customers; and using what is learned throughout your organization) are starting to become apparent.

Throughout this chapter is an underlying theme of the value of measurement and its role in determining a return on investment (ROI). As you work through this chapter, consider that asking "How do I measure ROI?" is preceded with questions like "What *is* ROI?" and "Does ROI even apply to this activity?" Don't overly focus on ROI unless you've first established that ROI is actually the appropriate end measure for your intended use of social technology. For example, a key performance indicator, or KPI (see sidebar) may be more appropriate and more informative if there is not a clear "investment" or financial return in the form of new, incremental revenue or costs avoided as a an expected outcome of your project. ROI is important, but determining why (and when) ROI is the appropriate measure can make even more difference to your success.

Quantitative Measurement

What should be clear at this point is that without meaningful and quantitative measurement you stand essentially no chance of ever seeing social media and Web 2.0 technologies adopted through your organization. Why not, and why the central role for metrics? Think back to the Good Guide— a customer-driven, handheld social application that directly empowers consumers—referenced in Chapter 4, "The Social Business Ecosystem." When your core customer—take the "advocate Mom," for example—has an application like the Good Guide and scans your product with her iPhone, comparing your company's carbon footprint and hiring practices with your competitor's, what will your marketing program do to ensure that your brand wins in this type of comparison? Without the coordinated, committed help of the *entire organization* you stand no chance of winning, and without quantitative measurement—the universal language throughout most organizations—you'll face an essentially undoable job in trying to rally your larger team to understand why their participation—beyond marketing—is essential.

Social media analytics are at the core of putting the Social Web to work in business. When time is taken to understand the quantitative tools and measurement points, the Social Web is transformed from a source of largely unstructured qualitative data to a conversational framework that can be viewed and tracked quantitatively. It is this quantitative discipline that enables two essential best practices when it comes to applying social media to your business or organization:

- Making sense of what people are talking about in a way that leads to *prioritized* insights in the context of competing capital efforts

- Connecting these conversations and the results of your programs designed to change these conversations for the better by addressing adverse conversations and building on beneficial ones

In traditional communications, the activities that parallel the study of conversations via social media analytics include press clipping and reporting, focus groups and consumer research, so-called pre- and post-campaign marketplace surveys, and similar. In each of these, there is a specific collection/identification/result process that underlies a fundamental learning process. This learning process is designed to anchor the brand, product, or service in the desires, needs, and reactions of customers, influencers, and others whose opinions matter with regard to what is talked about in the marketplace. In each of these measurement practices, there is a distinct set of metrics or an accepted method of stating a learned or observed outcome.

ROI, KPI, and Intangible Value

When defining your metrics program, be clear about the difference in the types of end results you are seeking. In addition to ROI—which is nearly always measured in financial terms like increased revenue, cost savings, or cost avoided as a result of an investment—you should also define target KPIs—numerical "key performance indicators" like conversions or new registrations—as well as intangible values associated with simply having a presence in specific social channels.

The New Media Sings the Old Media

Social media analytics is built around many of the basic practices applied to traditional media—who's talking, what are they saying—now applied to the (digital) conversations happening on the Social Web. So what's different? For starters, because social media is defined in some way as leveraging the massively scalable publishing capabilities afforded to each Social Web participant—in simple terms, recognizing that it is easy for reasonably well-connected people to command a reach that rivals TV within local markets or to reach more accurately defined niches and social circles. This means that the well-connected homemaker, or the hobbyist blogger, or anyone else with a defined passion and a basic command of social media publishing can amass a real audience and can exert real influence within it. Quantitatively measuring this reach and impact is just as important on the Social Web as it is any place else. Further, because each conversation is literally time and date stamped, signed by what is more often than not a real person and associated with a specific URL that is forever discoverable, these conversations form a robust body of information that is very useful in managing your business. This is what social media analytics is all about.

Sentiment, Source, and Volume

As a starting point in social media analytics, among the most commonly cited metrics are sentiment—also known as *polarity*—along with source and volume, measures of the origin and overall level of the conversations you are tracking. Start with these, but then push beyond them and understand the processes that drive what you observe.

As a starting point in social analytics, consider sentiment, source, and volume, an example of which is shown in Figure 6.1. *Sentiment* is the measure of the polarity of the conversation—positive versus negative with regard to the subject—and is useful in understanding not only the immediate issue of "Do people like _____?" but also the degree to which they feel this way. This is helpful, for example, in refining a brand advocate/brand detractor-centric tactical initiative.

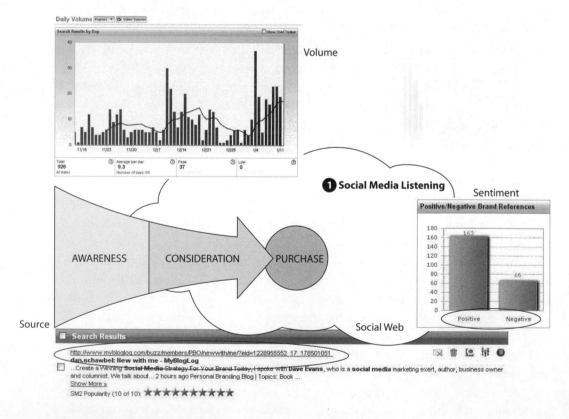

Figure 6.1 Sentiment, Source, and Volume

Source analysis has two facets: the identification and understanding of the author—covered in detail in the next section, "Know Your Influencers"—and cataloging and tracking the location of posts. The latter—understanding what is being said on Twitter versus Orkut or Facebook versus a blog—leads to an understanding of where you should be participating on the Social Web, information that is essential in planning, for example, a brand outpost program.

Volume measures are used to assess the overall conversational level with regard to your brand, product, or service: How many people are talking about a particular topic or picking up and reposting information? Volume analysis is most typically associated with conversational trends—the relative levels of positive versus negative over time, the number of conversations over time, or the sudden spiking of an adverse rumor. A typical trend chart is shown in Figure 6.2.

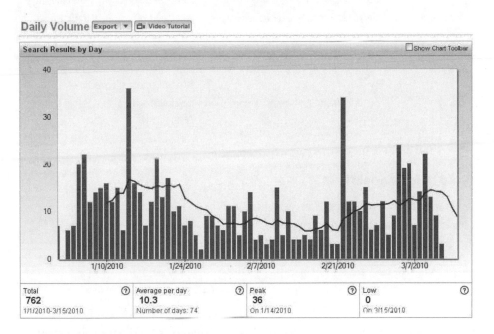

Figure 6.2 Social Media Analytics: Trend Charts

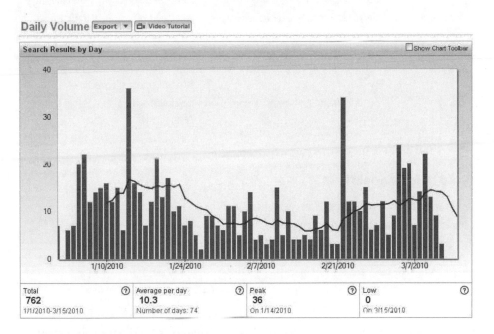

By building on the basic measurement of sentiment, source, and volume, a more practical and defined set of metrics can be established. In a post on Social Times, a blog published by Nick O'Neill that follows social media's technical tools and skills, Raj Dash lists the essential metrics, examples of which are shown in Table 6.1. As you work through this list, notice how they are built on the selected fundamental measurement areas, which are then set in a business context. The complete table can be found at http://www.socialtimes.com/2010/02/social-media-metrics/.

Even more importantly, rather than just accepting the examples in Table 6.1, use them as a starting point in developing a specific set of measures and sources that apply to *your* business. Always cite your own business objectives, your existing metrics, and then build off of those to develop your specific set of key performance indicators and related quantitative guideposts.

▶ **Table 6.1** Examples of Primary Social Media Analytics

Measurement	Sources	Details and Notes
Traffic Leads	Based on the sources of traffic arriving at your site.	Tie this to your current customers' behavior.
Membership Level	The number of fans and followers, or subscribers if the content is offered as a free or for-pay subscription.	How many of your fans are also followers? What percentage is active in more than one channel?
Member Activity	Number of members (registrants) versus actual unique visitors.	What percentage of your membership base is visiting you with some regularity?
Conversions	Google Analytics, Your conversion funnel.	What share of your social traffic is actually completing the activities you have defined?
Mentions	Social Media Analytics, Tweetdeck, similar counts.	How many people are talking about you? What are the trends over time?
Virality	Send-to-Friend, cross-posts, Diggs, similar.	How much (or how little) is your content being spread?

Nick O'Neill's "Social Times"

Writer and Industry Analyst Nick O'Neill publishes Social Times, a collection of reviews and commentary on a variety of social media topics including the use of analytics. You can follow Nick on Twitter (@allnick) and you'll find the Social Times online site here:

http://www.socialtimes.com/about/

Setting your measurements into your business context is an obvious first step; yet for the most part, businesses and organizations sometimes fail to formally recognize and measure the impact of social media on business. Without such measurement, it is a stretch to think that a social business program will ever take hold, let alone thrive, inside a run-by-the-numbers business. Because most businesses and organizations are in fact run by the numbers, this does not bode well for an effective connection between the Social Web and the inner workings of business, effectively relegating social media to outbound marketing applications.

This is really unfortunate, as purely *outbound* marketing is probably the *least* effective application of social media and social technology. Remember, the Social Web—unlike TV and American Football, both essentially built for use as an advertising platform—is not fundamentally a marketing channel. Rather, it is more of a forum or place for conversations, some of which may be of interest to you as they impact your brand, product or service. This creates the opportunity to talk, participate, and gain influence that can be helpful in marketing and more general business applications. Measurement forms the basis for quantifying this work.

The Need to Measure More

The significance of the lack of a formal measurement mindset around social media becomes clear when you consider that too many professionals using social media in business do not measure its effectiveness. A 2009 eMarketer study found that 16 percent of the professionals it surveyed measured the effectiveness of their social media programs. The other 84 percent? It's unclear why they are even doing the work they are doing, and likely less clear to their CFO that they should be doing it at all. Without a measurement program, social media marketing and its application to business is at best an experiment; at worst, it's a costly diversion.

If this sounds harsh, consider that nearly any business or organizational effort undertaken represents an opportunity forgone someplace else within that same business or organization. Every choice in business has an economic component and an associated opportunity (and time) cost. Failing to associate some sort of realistic, relevant metric with an economic business decision is a path to suboptimal performance.

> ### Webtrends for Facebook
>
> Facebook provides a comprehensive analytics package that offers an excellent starting point for understanding the performance of your Facebook business page. Webtrends builds on that, adding additional capabilities and metrics not available through the basic Facebook tools. For more information, visit Webtrends:
>
> http://www.webtrends.com/Products/Analytics/Facebook.aspx

In a Bazaarvoice study on measurement and expectations of social media, the majority of those businesses studied found that across a range of social channels and applications the CMOs either didn't know what they were getting from their social media marketing program, or had actually concluded that there was no ROI (meaning positive economic contribution to the business) associated with social media. The one clear exception to this near-universal lack of measurement and understanding? Ratings and reviews, which are the focus of the Bazaarvoice social commerce platform. Compared with programs launched on Twitter, LinkedIn, and Facebook, ratings and reviews (followed by a variety of implementations of brand platforms and corporate blogs) stood out as being *expected to make a positive contribution to the business*, and in many cases from a sales perspective. By comparison, and illustrating the importance of being clear as to the basis for ROI calculations, note that the focus of the Bazaarvoice offering is *commerce*. For many types of community platforms and social applications—covered in detail in Chapter 12, "Social Applications"—the ROI is derived not out of incremental revenue but out of *cost avoidance* (lower support costs online versus phone center costs, for example) in return for the platform investment. Whatever your program, it is essential to understand what is being measured and how the measurements will be used to guide performance.

What is most interesting—and most telling—with regard to the Bazaarvoice study is that when the measurement is clear and the social application is directly tied to the business, the expectation of CMOs is that their use of social media *will make a net positive contribution*. Further, the expectation is that the contribution made *can be measured*. This is at least in part a result of the focus and attention that Bazaarvoice has placed on its platform and its connection to business: Bazaarvoice goes to great lengths to educate its customers and ensure an understanding of the value of its platform. It is also in part a result of Bazaarvoice's dominance in its market segment. Because of the significant presence of large brands within Bazaarvoice's client roster, and given the direct and measured connection between the platform and the businesses it serves, it is no wonder that a large proportion of leading CMOs recognize the value of ratings and reviews as applied to commerce. More platforms, and more CMOs, need to be looking more intently at quantitative measures of social media.

Bazaarvoice

Bazaarvoice offers a strongly metrics-driven solution that can be used with online commerce platforms. You can learn more about the Bazaarvoice social commerce solutions here:

http://www.bazaarvoice.com

The takeaway is this: Apply the same sort of critical assessment to your social media program as you would apply to the running of any other aspect of your business or organization. Always begin by connecting your proposed social media effort to your business, and only then begin the process of evaluating specific tools or social applications. Like any measurement-driven program, the choice of tools follows the business objectives and the establishment of numerical goals.

Source and Sentiment Analysis

In Chapter 2, "The New Role of the Customer," you saw tools like Buzzstream and the Grasshopper business example. Buzzstream provides a view into the sources of influence within an area of interest—defined through keywords such as the name of your product or a competitor's—so that you can create relationships with the people talking about you. Your active listening program takes this one step further by connecting these sources with the actual business impact of the conversations in which they are a part.

Knowing who is talking is an important part of understanding the meaning of what is being said and then applying this in a useful manner within your business or organization. Combining the sources of the conversation—especially when the sources are actual (or potential) customers—with your listening data provides insights into how you can evolve your product, how you can reshape the customer experience, and where you *and your competitors* have points of relative vulnerability. As you consider specific listening tools and listening programs, consider how the data provided facilitates connecting the source of the conversation along with the actual conversation and what it means to your business processes that are driving the conversations in the first place.

One aspect of listening—known as *sentiment analysis*—deserves specific mention. Sentiment analysis is one of the meaning-related processes by which conversations are categorized. It's also one of the most talked about and one of the most troublesome. Without belaboring the point, human communication is complex: Anecdotal examples of the issues around sentiment analysis can be summed up in two words: "Dyson sucks!" Is this a positive comment—perhaps an expression of joy by a new customer of these amazing vacuum cleaners? Given the reputation for the Dyson brand, it's more than likely the case that this is a *positive* comment.

Sentiment analysis, important enough in its own right, is not an end in and of itself, though many would love it if it were. How great it would be if instead of actively listening all you needed to do was read a report and respond to eight negative posts or send "thank you" notes to a dozen loyal fans. Unfortunately, there's more to it. A lot more. Like the tip of an iceberg, sentiment analysis—and more specifically tracking and trending sentiment—gives one an indication of what is happening below the surface. Unlike the tip of an iceberg—which is a good indicator that there is more ice underneath *that is otherwise just like the ice you can see* above the surface—in the case of sentiment analysis, you generally have to go back to the original posts, to the original context of the conversations, to sort out what is really happening: you may find more ice, or you may find rocks. A strong negative comment may originate from a dedicated fan, or a dedicated detractor. You must dig in and understand these kinds of differences in addition to simply following the sentiment score.

TweetTone

Looking for meaning and emotion on Twitter? Check out TweetTone. It's a clever application that enables you to quickly look for different topics—all review a basic tonality analysis, all within the context of the individual tweets that gave rise to the tone results. You'll find TweetTone here:

http://tweettone.com

The challenge with automated sentiment—and one of three primary motivators for the consideration of workflow tools as a part of your listening program (the other two being data conditioning and noise elimination, along with scalable and trackable routing and follow-up) is that "meaning" is almost entirely context driven. One of the shortcomings of the automated listening tools is that they tend to consider the post—in which keywords of interest were embedded—in isolation: In other words, they see the immediate conversation, but not the back-story.

Consider Twitter as a channel: Because of its highly fluid and distributed nature, the short posts that define Twitter are actually interlinked conversations. One person says, "I bought a new Dyson—I love it," and another, seeing that post, replies "Dyson sucks!" as a humorous affirmation of the product, resulting in the "negative" post referenced earlier. Because replies are not always linked (in the technical sense) to their originating posts, the listening tool sees "Dyson sucks" in isolation and then applies its rule base accordingly. Somewhat humorously—or maybe by design—with the launch of the new Dyson bladeless fan referenced in the prior chapter, a whole new round of sentiment issues arises for Dyson as posts like "Dyson really blows!" start circulating. Oh well.

More seriously, none of this is a knock on sentiment analysis as an idea, nor is it intended as commentary on listening tools that include sentiment analysis in particular. The fact is that the current generation of tools—with all their attendant shortcomings—still provide more value than not using them at all. The challenge—and your responsibility—is to ensure that you are, at some level, tying the conversations you discover back to their original context so that you can actually deduce the intended meaning. This is also important from the perspective of workflow: the elimination of "noise," those results that while they match your keywords are not related to your actual search. Referencing the Dyson products example, conversations mentioning Esther Dyson are probably unrelated. The effort required to winnow the results to those which are relevant to your specific interests must be considered as an integral part of any listening program.

Here's a twist on sentiment analysis: You can, if you're savvy, get your fans to do at least some of the work for you. Jake McKee, while at LEGO, often turned to key people within the communities he worked with for insights into "brand sentiment." Fans would often let Jake know—via IM, where Jake maintained an active, open presence with fans—that there was something or other that he needed to pay attention to, adding within their posts whether this was a good thing needing more attention, or otherwise. This is one more reason, as if you needed one more, to actively build a base of loyal and alert supporters.

Know Your Influencers

Parallel to traditional PR and the associated marketing and advertising concepts relating to "influentials," there are metrics related to the social graph—the connective links, profiles, and updates connecting people on the Social Web—that define the sources of the conversations you are tracking with your social analytics tools. Just as with any other communications channel measurement, understanding how a particular source (typically an individual) fits into your overall intelligence and outreach program is essential in getting the most out of it.

From Journalists to Connected Enthusiasts

In traditional PR in particular, there is an established practice of identifying and developing relationships with key journalists and industry experts. These media connections are useful, for example, when rolling out a new product. By communicating in advance with these contacts, you can seed the general market awareness with comments from these individuals as they begin writing about your product launch. Sometimes this is done confidentially—for example, you may "embargo" a press release when you want your closest contacts to have this information and be aware of what is coming but not actually talk about it before a certain date. Or, you may want these advance recipients to talk about it first, conveying to them a certain "scoop" value. As a tip, include in your press releases a 140-character statement intended for re-use on Twitter, what Brian Solis calls a "Twitter Pitch."

However you do it, the basic process involves identifying and building relationships with the journalists and experts that write about your product or service, or who focus on issues relating to your markets. The same process applies on the Social Web, with one big difference: The people you want to reach and build a relationship with quite often don't wear nametags.

For any specific interest, cause, lifestyle, product or service there are people who blog about it, who post about it on Twitter, and who convey this information to those who "follow" or subscribe to the blogs, for example, of these people. This includes the wider public audience that extends beyond media professionals and specific analysts and influencers.

The challenge, of course, is picking out the influencers that are of interest to you using tools like Buzzstream and Sysomos, now part of Marketwire, and then measuring your progress in building a relationship with them. Table 6.2 shows a selected set of core metrics related to influencer relations and relationship development.

▶ **Table 6.2** Examples of Core Influencer Analytics

Measurement	Typical Tools and Services	What It Shows
Social Influence	Buzzstream, Sysomos MAP, Scout Labs (Lithium Technologies), Klout and similar tools	Provides insight into profile connections revealed by examination of social graph.
Reach	Facebook (fan count), TwitterGrader, Klout and similar tools	Provides an indication of connectedness within a community relating to an individual profile or page.
Frequency of Posts	Alterian SM2, Buzzstream, Sysomos Heartbeat and similar tools	Provides an indication of how active a particular person or source is.

Metrics like "social influence" are returned directly through tools like Buzzstream. Figure 6.3 shows the Buzzstream dashboard and the social influence ranking that is applied. Tracking this type of metric over time, as well as across influencers, allows you to develop a profile of the people likely to be helpful to you as you go about the task of quantifying what is being said and affixing a numerical score to the likely impact of who is saying it. This helps you in two ways: You can build relationships with your influencers, and you can better understand the larger social graph that is connecting participants in the conversations around your brand, product, or service.

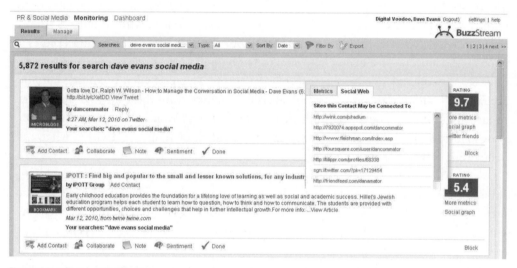

Figure 6.3 Influencer Identification

Identify Your Influencers

Understanding your influencers requires more than simple tracking: You will need to know who specifically is influencing others in your markets. By identifying them and then building an actual relationship with them, you can get into the subtleties of what drives the commentary they produce. This is an important insight, but it raises a question: How do you go about building these relationships? You meet them.

As you discover influencers, you can talk with them or interview them. You can dig in to their conversations and understand in detail what they like about your brand, product, or service and what they don't. You may not like what you hear, but that's OK. By understanding the subtlety of the conversations, the dynamics over time—is the negative sentiment rising or falling, is it cyclical, is it driven by your firm, or driven by your industry?—you can intelligently craft an overall *business* strategy. In short, you can learn a lot from your influencers, and it goes way beyond and is more valuable than simply enlisting them to push your message (as if they'd actually do that).

The first step in identifying influencers is to sort out who is connected to whom, who is influential, and who is not. It's not a fully automated process, so your gut instinct and skill as a marketer will pay off as you sort through the quantitative information that is available, and then combine that with your own industry knowledge, for example. Take advantage, too, of personal relationships that you may be able to build: if a conversation in a particular community is of interest to you introduce yourself (in the real world sense, for example through email or Twitter) to the webmaster or community manager in charge. Share your point of interest, and see if this person or team will help you understand the other influencers within that community. More information is better, and if nothing else you'll build a nice connection with a community manager that may pay off later.

Building on what you've learned or the knowledge gained from community managers you've met, tools like Buzzstream or Sysomos, or retaining a services firm like Oxyme will help you to quickly dig deeper so that you can then take the steps of building relationships with those individuals within the community who are relatively more influential or more connected. Look back at Figure 6.3, which shows a typical view of influencers through Buzzstream. Buzzstream gathers this information by crawling the social graphs of the people identified as the sources of specific conversations. What is presented to you is a summary of all of the possible publishing points associated with this person. You can then quickly scan these publishing sites for the people you are interested in and refine the list. Then, you drop the information you've gathered into a contact database and begin building an actual relationship.

The Role of Trust

Creating this kind of relationship is important. Figure 6.4 shows the role—and sources—of trust in consumer transactions. The same concept applies across all business transactions and is bound up in what is now called *social capital*. Social capital, briefly, is to social media and the reputation of your brand (and you!) what economic capital is to your CFO and your organization. Social capital plays a role in influencer relations: For example, by understanding who your likely influencers are, and by then taking a genuine interest in understanding their points of view, not only do you learn more about how your brand, product, or service is perceived in the marketplace but you also create the opportunity to gain social capital.

How? As an industry participant, for example, you very likely have general domain expertise. If you share this openly—and not from the point of self-interest—you will increase your social capital. Here's an example: An influencer contacts you about a speaking date, but you are busy. You can rearrange your schedule, you can simply and politely decline, or you can refer a competitor who you know will also do a very good job. If you can rearrange your schedule, that's great. If you can't, the best social option is to refer someone else who is qualified, because it is this act versus the simple declination that actually helps the person seeking your assistance. It's like the old retail cliché: "Do you have this shirt in blue?" A response like "We don't, but I know where you can get it..." is the one that is remembered and appreciated. Building social capital works the same way, and it most definitely applies to influencer relations.

Advertising Tactics/Media Trusted* by Internet Users in North America, by Age, April 2009 (% of respondents)

	<20	Total
Recommendations from people I know	96%	92%
Consumer opinions posted online	66%	72%
Editorial content such as a newspaper article	81%	70%
Brand Websites	82%	69%
E-mails I signed up for	55%	67%
Ads in newspapers	68%	66%
Brand sponsorships	77%	62%
Ads in magazines	70%	62%
Ads on TV	75%	61%
Ads on radio	73%	61%
Ads before movies	75%	53%
Billboards and outdoor advertising	65%	53%
Ads served on search engine results	46%	37%
Online video ads	35%	33%
Online banner ads	26%	24%
Text ads on a mobile phone	26%	18%

Note: *participants responded that they trusted each tactic "completely" or "somewhat"
Source: Nielsen Online, "Nielsen Global Online Consumer Survey," July 2009

105466   www.eMarketer.com

Figure 6.4 Relative Trust

Social Capital

Author and thought leader Brian Solis offers a clear, concise view on social capital and its importance in business. You can follow Brian on Twitter (@briansolis) and read his post on social capital here:

http://www.briansolis.com/2010/03/social-capital-the-currency-of-digital-citizens/

Apply Your New Influencer Knowledge

Once you understand—quantitatively—the people in the marketplace or stakeholders who matter to your firm or organization you'll want to do something with this information. Much of what can be done with influencer knowledge involves the use of the social graph and applications that navigate it. Tools like Buzzstream and Sysomos MAP are examples of how the social graph can be used to provide information that defines the people talking about your brand, product, or service. You can combine this with information that highlights the interconnections between people to create an assessment of how influence actually flows. This can be tracked over time and tied back to your social-media-based marketing efforts.

Influence ranking further allows you to prioritize your efforts. Like any other program, there is a cost to undertaking it that can be measured in terms of other opportunities foregone. The same applies to building relationships, with one caveat. When using influencer scores to prioritize your efforts, it's important to use more than the numerical influence score. While it's good to have highly influential people in your contacts database, it's also important to recognize that influence doesn't necessarily flow from the most influential directly to your prospects or others in whom you have an interest in reaching, Instead, a significant amount of influence actually flows along what are called *weak ties*.

Weak ties are the casual bonds that exist across members of a community. Think of weak ties as "knowing someone who knows someone who...." For example, in a typical Facebook or LinkedIn network, there are people you know directly and people who are connected to the people you know. These types of bonds are extremely important in understanding how information passes through a network, and ultimately how the information that relates to your product or service, or your brand, company, or organization, gets to the people who are considering some aspect of an offer.

Ripple6: The Role of Weak Ties

Ripple6 offers a community platform solution set that leverages the strengths of weak ties between community members. You can learn more about Ripple6 here:

http://www.ripple6.com/

Community tools like Ripple6 utilize weak ties, as do platforms like LinkedIn. Ripple6 creates connections between community members by facilitating the transfer of information between people (profiles) who are not themselves directly connected. It does this by making it easy to pose questions, for example, to people with whom you are connected and who in turn can post these questions to others in their networks who might have an answer for you. LinkedIn uses this methodology when it assists in introductions. LinkedIn very clearly shows the social graph as it applies between people: When a LinkedIn member wants to be introduced to someone specific, LinkedIn shows the member the chain that connects people he or she knows to the people he or she ultimately wants to reach, and then sets up the intermediate "pass along" process.

Influence flows across the Social Web in exactly the same way. By taking care to understand not only who your influencers are but also how they are connected to pockets within your market that you may not otherwise have a direct connection to, you can significantly increase the likelihood that the conversations you participate in will ultimately involve these people. This kind of quantitative information is especially useful in tuning an *outreach* program: Whether the goal is spreading your message further—think blogger outreach efforts—or building up your customer-driven intelligence program, knowing who is talking about the issues that matter to you and how these people are connected to others is vital.

Web Analytics

In the prior sections the basic metrics relating to the Social Web were defined. Social media analytics help frame the conversations in a quantitative context. Influencer metrics do the same for the source of the conversation. Between these you have the basis for success determination according to the business objectives you have set and the KPIs (Key Performance Indicators) that you have established. The next step is to tie these to your business, beginning with its online presence.

Website Performance

Web analytics—a representative look at Google Analytics is shown in Figure 6.5—is concerned largely with the performance of your website or online applications. By "performance" what is generally meant is how well your website converts visitors into customers, people supportive of your cause into donors or enlisted volunteers, or some similar transition that carries them all the way through your purchase or acquisition funnel.

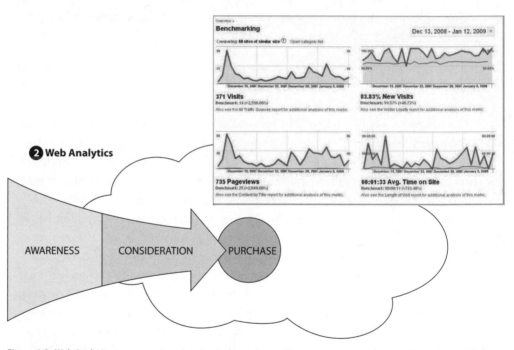

Figure 6.5 Web Analytics

Web analytics offer a number of measurement points. Table 6.3 lists a representative set of the more popular metrics associated with the performance of a website in a business context. The key to getting the most out of your web analytics program is understanding the individual measures shown in Table 6.3 and then moving beyond them. Far too many firms track the basics—bounce rate, time spent, page views—but then fail to move beyond these basic counts and into the actual analytics of what drives them and why they matter.

Measurement	Tools and Data Sources	Details and Notes
Bounce Rate	Webtrends, Google Analytics, Omniture, similar measurement platforms	Indicates the degree to which your landing page pulls visitors into your site.
Unique Visits	Webtrends, Google Analytics, Omniture, similar measurement platforms	Compare with membership (registered visitors) levels.
Time Spent, Pages Viewed	Webtrends, Google Analytics, Omniture, similar measurement platforms	Indicates the degree of engagement when used in combination with other measures of activity.
Referrer URL	Webtrends, Google Analytics, Omniture, similar measurement platforms	Provides indication of which social channels are sending visitors to your site.

Beyond the Basics

What's beyond the basics? Although simply "counting and reporting" is an important first step, understanding what is driving the measurements you collect is essential to running your social media program and connecting what you learn to your business. The application of web analytics to your business should provide insights into how your online assets—your website, blog, or community site, for example—are driving your business and contributing to the achievement of business objectives. In turn, understanding these business drivers should inform or connect to your internal intelligence processes.

By connecting the measurements to business processes, and by understanding how the process results drive the measurements themselves, you can use the trends you observe to steer your business or organization in ways that ensure success with regard to your business objectives. The necessary requirement here—especially as teams that span functional areas of a business or organization are brought under the increasingly large umbrella of social business and Social CRM— is a quantitatively based understanding of how processes translate into results. The measurements you observe are indicators of results but are not themselves the results. By taking the steps to connect the measures to the business objectives, you ensure that you are tying what you've observed or learned through listening, for example, to the processes that create the conversations in the first place. In this way the Social Web efforts—whether outreach, listening, participation, or other forms of engagement—become measurably tied to the ongoing operation of your business or organization.

Don't Overcomplicate

Note here that "going beyond the basics" doesn't necessarily mean moving to advanced or exotic measurements, but instead combining core metrics in ways that provide deeper insights and that show you how to tie actions and results to your business objectives. Again, the key insight in measurement is taking the time to understand how relatively simple measurements can be combined, trended, and reinterpreted to provide useful information. This means that it is important, especially in the early stages of any social business program, to measure aggressively. Measure everything you can. Sure, you may end up discontinuing the collection of some items, but you will surely discover others that are surrogates or even direct indicators that provide the data you need to make sense of newer Social Web-based consumer behaviors.

Consider a metric like *bounce rate,* the relative measure of visitors who land on your site and then leave immediately, without looking at anything else. Dig into bounce rate, slice it by source, slice it by date, trend it over time, and run correlation analysis against it. What's driving it? Do adjacent trends in blog activity or conversations on Twitter correlate strongly with the trends in bounce rate that you observe? *These* are the questions you really want to answer, because when you know what is driving your bounce rate rather than knowing only the number itself, you can actually develop a plan to reduce it—or to understand why further reduction has a diminishing economic payback.

Avinash Kaushik: Web Analytics

Author of *Web Analytics: An Hour a Day* (Sybex, 2007) and *Web Analytics 2.0* (Sybex, 2009), Avinash Kaushik publishes the blog Occam's Razor. You can follow Avinash on Twitter (@avinashkaushik) and read his blog here:

`http://www.kaushik.net/`

Connect the Dots

Moving beyond the basics of data collection is the difference between "12 people visited last week, up from 8 the week before" and "qualified visitors to our site increased following the release of the latest podcast program." Counting visitors is important, no doubt about it. Studying the ways in which people traverse your site, for example, before they choose to make an actual purchase gives you a way to spot "qualified" visitors earlier in the process and thereby the ability to implement specific practices that drive these conversions further. Connecting the next step—connecting the changes in qualified traffic to specific Social Web-based programs—enables another level of understanding. This is, of course, the path to understanding ROI, and in the larger sense being able to make the case across your organization for meaningful spending on social business efforts.

It's all about connecting the dots. Like the silos that exist inside organizations, data that is collected in isolation is less useful than data that is connected and thereby reflects holistically across processes. This leads to the larger question of "How are web analytics related to or indicative of interactions originating on the Social Web?" The connections between the two are found by linking the sources of Social Web conversations, influencers, and the incoming traffic to your website, support forum, or community application.

To see how the data collected through a Social Web listening program is connected to the data collected in a web analytics program, consider the application of basic correlation. Figure 6.6 shows a visualization of correlation. The data represented by Data Set 1 (solid squares) appears to be correlated—note how it falls along a common line—whereas there appears to be no relation in the data compared between Data Set 2 (depicted by the dots), whose data is scattered all over the chart. *Correlation* is the study of sets of observations, with the end goal being the deduction of a possible connection between the sets of data. There is a big caveat here, and it's an important one: Correlation and causation are two different things.

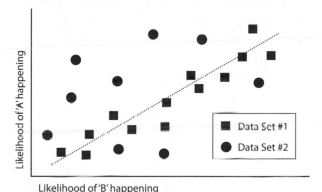

Figure 6.6 A Visual Chart of Correlation

Correlation is the more general of the two. Correlation implies that whenever *A* is observed, *B* is also observed. An example of correlation is the observation that "People who bought dog food on the Petco website also bought dog leashes." Purchasing one does not in itself *cause* the purchase of the other. However, the two tend to occur together more often than, say, people buying dog food and a bowling ball, something that may well be observed on occasion in the checkout line at a physical department store like Walmart.

Causation, by comparison, is a direct cause-effect relationship between *A* and *B*. When *A* happens, *B* results. Acquiring a dog, for example, fairly certainly *causes* the purchase of both the dog food and the dog bowl. Cause and effect can be seen in things like the increased checkout basket size that results when online shoppers are prompted to consider additional items based on what they have currently placed in their shopping carts: When people are told "others who bought dog bowls also bought dog leashes...," they tend to go look for a new leash.

Correlation has an application in connecting social media analytics and other web and business analytics. First, it's easy to do: Collect your listening results, clean them to remove noise and irrelevant results, and then attempt to correlate the listening results volume and sentiment with web traffic. If the patterns match—if the correlation is high—you've got an indication that some deeper connection is at work. *This is not proof of such a connection!* But it is an indication that looking further might be worthwhile, that what happens on the Social Web might be impacting what you observe at your website. The connection in this case is fairly intuitive, to be sure, but consider how this technique might be used to uncover relationships that are not immediately obvious,

Try shifting the dates, too: Lag the website traffic by a day or two days or a week and see if the relative measure of correlation improves. If so, you are seeing an indication that what happens on the Social Web has a *lifetime,* or a *transit time,* across the Social Web. This is certainly the case with brand advertising, for example, where a build-up time in awareness is observed. This is very different from, say, TV-based direct response or impulse buying (think QVC) where running a spot immediately triggers a known (or certainly knowable) buying response. It makes sense that these same conditions apply between the Social Web and your online purchase points or conversion funnels: It's worth your time to sort out the relationships.

If correlation is important, causation is the Holy Grail. When you nail down causation, you've got real power as the implication is that you can actually drive a particular outcome. The test for causation is tougher, and rigorous, systematic A/B testing should be at the core of your analytics practices because of it. This is as applicable to your use of the Social Web as it is to your use of any other marketing technology that can be optimized. By testing and comparing, you'll separate cause from correlation and identify the key activities and practices that will drive your business.

Take the time to examine the "usual suspects" in the context of web analytics— bounce rate, page views, time spent, and unique users—and connect these to your social media program by selectively changing elements of the social media program and noting the results. Building on what you learn, add your conversion results to the mix: Using Google Analytics, for example, set up conversion goals and then compare the results of your A/B testing around your social programs with your conversions. The result will be a quantitative understanding of your business, and the way in which your social programs support your overall business objectives.

Business Analytics

The business application of social media is—or should be—driven by its connection to business. In the previous sections, the links between social media analytics and web analytics were examined, with the result being a systematic testing process aimed at finding the relationships (correlation) that drive results and then extracting the key practices (causation) that you can replicate to grow your business. Figure 6.7 shows the relationship between social analytics, web analytics, and the starting point of your business analytics, shown here with their related commerce pipeline metrics.

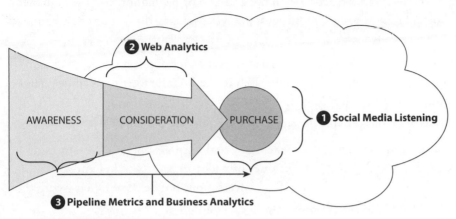

Figure 6.7 Business Analytics

    Initially, these techniques may be limited to marketing and your use of the Social Web as a marketing platform, as is often the case with social media marketing programs designed to create additional outreach points or places where people within your organization can participate with customers on behalf of the brand. The next section—where the focus turns to business analytics—takes the techniques that are useful in marketing and applies them to the business as a whole. In particular, in the case of social media and the Social Web, there is a measurable connection to business, expressed through a result against a set of established business objectives. That level of understanding needs to be the end goal, and you need to be relentless about getting there.

It's All About Business

In social business applications, *the connection to the business itself* is an order of magnitude more fundamental. In the simplest sense, it is Operations more than Marketing that drive the conversations: Therefore, it is the way in which the business is managed that becomes the focus, as opposed to how well the business is marketed. In true social business applications, the social processes and the software or technology that supports them are more likely to be paid for by the operations or information systems budgets than they are by the marketing department. The marketing department, by comparison, may pay for the programs associated with talking about the ways in which customers are benefiting from the implementation of a social business program, or in building the outreach or listening platforms that drive them.

    Looking at social business technology and software as a business infrastructure expense rather than as a marketing expense makes clear the ways in which the analytics are *required* to roll up. Social media analytics, web analytics, and influencer assessments must all be viewed in the context of their relationship to fundamental business analytics because they are the metrics that matter to the owners of the budgets and cost centers that are more likely than not going to be paying for the cost of implementing a social business program. Business analytics joins with social, influencer, and web analytics on two fronts:

- Business analytics, especially as related to commerce applications, provides an additional set of metrics that can be used in the overall effort to document success and provide insights for improvement.

- Business analytics provide the stepping-off point into Social CRM.

Because business analytics relate to the actual business operation, connecting business analytics to social and web analytics provides an end-to-end picture of the customer experience—manifesting itself as conversations on the Social Web—with the internal business processes that created the conversations.

Closest to web analytics are the business metrics associated with your online commerce pipeline (assuming you have one). For businesses that do some part or all of their business online ("pure online plays"), the commerce pipeline offers a number of measurement points. Social commerce platforms from firms like Bazaarvoice excel in not only improving close rates, increasing checkout value and the cross-selling of related products, but also in providing continuous, real-time quantitative feedback you can use to guide and evolve your business offering.

Offline and Nonbusiness Processes

For businesses that do not have a specific online commerce process—for example, for a cause that is collecting signatures or a business-to-business pre-sales funnel—the thought process and the approach to business analytics is still largely the same: The commerce pipeline is simply replaced with the defined conversion process. Tools like Google Analytics offer well-developed conversion analysis support that you can use to refine your online programs in the same ways you would any other commerce process. The connection is this: The objective is to pull together your various sources of data that supports measurement against KPIs along with the business process metrics around your established business metrics. This can be tied back to what you are observing on the Social Web. This basic metrics-driven methodology is what closes the feedback loop that the Social Web sets in place: It is this basic feedback loop that will drive a social business.

The feedback loop defined in the basic relationship between the purchase funnel and conversations that impact conversion is the connection between the operation of the business and its marketing effectiveness. This is equally true—though specific metrics may change—for commerce applications, for nonprofits and cause-related groups, and for other types of organizations. The remaining aspect of measurement and metrics is, therefore, to identify the key *business analytics* that can be shared across the organization and used to guide the overall processes driving continuous improvement in your products or services.

> ### Mind What You Measure
>
> Dachis Group principal Kate Niederhoffer offers her perspective on what to measure and why in the following post. You can follow Kate on Twitter (@katenieder) as well.
>
> http://www.dachisgroup.com/2009/11/three-masquerades-of-metrics/

Sources of Business Analytics

Business analytics can be pulled from a variety of places within the organization. The following sections cover two of the more immediately useful sources of business analytics when setting out to create a social business program. These areas are *commerce analytics*—after all, at the end of the day we generally are in business to sell something (even in some abstract manner)—along with measures of acceptance or rejection. The latter is particularly important as a class of metrics because it is very often a near-direct measure of what underlies the conversations observed on the Social Web, in support forums, ideation platforms, and traditional CRM systems. Between these two, a significant portion of what defines and drives a social business program can be found. This makes these ideal starting points.

Commerce and pipeline analytics are an obvious first choice. To the extent that one can directly tie social media analytics and (where applicable) web analytics to sales, for example, a very tight reporting loop is established. In these cases, it is very likely that the study of correlation and causation—identifying the specific relationships between various measurements and the economic performance of the business—will yield a fundamental set of metrics that can be used to guide the business vis a vis social media analytics.

What about nonbusiness applications of social business or its use by organizations where the direct connects are less obvious? This is where the studies of correlation and causation, combined with your own domain expertise around the processes that drive your organization, are valuable. You can employ correlation, for example, to literally find or discover useful quantitative measurements, and to then press deeper into the understanding of *why* these particular observations are correlated. Not only is this directly useful, you can often find new business fundamentals—especially as they relate to the emerging marketplace defined by the Social Web—that will help ensure that you achieve your business or organizational objectives.

Turning to the acceptance and rejection measures—take defect reports or calls abandoned as examples—a second and equally rich measurement area is found. Tracking a defects report, the issues that result in difficult or repeated service calls or call satisfaction are very powerful in identifying those specific aspects of a product or service that are likely to be talked about. In addition, these types of measures are very likely to be indicative of what will be said, and so can be expected to correlate strongly with the conversations observed and tracked through the social media analytics programs.

The net of the measurement discussion is this: Given that you already have a solid understanding of your business and your business objectives, begin an aggressive measurement program that ties social media analytics to your business. The eye candy—the sentiment charts, trend lines, and radar plots—are all cool. But the connection to business is what matters: Connect up web analytics and business analytics to get more out of your social media measurements, and more out of your social media and social business programs.

Review and Hands-On

This chapter covered the fundamentals of measurement and then showed how to take the basic metrics that are readily available further. By moving beyond counts and trends and into correlation and causation and by aligning social media analytics with business metrics, you can move your use of the Social Web in business to a whole new level.

Review of the Main Points

The main points covered in this chapter are summarized in the points that follow. The essence of Chapter 6, with credit to Katie Paine, is "Yes We Can! (measure social media")."

- Understand quantitatively what is happening on the Social Web, on your website, and in your business.

- Tie these measures together to create a complete feedback loop that includes the delivery of what is learned to the functional areas within your business or organization that can act on and respond to this information.

- Use quantitative techniques such as correlation to find relationships in available metrics that you may not have considered, and that once identified can lead you to new understanding of what the impact of social media and Web 2.0 really is.

- Move beyond basic metrics in all of your measurement areas, and press into a complete understanding how these metrics indicate where you are heading rather than simply where you have been.

By taking the time to connect the dots, to link together the fundamental sources of data that are available to you, you can significantly increase the likelihood of gaining acceptance and support for the organization-wide adoption of social business practices. This sets up the truly collaborative relationships between your business and customers, or between your organization and its constituents, that drive long term success.

Hands-On: Review These Resources

Review each of the following, and consider subscribing to those that you find especially useful or relevant to your business or organization:

> Avinash Kaushik's blog, "Occam's Razor"
>
> http://www.kaushik.net/
>
> Nick O'Neill's "Social Times"
>
> http://www.socialtimes.com/about/
>
> The Dachis Group's Kate Niedehoffer
>
> http://www.dachisgroup.com/author/kate/

Hands-On: Apply What You've Learned

Apply what you've learned in this chapter through the following exercises:

1. Identify the primary social, web, and business analytics that matter to you.
2. Run a correlation analysis on metrics you've identified, and then investigate why certain metrics are correlated more strongly than others and how this correlation might be used to further your understanding of how the Social Web is impacting your business or organization.
3. Develop a basic dashboard or incorporate one or two new business fundamentals that you identify through the above into your current business scorecard.

Five Essential Tips

7

This chapter pulls together the three basic things you've simply got to get right if you are going to make effective use of the Social Web in business, along with two behaviors to avoid (and what to do instead). The chapter concludes with a set of best practices that will help guide the implementation of a social media program throughout your organization.

Chapter Contents

Three Things to Do (and Why)

Listen, collaborate, measure.

Three words, simple in concept yet difficult in practice. At the core of social media—and indeed the deeper application of social technologies in a business context—is a process that is very nearly the reverse of traditional marketing and communications. Where traditional communications and advertising planning starts with a message and a target audience or target influencer, social media begins with an understanding of what consumers and influencers are saying about your brand, product, or service and then builds on that through participation (yours and theirs) for the purpose of encouraging higher forms of engagement, up to and including collaboration. This stands in contrast to prescribing and directing a message with the intention of persuading or driving awareness and conversion.

Taken together, listening, collaboration, and measurement create the basis for the highest levels of engagement. The objective of listening—simplified—is to enable a strategically directed response that leads to collaboration. This collaboration occurs in multiple ways: between the customers and business, between and among customers themselves, and between customers and employees. In other words, the end result of an effective social business program is a business-customer paradigm that is more or less equal in terms of who is listening, who is directing, and how it is that products and services are inspired or evolve over time. Around this entire process is wrapped a measurement methodology that ties it all back to the underlying business objectives.

The next three sections present, in order, listening, encouraging collaborative activity, and the measurement of conversations that are applicable to your social business program.

Listen Intently, Respond Intelligently

Listening forms the basis of your social business program. It is one of the tangible, measurable connections between your business and your marketplace; it's a direct link to your customers. By developing a baseline of existing conversations, you can more quickly spot irregularities. If a sudden new interest or accidental or unpaid celebrity endorsement kicks off a wave of excitement, or a negative event or rumor around your product or service is suddenly running through the market, you'll see it in time to do something with it, or about it. Combined with a response strategy and a current understanding of marketplace conversations, you can build on the positive conversations and effectively respond to those that are negative.

Listening is a core skill for communications professionals. After all, communication begins with listening, right? Careful listening—in the context of the Social Web meaning listening, analyzing, and thereby understanding both the subject and the source—enables the ability to make sense of conversations and join into them. Rohit Bhargava, Senior Vice President, Strategy & Marketing with Ogilvy 360 Digital

Influence, refers to this process as *active listening*. In simple terms, *active listening* is built around paying attention to conversations and then responding based on a combination of strategy and measurement. Active listening is a key to understanding what to do and why on the Social Web, because it is the almost singular act that says to your customers, employees (for internal social technology implementations), or other stakeholders (the larger collection of members, staff, persons served, as with nonprofits or municipal organizations, for example) that you are truly interested in their ideas and what they have to say about your brand, product, or service. A listening program, integrated into your business practices, provides the intelligence you need to put these conversations to work.

By establishing listening as a core practice, and using what is learned to shape your response, you invite your customers into the processes that lead to collaboration. Given the opportunity and the tools, your customers will readily work together to create a better understanding among themselves with regard to what you offer. The Social Web provides the infrastructure for these conversations: Applications like social networks and support forums, for example, enable content sharing and similar participative actions that occur in and around online marketplaces. Ratings, reviews, recommendations, and content showing your product or service in use are among the first steps that are taken when it comes to sharing information in the marketplace that helps inform others' decisions, precisely because these are the things that help consumers make smarter choices. In the business applications of social media, this is core.

You can tap your customers' willingness to share information and improve the choices they make by connecting these conversations to your business. The first step in this process is active listening, using the information that is being shared for your own intelligence.

Create a Baseline

Given the relative newness of the Social Web, there generally are no historical metrics that answer basic questions such as "How much conversation should one expect?" or "How many negative posts is too many negatives?" Some would say "One negative is too many" but that's probably not realistic. In any marketplace for any product or service, there will always be a range of opinions. It is, therefore, essential to establish your own baseline—think of this as a starting point—and build your response strategy off of that.

Beyond the practical problem of developing an accepted baseline, the common or "best" practices that might provide guidance when starting out are likewise just emerging. But even more, as a brand or organization moves toward a social business orientation, the unique differentiators that apply to a specific product or service, for example, begin to dominate in importance across conversations. Rather than the generic metrics—like number of units sold—social business is about understanding the specific ways in which your customers are talking about your products, again making it mandatory that you dig in, discover the metrics, and govern your business.

As an example, you may find little or no mention of your brand on the Social Web. In this case, your objective may be to build a conversation, and your baseline is the low background measure against which you can assess success. Or, there may be substantial conversation, with some relative distribution between positive, neutral, and negative. Tools like the Net Promoter Score factor in here: a score near zero indicates a roughly equal balance between promoters and detractors, something you should be able to see (through measurement) on the Social Web. In this case, your baseline is the relatively equal distribution of promoters and detractors, and your response strategy may be directed toward increasing the measured share of promoters. Whatever your specific starting point, it needs to combine active listening and influencer identification with a marketplace performance assessment such as the Net Promoter Score so that you can both tell what's happening now and be able to assess performance against business objectives as you progress.

That is, you need to begin with some data—what customers are saying, what they are concerned with, etc. Later, through collaboration you'll convert that to the knowledge you'll need to truly engage with your customers. At the outset, however, what matters is extracting enough *data* to sort out exactly where you are *right now*. Here's the good news: Most of the commercial (meaning, "for fee") listening services provide historical information ranging from a few months of history to two years. You can use these tools to construct conversational baselines immediately.

Conversational baselines are obviously handy when the desire to "act now" is present (as if that's ever not the case!). Historical data provides the context for many of the programs that you'll implement going forward. Using a basic listening platform— whether a service like Google Alerts, a modestly priced DIY (Do It Yourself) tool like Alterian | Techrigy's SM2, Radian6 or Scout Labs, or the full-service offerings of TNS | Cymfony or Neilsen's Buzzmetrics, you can establish a conversational *baseline*. Figure 7.1 shows such a baseline. The listening program was "turned on" on January 1st, and a social media effort to encourage conversation was started shortly after. The listening platform provides historical data against which any change in conversational levels can be measured. The practice of creating your own baselines and understanding their significance—along with any changes that happen over time—is essential in making sense of the conversations that you are interested in.

As an important side note, *establishing a listening baseline can help you spot and manage a crisis before it's too late*. Whether it's a rumor about your brand, or an actual (negative) event that takes place with your product or within your industry, trying to sort out who is talking and how the conversation is connected to your organization after it has become widespread is too late. Instead of fighting the fire, you'll be swamped trying to figure out where it's coming from, losing valuable time at a point in the crisis management process where literally *minutes* count. With an effective baseline program in place, and an understanding of who your influencers are, as soon as you detect a rise in comments or the presence of a new and potentially damaging thread, you can be ready with a response that is directed to those who can help you.

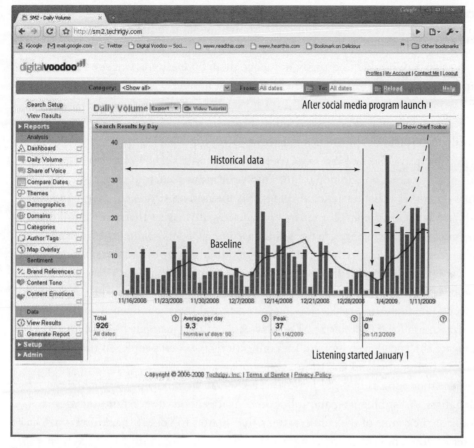

Figure 7.1 Baseline for Conversation

Find Your Influencers

Moving deeper into listening, *who* is participating in the conversation is often as important as *what* is actually being said. Being able to identify participants who are more broadly connected, or who have a specific connection in your marketplace is clearly important. In PR, for example, you connect with media influencers and similar professionals by researching or subscribing to a database of known journalists, writers, analysts, media influencers, and so on. These people sit at the entry points of the media channels that convey your message to large, defined audiences. In this setting, getting your information to specific people is as easy (or as hard) as the readiness of your own contacts database enabled. (Getting them to do something with it, and more importantly what you wanted them to do with it is, of course, much more difficult.)

By comparison, one of the aspects of the Social Web that makes it more challenging than traditional channels of communication is that the influencers—in the conversational leadership and direction or tone-setting sense—can be literally anyone.

How do you find them? Sure, there are A-list bloggers within most or larger industrial and social/lifestyle verticals, and there known media pundits and subject matter experts who blog, write columns, host news shows, or produce similar commentary. While you may not be able to directly influence them, at least you can spot them and build appropriate relationships with them. But what about the smaller-scale or niche bloggers whose 1,000 or 10,000 or 50,000 subscribers also comprise a meaningful slice of your customer base?

Influencer identification—as a part of your overall listening program—is all about spotting and building functional, productive relationships with these individuals. This means taking an additional look into your influencers to pick out specific behaviors—what is it that a particular blogger is focused on within the larger industry covered, and what are the larger industry or cause-related issues that most or all of the bloggers you are following are themselves focused on? Understanding the interests and hot buttons of groups or specific types of bloggers that matter to you is as important as picking out specific bloggers. These people too are influenced by their peers and operate with the benefit of their own collective knowledge. That means you need to understand this as well. The tools used to develop marketplace and specific influencer profiles—recall Buzzstream from Chapter 2, "The New Role of the Customer,"—include crawlers that navigate the Social Web looking for connections *between* people, so they can be used to spot both individual and group behaviors.

One other point is in order here: On the Social Web, it's not so much about the journalists, A-list bloggers, and influencers as it is about understanding who is repeatedly at the center of the conversations that matter to you. If the A-listers are at the center of your conversations, congratulations! You've got mail! More likely, it's the enthusiasts, individual industry professionals, consumers with a knack for social media, and similar with whom you'll want to create relationships. These people don't have nametags and titles. Instead they have something that's even better: a personal profile and a social graph that links them to the people who make up your target market. The challenge is finding these sources of influence, and tools like Buzzstream and Sysomos are designed to not only pick up on the listening aspects of your influencer research and baseline construction, but also to identify and connect you with the specific sources that are important to you.

In a socially connected setting, the influencers in a decision process are very often the actual users of the product or service who have also established a meaningful presence for themselves online. This person might be a homemaker who blogs about health, nutrition, or family vacation planning, or a photographer who publishes reviews of cameras along with techniques for lighting and subject composition. These are otherwise ordinary people, with a specific passion or interest, who have also made it a habit to publish and share what they love, hate, find useful, or otherwise want others like themselves to know about. These are precisely the people you want to find and build relationships with.

With the combination of listening and influencer identification programs in place, you can take a big step toward designing your business based on what your customers want. It's important to understand that this goes beyond "designing the products they ask for." Sometimes customers don't know what they want, or they don't know what is possible, or they want the wrong thing. Don't confuse listening and influencer identification with the wholesale turning over of your business design to your customers. At least as regards your brand, product, or service, it's still your ship: Your customers are the crew, and so can make or break the voyage.

Bring Social Learning (and Technology) In-House

Using your listening program to discover and track important memes (thoughts and trends) and to spot influencers and create valuable relationships is Step 1. Connecting these to your business by identifying who within your organization needs to know about this, and who has the ability to do something constructive with it, is Step 2.

Social business is highly focused on the combination of getting marketplace information where it needs to go and ensuring that internally you have the kind of organization that can benefit from it. To do this, look at internal (enterprise) software applications such as Socialtext, Lotus Connections, SharePoint, or internal communities built using Jive Software, Lithium Technologies, and Salesforce.com. Dell's Employee Storm and Philips' use of Socialcast are examples of social technology applied internally to create powerful connections to customers. These connections were built to implement effective responses to conversations using the same types of applications *inside* the organization as were used by the customers to create those conversations *outside* the organization.

Very often, implementing a social business program means that before you get started with more engaging social technology programs that are outside your organization, you'll want to get to work within your organization, building cross-functional support and the capability to act on what you'll learn in the external marketplace. Going back to the purchase funnel and to touchpoint analysis, the challenge of managing conversations hinges on your ability to guide the conversations so that they help you. Because you cannot control the conversation directly, you instead manage and influence them through your own actions, through the products, services, and messages you deliver into the marketplace. Your overall response strategy—listening, and then bringing relevant information inside your organization, respectively—depends on your organization's ability to effectively connect external conversation with internal care and capability. Think of the actual response as step 3 following steps 1 and 2.

Having an internal, workflow-based process that receives, analyzes, and routes the conversations that matter to you is essential. Often overlooked, these processes and the people across your organization that are parts of them should be in place sooner rather than later. Setting them up can be a challenge—most people don't arrive at the office looking for more to do—but this is again where "listening" is such a great starting point.

Bonus: Listening Is Low Exposure

The previous sections articulate an end-to-end listening and response process: listen, analyze conversation and spot influencers, and then connect this information with the customers, offering it internally to employees who can address it as required and respond, thereby closing the loop and creating a genuine sense of appreciation in the process.

As an example, consider an experience I had with Boingo, the Wi-Fi hotspot services provider. I was in Newark airport's Continental terminal, and the connection was decidedly slow. I tweeted this information—in a helpful rather than snarky manner—to @Boingo. With 5 minutes, I had a response, asking me to run a quick line-speed test. That was nice, but what was even better was what happened a few days later. In my Twitter stream I saw a tweet from @Boingo: "People who are always on our radar: ..." and among the names listed was me, @evansdave. *In the eyes of Boingo, I was now an individual. I was recognized by Boingo as a specific customer.* As crazy as it sounds—or maybe not crazy at all—as the line from *The Grinch Who Stole Christmas* goes, my loyalty to Boingo "grew ten sizes that day." Even in the rare months that I don't travel—months that I know I will probably *not* be using a Boingo hotspot—I still happily pay the service fee. *I want Boingo to stay in business.* Listening and paying attention to what specific customers are saying is a great first step in building loyalty.

There's an additional insight in the Boingo interaction, very much like the insights into the Freshbooks case presented in Chapter 5, "Social Technology and Business Decisions." Businesses typically are not cold corporate entities, but rather are made of individuals who enjoy what they do and take pride in the end result. It wasn't the abstract "Boingo Incorporated" that won me over: It was a one or more specific employees who were enabled to respond to Boingo's customers in ways that resulted in a positive experience—even in the face of a negative issue—and to therefore earn customer loyalty. It is the implementation of these internal processes—flip back to the Freshbooks case too—that tap the collaborative, equal-footing relationship with customers that define and drive social business.

If you're not sold on the value of a formal listening program, consider this: Unlike developing an external presence on the Social Web or changing a business process because of what has been learned, listening is an activity that is in itself low exposure. The response aside, you aren't actually required to do anything: You are simply paying attention to what is already being said. Basic listening provides a way to gauge your actual requirements should you decide to begin responding (as @Boingo and @Continental and many others now do). Listening gives you the insights and information you need to make smart choices in how you might implement social technology in support of your business objectives.

In summary, you can use listening to build the social connections between your organization and your marketplace by first understanding what is being said and how it impacts you. You can do this without incurring significant costs (your time aside!) and without creating exposure. In effect, you can leverage basic listening to shape your organization so that when the time comes it is able to respond by measuring the volume of conversations and sharing what you find within your organization. You can further leverage this basic data to encourage interest and involvement across the *internal processes* that span work teams or functional groups, again building the cross-functional discipline that you will ultimately need to be effective in your use of social technology. Getting your business ready to do business on the Social Web is a big part of the challenge ahead, and an effective listening program is one of the best starting points.

Encourage Collaboration Everywhere

Second of three "must do" activities that form the basis of this chapter is *collaboration*. Collaborative activities sit at the top of the engagement processes. As such, moving your customers, members, and employees toward collaboration is a definite "must do" in your list of both marketing and (larger) business goals. Collaboration, whether internally across functional work teams, or externally (involving customers in product and service design, for example) is the inflection point on the path to becoming a social business.

As a basic framework for an organization-wide path toward collaboration (meaning "driving high levels of engagement, as defined in the social context"), consider the following set of steps developed at Ant's Eye View:

1. Define your objectives.

   Begin with a clear view of your *business* objectives and an understanding of your primary customer base or applicable segment of it.

2. Listen.

   Implement a listening program to understand the specific conversations around your brand, product, or service. Use this same program to validate the actions you are considering, and then use it to measure or otherwise understand the impact of those actions.

3. Organize.

   Organize internally and externally around what you learn through listening. Create cross-functional teams, for example, that respond fully to the customer need rather than just the functional issues you discover.

4. Engage.

   Engage the customer through participation. Respond in the channels in which your customers are talking, implement the collaborative solutions that result, and then give your customers credit as this will encourage them to participate more.

5. Measure.

   Aggressively measure everything until you have adequate baselines to assess the impact of the programs on which you embark. You can always discontinue the collection of unneeded or uninformative data later. You can't, however, make decisions based on information you don't have.

Taking these steps together, collaboration occurs—or at the least is facilitated—in the fourth step; Engagement is a direct result of the preceding three steps. Collaboration, in this context, requires the active participation of both the customers and the employees—of the marketplace and the organization itself.

It's About Me…and Us

Referring back to the process leading to collaboration—content consumption, curation, creation, and then collaboration—compare "content consumption" as applied to traditional marketing and business processes with its social counterpart. Consumption—whether of your mass market communication or the video assets you've placed on your website—is often described in terms of "engagement." Look more closely, though, and what's happening is actually a relatively passive and in most cases solo activity. Call this "traditional consumption" for lack of a better term: Whatever the term, this type of engagement is a relatively low-involvement form.

Now move to the social sense of engagement: What does it really mean for customers to be engaged in ways that engender conversation or sharing or the creation of new content? As people become more connected, their desire to be part of something larger only increases. When someone posts "I am standing in line at Starbucks…" or "Waking up to a beautiful day in Austin" on Twitter, the motivation is not sharing the fact that some particular activity is happening right now. Instead, it's all about telling *yourself* that *you are part of a larger community*, and telling that community that you *appreciate* it being around you.

This is the kind of attachment that manifests itself in the relatively higher levels of socially inspired engagement—and in collaboration between community members, for example. If you see Twitter (and social media in general) as a big, meaningless, narcissism-fest think about that last point again: Participants truly value their communities and the tangible expressions of belonging. When one *belongs* to something, one takes personal ownership for it: This shows up in member-to-member curation, in solutions posted in help forums, in the entries developed over time in Wikipedia, and through many other similar expressions on the Social Web. This sense of participation and belonging is more encompassing it may seem: It's not just "my own needs" expressed through "my own activities."

In reality, yes, it's "all about me," but this includes "my knowing who's (also) in line at Starbucks." Whether connected through SMS, Twitter, Foursquare, or whatever, it's about my knowing what is happening around me, and in particular with and among the people I am connected to through my entire (meaning, "across networks") social graph. It's about a larger, social view of what's around, and the participant's specific role within it. In a resounding setback, Facebook was called out when it botched its privacy changes in mid-2010: That said, the fact is that people willingly and knowingly share a *lot* more personal information than ever before, precisely so that *they can see* some sort of reflection in the world around them that they exist. The consequences and push-back for mass marketing are huge, as the coincident drive toward alignment with brands that recognize individuals accelerates. Again, this observation:

> *"As people take control over their data while spreading their Web presence, they are not looking for privacy, but for recognition as individuals. This will eventually change the whole world of advertising."*

ESTHER DYSON, 2008

It's Also About Engagement

Across multiple forms of media—social media being no exception—*consumption of content* is typically the most likely activity. However, beware! Whether you're reading the paper, watching TV, or listening to the radio or a podcast, consumption is by all counts a fairly passive activity. Even when the activity involves social media (reading blogs, for example), 80 to 90 percent of the audience limits its activity to consumption. While this can be helpful from a marketing (awareness) perspective, it doesn't directly connect customers around the brand, product, or service in the kind of social context that leads to the higher forms of engagement.

It's important to get beyond content consumption and bring your audience to the level of a genuine connection. This means participating with them, getting them into the game, and placing yourself in it with them. The easiest way to do this is to do this is through social activities—not unlike real life—and to do it in the online social spots where your audience is already present.

As a starting activity, consider *curation*. Curation is built around activities such as rating, reviewing, and otherwise passing judgment on the content (or conduct!) of others in the community. Because this content has been made available in a social setting, curation is a natural next step. What does curation look like? It can be as simple as rating a post as "useful" (or not!).

Curation matters for two reasons. First, it is a reflection of the sensibilities and value system of the audience and/or community members. Curation and the general act of evaluating and rating content—videos, posts, articles, etc.—make it easy for others to quickly find what's valuable and learn about what the community values. Curation drives positive community experiences for the benefit of its members: Curation in the community and membership context helps provide a better experience for its members and thereby encourages the collaborative activities seen in the higher forms of engagement. Recall that these higher forms of engagement are what one is after through the adoption of social technologies. In consumer products, for example, these higher forms of engagement lead to better products and to better understandings among customers as to why these are in fact "better" products.

Importantly, engagement readily happens in the places where consumers and stakeholders naturally associate (which is why they join up and spend time there). Thought leaders like Jeff Jarvis talk about engaging customers on their terms, as an alternative to traditionally controlled forms of media: Pepsi elected not to participate in Super Bowl XLIV (That's "44" for non-Romans). The Super Bowl is an event where millions of consumers gather in no small part to *watch the ads* (along with some football).

In an advertisers' context, the Super Bowl is considered as a sort of crown jewel, and it is often a career make-or-break opportunity given the correlation—for the present anyway—between ad and media budgets and advertiser and media planner career trajectories. In a bit of a challenge to this, Pepsi is looking to expand its highly integrated program in the direction of increasingly *social connection points*: marketing touchpoints that put consumers in near-direct control of the tangible expression of the brand message in their world. Programs like Pepsi's Refresh project, while still built around a multimillion dollar budget, channel spending into social projects that consumers suggest and vote on. This program directly defines the Pepsi brand according to the lifestyles, passions, and causes of its customers rather than those of its ad agencies.

If that last line sounds harsh, consider the millions of dollars spent over the past ten years on Super Bowl ads that consumers, by their own words, simply "did not get." Pepsi's Refresh avoids this fate by asking its customers directly "What do YOU want us to do to make our brand relevant in YOUR life?" This is the "higher calling" that was referenced in Figure 3.3.

Pepsi's Refresh project, shown in Figure 7.2, along with its Juice program integrated into BlogHer (covered in detail in Chapter 3, "Building a Social Business") are solid examples of moving toward a participant-controlled social marketing and business orientation that encourages collaboration.

Social programs in organizations like Pepsi, Starbucks, and Dell go beyond awareness (consumption) and instead push for collaboration between the businesses and their marketplace stakeholders. They are part of an overall, holistic marketing program. Programs like Pepsi's "Refresh," Starbucks' "My Starbucks Ideas," and Dell's "Take Your Own Path"—each different in its approach and use of social technology—connect the brands into the specific communities where customers and potential customers are found. Curation, along with basic content creation, occurs naturally in these communities, making them ideal for participative marketing efforts and the use of social technology.

Building on consumption, curation, and content creation, collaboration is the end objective in the process of creating advocates, evangelists, and brand ambassadors. Getting people in your audience to work together collaboratively is very powerful. Working together to produce a common outcome, participants around your brand, product, or service bond with each other; and as they do, they develop a strong loyalty for the communities in which they are able to collaborate.

Figure 7.2 The Pepsi Refresh Project

Connect Collaboration to Your Business

With a collaborative context defined, the challenge is to connect the engagement process as defined in the social context to your business or organization's objectives. Starbucks and Dell, using a range of social technologies, have done this really well. They have used consumption, curation, and creation through their respective "Ideas" platforms as a way to *invite* collaboration, and then used what they learned to improve their products and product experiences. Google will offer up plenty of analysis and commentary on these cases: Check them out and see how their implementation of what amounts to a suggestion box—done right—has changed their businesses.

Collaboration extends into tactical marketing programs as well: Pepsi's Refresh is one way of involving customers directly in building a relevant brand, clearly a long-term strategic social-media-based proposition. By comparison, in early 2010 announcements from other big consumer brands like Unilever and Coke indicated that they too would be de-emphasizing branded microsites and similar media programs as components of online marketing. Instead, they increased investments in building a presence in globally significant social networks like Facebook. Coke, for example, has literally millions of fans collected around its Facebook business page.

Building on what was learned by participating in Facebook—and its very favorable experience with its fans through its business page—Coke created a stand-alone collaborative site for NCAA fans. Built on the Posterous blogging platform (you can learn more about Posterous here: http://posterous.com/), Coke's NCAA marketing tie-in, "The Department of Fannovation," encourages NCAA fans to submit ideas on improving the fan experience for NCAA athletics followers. The Fannovation campaign creates a connection between "new" NCAA fans and Coca-Cola, and importantly does so in a way that new fans in particular are likely to gain additional awareness of and thereby *consider* Coke as a first choice in refreshment. Fannovation—built as noted on a blogging platform that was configured to encourage curation and hence participation (content creation and collaboration)—was further promoted through adjacent social channels including Facebook and Twitter.

Note that Coke's "Department of Fannovation," like Dell's "Digital Nomad" and "Take Your Own Path" communities, is not a purely brand-centric application. It is instead built around a passion of a subset of Coke's audience—that is, being an NCAA fan. Coke is a participant in the application, but at the center is the excitement of being an NCAA fan. The application carries right into collaboration as well, by encouraging fans to create and submit ideas, and then rate (curate) them. The result is new learning for Coke in the ways it can take itself to market—and in using a range of social channels for campaigns as well as the promotion of those campaigns—and a whole new set of quantitative measurements that can be used to further improve its social presence and related activities. By tying these projects to Coke's larger brand essence, Coke reinforces its role in its customers' lives, not as a soft drinks vendor but as an expression of the connecting point—the higher calling—between the activities and lifestyles of its customers and the brand itself.

Beyond consumer businesses, business-to-business brands—like Element 14, American Express, HSBC, and Indium—are using purpose-built communities, business-oriented networks like LinkedIn, and blogging to get closer to their own customers. In all of these efforts, the rationale is simple: Fish where the fish are, at least at the start. You can create your own pond later. More importantly, respect your audience by getting involved in the activities that they are themselves involved in. Become part of their community by bringing your brand to them. Combined with a longer-term strategic plan, these types of real-world, tactical efforts built around platforms that already exist are a great way to get started.

Measure Social Media

Now that listening and collaboration have been discussed, the final "must do" topic for this chapter is measuring the impact of your social media efforts as they are connected to your business or organization. Measurement is the key to understanding effectiveness, and ironically is too often overlooked or simply dismissed out of hand. This is no longer acceptable: social media can—and should—be measured, and done so in ways that press the application of metrics beyond correlation and the use of surrogates.

Take a step back in traditional marketing and advertising measurement. Common measures like reach and frequency are accepted *surrogates* for effectiveness: One generally measures reach and frequency often, but conducts formal pre/post studies of actual efficacy only occasionally. While these traditional measures of advertising are themselves concrete—reach and frequency can be directly measured, for example— they have become *surrogates* for the more important measures of effectiveness, derived generally through the observance of correlation and *implied* causation.

It's important to note the distinction, covered in Chapter 6, "Social Analytics, Metrics, and Measurement," between causation and correlation. It's important to recognize that measures such as a blogger's reach, or the number of comments in regard to a post, or the number of times a photo was viewed or shared are also concrete, easily obtained measures of the use of social channels. Make *measurement* a formal part of your social media program.

In addition to the more obvious quantitative metrics (views, measures of content sharing or pass-alongs, comments on a blog as a ratio to posts and similar), social analytics often involves dealing with large amounts of unstructured data (comments, recommendations, videos, and text posts, for example) that present a challenge when looking for concrete measurability. This same condition has long existed within traditional media and the metrics that define it all along: Verbatim comments are an oft-cited component of a typical advertisement effectiveness or customer feedback program. Social media analytics tools (see Chapter 6) provide much of the "horsepower" needed to make sound use of this unstructured data—for example, by extracting trends in positive versus negative comments, overall conversational levels, and similar.

K. D. Paine

Tired of hearing "The problem with social media is that you can't measure it"? Encourage people within your organization to look at K. D. Paine's PR Measurement Blog.

http://kdpaine.blogs.com/

Link Social Analytics with Business Analytics

Given the direct measurement of activity in and around social channels, it's also important to link this with your existing business analytics to create an understanding of how social, web, and business analytics fit together. Far from isolated, the social analytics both drive and are driven by what happens at the intersection of your business and the output side of the purchase funnel. Comments, ratings, recommendations, blog posts, and videos tend to reflect what happened when a brand, product, or service was put to the test more than they reflect what was promised in the advertising or other promotion that helped drive purchase, although commentary to that effect is often present. These comments, ratings, and recommendations are valuable when creating and refining a social business strategy: They can be tracked and used as guides when developing a response to a negative event, for example.

Beyond using social media for outreach or promotion—for example, in creating a brand outpost or using a channel like Twitter to convey sales information or collect customer comments—the Social Web can be used as a part of a real-time feedback system that keeps you firm or organization on track. You do it; they talk about it. You do it a different way, and they talk about it in a different way. This basic feedback loop sets up a strong measurement and testing application that you can use to build your business.

As a starting point, consider the Net Promoter Score. Created by Fred Reichheld at Bain Consulting, the Net Promoter Score is straightforward, well-documented (a benefit to you when presenting social technology and gaining internal support for its use) and easy to apply. Built around a 0-10 scale and the single question, "How likely are you to recommend my brand, product, or service?" the Net Promoter Score nicely captures in a single metric what underlies the majority of the significant connections between the Social Web and your brand, product, or service.

How can the Net Promoter (NPS) methodology help you? Consider the application of NPS by Austin-based B2B technical and lab furniture manufacturer Formaspace. Implemented in earnest in 2009, NPS provided a whole-business marketplace view that was fully auditable. It was implemented at the C-level and is now followed by every department at Formaspace.

I spoke with Formaspace CEO Jeff Turk about the implementation of the Net Promoter Score. Jeff described the effort like this:

> *"We don't really look at NPS in terms of expecting a single "great leap forward." We had a formal and frequently measured quality assurance and customer satisfaction system long before implementing NPS. We also know our most vocal customers quite well, so we had a very good idea what they would have to say about us before implementing NPS. We look at NPS as a source of continual incremental improvements.*

"The NPS system gives us a lot of small bits of feedback that incrementally add up to very high customer satisfaction. Some suggestions have included specific changes to furniture assembly instructions, asking for e-mails at certain times in the delivery process, and letting us know when we need to give kudos to a particular staff member."

Look back at the implementation and you'll see that the company knew its customers and what they would say. NPS was used in the context of a larger measurement program. NPS was used to drive continuous improvement and thereby loyalty. The implementation of NPS at Formaspace exemplifies exactly the processes articulated in this book thus far, and it has paid off. Formaspace was originally acquired as a turnaround opportunity in 2006. Recovering and rebuilding customer loyalty was absolutely a key measure of whether its new owners were turning the company around. Based on prior customer satisfaction and loyalty surveys, Jeff and his team estimated that its NPS score would have been negative in 2006, and in the 30 to 50 range between 2007 and 2008. The measured score was 77 in 2009, and the company's goal is to surpass 80 in 2010. That is impressive.

There's a bigger insight here too: Paying attention, in detail, to customer conversations and measuring and tracking results doesn't just boost measures like the Net Promoter Score: it actually drives business. Again, listen to Formaspace CEO Jeff Turk:

"When we took over the company, it was doing so poorly at servicing customers that it sprouted competitors left and right. Today it would not be an exaggeration to say that Formaspace is the go-to resource for companies that use technical and laboratory furniture. We are rapidly becoming known as the "it" brand—so much so that our furniture is on the Discovery Channel, ABC's Grey's Anatomy, *in NASA's mission control center in Houston, and will soon be seen on the sets of more than one major motion picture. Many people import furniture from China: Ours is in sufficient demand that we send it the other way."*

Because I am a former product manager, this last exchange really hit home. When I served in this role at Progressive Insurance Company, before we turned fully toward a *customer* orientation, we too were sprouting competitors. Nearly all of Progressive's early competition came from former Progressive product managers and executives who simply copied the Progressive rate books and undercut the prices. Whether it's extreme price sensitivity (technically referred to as high elasticity) such as was the case at Progressive, or poor quality or bad service, negative factors like these are invitations to more competition and lower margins. Formaspace engaged its customers, turned high quality to its advantage, and put itself—in brand-speak—on a different ladder. To learn more about Formaspace—and to see the great products they build—check out Formaspace.com.

As an important note, the Net Promoter may not be for everyone (see sidebar), nor is it the only metric available to you (although if you had to choose only one, it would be a very good choice). Instead, the Net Promoter Score is a great place to start if you don't have a central dashboard or other in-place methodology for measuring success, as it provides an understandable basis for linking the experiences you create in the marketplace with your organization as a whole, where these experiences are (largely) created. Obviously, there are other metrics that may be specifically applicable to your business or simply a better cultural fit within your organization. One way or another, however, a metric or set of metrics that link your business—as a cause—with the conversations and customer behaviors you observe on the Social Web is fundamental to your success when implementing social business technology.

Alternatives to the Net Promoter Score

As the Net Promoter Score (NPS) has gained in popularity, so have the discussions of its potential limitations and the rise of alternatives. As you are reviewing specific metrics and in particular the use of the NPS methodology, consider searching the Web for "alternatives to Net Promoter Score" as well.

The Net Promoter Score—or your preferred equivalent—provides a quantitative assessment through which you can capture and track the degree to which your customers will sing your praises. In a marketing environment that is increasingly driven by trust in "others like me" and more so the recommendations of people who are known, the Net Promoter Score stands as a central social metric.

Again, is the Net Promoter Score perfect for all situations? Of course not. What single metric is? That said, adopting the Net Promoter Score and supporting methodology pays big benefits:

- It creates a consistent, trackable metric that can be presented and placed into context across an organization.

- It is naturally aligned with the conversational dynamics on the Social Web. If most people would highly recommend your brand, product, or service, then the conversations about your brand, product, or service will reflect that.

- It is quantitative. The Net Promoter Score "translates" unstructured data like the characterization of the recommendations that people might give on your behalf into a number. You can work with numbers.

Having a consistent metric that can be shared across an organization, is vital. With a metric like this, everyone can "speak the same language" when it comes to assessing performance. Recall the Formaspace case: the context of a single metric like NPS is as important as the metric itself, and the verbatim responses (that is, individually detailed conversations with clients) that are often gathered as part of an NPS implementation are extremely valuable as well.

Having one or more metrics that apply to all divisions, departments, groups, and functions may seem a stretch, but consider this: Everyone who plays a part in creating the experience that your customers, members, or constituents subsequently talk about is "covered" under a single metric like the Net Promoter Score. Referencing the earlier sidebar, "Alternatives to the Net Promoter Score," if NPS isn't right for your organization, develop your own simple, easy-to-understand metric that is. Take a look at Fast Company's "Business Advice from Van Halen" (March 2010) for more on the power of simple, insightful metrics applied to business.

To see this, deconstruct an experience. Suppose you consistently see on Twitter that the prices charged for your product or service are too high. As a result, some people—even many people—fail to recommend you highly and unconditionally, and instead say things like, "If you can afford it…I'd highly recommend them." On the Net Promoter Score, that's about a six, on a good day maybe an eight. Not only do sevens and eights not count (you throw those out, because the recommendations—like the one in this case—are weak), the six actually counts *against* you.

Get Everyone on the Same Page

If there is an emergent reality of social business and "managing" conversations on the Social Web, it's this: Social business is bigger than marketing. It is a holistic approach to organizing a business around its customers—going as far as to integrate its customers into its formal business processes—and to thereby consistently improve and evolve in ways that generate customer delight. The big question is, who is responsible for internal alignment of business processes? The CEO, the COO, and CMO, right? Partly, but not completely. How about the supply chain manager who is negotiating better prices from suppliers while failing to maintain quality standards? How about the HR manager who is vetoing training that would otherwise increase retention and thereby reduce the cost associated with turnover in *your* department? How about each and every employee who leaves a light on or uses two paper towels in the washroom where one would do instead?

This may seem petty—and counting paper towels (or admonishing employees to only ride the elevator when rising more than two floors…true story) is a bit extreme. But what it all boils down to is this: *Each and every officer, director, employee, and supplier is potentially responsible for some aspect of the experiences that are associated with whatever it is that is produced and sold by your firm or organization.* The power of a metric like the Net Promoter Score is that it puts everyone in the business on the same page of customer accountability. The question to the customer is, "Would you recommend us?" The customer's response is based on the sum total of all of the moving parts that resulted in a particular experience, upon which the likelihood of a recommendation is predicated.

When the entire organization is looking at a holistic metric like the Net Promoter Score (or your preferred equivalent), *questions get asked that wouldn't otherwise be asked*. Innovations arise that would not otherwise arise. The business actually runs—from the ground up—in ways that delight the customer. We had a universal metric at Progressive Insurance, where I spent a number of years as a product manager: We used the Combined Operating Ratio, or COR, a fundamental measure of performance that everyone understood. It predated the Net Promoter Score and was a *fundamentally different* measure to be sure. While the COR was a business operations performance metric instead of a customer experience metric, *by sharing the COR across the entire organization everyone became focused on their specific impact to the proper operation of the business*. The result was an organization that worked like a team.

Whether you follow the Net Promoter Score or an alternative yardstick, beyond the core measures that indicate the relative likelihood of favorable conversations, you'll want to connect these metrics with your current business analytics. What's required first is a baseline. You can generate a baseline for your social analytics using any social analytics package that supports raw data export: Alterian's SM2 is one such platform that provides this capability. This makes it easier—but still not simple—to integrate social and business metrics. The objective is to identify and track the social measures that have predictive or associative value when used with your current marketing metrics.

By beginning with the connection of your marketing metrics and the social analytics, you'll discover up front the degree to which the Social Web is impacting your marketing program, either positively or negatively. Begin by creating a baseline: Social analytics tools like SM2 provide two years of history so you can actually run regression analysis on social metrics such as daily volume and sentiment against the business metrics you have collected over the past years. You'll end up throwing a lot of your work away, but that's OK: You'll find the subset of key business indicators that are closely aligned with social analytics. With this work completed, you can assign relative values to the change in social analytics by matching the values of the corresponding changes in business metrics.

However you do this, the important step is "to do it." Begin with the data you have, and line it up over a period of years with the social data. You'll come away with a defensible case for why you need (or why you don't need) to invest in social-media-based marketing, and you'll have created the baseline data that you need to evaluate a social business strategy.

What Not to Do (and What to Do Instead)

In the prior section, I presented three "must do" activities: establishing a listening program, encouraging collaboration externally and internally, and aggressively measuring (because you can). These three activities are built around the main lessons of Part

I of this book: Listening and understanding the root causes of the conversations you discover, moving customers up the engagement path toward advocacy by encouraging collaborative activities that inform your business and strongly tie your customers to it, and taking the time to measure and establish a quantitative basis against which to assess the business value of your social media and social business program.

The next section covers two of the universal challenges that face businesses wanting to take advantage of social technologies: These are the difficulty of facing up to the changes required in some form for most business, and the tendency to assign all of this "social stuff" to marketing, as if it were something marketing alone could control.

Ignore Change at Your Peril

Wouldn't it be great if the world stopped changing, or it changed so slowly you could ignore it? Actually, no, it wouldn't, because in that case you wouldn't get your next promotion because that would change things. One way or another, change is something to get used to and ultimately to embrace. "What's next" is change, and that change is coming to a marketplace near you.

Gearing up for change, then, is part of getting an organization ready for social business. This includes instilling a culture of learning (so that new collaborative tools such as wikis, Yammer, or Socialtext are embraced rather than pushed off, along with a culture of openness (so that employees are comfortable suggesting what may seem like wacky ideas to others in the organization).

Watch out for resistance to change that is hidden—businesses can position themselves, for example, as "forward thinking and innovative," yet be very rigid inside when it comes to how they go about running themselves. If the internal vision held by an organization for "innovative and forward thinking" collides with that of its customers in the marketplace, the kinds of internal changes required to adapt may be tough to implement. In particular, in organizations with a strong leadership figure—a founder or a CEO whose personality is an active part of the brand—the inclination of that business leadership to actually embrace change is a factor. I've been fortunate to consistently work with businesses headed by leaders open to and supportive of change: Your mileage may vary.

The Status Quo Is a Dead End

While "doing what has always worked" may see a firm a few more miles—or many more miles—down the road, market evolution is a fact of life. To adapt—and to be sure, there are countless management handbooks and articles on this topic—some degree of flexibility is required. In start-ups, it's the ability to move from what "we knew our customers wanted' to "what they were actually willing to pay for." Surprisingly, a lot of start-ups fail by missing this signal. In established firms, it's more likely exhibited as an aversion to risk or the failure to hire (or even the tendency to actively screen out) "change agents."

As an example of the former, consider a business line leader who approaches an executive with a breakthrough idea, only to hear "Sounds great, but if sales dip you're fired." The chance of implementation is zero, and there is even less chance of another breakthrough even being looked for in the future. The latter example—screening out change agents—happens slowly, as companies mature. The kinds of risk-taking, entrepreneurial minds that are were attracted to Walmart or Southwest Airlines 40-odd years ago (when Southwest had a handful of airplanes and Walmart had less than a dozen stores) may not see the allure of joining what are now among the largest businesses in their respective industries, or any industry. It's up to the HR departments and hiring managers to ensure that organizations remain attractive to fresh minds as they these firms age.

The ability to support calculated risk and to adapt to change matters: It brings out contributions from those who will willingly take the personal risk in the context of the workplace—the risk to a future career path, for example—that is associated with innovation. In organizations that predictably and measurably benefit from social business practices, the in-place leadership often sets examples of acceptable failure—making risk-taking within limits OK—and rewards innovation and process change when it is grounded in business objectives. Again citing Progressive, we had what we called the Armadillo Award. It was a huge motivator, as it recognized individuals who failed in big (but smart) ways. Like Armadillos, sometimes despite the best planning and intentions, when you step out into the fast lane…you know the rest.

The Negative Conversations Are Already Happening

The fear of negative events and negative conversations is often a factor in a decision not to embrace social-media-based practices inside or outside the organization. Not always irrationally, no one wants to intentionally steer into bad publicity. At the same time, and as said before, the negative conversations are already happening. It is rarely the simple presence of a firm itself on the Social Web that *causes* negative conversation to flow. To be sure, this does *not* mean "Just go running in…it will all be fine."

Instead, as has been outlined—flip back to Chapter 1, "Social Media and Customer Engagement," and see the sidebar reference for the USAF/Altimeter response matrix—listen first and understand what is being said. If there is some negative, examine it. If it's factually incorrect, you may have an opportunity to correct the error. If it's an all-out assault on your brand, you'll want to plan thoroughly first. But then, this is the whole point of adopting a social media program: Build an understanding of how your brand, product, or service is viewed on the Social Web—and based on that, create your roadmap for future activity.

As an example, suppose that a service issue results suddenly in a fast-growing, negative conversation. In January of 2010, India's Café Coffee Day, a higher-end chain coffee outlet, caught the full force of an attack when a group of bloggers meeting in a Café Coffee Day were asked to pay a cover charge (presumably for sitting and talking in a coffee shop) in addition to the drinks and snacks they had already purchased. On the one hand, restaurants in particular need to balance the needs of current customers—enjoying conversation after a nice meal—with the needs of those waiting for an open table. In this case, there were open seats and the group was spending money: predictably the request for a cover charge resulted in a localized (to that store) uproar that quickly spilled onto the Social Web. The chain's preexisting participation in social media saved it.

A brand that was used to less than 10 posts per day from customers on Twitter suddenly had a spike. Numerous posts were logged in a 24-hour period as people jumped in—in technical terms, "piled on"—to the conversation. The brand team actually handled the event pretty well. Because they were already listening (again, credit to them for participation in social channels in the first place), they were able to spot this and respond quickly. They took action publicly (reviewing, for example, the motivation of the store owner in requesting a cover charge when no such corporate policy existed). The online team issued an apology, made amends, and wrapped it up.

But the "piling-on" continued, and that's what brought the brand advocates, who were also seeing what was happening, out in support of the brand. The advocates saw the event, saw the appropriate response from Café Coffee Day, and then took action as others seeking to cash in on the notoriety of the thread kept reposting, after the fact. You can see the positive (up) and negative (down) comments in Figure 7.3, and you can see that the positive comments rose as fast as the negatives. The entire event was over in a few hours, and the online storm died out in a just a couple of days.

Two things in the Café Coffee Day event are important to recognize. First, the brand was present in the social channels and so they recognized what was happening quickly. Then, second, *they knew how to respond*: Listen, acknowledge, correct, and move on. The result was the emergence of a supportive crowd as the brand advocates moved in and a fairly balanced conversation resulted—for every hater there was roughly one lover. Had the brand team not been involved, the event would have simply gone out-of-control, unanswered, *because without the brand's public recognition of the actual wrong, and the apology from the brand team to the bloggers involved directly, the defenders would have had no ground on which to stand*.

Even worse, real brand damage could have accumulated over time. For example, the offending store owner—most likely totally unaware of anything "social," would have committed the act again, restarting the entire cycle and doing significant harm to the brand as other similarly enterprising managers caught on to an opportunity for added income, below the radar of corporate management. The initial tweets, posting on the Social Web, combined with the brand team's active listening program actually paid a real benefit to the overall Café Coffee Day operation.

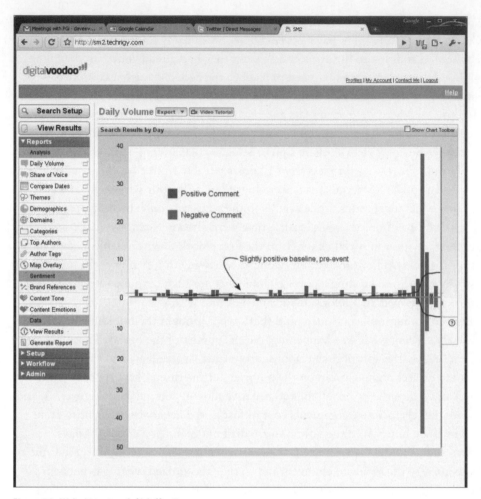

Figure 7.3 We're Listening: Café Coffee Day

Start By Listening

So if avoidance of change is at the top of the "don't do" list, what is the right thing *to do*? Instead of avoiding change, develop a listening-based and policy-driven response channel. Yes, social media can be tricky. And yes, conversations that you can't control can be a challenge. So, start by listening—actively listening. Begin collecting social data, create a historical baseline, and use this to chart your way forward and to pull in the rest of your team.

By establishing a solid baseline, for example, you set up robust measures of success. That is always helpful. Second, you develop a sense of when conversational levels or topics "aren't right." You can use this knowledge to trigger responses when situations that warrant a response arise.

In addition, create a strong internal policy that governs your organization and its application of social computing. Include notification rules, disclosure, topics that are off-limits—like trade secrets, for example—and expectations for conduct. Not only will this give significant comfort to your legal and HR groups, it will make your social-media-based marketing and business programs more likely to succeed. Refer back to Chapter 3, "Building a Social Business," and Chapter 4, "The Social Business Ecosystem," for more on the use of social computing policies, and in particular for pointers to IBM and other great starting points when developing your own social computing policies.

Marketing Can't Do Social Media Alone

Next on the "what not to do" list is limiting social media to marketing. Managing (or leading) change while getting your organization ready for the adoption of social technologies is very often among the most challenging aspects of implementing an effective social media strategy.

The starting point for social media *is often marketing*—probably because the initial social applications were promotional or advertising related or the conversations seemed most related to marketing and sales. However, the application of social media in *business* carries far beyond marketing. This is evident in the view of the purchase funnel and the role of the conversation as it impacts the marketing—think sales or membership or donor campaigns here— functions within the organization.

It's what happens after that makes clear how far beyond marketing social media and social technologies can be applied. Consider a conversation about a service and about an employee who is particularly adept at making customers feel great. This person is a source of positive referrals and so is a contributor to an elevated Net Promoter Score. What you need are ten more just like this one, and by listening to conversations and carefully measuring results and following the customers associated with this agent through your CRM Program you've made the case to hire more.

Hiring "ten more just like this one" means getting HR to understand what makes a stand-out employee...a stand out. It means that the hiring team has to understand how to assess the skills that this person is bringing in the context of the conversations that are being created, not just in terms of the right degree, the right background, and three decent references. This is not to trivialize HR and the hiring process: I have deliberately simplified this example to separate what is important in making the proper hire—understanding how this person is likely to impact conversations about your brand, product, or service—versus knowing how to properly hire someone.

When social media is seen as a marketing function, the application is generally aligned with the outbound communication needs of the business—the "let us tell you about ourselves" part of the conversation. By comparison, the conversations that exist about your brand, product, or service on the Social Web—and impact that they have on marketing—are not a result of marketing but rather the combination of HR, legal, operations, customer support, retail, and warranty policies…all of which exist *outside* of marketing.

Don't underestimate this. As interest develops in social technology, take the time to look across your entire organization and create a cross-functional team with representatives from all of the primary departments. You'll need Legal and HR for social media policies, for example, and you'll need Operations and Customer Service if using Twitter as a service channel appeals to you. Think about how you'll build a larger team to properly implement your ideas.

Create a Shared Sense of Purpose

So, if you want to hire that next killer associate, you've got to make the case for hiring the kind of people that understand the holistic operation of the company, and their place, however big or small, in the generation of conversations and recommendations on the Social Web. This means that when you are thinking of social media, you need to be outside of marketing.

As you consider the role of social media in business, and you move the focus beyond marketing, you cannot think only in terms of tactical campaigns. Moving the application of social media beyond marketing requires that you anchor your programs in your business strategy. Social technology and technology applications must be aligned with the overall business objectives and strategic efforts. If not, they will be limited in efficacy to marketing, or to IT, or to HR, whichever organization sponsored the tactical project that included some aspect of social technology.

Social business is all about the spread of social techniques into the organization, beyond marketing or communications. Social business means picking up on the dynamics of the purchase funnel and feedback cycle and then applying analogous thinking across the entire organization.

For example, customers are creating and sharing content among themselves for the purpose of improving their own decisions. They are curating what they create to make it easier to find valuable content, or to indicate to whom it is most likely to be valuable. They are rating and tagging each other so that they know who they can turn to for what: The Advocate Mom—the mother who sits at the center of her online friends networks on all matters "family"—is a powerful resource when your baby is crying and all you have to go on is a kid's tongue that is purple and fuzzy. People seek the answers to the questions that matter to them, and they organize the people around them in terms of what they know, who they know, and how they might be of help.

Why is that kind of care in developing and identifying specifically valuable resources limited to promotional marketing? Change the name in the previous scenario, apply it to an office, and you'll find a very empowered, very flat, and very efficient organization from the standpoint of sharing and improving collective knowledge. It is exactly this kind of application of social technology that drives social business.

In social business, there are external dynamics (customer, member, community, or similar) and internal dynamics (between the people who make up your organization) that can be made to operate in a more productive and more innovative manner. Marketing is a part of it, especially so in organizations that include product development as a part of marketing.

By connecting the internal efforts of your team, by improving the way in which knowledge is shared, with the external marketplace dynamics—tapping conversations and looking for competitive opportunities—the benefits of applying social media and social technology to your business are most readily realized.

Best Practices in Social Business

In this final section, it's the dos and don'ts (actually, the "do this insteads") that get put into practice. Following is a quick look into five specific examples of how social media and social business best practices are being used now to build better organizations.

- Listening

  Always begin with a listening program, and incorporate this into each of the following items. This provides the starting platform to keep you on track.

- Customer-driven design

  Focus your listening, and invite customers to provide specific inputs. Use this to evolve your product or service offering and to connect your customers deeply into your business organization.

- Crowdsourcing

  Rather than trying to make sense of 10,000 ideas, let your customers sort out the list. They'll vote for what they want and pass on the rest. You can focus on what they want.

- Knowledge exchange

  How much faster can problems be solved when everyone involved—including your customers and your employees—work together to solve them? Collectively solving problems is a great way to show your customers you love them.

- Gaming: Incentive for sharing

  What can you learn from a gamer? A lot, actually. Adding a game-based challenge to basic activities like content posting can turn spectators into participants.

Threadless.com: Customer-Driven Design

What happens when you build your business around collaboration itself? For starters, your customers get involved in your products and services right from the start, which in turn can give you a continuous source of innovative suggestions on how to evolve.

In addition, directly involved customers can become the core of your most ardent supporters—or most vocal detractors.

Threadless.com—shown in Figure 7.4—offers T-shirts for sale. That sounds simple enough, but Threadless does it one better. Rather than selling their designs (or worse, designs that people could buy elsewhere), Threadless sells only the designs that its own customers create.

The Threadless model works like this: People submit T-shirt designs, which are then reviewed and put to public vote. The winning designs are produced and sold, and the creators of the selected designs receive a cash reward as well as additional cash on future reprints. Threadless customers—through collaboration with each other and with the business itself—have a direct hand in shaping the product.

Figure 7.4 Collaborative Design: Threadless

Threadless is a great example of a collaborative business. Founded in 2000, Threadless is also a testament to the viability of a collaborative business. According to the Small Business Administration, on average new businesses have slightly less than a 50/50 chance of making it five years, let alone twice that.

Threadless

You can learn more about Threadless and its history by visiting Wikipedia:

http://en.wikipedia.org/wiki/Threadless

Dell: Customer-Driven Design

Dell turned to its customers, initially through surveys and polls and then more formally through its IdeaStorm platform, for suggestions on what customers wanted to see more of (or less of) in the product line. Where Threadless encouraged its customers to design the entire product, Dell was after the ideas that informed its future product options and the way they were offered to customers.

In 2007, building on the Salesforce.com Ideas platform, Dell launched IdeaStorm. Like the My Starbucks Idea program, IdeaStorm is a transparent adaptation of the classic suggestion box. What makes this suggestion box work is the fact that voting—done by other customers and potential customers—is out in the open. The better ideas move up as they are discussed. Ideas faring less well sometimes get combined in the process, strengthening their chance of making it into the idea pool from which Dell's product managers ultimately pull ideas.

The suggestions implemented through the IdeaStorm platform include Dell offering the Linux Ubuntu operating system as a preinstalled option. Additional ideas receiving higher than average attention included aspects of customer service, suggestions regarding the website (a primary source of income for Dell), and suggestions that preinstalled promotional software be optional. Looking at these ideas, it's clear that social technologies have applicability and impact that extend beyond marketing.

Crowdspring: Crowdsourcing

If you've never tried a true crowdsourcing application, here's your chance. For a couple of hundred dollars, you can get a snappy new logo and card design for your upcoming birthday party...or just about any other event that you wanted "branded." Of course, if your business needs a visual makeover, you can use Crowdspring to do that too.

Crowdspring attracts artists—designers, typographers, CSS wizards, and more—who compete for projects. Unlike eLance, where project awards are made *before* the actual deliverable is prepared, Crowdspring participants see the actual designs as they are evolving—in public and in view of competing designers—as the process occurs. You pay after the fact.

What really makes Crowdspring work, however, is the participation of the buyer in collaboration with the designers. Take a logo design as an example: Imagine that you want a logo for your new business. First, you create an account and define what you want—color preferences, style choices, and maybe some examples of logos you like. At this point the designers review the project, and those wishing to compete jump in and start offering design ideas.

Now, if the buyer doesn't participate beyond this point, the designers will offer a range of styles and the buyer may pick one, but this isn't the optimal path. One of the Crowdspring rules is that buyers have to pick a winner based on what is offered: This means it's in the direct interest of the buyer to improve what's offered. The best way to do this is to participate alongside the designers, not as a designer but rather through feedback on the designs being produced. As the buyer actively signals which of the submitted designs is favored, the designers will all start shifting in that direction.

The more the buyers participate, the more the designers participate. Disclosure: I've used Crowdspring multiple times, and each time I have seen the number of participating designers go up, directly in response to my participation. My good friend Dr. Tom Hill aptly quotes Saturday Night Live's "Hans and Franz" on this point, "Hear me now, believe me later." If you want people to participate—in any social application—show them you are serious by participating yourself.

After ten days, buyers choose the design they like, and the logo (or whatever design work you requested) is delivered. It's really quite amazing how well Crowdspring works.

> ## Crowdspring
>
> You can check out Crowdspring and see how it works and what others have used it for here:
>
> http://www.crowdspring.com

HARO: Knowledge Exchange

HARO—an acronym for Help a Reporter Out—is a knowledge exchange that was created by Peter Shankman. The basic proposition of HARO is that for every person who has a question, somewhere there is also a person with an answer. The trick is to put them together, and this what HARO does.

The context for HARO is news reporting. Reporters are often in the predicament of having to report on something they themselves don't fully understand. This is *not* a knock on reporters: It is simply the reality of a technically complex world.

Even if a reporter is the "science journalist" for a magazine or paper, it's unrealistic to think that this person would simultaneously fully understand a nuclear power reactor, the inner workings of a rocket motor, and the various competing ideas and technical underpinnings for what to do about global warming. Yet, in the course of a week, that reporter may be asked to cover all three.

This is the classic expertise-sharing problem that led Dr. Vannevar Bush to conceive of the Memex, the theorized mechanical device that provided the fundamental insight in creating the World Wide Web. Peter Shankman has applied this same thought to the job of the reporter and the challenges they face in getting accurate information about a variety of topics, even within a chosen focus area.

On one side of HARO are reporters: Reporters need information. Typically, information costs money (except online, where it's assumed to be free!). So here's the dilemma: How do you get reporters the information they need without paying for it, at least directly in cash, since that would introduce a whole host of issues with regard to reporting?

The insight was this: Experts seek recognition, and being cited as an "expert" in a publication can be very valuable as a way to advance the career of an engineer, doctor, sociologist, prosumer (a sort of professional-grade hobbyist) and a lot of other people. HARO puts these two needs together through a searchable exchange. Reporters go looking for experts, and the experts—who have signed up and completed detailed profiles about their expertise—are thereby available for interviews by those reporters.

HARO

You can learn more about HARO—and perhaps even sign up yourself—here:

http://www.helpareporter.com

You may also want to learn more about Peter Shankman, who developed HARO: Peter is the author of *Customer Service: New Rules for a Social-Enabled World (Que Biz-Tech, 2010)*. You can follow Peter on Twitter (@skydiver).

Foursquare: Game-Based Sharing

Beginning with phones that included GPS or similar location tracking, applications such as Brightkite, Dodgeball, Loopt, and Latitude have made the simple act of "being someplace" talkworthy. (Just how talkworthy they are is, of course, left to the participants in any given conversation to decide!) Each of these tools in some way traded on the value of knowing where others you knew were right now.

Early applications included things like meetups, coffee shops, and dinner dates. Depending on your motivations, the ability to see where your friends are can be useful information. But beyond basic location awareness, these early applications didn't do much. That was a problem.

Enter Foursquare. Along with applications like Gowalla and rebuilt versions of earlier applications, Foursquare combines location awareness with collective knowledge to produce an order of magnitude more useful experience.

Using Foursquare, upon arriving someplace one "checks in." The GPS in your phone knows where you are, and Foursquare tells you what's around you. Typically, you'll see the name of the place where you are and some others that are nearby, and you simply click Check In.

What makes Foursquare relatively more popular is its game-based functionality. As you check in, you accumulate points. Check in someplace new and add that venue to the Foursquare database—there's a form for this right on your phone-based app— and you get six points. Even better, hit three places in the same day, and you get a traveler badge. Go out on a weeknight, and you'll earn the "school night" badge. You can see your points and badges when you log in online or open Foursquare on your phone (see Figure 7.5).

Figure 7.5 Foursquare Badges

Once you've checked in, you'll see a list of your friends *also using Foursquare* who are nearby, along with tips about the place you've checked into. The tips are one of the first big "value adds" of Foursquare. Checking into a restaurant, you can see what's good (or alternatively, what's good that is right across the street). Checking in at a grocery store alerts others in your friends' list that you're there— and they can ping you to ask you to pick up some milk (since you actually know each other, the relative tolerance for such an imposition is known by both parties) and thereby save your friend a needless trip in the car.

Sharing Location Data

Foursquare and Twitter both allow you to follow people, and allow others to follow you. Unlike Twitter's basic posting features, however, that let followers know what you are doing, Foursquare tells them *where* you are. This means it's also telling people where you *aren't.* If you check in at a movie theater, it means you aren't going to be home for about 2 hours.

Rather than uninstalling the application, this means you need to think about your own follower/ following and "friending" policies. Location-sharing applications raise the bar in this regard. My good friend Susan Bratton talked of the "gluttonous social behavior" many have engaged in—amassing thousands of followers simply because they could. Many are now rethinking that behavior.

Before accepting a follow request with location-sharing tools, take a minute (or more…) to think through the potential impact of what you are sharing. Twitter has taught that not everyone really wants to know what everyone else is doing right now. Foursquare may teach that even fewer people want *anyone* to know *where* they are doing it.

Foursquare: Beyond Meetups

The Dachis Group's Peter Kim takes the possible social business applications for Foursquare further, extending the application well beyond simple meetups and check ins. You can read more about Peter and Foursquare here:

http://www.beingpeterkim.com/2009/11/foursquare-social-business-design.html

Review and Hands-On

Applying social media principles effectively in business is both straightforward and challenging. It is straightforward because there is actually a process around which you can organize your efforts. It is challenging because much like the rethinking that occurs when applying social media in pure marketing applications, applying social technologies at a business level may require a redesign of the business itself.

Review of the Main Points

The tips and best practices covered in this chapter are summarized in the points that follow. Get these things right and you're on your way to a solid implementation of social technology in business.

- Listen, collaborate, and measure. These are the three fundamental practices that lead to successful implementations of social technology in a business context. By listening first, knowledge about the current conversations can be shared with the larger organization, making collaboration between the business and its customers easier to implement. By always looking for metrics, and thinking though how they are applied, the actual results can be evaluated in the same terms as any other business project.

- Don't shy away from social media and social technology because it's scary. Instead, follow the three essential practices of listening, collaborating, and measuring.

- Don't limit your view of social media to marketing. The root causes of the conversations that drive the success of your firm or organization are often outside of marketing. Trying to use the Social Web effectively without cross-functional support is like bringing a spoon to a gun fight. It's not going to turn out well.

Hands-On: Review These Resources

Review each of the following, and ensure that you have a complete understanding of how social media and social technology is used.

Threadless

http://www.threadless.com

Foursquare (You will need an account with Foursquare and a GPS-capable phone or similar hand-held device for this.)

http://foursquare.com

HARO

http://www.helpareporter.com

Hands-On: Apply What You've Learned

Apply what you've learned in this chapter through the following exercises:

1. Prepare a short presentation using Threadless or Dell's Digital Nomad project as the subject, or any other collaborative business design application that you choose. Talk to your team about what makes the application work and how social technology has been built into the business.

2. Looking at your own firm or organization, list three ways that your customers could collaborate directly with each other to improve some aspect of your product or service.

3. Develop an outline for a business plan based on exercise 2 that involves multiple departments or functions to implement. Win the support of those people.

Social Business Building Blocks

Part III breaks the prior topics—social business fundamentals, best practices and metrics—into a set of building blocks that you can use to evolve and expand your social media marketing efforts across your entire business or organization. Each chapter includes selected examples that show you how the components covered so far fit together to create "social business" processes and applications in a way that makes it easier for you to implement smart social business programs.

Engagement on the Social Web

"Engagement" takes on a new meaning on the Social Web—or at least one that is different from what is typically implied in a marketing context. This is because "engagement" on the Social Web—like all other aspects of "social anything"—is defined by participants *rather than the creators of a marketing message or software application. In this context, the term "participant" means a customer or stakeholder; the term "engagement" is less about exposure and click-throughs, and instead more about participation in activities that might be described as "I'd actually spend all day doing this if I could." Getting engagement right is a key to getting social technologies working for you.*

Chapter Contents

Engagement as a Customer Activity

The Social Web creates an expectation from the customer's perspective—whether a prior, current, or potential (future) customer—of a two-way relationship with brands, products, and services that was nearly unthinkable just a generation of business ago. Customers now have a real voice that—in advertising lingo—*resonates* with others who share their lot: Just as soon as your awareness campaign has done its job, they'll use their new collaborative tools to vet your claims and promises. They'll ask questions *of each other* and share outcomes, and in the process exert influence on pending or potential decisions of all involved. It's a kind of group-think, gone wild.

At the heart of engagement is a fundamental connection between the business and the customer, a connection where the customer is not a "target" but is rather an equal partner. This shift in perspective is significant and will be difficult for many businesses to fully embrace. Altimeter's Jeremiah Owyang put it this way:

> *"Companies know the problem will get worse before it gets better.*
> *Organizations realize they are no longer in charge. They often lack a*
> *credible strategy that empowers their employees to catch up with their*
> *customers."*

The very term "engagement" needs to be rethought in this context.

Among marketers, engagement is generally taken as a measure of how involved someone is with a piece of content or an activity that is provided through email, a banner ad or a website. Traditional marketing and the time-tested and proven efforts that move potential customers through the purchase funnel still apply. In this view of engagement, however, the customer is seen as rather like a fish by a fisherman, with the measurement of "engagement" resting on the amount of time spent by the fish as it considers the lure.

It's important to understand whose perspective we are viewing engagement from, because in social marketplaces it is the perspective of the fish—not the fisherman—that matters most. Measuring engagement in a traditional context still matters: Knowing which ads "get bites" and which don't is of obvious interest. From the fisherman's point of view, it's good to catch the attention of a fish—but simply attracting attention isn't enough. To move from attention to serious involvement, you need to adopt the fish's point of view. Ideally, you want the fish to design the lure for you, to show you where in the pond it spends its time, and to invite its friends to the party.

Learn to Think Like a Fish

When you turn your perspective around to the viewpoint of your customers, the mechanics of engagement change. From the perspective of the fish, it is not the lure that is "engaging." Rather, it is the act of eating, driven by a more fundamental interest—like the instinct of survival—that results in the fish being "engaged." The lure looks like a meal, and fish think a lot about eating. Simply put, successfully catching a fish is not driven by the need to catch a fish: It's driven by appealing to the *needs and interests* of the fish.

The Social Web works more like fishing, from the perspective of the fish, than it does like *target marketing*. Take a look at Figure 8.1, and read the copy for a quick diversion and an insight into a brand that understands that building a great lure starts with thinking like a fish. The central question around engagement on the Social Web, therefore, shifts from an interest in a creative campaign (the marketer's perspective) to why a potential customer would be interested in spending time in the activity associated with that campaign (the customer's perspective). This is where the notion of building social media marketing and business programs around *passions, lifestyles, and causes* fits into engagement. By seeing the Social Web—and engagement—from the perspective of the participant, the necessity of building around the activities that occupy the minds and hearts of customers and stakeholders becomes clear.

Figure 8.1 Storm Lures: Think Like a Fish

The connection between social media marketing and social media as applied to business is built around the processes of engagement that lead to collaboration and brand advocacy.

By creating activities that connect to lifestyles, passions, and causes, the brand, product, or service takes on a new relevance for the customer. On the Social Web, the specific point of engagement generally occurs in a social context. A support forum or ideation platform, for example, provides a significant attachment point between a customer and a business based on the desire of a customer to share an idea or experience with others, and to learn more about how to apply this knowledge toward the end-goal of "becoming better" at the associated activities of that customer which drove the actual purchase. Customers want to feel empowered and accomplished: Creating a space where customers share experiences and learn from each other is a powerful way to connect your business or organization to them.

Social technology solutions accomplish this by appealing to lifestyles—think Harley-Davidson for example, whose brand *is* a lifestyle—or by aligning themselves with a shared passion or cause, in the way that Dell has done with its "Take Your Own Path" community for entrepreneurs and (separately) its Digital Nomad's community programs.

Engagement Points

What are some of the typical engagement points—built around associated activities that run beyond the immediate purposes of marketing—used by businesses on the Social Web now? Table 8.1 provides examples of social technology and its application in innovation, support, marketing, and demand generation. The engagement activities are tied to business objectives and in turn drive the selection of the engagement platform that is ultimately used.

▶ **Table 8.1** Engagement Programs Beyond Social Media Marketing

Brand	Engagement Activity	Engagement Platform
Starbucks	Ideation: Transparent suggestion box seeking innovative ideas, with visible participation by the Starbucks team.	Salesforce Ideas/ "My Starbucks Idea"
Dell	Member-driven answers to technical questions, with Dell playing a supporting (participative) rather than primary (controlling) role.	Lithium Technologies Support Forums/ "Dell's Support Forums"
Coke	Suggesting and voting on ideas to improve the experience of being an NCAA fan, building on the participant experience rather than (purely) marketing the brand.	Posterous (blogging)/ "Department of Fannovation"
PGi	Developers speak openly with each other as they develop applications using PGi's programming tools and thereby drive demand for PGi's services.	Jive Software-Based Developer's Community/ "PGiConnect"

While Table 8.1 may seem like any other list of tools—leaving you to figure out where to apply them—the easy way to put the information contained in this table to use is by looking at the "Engagement Activity" column. Compare these activities with your own business objectives and look for relevant, interesting ideas on which to build. It's always a better idea to start with the end application or business objectives and then choose the tools than it is to pick a tool and try to come up with a use. Picking tools first is actually a common mistake. It's not unheard of to read a case study or the description of capabilities around the newest Web 2.0 technology and think "Hey, I should apply that tool to my business." Too often, the result is an expensive implementation of someone else's solution, minus the results that indicate a business success. Don't make this mistake.

How do you avoid this? Start with the desired end results, and have a clear statement of desired outcomes in mind. If the objective is to reduce support costs, and the measures of interest are economic indicators of ROI that back up the decision and quantify results, then look, for example, at the engagement points built around the activities related to customer support. Ready-to-use support forums and the white-label (Do It Yourself, or DIY) platforms that can be used to create self-directed support environments or the ready-to-use support services like GetSatisfaction are great starting points. They are relatively simple to implement, and because they are built on pretested platforms, they are lower complexity implementations and therefore lower risk. The DIY platforms also provide metrics—the number of participants, solutions generated, metrics around solution quality, as evidenced through participant-driven ratings, and more—that can be integrated into your overall KPIs and ROI calculations as appropriate.

The previous example—use of social technology in customer service—cited cost reduction and/or improved satisfaction in and around customer service. As another example, you may be looking to create or enhance *innovation* processes. If so, the ideation tools will nicely fit here—for example, Salesforce.com's "Ideas" platform or the equivalent, perhaps built on Lithium's support community or even something as low-cost as Posterous (as Coke did with its "Department of Fannovation"). You can use social technology to solicit new product ideas or product options, to ask for suggestions for customer process improvements, or just about anything else. The only real caveats are that you'll need to be transparent—people need to see who has suggested what and what has happened as a result—and you'll need to be prepared *to do something* with the suggestions you receive. What that something is…is up to you. It's still your business.

It's Still *Your* Business

How often do you hear someone say, "When it comes to the Social Web, if your customers tell you to jump, your only response should be along the lines of 'how high'"? Or perhaps you've been told, "You need to be 100 percent transparent." While these make great rallying points—and from 30,000 feet they are correct—they aren't all that useful when it comes to the task of *actually applying* social technology to your business or organization. Sometimes customers get it wrong, and "100 percent transparency" could be taken to mean being so transparent that your competitors know (as a result) what you are planning. Remember, it is still *your business*. You are still running it, and you are still responsible for its performance as measured by some combination of customers, shareholders, management, and colleagues. The Social Web doesn't change this per se—what it changes is the way in which your customers expect to be able to participate in—to engage with—your business.

What the Social Web really does—and the reason that traditional measures or views of things like engagement are shifting—is driven not by the necessity to cede control fully to customers but to involve them meaningfully in the processes that produce and deliver the products and services that they buy from your firm. So, when a customer says "jump," you should ask "why?" and then *listen* to the answer and evaluate it jointly with that customer in the context of the your business objectives.

This realization shapes the firm or organization's response to ideation, support, and similar social engagement applications. Suppose, for example, that customers were to ask for something that you could *not* legally or responsibly do. Consider for example regulated businesses—airlines, pharmaceutical firms, and banking and investment firms to name but a few—and the sometimes less-than-clear processes that govern these businesses. As product manager or marketing director, you are bound by regulations that may be at odds with what customers are requesting. Suppose it was your business and that your customer was making the request: What would you do?

In respect to the customer's participation, you've got to do something or you risk alienating (to put it nicely) your audience. In a case like this, the only viable response—which by default makes it the best response—is to clearly explain why this particular request can't be entertained and to offer instead an alternative if one is available. When customers have the information they need to understand *why* something is happening (or can't happen) they generally end up supporting you. This is where the combination of participation and transparency can really pay off. Honest, open conversation includes "We're not allowed to do that by law" or "Our company has made a strategic and top secret call." This kind of frank honesty—sometimes the answer is "No" or "We can't talk about it"—is especially applicable in regulated industries where social media and the adoption of social technology is nevertheless expected by customers and stakeholders. Importantly, your practice of *consistently* open, forthright participation on each and every interaction is essential in building trust: Trust happens not on the first interaction, but on the second, fifth, or hundredth interaction. Building a relationship is done by working at it over time.

As an example of the difference that the right information shared at the right time can make, consider the following: I was on a flight heading for Cleveland one evening, and as we approached the airport, we began circling. If you've flown more than once you know that planes fly relatively direct routes between cities, and so circling generally means only one thing: you are being delayed. Tensions on the plane started rising as we circled for 5 minutes, then 10, then 15.

At this point the pilot came on, explained that we were in fact being delayed, and asked passengers what they wanted to do: The choices offered were either circling for another hour—the estimated time of delay—or diverting to Milwaukee and spending the night there. In a unanimous cry, the plane's passengers opted to circle for *an hour or more*. However, the pilot then continued explaining the choices more completely: if we diverted, rooms would be provided, etc. and that, oh by the way, we had *less than 45 minutes of fuel* remaining. Everyone yelled "Let's go to Milwaukee!" and off we went.

What's important in this somewhat humorous example is that regardless of how the decision was actually made, the passengers were given the opportunity to participate, to be included in the process, early on. Imagine how different this would have been if the pilot had said, "We are on our way to Milwaukee, unless you all want to risk running out of fuel." When given all of the information needed to make a decision, customers are generally a pretty reasonable group. When kept in the dark, when looked at as a mob to be controlled, predictable challenges arise. No one likes to be told what to do, and even less so in a dictatorial manner. Yet, that is exactly how too many customers are treated. Engagement in a social technology context depends on active participation and collaboration, not control.

The point is this: When implementing an engagement strategy on the Social Web, you will ultimately present yourself (or your brand) as a *participant* and as such you will have to participate alongside your customers or constituents. *How* you participate is up to you: It's not an all-or-nothing thing. Just because a customer demands it does not in itself mean it has to be delivered. What it does mean is that a response is needed, and that this response needs to affirm in the minds of your customers or stakeholders that they have been heard and that their point of view has been considered. If the request made in a support forum is in-line with the existing community policies—if the suggestion for a process change made via an ideation or support platform is not inflammatory or otherwise at odds with the stated Terms of Use that govern everyone's conduct within the application—then a response that indicates review, consideration, and thought is expected in return. This includes the possibility of politely, accurately, and clearly explaining why a particular request *can't* be honored, or at least not in its present form.

Customers to the Rescue

But wait...it actually gets even better. Other customers are also involved, so if the idea is crazy on its face, very often the other participants involved will handle the situation themselves. In the cases of Dell, Starbucks, or India's Hindustan Times (shown in Figure 8.2), all of whom use public ideation platforms for assistance and fresh insight supporting their innovation programs, or Coke's Department of Fannovation program, participants vote up and down on various ideas. Product and marketing managers can then focus on the ideas that have a lot of support and needn't worry about those which don't. Simply put, you don't have to be the person that says "no" to every wacky idea: Other customers will say it for you.

Figure 8.2 Hindustan Times: Talk to HT

The same holds true in support programs. Dell manages its customer support forums using a small number of moderators by *empowering other customers* who offer technical solutions based on their own experiences. This approach yields evident process changes that can be acted on after a sufficient number of customers have "approved" the solution, providing a better support experience while at the same time elevating the ideas that will result in likely business gains for Dell when addressed through subsequent product innovations.

What's nice about these applications and implementations is this: You can focus on building relationships and managing the processes that support them rather than the specific conversations. For example, by building trust—by implementing clear practices that engender in your employees a genuine, visible concern for your customers—you set an entire context for the conversations that involve your brand, product, or service. Your customers will sort out many of the conversations for you, so that you don't have to respond to every single comment, suggestion, or idea that arises. When you do choose to respond—or when it's clear that you are expected to respond—you can focus on the requests and suggestions that have a large following or which, if left alone, may generate one. If you can't implement a specific idea, you can explain it once and move on. And, if you think you *might* be able to do it given an internal process change, design change or similar effort you've got at least the beginnings of the *customer* support you'll need to make the business case inside your organization for pressing for the required change or innovation.

This brings up an additional point about true engagement solutions: By connecting with your customers and participating with them in conversations—by inviting them to collaborate with you and placing in them an *appropriate* degree of trust and control—your customers will actually enable you to take up their case inside your firm or organization. Rather than stopping at the first "No" from legal or the C-suite, for example, you'll actually find yourself championing the cause on behalf of your customers. That's the point where you know you are on the way to a social technology–driven business and to long-term success.

Advocates in the Making

Ultimately, engagement is all about driving collaboration and the development of brand advocates. It may be reserved or casual, or it may be spontaneous and enthusiastic. But in the end what you are after as part of the leadership team within a business or cause-related organization—and especially so as a marketer—is a customer base that spreads beneficial word of mouth for you. Peter Drucker noted that "the purpose of business is to create and keep a customer." With the advent of social technology, the objective now is for *customers* to create (more) customers.

Looking at the awareness-driven purchase funnel and connecting it to the Social Web creates a closed-loop feedback path. Cyclical behaviors that surround social media and the purchase funnel feedback loop often resist definition in terms of starting and ending points: it's an iterative process, not a line with an ending point. Listening leads to innovation and product or service design that delights customers, and in turn drives beneficial word of mouth that shows up as favorable posts in listening exercises and social media analytics. Life's a circle, right? So is business.

To make it simple, assume that if at some point in the cycle customers are actively promoting a brand, product, or service, then this is the "result" desired. In other words, as a marketer it's less about creating awareness (though awareness still matters and is the right focus of your advertising efforts) and more about creating advocates and evangelists. Imagine the delight of our fisherman-friend if the first fish that spied that lure told three others, "Hey, you've got to check this out." That's what you want on the Social Web, too.

Engagement as a Business Activity

Customer engagement is the prerequisite for advocacy. Mentally jump back to the engagement process defined in the opening chapters: Starting with content consumption, and then proceeding through curation, creation, and collaboration, there is a stepping-off point—collaboration—that connects trial, purchase, and advocacy into the engagement process. That leads to the choice of *collaboration* as the new benchmark for engagement: When your customers or constituents are collaborating with each other and sharing the results of those efforts with other participants, *then* they are engaged in your business or organization.

Combining this definition of engagement and the benchmark of collaboration with the larger engagement process leads to a powerful end result: the development of customer advocates. Tangible results—the emergence of customer advocates, for example—become *measurable* end goals of the social business. In the next section, customer-led advocacy (or stakeholder-led, for governmental services and NGOs, non-profit organizations and similar) will be tied to the business objectives and business fundamentals that punctuate a quantitative management process.

Create Advocates Through Engagement

Having established the path from *consumption*—think traditional media and "traditional-media-like" activities in a digital context (banner ads or video pre-rolls, for example)—to collaboration and advocacy as a sort of process template or design guide for your social business engagement programs, the next step is connecting the resulting expressions of *advocacy* to your business.

Recall Fred Reichheld and the Net Promoter Score: A base of customers or constituents that are highly likely to strongly recommend a brand, product, or service is a fundamental condition for driving long-term profits and sustained growth. This is precisely what advocacy is all about: Advocates will readily and favorably recommend brands, products, services, and causes; which in turn leads to a competitive advantage by reducing expenditures required to overcome a lack of referrals or worse (detractors, for example). Offering price breaks, discounts, rebates, or similar concessions intended to offset inferior quality inevitably eats away at margins. Over the long term, any unnecessary expense and the associated deterioration of margins will obviously hurt the business or organization.

What is perhaps less clear—though equally valid—is that sustainable higher profit margins—think Whole Foods versus the other food stores against which it competes even if not directly—lead to enhanced opportunities to innovate, to the ability to attract and retain higher quality employees, to support higher quality suppliers, to use better raw materials, and to realize other similar business benefits. Each of these has a distinct, measurable payback of its own.

Consider innovation and the ability of a firm to afford the programs that support and drive innovation. An enhanced ability to innovate means your business or cause or program is less likely to be stymied by a change in the legal or business environment (as when AT&T was forced to open up its local lines to upstart MCI) or technology (say, from horse-drawn to horseless carriages). The latter example may seem obsolete; but Fisher Body, which is still going strong, is the classic case of innovation and survival after its core business—depicted in its logo (shown in Figure 8.3)—dried up in the face of technological and industrial change.

Figure 8.3 Body by Fisher

Fisher's founders had originally made horse-drawn carriages. Seeing the opportunity for innovation as Ford and other auto manufacturers sprang up, and having access to working capital, they adapted what they knew about *carriage* building to become a premiere *auto* body builder. The result was a firm that became a household name building car bodies for General Motors long after the original business—horse-drawn carriages and the firms that made them—had disappeared. The point is this: Innovation is the lifeblood of business, and the opportunity to rapidly innovate is enhanced through the process of engagement and collaboration with customers that is enabled through social technologies.

While much of the interest in social media *marketing* is driven by sales and demand generation, innovation as a result of the adoption of social business practices can pay an additional dividend: higher sustainable margins that enhance your ability to attract and retain higher caliber employees. Investing in better employees across the board pays big dividends when your firm or organization sets out to transform itself—for example, into a social business that is connected more directly to its customers. This type of transformation can be upsetting, and so employee "buy in" as well as their innate ability to step up to a more complex job is absolutely essential.

Why? Because superior employees are both more capable and more willing to learn new skills, to consider different ways of doing things, and to look for and champion new solutions. This is critically important. When you connect your business to your customers, those customers will no doubt ask for things that your firm has not considered—or has even decided against. Your ability to innovate and address these suggestions and ideas, to rethink past decisions, and to question established practices will rest entirely on the willingness and capability of your employed or retained work-force. All other things equal, better people will produce a better outcome.

Respond to Engaged Customers

The Social Web—combined with more specific engagement programs that encourage transparent and visible collaboration—is the central to the conversations happening through social media in a business context. Understanding and collaboration in *response* to the conversation often matter more than the conversation itself: The conversation and what is learned from it via social media analytics is more often than not a statement or reflection of something that has already happened. Simply put, it's less about what's already happened and more about what you do next as a result of knowing about it.

For example, when a constituent or potential customer conveys a favorable rec-ommendation, it is usually built around a prior experience. Further, that experience was created by a business process that is currently in place within your organization. This means that a social media analytics program—by itself, independent of support and ideation programs—is reporting on artifacts of history, not on indications of what direction the future should take.

What does this mean for social business and the design of processes built around social technology? It means that your real work begins *after* the initial analytics are collected, *after* sentiment and trend patterns have been reviewed and charted. This is a particular "watch out" point when implementing a dashboard-style social analyt-ics program. A screen full of charts and graphs can make it feel like real work is being done: The reality is closer to reading yesterday's newspaper. The game is, after all, in getting a fix on what's next and not so much what was. Listening, analyzing, and responding are, of course, on-going activities: But at the same time, actually addressing process issues that are driving negative conversations or implementing suggested inno-vations to further strengthen brand loyalty or enhance competitive advantage create the real payoff following the adoption of social technology in business.

Given these factors, albeit a simplification, the real work begins with the devel-opment of the *response* to whatever it is that is being talked about and passed around with regard to a brand, product, or service. The biggest challenge of running a social-technology-based business can, in this view, be clearly seen: The challenge is setting up your team internally to collect, analyze, and respond to what is learned or observed on the Social Web. This is what participation is all about and what engagement feels like.

The challenge of social business, therefore, comes down to balancing what *you need to do*—recall the point about regulatory issues driving some aspects of customer policy development—with what your constituents or customers are *asking you to do*. A great example of this is the promulgation of the 3-hour rule governing airline flight delays, implemented in 2010. The new legislation requires that airlines limit tarmac delays—delays that occur after boarding and pulling away from the gate—to 3 hours. Otherwise, steep fines kick in.

On its face, and in particular from a customer's *initial* perspective, the rule looks fine. Who really wants to sit on a plane for longer than necessary? Even more so, given—and I say this carefully and respectfully of all involved—the visible discontent of the traveling public with the end-to-end flying process, many customers are all too happy to see the airlines (as organizations) get hit with a harsh regulation.

From the perspective airline's operational staff—and in fact from that of seasoned travelers as well—the rule looks very different: Airlines will (now) be stiffly penalized for on-ground delays, so the rule introduces yet another risk into a business system that, like most business systems, is designed to *reduce risks* or at the least to understand and control and price for them. Businesses routinely trade risk for revenue/margin rewards. In the case of 3-hour rule, it *adds* the risk of a financial penalty into the system.

From the airlines' perspective, this added risk means that for flights that had a chance of leaving—albeit delayed—the "sure bet" is to simply cancel the flight. The financial penalties, if the 3-hour limit is crossed, can greatly exceed the total revenue value of the flight itself, so canceling the flight begins to look like the better option. Obviously, a cancelled flight is at odds with what most passengers actually wanted in the first place, which was of course to go someplace. In the end, everyone loses.

Airlines will very likely do the obvious thing: If there is a chance of a lengthy delay—that is generally caused *not* by the airline but by the airport, the air traffic control system, or weather—the flight will simply be cancelled, avoiding the risk of a potentially large, and unknown until after the fact, fine. Shown in Figure 8.4, the immediate response—requests for exemptions, for starters—are headlines as the rule is challenged. Reactive and punitive rules rarely help in business: Instead, appealing to and collaborating with customers to develop a better solution is the way to go.

As a result of the 3-hour rule, airline marketing and communications managers will no doubt be pressed to explain the increase in flight cancellations to passengers, further straining relations as a "blame game" ensues. Making matters worse, the number of flights delayed, along with the average delay time, will likely *drop* as a result of the legislation—driven down not by more people arriving on time (the intention) but rather by the removal of the longest delays—including those associated with flights that might may have faced a lengthy delay—from the underlying calculation of average flight delay. On the one hand, passengers will see advertising claims for improvements in on-time performance as airline marketers one-up each other citing these now recalculated figures, and on the other hand these same passengers will be more likely to directly experience an actual flight cancellation. That will make for some tense moments in the airports.

Figure 8.4 Requesting Exemptions from 3-Hour Rule

This is where social business fits: Suppose the airlines and regulators had spent (or do so in the future) more time with customers, explaining the entire process, and seeking input? Rather than relying on a handful of anecdotes—"Next up on Breaking World News, Meet 83-year-old Mildred W., who was trapped on a flight for 11 hours when she tried to visit her great grandkids in Mt. Pleasant," and the testimony of *representatives* for airlines and passengers who may well have an agenda that is at odds with those of *actual* passengers or *actual* airline employees—what if they connected customers directly with employees and asked them to sort it out?

Consider that alternative: Would it not produce a better solution if a) the actual participants in the process had a say in it, and b) those directly involved—including passengers and employees—understood the entire process and why longer delays might actually be in everyone's best interest? For example, what if instead of fines (which do not flow back to the customer as a benefit in any appreciable form) the airlines were required to provide wholesome meals if the delay crossed a dinner hour? Or what if they were required to keep essential on-board services (such as the bathroom and air conditioner) functioning? What if airports were required to provide free Wi-Fi, including on the tarmac? Some of these are now present in some airports and on some airlines that have a demonstrated commitment to traveler/passenger well-being, while in others this same customer orientation is clearly missing.

Crazy ideas? Perhaps, but chances are by working together the result would be both a better flight experience and a better "delay experience." If you still doubt whether or not directly involving customers in the process makes a difference, the next time you see someone volunteer to give up a seat on an overbooked flight for $200, ask that person why they opted to take the later flight. Evidently, being delayed for an extra day or night has a market price. Meet or exceed the market price, and "delay" becomes "delight."

It goes further than this too: There's also a point here about the *manner* in which gate agents ask for volunteers. Jake McKee shared an experience with me on this point: Jake once heard an agent looking for "next day" volunteers ask, very sweetly, if perhaps those without families waiting at home would mind giving priority for the immediate flight to those with waiting families. Whether or not this changed the actual list of volunteers is immaterial: At that moment, the airline—through the considerate act of its employee—appeared human and compassionate. It's amazing what happens when a company is seen as a collection of people rather than an impenetrable process. The adoption of social technology in engagement processes are direct enablers of the "company as people" view.

At the end of the day, it was not the hours-on delays that caused the 3-hour rule; it was the dehumanizing experiences suffered by too many for too long. This rule could have been avoided by asking customers for ideas and then listening to them and acting on them. The social business question that arises is, therefore, this: What are the social technologies, tools and processes that need to be put in place to connect customers and businesses in ways that drive *collaborative* conversations? These are the kinds of things you want to be thinking about as you work through concepts like engagement and participation and the expected benefits of the application of social technology within your business or organization.

The combination of active listening, touchpoint analysis, and collaboration (via engagement) makes obvious the root causes of dissatisfaction and equally so the potential solutions (ideation and innovation) that drive enhanced satisfaction. Getting to the root cause of the customer's issues with airlines, more than anything else what makes airline travelers nuts is the feeling of an almost total loss of personal control from the moment you contemplate purchasing a ticket until the moment you successfully retrieve your bags on the return flight. At the same time—and again very much the subject of social business—consider the *employees* of the airlines and their role in all of this: They have ideas, too. Compare the happy, motivated, and consumer-oriented people at Southwest Airlines, Alaska Airlines, and Continental Airlines in the United States or India's Kingfisher or Dubai's Emirates—to name just a few—with the frustrated, underpaid, unhappy, and impolite representatives of those airlines known for poor service. Employees—and their own levels of engagement in the businesses they are part of—are a huge component of a social business.

It's Eighties Night!

As a practical example of the connection between operations, marketing and social business, consider JetBlue's terminal (T5) at JFK. All airlines have delays—they are part of the trade-off between the reality of weather and a highly interconnected flight system and the overriding concern for passenger safety. JetBlue's T5 is the kind of place one actually looks forward to visiting—shops, restaurants, plenty of free, robust Wi-Fi, and pleasant open space. I spent an extra few hours there one evening when all but one of JFK's main runways had closed due to ice. As I looked around, I was struck by the relative calm, with a large number of people watching Hulu on their laptops and patiently waiting.

The robust Wi-Fi in T5 is no accident: JetBlue actually takes a further step in ensuring that its T5 runs smoothly from the perspective of travelers by recognizing that Wi-Fi (alng with food, drinks, and engaging activities in shops and restaurants) is both essential to maintaining a sense of calm (when people are productive or happily diverted, things work better!). WiFi is also largely a function of external providers: so JetBlue works with its external Wi-Fi support services to ensure that their services, too, keep pace with the needs of its customers while in T5.

By comparison, I was on an American Airlines flight home from Boston that happened to connect in St. Louis a year earlier. Just as we were about to leave St. Louis, a tornado was spotted. We had to deplane (understandable) but then in a completely baffling series of missteps, 5,000 passengers were herded into the baggage claim area (the "safe" area), which as you've no doubt guessed placed all of us on the wrong side of the security check points. Even worse, because no thought had been given to the actual capacity of the baggage area, many people were actually forced outside, into the storm as the dark, lower-level baggage area overflowed!

The storm passed in less than 10 minutes. The impact of the mess created by a total lack of disaster planning (as noted earlier, regulatory fines evidently go everywhere except into services that would actually benefit customers) lasted well into the next day and at significant out-of-pocket personal costs as thousands of travelers and families scrambled for food, cabs, and hotel rooms, all of which were suddenly re-priced at "rack rate."

Social business is all about connecting customer feedback and business processes, about creating systems that trigger and cultivate advocacy. Recovering from its own near meltdown, JetBlue has reexamined it operations-driven processes to match its differentiating marketing prowess: The result is the steady rise in the creation of

JetBlue advocates. The challenge for JetBlue going forward will be to scale its current customer experience. Here again, social technology (used to connect employees and passengers to drive service innovation) comes into play. The combination of active listening—understanding what is happening (positive or negative) right now, along with collaborative systems that facilitate ideation and innovation inside of JetBlue as it grows—are all part of what defines a social business.

If you're wondering about how powerful the combination of operations and marketing really is and about the kinds of conversations this kind of alignment can generate, go to Twitter and search "JetBlue T5." Figure 8.5 shows the typical results. My favorites? From FlyBoyVancouver comes "T5, of course!" in response to the posted question "What is the best airline terminal in the world?" right along with CrazyLoud1's "It's 80s night at T5!" Kind of makes you want to Fly JetBlue to New York, doesn't it? That's not a coincidence. It's by business and experience design.

Connect Customers to Employees

In the previous section, I covered three scenarios: One past (St. Louis, hopefully having since rehearsed for the next weather event), one present (the ongoing business benefit of JetBlue's T5 investment in social business), and one future (the actual implementation of the new "3-hour" rule). It will be interesting to see which airlines simply pass the buck to customers—creating more delays, while simultaneously claiming better on-time performance—and which ones will stick up for their customers and sort out a better and perhaps completely new boarding-to-take-off procedure when lengthy delays are likely.

The summary idea is this: Higher forms of engagement, built on the building-block processes for realizing a social business and then powered by collaboration, offer ways to bring customers and constituents back into alignment with the business and its employees. Social technologies provide a way to return a sense of control—in an appropriate manner that is consistent with the norms of your business or organization—that invites collaboration. In the case of the airlines, what sorts of solutions might passengers come up with if only they were given the chance?

This is where ideation and similar platforms enter the picture. The ideation platforms, as they are commonly called, make it very easy for interested people across a variety of applications—products, services, legislation, policies, and more—to not only contribute ideas but to *curate* the contributions of others. This has two direct benefits to business and/or the operation of an organization.

First, it encourages involvement, which in turn drives *participative* collaboration. Second, it provides a venue for discussing why not all ideas can be implemented, or can only be implemented in the future. In other words, it provides a venue that reestablishes your control of your brand, product, or service by recognizing that your customers or constituents have a voice in it. They get to ideate, and you get to moderate.

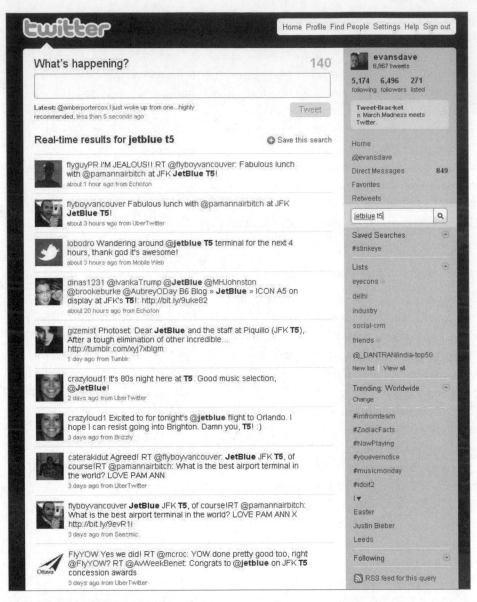

Figure 8.5 Eighties Night at JetBlue's T5

Structured "suggestion boxes" built around an open, visible process provide a very doable way of connecting your business to your customers. Yes, you need to participate: But at the same time, you don't have to give up control, and you certainly don't have to do everything that is suggested, even if it is a popular idea. What is required is participation, some feedback, and a reasonable degree of incorporation of what is offered by participants in the ideation process into your business, organization, or delivery channel. A different way to approach your customers? Yes. Impossible to implement? Hardly.

Extend Engagement

The prior sections covered engagement, first as a *customer* activity and then by its counterpart, engagement as a *business* activity. From the customer's perspective, engagement is all about the simple act of spending time in activities that are relevant, of interest, or otherwise satisfy a purpose or desire. This may or may not include your branded microsite or online game or what have you. Truth be told, as engagement is defined in the social business context it probably does not. This is not to say that these elements aren't useful as a part of an overall marketing campaign, but rather to say that they are less effective as social media components when compared with elements that are centered around interest in a lifestyle, passion, or cause.

The tendency or behavior to associate around passions, lifestyles, causes, and similar personally relevant activities is what underlies the recommended approach to participating in a community as a business. Look for community anchors that are centered on a passion, a lifestyle, or a cause and use them as the basis for your social technology efforts. Around these one can then add and connect to the brand outposts in places like Facebook, Twitter, Linked In, and similar sites.

Extending engagement as a business tool requires a different set of actions than engagement as a marketing concept. From the perspective of your business, engagement looks a bit different: It's still centered on passions, lifestyles, and causes but the goal is collaboration, expressed as learning or a suggestion that leads to innovation or similar business benefit. The challenge facing the marketing team—and by extension the other functions that support the overall customer or member experience—is in converting the energy of customer or stakeholder passion, for example, into energy that produces a business benefit.

This conversion of passion into a business benefit might occur between customers—for example, when a customer who becomes an evangelist emerges as a true advocate for your brand, product, or service. Or, it may occur between a customer and an employee when a customer service agent discovers a passionate customer with a specific suggestion or viewpoint. In the past, an invitation may have been extended to such a customer to join a customer advisory board. While that may still be a good practice, why not ask this person to lead a discussion or support forum, or enroll this person in a research community? One caveat applies: Whenever you create a community that has a defined starting and stopping point—generally the case with purpose-driven research communities—be sure that this is communicated to participants in advance.

Collaboration

Research communities are one of the ways that you can begin to engage customers and constituents in a collaborative process. Because participants know that they are engaged in a research and learning effort, they are already in the mode of sharing what they think with you. Unlike focus groups—typically one-off events, too often with but a small number of screened participants—research communities provide a context for more natural participation. This is not a criticism of focus group methodology: Clearly, they are one of the tools that remain important in the discovery and design processes for marketing campaigns, product features, and a lot more. Research communities combine the basics of focus group research with the social structures and potential for collaboration found in social networks.

The business advantage of a research community over a focus group is in its longevity and continuity. Participants may be involved for months or even years. This gives you the opportunity to develop real relationships with participants, and for the research community members themselves to become very familiar with the brand, products, or services being evaluated. As a result, the level of feedback—and the insights that you can carry back into your business—can be quite substantial.

Research communities can be launched using services that provide turnkey implementation as well as participant recruitment and community management, or they can be built up from the ground just as you would build any other community. Service providers such as Communispace and Passenger offer these types of purpose-built communities as turnkey services. Take a look at these offerings if you are interested in this type of collaborative social application.

Research Communities

Using a community platform for extended research can provide in-depth insights into brands, products, and services and the ways in which customers are likely to perceive them. One big caveat: Because these are often fixed-time programs, be sure that participants understand the terms, expectations, and when (if) their stay in the community will end.

Passenger and Communispace are two leading providers of research communities. You can learn more about them here:

http://www.thinkpassenger.com/

http://www.communispace.com/

In addition to research communities, tools like forums, ideation, and innovation platforms have a natural place in your collaboration program, making it easy to extend these tools inside your business or organization. Support forums, for example, provide a context for issue identification and resolution, and they do so in a manner that naturally involves your own employees or staff. Support forums are a great way to involve and empower customers and then connect them with your employees. By letting customers answer questions for each other on basic or unusual (highly specific) cases, you can redirect your own support efforts to other venues and provide a more complete customer support experience while also keeping your budget issues in line.

As an example of the benefits of self-directed customer support, I was on my way to Gold's Gym one morning. It was about 4:30 AM. I had a full day planned including a conference call at 10:00 AM. As I was checking my calendar my newly updated Google G1 froze up. I tried the obvious: I turned the phone off and then turned it back on. Halfway through the startup sequence, the process hung on the "android" logo. I was stuck in about the worst situation a digital nomad can be in: My connection to the Internet was gone! I was outside the spacecraft, without a tether.

At about 6:30 AM, between workout sessions, I visited a nearby Starbucks, opened my laptop, and searched via Google for "g1 frozen android cupcake," as this seemed like a reasonable starting point. (I included "cupcake" as this was the operating system update that had been installed a day or two prior.) Near the top of the search results was an entry whose visible description read "freezes with android logo following cupcake upgrade…"

That looked promising, so I clicked into the result and found myself in the T-Mobile support forum. About five posts down I saw the recovery process for a frozen G1, outlined in detail. I followed the steps, and in less than 3 minutes my phone was functioning, albeit in its basic (default) configuration. I reinstalled the apps, one by one, later that day, after my conference call was completed.

The point here is this: At 6:30 AM, much less 4:30 AM, it would have been a stretch to expect live phone support. But in my case, I wouldn't have been able to call anyway: My phone was dead, and I haven't a clue how to use a pay phone! Because T-Mobile had created an online community for Android support, I was able to quickly self-serve and resolve my own problem. Had I not had my laptop, I could have done the same thing from any library or other municipal facility in Austin: And I wouldn't be alone—about 70,000,000 Americans regularly access the Internet from public libraries, schools, and similar public facilities in public, government and municipal buildings.

Not only did T-Mobile save itself the cost of a call, I was delighted, even in the face of a failure. As an occasional user of first generation devices, I expect a few bumps when using them. Hey, even Apple products freeze. What's delightful is when the recovery from said bumps occurs in minutes and without disrupting the rest of an otherwise fully booked day. My conference call went off as planned, and yes, I recounted this story at the start of the call: I'm an advocate for both Google and T-Mobile.

You may be wondering here, "Wait…if Google's update *caused* the problem, why is this guy an advocate?" Here's the answer: Google has provided enough other value—through Gmail, its applications and Google Docs, its search tools and social APIs—that I waited for the T-Mobile G1 to be released while all of my friends were sporting their iPhones. I understood that in being an early adopter of the G1 that "bumps" were going to happen. What keeps me an advocate is that when they do happen, there is a ready solution. Who among us is perfect, right? This last point is actually worth considering: Again calling back to engagement as a participative, collaborative experience, these higher levels of engagement are essential in building durable, long-term advocates.

What Else Can I Do?

In addition to support applications, also consider the role of discussion forums. Discussion forums—the long-standing staple of member-to-member communications—offer an easy-to-implement collaborative platform. The twist is this: In addition to members, your own employees can also participate. The rule to recall is this: Any time an employee (or anyone else with a nonobvious interest in the brand, product, or service) is participating, a clear disclosure must be made. This is another reason why time spent early on—preferably with your legal support team and HR, developing effective, relevant social computing policies and then distributing these throughout your organization—is time well spent.

Discussion forums are particularly useful in providing both engaging activities, and in surfacing ideas that provide insights into future innovations with the built-in benefit of having been generated by customers. Visit any of the Meredith Publishing properties: Better Homes and Gardens, American Baby, or any of its roughly 20 other online properties. Powered by Pluck, now part of the Demand Media online community solution set, Meredith Publishing has implemented a set of communities that facilitate both extensions of the (print) magazine articles and activities, and provide ideas and direction for future magazine as well as online subjects and activities.

Collaboration extends beyond business: Nonprofits, NGOs, and governmental agencies themselves are all part of the social business evolution. In an especially insightful remark, Ian Wilson, Librarian and Archivist of Canada Emeritus, noted the following:

> "Governments will collaborate with experts, lobbyists, trade organizations, and service partners. Policy will therefore evolve and the citizen will become more engaged in the political process. To my mind social media will deliver one of the greatest leaps forward in democratic participation seen yet in our world. Government had better be ready."

In India, the work and writing of Shashi Tharoor has been significantly promoted both within and outside this democratic country through social media and the Social Web. Mr. Tharoor, no stranger himself to the challenges that can sometimes arise out of the use of the Social Web, is a leading intellectual figure in the application of social technologies to the tasks and processes of building constituencies around, and providing a voice for, social media participants.

Advocacy

Collaborative activities, in a business context, are designed to move current and potential customers up and through the engagement process toward true brand advocacy. Brand advocates are, of course, an essential factor in a brand's overall success: Not only do they promote the brand and any associated products or services, they will defend the brand when it is being attacked. The earlier example of India's Café Coffee Day and the bloggers who were rightly offended by an overly enterprising store manager made clear the beneficial impact of brand advocates.

There is a larger play to be made, however, using social technologies. Similar to the diffusion that is observed in PR—where easily identified journalists or industry experts active in traditional media give way to a foam of enthusiasts present on the Social Web, the development of brand advocates requires a deeper dive into the conversations that surround a brand, product, or service so that the advocates—and the topics around which advocates may form—can be identified and nurtured.

The degree to which a brand participates via social technologies is a good indicator of the contribution that such participation has. In the Altimeter report "Engagement db 2009," the case is made that an active social presence is associated with successful brands. *To be clear, the report does not claim that an active social presence causes or directly drives enhanced business success.* Recall the difference between causation and correlation. The report does, however, note that there is a very strong correlation between successful brands and an active social presence.

Most useful is the following realization: Whether social activity drives business success or business success provides a context for an active social presence is not the issue. Instead, the connection—the correlation—between the social activity associated with successful brands and the success of those brands arises out of the combination of business acumen and significant time spent in defined, measurable activities that engage customers. The result is a higher-than-average generation of brand advocates, further driving this (positive) cycle! In other words, it's not the social activity that matters per se: It is what happens in and around a business or organization and its marketplace as a result of this social activity. More engagement + better experiences = more advocates.

To test this idea, consider a successful business—in the profit and loss sense—that largely ignores the conversational (social) issues that surround it. Walmart in the early nineties comes to mind, with issues ranging from hiring and pay differentials to product pricing practices and new store locations. While Walmart was being attacked on all sides, its public policy, summed up, seemed to be "We can't hear you." As businesses took to the Social Web, Walmart tried as well—unsuccessfully—to create an early presence in places like Facebook. Each time it tried it was overrun by hard-core detractors, or worse stumbled over its own efforts to "control" social media.

Compare this with Walmart now: Stores are changing, becoming more open, designed and located with more input from communities, with attention to the kinds of products stocked and the quality of these products. Walmart has introduced organic foods and is working with Bazaarvoice to implement a comprehensive ratings and reviews program across its product lines. These are all efforts that would be widely praised if just about any other retailer were to have implemented them. Yet, if you search Google for "walmart brand advocates" the top results returned are still things like "Why do some people advocate boycotting Walmart?"

The insight is this: Business success by itself does not translate into overnight Social Web success, and in particular when a historical view of the business involved presents a picture that is counter to the norms associated with the successful use of social media and social technology. Furthermore, even when these brands involve themselves in social media, the results are typically lackluster, or worse, actually contribute *at first* to the further negative perception of the brand. In the case of Walmart, time will tell: tarnished reputations on the Social Web, correctly managed, do heal. Walmart appears committed to this and over time will benefit from a sustained effort to reinvent itself. As noted earlier, building a new reputation takes time. Walmart is most certainly on the right path and will ultimately get there: It is an organization built on clear goals that serve the needs of its customers, and it is run by smart people.

Back to advocates: It really is about the combination of business savvy and a genuine intent to place customers—and not the brand—at the center of the social experience. Brands like Starbucks—who openly and deliberately called on customers to help it find its way forward—and Zappos, eBay, Microsoft, Google, Nike, and SAP have all undertaken specific programs to overtly reach out and connect—to engage—with customers and constituents. The result is an increased momentum—call it brand mojo if you want—that places a further distance between these firms and their competitors while decreasing the separation between the businesses and their customers. The overall result is the emergence of brand advocates, and in particular brand advocates that are unexpected and/or nearly invisible (except to the potential customers they influence!).

When Comcast undertook its Twitter-based customer service program, the initial observation was simply: "A lot of people are complaining about us on

Twitter—maybe we should pay attention to that." This is a really insightful first step. It was not a corporate strategy to do something about the firm's image problem on Twitter, but rather a decision to go out (so to speak) and *engage customers where they are*, a point stressed by Jeff Jarvis in his work relating to creating a social business. Based on what they found, and what the firm's internal customer advocates did next, the result was profound: In the words of Comcast CEO Brian Roberts, "It has changed the culture of our company."

In addition to looking at social technology as a marketing application, and beyond the actually engagement points—support forums, communities, ratings platforms, and similar—that help shape a social business, look to your own purposeful and decided participation as a way to build a force of advocates. Combined with a decent business model, an orientation that positions your firm as the advocate for your customer is a smart play.

Review and Hands-On

Chapter 8, the first of the "social business building blocks" chapters, covered engagement in detail. Importantly, this chapter viewed engagement from the customer's perspective rather than a marketing or business perspective. This distinction is more than semantic: Analogous to catching more fish by learning to think like one, getting it right in social business means engaging your customers from their point of view. In short, it means becoming their advocate, so that they might become yours.

Review of the Main Points

The key points covered in this chapter are summarized in the following list. Review these and develop your own practical definition for *engagement* in the context of a social business.

- Engagement is a customer-centric activity.
- Move beyond ratings and reviews—useful as always, no doubt—and get into support services, ideation, and discussions.
- Implement a strategic approach to social business that specifies a plan to create advocates and then measure your performance.
- Connect customers to employees using collaborative applications.
- Finally, it's still your business. Placing customers at the center of what you do doesn't mean handing them the wheel.

Chapter 8 sets up the primary activity that differentiates a social business from all others, engagement, and a collaborative approach to working with your customers that builds your advocates. A business that steadily builds its own base of advocates is a business that steadily and surely wins over the long term.

Hands-On: Social Business Fundamentals

Review both of the following and apply them to your business or organization as you create your plan for integrating social technology into your fundamental processes.

> The "Engagement db" report from Altimeter (use Google to search for "engagement db"). Try the self-ranking; where does your firm or organization fit?
>
> http://engagementdb.com

> The whitepapers in Jive Software's resources library, in particular "Social Business Software Adoption Strategies." Look for the similar resources offered by other social business software firms, and begin building a library.
>
> http://www.jivesoftware.com/resources

Hands-On: Apply What You've Learned

Apply what you've learned in this chapter through the following exercises:

1. Make a note of every recommendation you give or receive over the next week. Rank them according to the degree of enthusiasm on the part of the recommender.

2. Review your own engagement programs, and carefully examine how you are measuring or evaluating engagement, and from whose perspective you are defining "engagement."

3. Assuming that you have an appropriate social computing and social media use policy for employee use in place now, design a plan for an ideation, support or discussion platform that will actively solicit customer-led conversations about your firm or organization, or about your brand, product, or service.

   NOTE: *If you do not have a social media and technology use policy in place, now would be an excellent time to create and implement one.*

Social CRM

Beginning with a definition, this chapter explores Social CRM, along with the tools and best practices that enable it. You'll see how to create a platform for business intelligence and customer-led design. Whether you're running a local pizza shop and want to know how to deliver a consistently excellent experience, a nonprofit seeking to drive donations and participation, or a Fortune 500 company looking to win globally, the combination of off-the-shelf tools and a bit of creative wizardry will provide a leg up.

9

Chapter Contents

Social CRM and Business Design

With the engagement process (covered in Chapter 8, "Engagement on the Social Web") more carefully defined as it applies to social interactions (participation, friending, collaboration, and similar activities) the logical next step is to put these activities together to drive business processes. Simply, given a sequence of activities that lead to collaboration—in the process involving customers along with the business (and its employees)—a big part of the business benefit in adopting social technology is putting customer and employee collaboration to work.

Social CRM involves observing, measuring, and connecting what is learned via the Social Web to those places within your business where the underlying experiences that are talked about are created. As customers begin to connect, they will form and publish opinions and put forth suggestions with regard to what they like or dislike about a specific brand, product, or service. With that comes also what they'd *like to see*, or what *could have been better*. Social CRM provides an organized way to take that information through to the next step, driving process improvement, innovation, and more.

Customers and constituents have always been willing to offer up ideas for improvements and suggested new features. The difference—and driving the new challenge—is that the suggestions are now public. This means that it's easier for you to pick up on them, and that whatever happens, others will be watching. Again, note that the public nature of the conversations is *independent* of whether or not the organizations being cited have enabled or approved of the commentary. The conversations are happening regardless, so if you're on the fence about social media, consider this as one more reason to jump in.

The challenge that the higher levels of engagement—like content creation and collaboration— present from the perspective of a business or organization is in sorting out what to do with this *newly accessible* information, along with how to do it. Customers have a basic expectation of your presence on the Social Web—after all, you're already on their TV sets and radios, and you're already in their magazines and wrapped around the online content they view. As you develop a social media *marketing* presence, your customers will also expect you to be active in the related social places where they are talking about your products or services, the places where they exchange ideas about your business (and how it might serve them better) with others who share that same interest.

Social CRM: A Social Extension of CRM

The previous chapter covered engagement in the context of social technology and social interaction. Engagement—in social business terminology versus advertising and marketing—arises out of collaboration and the active realization of a shared interest.

Two mothers facing the same cold and flu outbreak at school are very likely to compare notes through an online forum, or as part of a conversation in a discussion space like Blogher's "The Juice" that was referenced in Chapter 3, "Building a Social Business." When I was a kid, parents of school age children would sometimes deliberately send healthy younger kids over to a sick child's home in order to "catch" chickenpox. Pox parties, as they were called, served to "inoculate" before the days of actual vaccines. (The thinking being that it is much better to catch chickenpox as a child rather than to catch it as an adult.) Rather than "parties," parents now use social media—forums, for example—to compare notes on vaccine programs, cold remedies, and general health and nutrition with regard to their families.

What all of this adds up to is an opportunity to participate—something you may already be doing in some form through a social media marketing program—that leads to an opportunity to learn and adapt your products and services according to the experiences and desires of your customers. This is the entry to Social CRM, a more formalized process by which these customer conversations are picked up and used to drive change and evolution of your business. Paul Greenberg provides the following definition of Social CRM: the link to the complete discussion leading to this definition is included in Appendix A, "Terms and Definitions."

> "CRM is a philosophy and a business strategy, supported by a technology platform, business rules, workflow, processes and social characteristics, designed to engage the customer in a collaborative conversation in order to provide mutually beneficial value in a trusted and transparent business environment. It's the company's response to the customer's ownership of the conversation."
>
> PAUL GREENBERG, July, 2009

Note in Paul's definition the recognition that it is the customer that owns the conversation, and that the conversation is happening *in public*. From the perspective of a marketing manager or chief executive officer, entrepreneur, or associate director, this ownership and visibility make all the difference. It essentially mandates a response, in particular when the conversation is negative.

From a business perspective, the essential point is that an intelligent, relevant response is now a typical expectation—even perhaps a requirement—in many Social Web settings and certainly from the perspective of your customers. This is the connection point between the Social Web, social media marketing, and social business: The experience created in the presentation, delivery, and use of a product or service drives a conversation. This sequence implies a connection between that conversation and the business or organization that created it. Social CRM provides a framework for measuring, connecting, and leveraging this entire conversation cycle.

Oil and Water

Beware: some businesses and organizations will find that, like oil and water, the principles of social business simply "do not mix" with their own existing practices. Whether it's a case of "not invented here" or "we know our customers best" or most any other reason, some organizations will find it tough to listen openly to their customers, and tougher still to rebuild their internal communications channels to support receiving customer conversations and then applying them constructively to their next generation of products and services.

If you're familiar with Yelp and Amazon's ratings, you've no doubt asked yourself "What if someone says something really ugly about *me* or about *my business or organization*?" For many firms who would otherwise be interested in social media marketing, one of the roadblocks to the adoption of social technology is the idea that "If my business participates…any (negative) conversations will grow louder." But this assumption isn't quite right, and in many cases is the opposite of what actually happens. Here's why: When you participate in the conversations that matter to you, any negative conversations can actually be *reduced* over time. And, when they are not, it's a pretty clear indication that a serious social *business* program is in order!

Brent Leary

Brent Leary is co-founder and partner of CRM Essentials LLC, a CRM consulting/advisory firm focused on small and mid-size enterprises. You can follow Brent on Twitter (@BrentLeary) and read his blog here:

http://BrentLeary.com

How's that? It works like this: At the outset, recognize that customers talk about their experiences, including those that involve your products or services. If they love it or hate it and it matters to them, they'll talk about it. If the conversation is negative, it may be that they don't understand how to use your product correctly, for example, or that it doesn't work as well as they'd like. Once you've gotten that feedback—through your listening program—your next step is pretty clear: Reset their expectation or explain the correct use of the product or make the actual product better. If you do these things—giving credit to your customers for their ideas and including them in the collaborative change process that results—the negative conversations *will* decrease over time. *Failing* to address the expressed concerns or not participating at all are the sure roads to *amplified* negative conversations.

The many review sites that are now popular have accelerated the feedback process and, in general, raised the stakes for businesses of all types when it comes to the impact of conversations around brands, products, and services. Over the past few years, building on the general tendency to rate and review everything, business review sites have sprung up—for example, Angie's List (http://www.angieslist.com)—that include ratings and reviews for local businesses and service organizations. Many of these include or even focus on local businesses—plumbers, auto service providers, home contractors, and physicians. As individuals face increasingly complex choices with regard to their healthcare, for example, where consumers are simultaneously expected to take a more active role in managing their health and managing their use of healthcare services, it's natural to expect an increase in the use of customer-generated ratings and reviews. This is exactly what's happened, and it's given headaches to as many physicians (and other businesses) as it has helped.

The Wrong Way to Control a Conversation

Coincident with the rise of customer-driven ratings and reviews, a second practice—which may affect you as a consumer and of which you may not be aware—some businesses are now attempting to *curtail* the customer's right to post a review! It works like this: Buried somewhere in a "service" contract is a clause aimed at controlling bad reviews: by signing the contract, one may also be agreeing not to post negative reviews! For example, a physician's office may use a "standard" office agreement that might include a clause like this: "As a patient of this office, I agree not to talk publicly about my treatment…"

A clause like the one cited above sounds innocuous: Why would anyone talk publicly—beyond a verbal conversation with a friend or family member—about a private office visit? But in the context of ratings and reviews, it's obvious where this leads: Post a negative review, and the result may be a lawsuit claiming breach of contract. *This is the wrong way to control negative conversations.*

Obviously, there are issues in this example that go beyond the scope of this book: For example, it's not clear that such clauses—which may be seen as limiting or removing entirely an individual's right to free speech—are even enforceable. There are issues as well on the slander side—Social Web or not, if someone says something *untrue* about your business, you may have legitimate recourse. But set all of that aside for a moment: The question that pertains to social business is, "Is this the correct way to approach a well-connected consumer, or *any* consumer for that matter?" Probably not.

The bottom line is this: If the (negative) review is accurate, then the right way to use it is as a business input. From *The Washington Post,* the following excerpt is taken: You can search via Google for the following quote and find the related reports, discussions, and practices. While the subject of the following review happens to be a doctor, the same issues apply across nearly all business segments and organizational disciplines:

> *"A veteran District internist has attracted nearly 40 comments on one site, compared with the more typical one or two. Most are negative, focusing on his off-putting demeanor, dirty office and hostile staff."*

If the office condition is as the review represents, then the right response is to address and correct the issues noted in the reviews. After all, whether a negative review like the above is digital, a printed page editorial, or delivered via word-of-mouth at a cocktail party, the result is the same: *It's a customer loss for that business*. Why not pick up on the clue and fix what needs fixing?

This matters more than may be obvious at first, and Social CRM is a factor here. Beyond exposing the immediate problem(s), there is actually a deeper business issue that needs to be addressed. The comments in this review arise not so much from an untidy office, but rather from a business attitude that—without words—sends a very clear message as to that business (owner's) view of the customer. Obviously, a hostile staff and poor office conditions suggest but one thing: The customer is *at the bottom* of the "what matters most" list. It is this attitude and the resultant manner in which the business operates—more so than any physical manifestation —that drives negative reviews. Think about it: Would you write a scathingly negative review about a sweet old man running a hardware store that was a bit messy? No. But you'd very quickly write it if that same store owner made you wait, yelled at you, or otherwise made you feel anything less than appreciated. These are the deeper nuances that Social CRM uncovers, and these nuances—done right—are extremely powerful as brand touchpoints.

As someone with a leadership role in the design or marketing of a business or service organization, one of the most important decisions is how much (or how little) your organization will value hearing feedback and improving based on it, or on the internal practices that lead to an unkempt store or hiring and HR policies that result in employees that are hostile toward customers. Looked at in isolation—in a book, for example—it seems so simple but ironically is all too common in practice. The statistics collected around *how and why many small businesses fail* make the case for valuing feedback and exhibiting genuine care for customers. Again, this is simple in concept, but more difficult in practice. Social CRM can provide a big boost, provided your organization is set up to accept and respond to feedback.

This is what Social CRM is all about: the constructive use of customer feedback. Tap into the conversations about your brand, product or service and extract the data that is applicable to your firm or organization. Then—unlike basic social media monitoring and analytics— identify the sources of these posts, create relationships and connect the reported experiences *deeply* into your business, to the office manager who oversees the cleaning crew or front office staff who greets your customers. Develop an operational response that *changes* rather than masks the conversation. The result—as the conversation improves—is typically more business. At the end of the day, in one form or another, that is generally the goal. The good news is this: The fact that you are reading this book suggests you care enough about your customers to want to run your business in ways that please them. Kudos to you.

The Elements of Social CRM

Table 9.1 shows the fundamental components of a typical Social CRM program along with a handful of representative examples, broken out in boxes that parallel the basic processes of engagement. Noteworthy with regard to Social CRM are the many ways it is similar to the relationship (or lack thereof) between social media and traditional media. Social CRM is *not* a new type of CRM but is rather a fusion of the principles of CRM—data collection around a specific customer or transaction, analysis and projection of a next action with regard to that customer—with the norms and technologies that are associated with the social elements—like collaboration—that are associated with Web 2.0.

▶ **Table 9.1** Representative Elements of Social CRM

Social Activity	Platform Examples	CRM Function
Listening	Alterian SM2, Radian 6, Rapleaf, SAS Social Media Analytics, Nielsen | BuzzMetrics	Collecting raw inputs, organizing conversational data, and quantifying primary conversational measures including volume and sentiment.
Responding	Twitter (external), Yammer and Socialtext's Signals (internal), Socialcast and its integration with SharePoint	Managing a basic, participative process: Listening, understanding, responding, asking questions, and acting.
Connecting	BuzzStream, Rapleaf Faceconnector, Lotus Connections	Identifying specific influencers and linking more information about them—at their option—to listening and business data.
Collaborating	SalesForce.com, Lithium, Socialtext, Lotus Notes (internal), SharePoint and Socialcast	Tapping the ideas of influencers and the suggestions of customers to improve products and services, and thereby manage conversations.

Referring again to Table 9.1 and the general ascension in engagement as a business moves from listening to collaborating, if the approach taken to Social CRM is a new way to collect customer data and then use that (only) to push a sales message, the result will be at best suboptimal. At worst, it will be an outright failure in the same way that using social media sites to push a marketing message are less effective or downright harmful when compared with directly participating in social activities, alongside and in support of customers. Social CRM *is different* from traditional CRM, and "social" is a big part of that difference.

Social CRM: Engagement Drives Innovation

Social CRM and its potential for driving beneficial change and innovation are built around the underlying *engagement* process. Social CRM brings to that process the same sort of discipline and quantitative rigor that (traditional) CRM brings to sales programs and customer relationship efforts.

Beginning with listening, sifting, measuring, and routing conversations, a Social CRM process is decidedly customer and constituent focused. Rather than using the process to identify the next sales opportunity—which is a great business goal and direct benefit of traditional CRM—Social CRM seeks to understand what customers really want, and to take that information and feed it into the organization where it can be translated into new, superior products and services. Starbucks' "No Splash Stirring Stick," shown in Figure 9.1, is an example of just this sort of customer-driven innovation.

Figure 9.1 Starbucks' No-Splash Stick

Looking at the use of social channels by Australia's Telstra, India's Café Coffee Day and the *Hindustan Times*, Germany's Tchibo, IBM's IdeaJam, and other businesses including Comcast, Dell, Starbucks and dozens of others around the globe, listening is being taken a step further: These firms and many others are using social software like support forums—perhaps recast as ideation platforms—along with existing social communities like Twitter and Facebook to build robust *customer service and response* systems. Whether responding to ideas, crises, calls for help, or requests for information, these response systems serve to connect these businesses to their customers in ways that are fundamentally more compelling to those customers than are the more common—and highly controlled—traditional feedback channels.

Getsatisfaction.com: The Company-Customer Pact

Get Satisfaction provides a spot-on "Company-Customer Pact" that establishes the ground rules for support programs that begins with this simple reality: "We, customers and companies alike, need to trust the people with whom we do business."

You can read the entire pact here:

http://getsatisfaction.com/ccpact/

In addition to creating a closed-loop feedback, and engagement process, the firms and organizations adopting Social CRM practices are measuring these social activities and tying the results to their business objectives. This includes understanding and measuring *not just the transactional activities*—posting content, reading or writing a review, and similar activities—but also digging in and understanding *who* is involved. Identification of influencers, right along with conversational analytics, is fundamentally important.

Social CRM and the Social Web "Bill of Rights"

Joseph Smarr, Marc Cantor, Michael Arrington, and Robert Scoble offered a point-of-view on the use of personal data—not just identity, but also their activity streams ("Bob just uploaded a photo…") and the relationships they form (part of their personal social graph). The Social Web Bill of Rights is worth reviewing as you think through your Social CRM strategy.

You can read more about the Social Web Bill of Rights here:

http://opensocialweb.org/2007/09/05/bill-of-rights/

Social CRM—when viewed as a process rather than an application—looks very different as compared to traditional CRM programs. Figure 9.2 shows the complete Social CRM process, identifying the components covered in the prior section. As you look at Figure 9.2, consider how different the impact of Social CRM is when looked at from the business perspective as compared with traditional CRM: Much more than marketing and traditional media, social media expresses itself internally through Social CRM—in collaborative processes that facilitate customer-driven innovation—as much as it does externally, where conversations circulate between customers themselves. Social CRM is the process and toolset through which you can tie all of this into your business and put the Social Web to work.

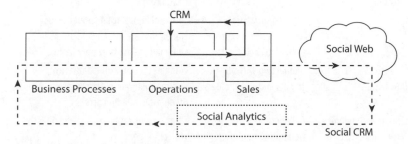

Figure 9.2 Social CRM in a Business Context

Build a Social CRM Program

Implementing Social CRM is both easier and more difficult than it might seem at first. It's easier because many of the Social CRM components are found in tools or applications that you are already using or could quickly adopt: platforms like Twitter, for example. At the same time, implementing a Social CRM is more difficult than it needs to be because not all of the applications involved work together as smoothly as they should. Depending on which platforms you (or your IT staff) choose, there will likely be gaps. It will fall to you to fill them.

Table 9.2 shows a sampling of the components that are available, from which you can assemble an overall solution. As you review the table, note the applications or solution providers you are working with now. As well, work through the sequential activities—listening, responding, connecting, and collaborating—and mentally check off what you have covered versus what you will need to spend more time considering for inclusion in your overall social business strategy.

▶ **Table 9.2** Social CRM Components

Component Examples	Used For	What this offers
Alterian SM2, Buzzmetrics, Cymfony, Google Alerts, Radian6, SAS Institute	Social media analytics	Quantifying conversational data; facilitation of monitoring and response.
CoTweet, RightNow, Rapleaf, Twitter	Listening, Responding	Source of conversations that can be monitored and used to drive response program.
BuzzStream, Gist, Rapleaf, RightNow, SAS Institute	Responding, Connecting	Prioritizing influencers and developing relationships.
BuzzStream, Gist	Tapping social profile data; connecting customers to conversations.	Source of information about the individuals that are influencing others in your marketplace or supply chain.
Appirio Cloud Connectors, Faceconnector, Informatica	Connecting with customers and stakeholders	Combines social profile data with existing customer data to improve the relationship building process.
IBM's IdeaJam, Lithium Technologies Social CRM platform Salesforce.com Ideas	Collaborating, Generating new ideas	Spurring innovation by working directly with customers.
Lithium Technologies: Reputation Engine, CRM Connect, Social Web Connect	Support, Collaboration (internal and external)	Identifying key participants in communities; combining social profiles and conversational data.

Taking the components shown in Table 9.2—or any of the others available in the market that perform similar functions—you can create an overall Social CRM program that matches the needs—and budget—of your business or organization.

Many of the social technology and traditional CRM solution providers—including those in Table 9.2—have already started creating linkages between their programs that can make this somewhat easier. Radian6, for example, has an integration program with Salesforce.com, while Scout Labs has been acquired by Lithium Technologies. The end result is that you can pull the conversations and the people behind them into a database and develop a contacts list that can be matched and integrated with your own customer data. Remember too, that in addition to ready-to-implement solutions you can always—and sometimes have to—build your own tools. As you evaluate Social CRM solution providers, be sure to ask potential solution providers about their own professional services: many offer these services or referrals to certified partners as a way to make it simpler and quicker for you to implement an integrated program.

Social CRM Use Cases

Altimeter's Ray Wang and Jeremiah Owyang have produced a useful summary and "next steps" guide that is very helpful when sorting out your Social CRM strategy. The guide is useful as a both a learning document for your team as well as a guide to choosing Social CRM solution paths.

You will find the guide here:

www.slideshare.net/jeremiah_owyang/social-crm-the-new-rules-of-relationship-management

Hope Is Not a Strategy

As you begin to craft your Social CRM program, the guiding idea is this: An effective Social CRM program begins not with hope but with a grounded, well-defined social media strategy *that extends across the organization.*

This is not to say that there is no room for experimentation: there certainly is. It is to say instead that the stakes are significantly higher with social business and investments in Social CRM than the similar entry costs (in time, dollars, and opportunity cost) for social media marketing. Where social media marketing can be "trialed" in places like Facebook or Twitter, or backed into via a discrete listening program using a free tool like Google Alerts, a Social CRM program—even a "light duty" implementation—directly involves your customers and brings them into your business. By opening up the formal listening/response/collaboration channels with customers—which is what Social CRM does—you are making a significant commitment to the formal inclusion of your customers as a component of your business.

A solid social media marketing program begins with business objectives, an understanding of the audience, and a thought-through measurement program or success assessment methodology. Social CRM is no different, and adds the requirements of creating a cross-functional team within your organization to deal with the feedback, ideas and suggestions when they start flowing. In Chapter 2, "The New Role of the Customer," I talked about workflow and the routing of critical information—at scale—directly into the parts of your organization that need to see it. These kinds of considerations and more are the added requirements in building a social business and Social CRM program. Without the ability to effectively route and track potentially large amounts of conversational data (workflow), your Social CRM efforts will quickly bog down.

Integrate the Social Experience

BatchBlue provides BatchBook as an integration tool aimed specifically at small businesses using Google applications. BatchBook connects social data with your in-house data and the Google apps you are using now.

`http://www.batchblue.com/google/`

Gigya provides integration tools across registration, social activities, and measurement as a part of its social business solution set.

`http://www.gigya.com/public/solutions/overview.aspx`

Create a Social CRM Plan

Creating a Social CRM program—organizational buy-in aside—is a straightforward process. Like social media marketing, start your Social CRM business plan with your *business objectives.* What do you want to achieve from your business or organizational perspective? *What do you want your customers to gain* as a result of this program? Be clear as well in identifying which of your customers or audience will be the focus of your initial efforts. Plan accordingly, allow time to do this "prep work" correctly, and provide plenty of opportunity for others in your organization who may be similarly interested to join with you. Here's why: One way or another, you will need the support of your entire organization. What is talked about on the Social Web is the net result of the actions of your entire organization, and there is no getting around that. If you charge into a Social CRM plan *alone,* you risk alienating the very people you need to succeed.

Begin with a team and an initial plan based on your business objectives; combine that with your listening program results. Use the conversations circulating now to shape your early programs. If you have not undertaken a best-practices-driven listening program, you'll want to initiate one. Add to this a set of metrics that are relevant to your firm or organization and define how you will recognize success. The following questions take you through the balance of the considerations as you undertake development of a project specification around Social CRM.

- What are your Social CRM objectives? For example, are you looking to improve your organization's innovation processes, effect service improvements, understand and respond more quickly to competitive offerings, or develop a customer-based influencers' program? Watch out if you answered this question "all of the above." Start with a manageable objective.

- What is your organizational culture? This matters because you are potentially pressing for internal and operational changes. If you've read *Who Moved My Cheese* (G. P. Putnam's Sons, 1998), you'll understand the significance of accounting for culture and planning for change. If you haven't read it, from the title alone you can guess the issue, and why this matters (and, why the book was a best seller!).

- What drives your delivery experiences? Regardless of whether you are manufacturer, a service firm, a nonprofit, or municipality or something else altogether if your organization serves someone—and I'm assuming it does as otherwise you probably wouldn't be reading this—then there is a process by which you create the experiences that drive their conversations about your brand, product, or service. Understanding that process is key to implementing Social CRM.

- Who else needs to be a part of your Social CRM program? At one level, the answer is "your entire organization." However, this answer doesn't really help you at a planning stage or early implementation. Who are your allies in Operations, Marketing, Customer Service, Human Resources, and Legal? What are the roles and expectations for each? Build *that* team.

- Speaking of your legal department or other similar control department, do you have social computing policies in place now for your organization? If not, add this to your task list: With employees directly participating in a Social CRM program, ensuring that they understand how to communicate outside the organization (and when/when not to) through social channels is essential.

- How will you measure success? Effectively tapping the results of a Social CRM program will necessarily involve tying business analytics to social data. What are your primary social and business KPIs, and how will you use them to tune your program and demonstrate—quantitatively—success?

Following are specific suggestions and methods for accomplishing each of the previous tasks.

Social CRM Objectives

The kick off for a Social CRM program is like that of any other marketing or business program: You start with your business objectives, combine them with the behaviors and interests of your expected participants, and use this to plan and implement your program.

One of the easiest ways to sort out which types of Social CRM solutions are right for your applications is by posing and answering questions like the following: Are your primary business objectives related to addressing an existing condition, improving margins through the work of brand advocates or through expense reductions, or focused on innovating and creating something new? Formulate your own additional questions like these for your specific situation as well.

If the answer is "addressing an existing condition," then at the top of your list might be tools like a listening platform and influencer identification, combined with a participative channel such as Twitter or similar. Gather and analyze relevant conversations, and then use a simple conversational channel to keep that dialog going. This combination provides the intelligence and precise targeting that you'll need. You can use "do it yourself" listening platforms like Alterian's SM2, Sysmos, or Scout Labs, along with an influencer identification tool like BuzzStream or Rapleaf to gather the background information you'll need to develop a conversational baseline and then track your progress.

For example, you can use listening tools to prioritize influencers as you identify the specific sources. You can then connect, through workflow processes, this listening data into your organization—into customer service, for example. You can use Twitter combined with a tool like TweetDeck, HootSuite, or CoTweet to look for specific issues and efficiently respond to them in the channel where the issues are being discussed. Even better, you can do this in real time or near real time, depending on your staffing levels, and you can use what you learn to inform your corporate blogging program or other aspects of your social-media-based marketing efforts. When creating your Social CRM program, look for the ways in which one activity (listening, for example) informs another (like internal product review meetings and product design efforts).

Alternatively, if you are looking for margin improvement through cost savings, then your focus might be the Web 2.0 tools and technologies that enable delegation of work to your customers. Dell's support forums exemplify this: Relatively few moderators and community managers acting together manage literally millions of customers (translation: Cost Savings) while the customers themselves bear the real load—much to their liking—in addressing the actual technical support issues that are the subject of the support community.

From influencer identification and relationship development to margin improvement to direct cost avoidance, Social CRM has applications across a range of business and marketplace challenges. The first order of business is, therefore, to sort out very specifically what you intend to accomplish and to clarify the business objective(s) involved. With that done, you can make your technology selection.

Social CRM applies internally—inside your organization—as well. The same triage process used to identify and connect a Social CRM program around business objectives can also be applied to internal process change and innovation. If you are seeking ideas for improved future products or radically new designs, or are looking for insights on how your organization might restructure itself (including "virtually"), then consider platforms like the Lithium ideation platform or collaboration tools from Cynapse and Jive Software. *They can be applied internally*, as Dell did with its "Employee Storm" platform, the internal counterpart to its customer-facing Idea Storm. Be sure to connect the outputs of external efforts to your internal work process: The concluding section of this chapter, "Enterprise 2.0 and Internal Collaboration," covers this aspect of Social CRM.

Looking back at Table 9.1 and Table 9.2, use your business objectives to refine the available technologies. After using your business objectives to narrow the choice of solution providers, ask the solution providers themselves to come back with a report or proposal on how they would approach your situation, and how their tools and methods apply. They'll be happy to do this and to share their case studies with you. Nothing like spreading the workload! Plus, it's a really smart way to generate a wide range of options quickly and to gain a broad perspective on what is available. *This book will slowly go out of date: Your good habits of due diligence and self-education won't.*

Organizational Culture

Along with business objectives, consider your organizational culture. How siloed is it, and why? What are you peers likely to think of a change to the way in which they work? It's quite important to get a handle on this before you start narrowing solution choices.

If your organization is broken into specific teams with minimal interaction, look for tools with automated workflow capabilities that invite collaboration across distributed teams. You'll need to send specifically filtered information to specific individuals and to have the responses shared with other internal stakeholders. If your organization is "flat," then posting a report on SharePoint, Basecamp, or Notes and inviting comments might be fine. Whatever the case, be sure that you understand and plan for the ways in which the teams that are necessary to the success of any implementation program will be looped into the process.

Your Delivery Experience

One of the more insightful aspects of Social CRM is its relationship to the processes through which your customer experiences are created. As distinct from the more sales-process-focused traditional CRM, Social CRM is all about aligning your business with your customers. This necessitates understanding the points of contact between your business and your customers.

Social CRM and the general management of conversations and adoption of Web 2.0 technologies to drive innovation depend heavily on understanding the experiences that create conversations. For Social CRM programs that are intended to change perceptions, sustain positive word-of-mouth, or address a negative situation, the identification of the root cause of the experience is essential, as generally speaking it is an underlying business process or practice that forms the root cause of these conversations.

As a well-understood example, Zappos focuses on high levels of customer satisfaction as the "root cause" for nearly everything that is said about the firm and the ways in which the company is able to operate internally. Zappos grew based on customer referrals, driven by satisfied customers, as a result of its understanding of how to create the experiences that would drive delight. For example, Zappos relies on measures of customer satisfaction more than talk time in its customer service teams. *They are able to do this because its employees understand the importance of a satisfied customer.* Compare this with call agents that are held to strict call-time standards, where getting the customer *off the phone* is instead the focus. With its various processes of delight understood, Zappos pushed the *ability to act* based on these principles out into the organization, to the very edges of its business, where its employees come into contact with customers. Employees are empowered—and expected—to "do the right thing" for Zappos' customers. And they do it.

The idea of employee empowerment is worth noting, as it too is a factor in your Social CRM program. Think about the last time you were in a restaurant, for example, and you brought an issue to a server's attention only to hear "Let me check with the manager…." Compare this with an experience where that same server is able to resolve the issue right on the spot: Some establishments have specifically trained and empowered employees to make decisions based on judgment and an understood business norm of customer delight. Which experience are you more impressed with—"I can take care of that for you" versus "Let me check on that"—and more likely to talk about favorably as a result?

Taking the idea of understanding "root causes" one step further, and again to reinforce the deep, organization-wide nature of Social CRM and the adoption of social technology, Zappos carries its mission of "customer delight" right through to its hiring practices. From Zappos CEO Tony Hsieh comes the following, which is about as "root cause" as you can get:

> *"We interview people for culture fit. We want people who are passionate about what Zappos is about—service. I don't care if they're passionate about shoes."*

By understanding your own delivery experiences and company culture, you can identify the planning scenarios—for example, changes to customer service policy or the design of your in-store checkout queuing system or online shopping cart—that will shape the use cases at the heart of your Social CRM planning process. Connect these with the identified root causes of conversations—positive or negative—and use this information to guide your planning, implementation, and measurement process.

Your Social CRM Team: It's Bigger Than "Just You"

Pick your team wisely. Though simple in concept, it's harder in practice but will make all the difference. Start with your work team: Whose idea is this "social technology" effort, and how much support for it is there? You can do Twitter alone, and many organizations have successfully kicked off what became social business programs in exactly this way. At the same time, you can't generally support a community or an ideation platform by yourself. When building your team, look back at the business processes that create the experiences you want to impact. A great starting point for your team includes someone from each of the units or functional areas who is a direct contributor or controller with regard to these processes.

As an example of what this looks like in practice, consider the efforts of Philips' Consumer Business Units, a client of mine in The Netherlands. The mainstays of Philips' implementation of social media and social business practices are built around a defined engagement process, one that depends on the participation of cross-functional teams that support their social business objectives. Marco Roncaglio, Director of Online Marketing, stressed the importance of the combination of process, dedicated resources, content strategy, and a cross-functional support team.

I asked Marco about this program and about how he and the larger team around him were approaching this:

> "In order to step up and leverage the social technology opportunity we
> felt that we had to combine a bottom-up approach—wide endorsement
> and adoption— with a top-down approach—key champions and leader-
> ship. As we are developing our long term vision, our social media content
> strategy and formally allocating dedicated resources, we are also putting
> in place an organizational foundation to support the business objectives.
> We have created a cross functional team, developed a very specific seven-
> step social media marketing planning and implementation system so that
> we can identify and spread best practices, established core solution and
> technology components (for example, listening tools, blogging and similar
> platforms) and of course defined the business principles and social com-
> puting policies that apply immediately, across the organization."

The approach that Marco and the combined teams across Philips' Consumer Business Unit have taken is instructive in this regard: They have carefully defined what they want to accomplish, gathered together the resources (people, budgets, tools) needed to succeed, and established the metrics and policies that will guide their efforts.

Gautam Ghosh

Gautam Ghosh is an HR professional and colleague of mine in India with a passion for internal collaboration: You can follow Gautam on Twitter (@gautamghosh) and read his blog here:

http://www.gautamblogs.com

When building your team, include your legal team or similar policy advisors. While we all know it's easier to beg forgiveness than to ask permission, as you move from a contained, experiment-driven approach to social media and even limited forays into social business, the stakes will begin to rise. The cost of forgiveness may become unacceptably high, and so to not involve the parties that really need to be involved—like corporate legal—borders on recklessness and irresponsibility. Take the time up-front to get important stakeholders involved early.

On the specific issue of legal involvement, recognize that the professionals in your legal team—like your IT department and your corporate systems administrators—have jobs to do, and those jobs generally involve protecting the business as well as protecting you in the context of the business. Rather than viewing legal as an adversary, take the time to understand the issues that are specific to your firm or organization's use of social technology and then factor them into your Social CRM plan.

If the idea of pulling legal, finance, HR, and others into the process seems daunting, consider the following:

- You have something to add, and so do these other teams. A law degree or HR certification on their part does not mean that you can't understand their perspective or their concerns, anymore than your business, marketing, or engineering degree means that they can't understand yours. Ask questions, understand their points of view, and offer (them) the information they need to really understand why you believe the program you are proposing will be beneficial to your business.

- Involve these other teams early. People love "ownership" and "stakes" —we're social, remember? As soon as you have your basic business case in order—objectives, audience, metrics, goals—start building your wider team. Make sure that there is (still) an opportunity for them to change things or add ideas of their own. You'll look "smartest" when you are able to make them feel "great" about what you are proposing and proud of their role in it.

- Ultimately, the adoption of social technology is a business decision. Legal, HR, and Finance should be part of your program to help you build the business.

Social Computing Policies

Speaking of your business or organization's legal counsel, this team is central to your development of social computing policies. Social computing policies are an absolute requirement for Social CRM, so right there you have a reason to create allies in Legal. *Moving forward on a social technology program without first establishing the ground rules—aka "social computing policies"—for participation within your organization is a very bad idea. In the best case, failing to develop such policies ahead of time will expose your program to the possibility of avoidable setbacks. In the worst case, those setbacks will actually happen, and your program will fail as a result.*

For many applications of Social CRM, there are a handful of primary considerations that are common across the promulgation and adoption of social computing policies. For example, advising those who may be using social tools to post in a business context to avoid the use of the first-person *plural* (saying "we" implicates the firm along with the person posting) and instead always using the first-person *singular* "I," or posting "forward-looking" financial or operational information—talking in advance about an upcoming product launch—or failing to disclose one's relationship with the company or organization (all of which are potential offenses under the law). All of these are essential practices that employees in an organization using social technology must understand.

As a starting point, take a look at Altimeter's compiled examples of social computing policies: The easiest way to get a comprehensive set of social media policies in place is to craft a couple of relevant examples, and then take them to your legal department and ask them to review and develop a version for your company

247

■

BUILD A SOCIAL CRM PROGRAM

Social Computing Policy Examples

Altimeter has compiled a representative listing of social computing policies, including large and small businesses as well as nonprofit and service organizations. You will find the listing by searching "social computing policy examples" or by visiting the following URL:

http://wiki.altimetergroup.com/page/Social+Media+Policies

Measure Impact and Results

Finally, develop your plan for measurement in advance. Alongside your business objectives—step 1 in the planning process—pick off the financial or quantitative Key Performance Indicators (KPIs) that are relevant to the Social CRM program you are designing.

An important note here: While I have stressed the importance of quantitative measures, not all relevant assessments are purely numerical. Your business and marketing "gut" is part of this too. It's important to strike a balance between the needs of your Operations or Finance departments and those of the other members of your team. This is why it's essential to understand your company culture, and to build your team earlier rather than later: If your organization is driven by numbers, you'll need lots of numbers. If not, then maybe you can do with less. On this note, remember too the reasoning behind involving a wide range of people within your organization: By doing so, you'll be exposed to the ways in which each evaluates performance. As a result, you'll know how to structure your KPIs or financial ROI objectives and measures.

SAS Institute: Social Media Analytics

Launched at the SAS Global Forum in 2010, SAS Institute's Social Media Analytics toolset integrates with SAS' CRM and business intelligence components to create an end-to-end analytics tool that ties social analytics to business decision processes.

http://www.sas.com/

In the end, the key is to build a set of stakeholders into your Social CRM program *early,* along with a defensible set of metrics that put your plan on the same evaluative basis as any other capital program inside your organization. By doing this, not only do you increase your likelihood of gaining approval for your plan, you increase your probability of success outright. Most organizations run on numbers for a reason, and including the necessary measures and a range of people from across the organization means you'll all know when you're heading toward success, and that everyone gets a share of the credit when you get there.

Enterprise 2.0 and Internal Collaboration

It might surprise you to find a discussion around what is often referred to as "Enterprise 2.0" in a social media marketing book, but it fits here. If you don't know what Enterprise 2.0 is, don't worry—you don't need to understand it in depth to see how it fits with social media and Social CRM. In fact, the same basic technology that powers Social CRM—the communities and social networks that people frequent—also powers Enterprise 2.0. Enterprise 2.0, simply put, conveys the idea of a socially connected organization in which employees collaborate, facilitated through the formal adoption of Web 2.0 technologies, *inside* the organization, in an analogous way to what is happening through Web 2.0 *outside* the organization.

Enterprise 2.0 is the analogy to consumers' (or anyone's) collective use of social media and social technologies, applied to the collaborative and shared tasks and processes *within* a firm or organization. In the same way that a family considering a vacation may use a travel blog and the associated comments on an online travel community or relevant ratings and reviews to plan a trip, employees in an organization or the staff members of an advocacy group might use an internal blog, support forum, or the personal profiles of each other to build relationships and collaborate in the pursuit of business objectives. In fact, they may well have used a social tool like a wiki to create those business objectives in the first place.

Here's the connection to Social CRM, and to the Social Web and the larger use of social technologies: Enterprise 2.0 involves the adoption and use of Web 2.0 technologies for internal collaboration, relationship building, and similar activities. When a business is truly connected to its customers, or equivalently an organization is connected to its stakeholders, it *must be able to respond in a timely manner* when customer or stakeholder issues arise. Enterprise 2.0—the adoption of social technologies inside the organization—facilitates an organization's ability to respond to its customers.

Ted Shelton

Ted Shelton is CEO of The Conversation Group; Ted's prior roles include Chief Strategy Officer at Borland. Ted's firm focuses on the transformative impact of social technologies on business. You can connect with The Conversation Group (theconversationgroup.com/), follow Ted on Twitter (@tshelton), and read his blog here:

tedshelton.blogspot.com/

The social business framework can be thought of as layers, starting with the innermost core, Enterprise 2.0. Social business practices build outward—including social media marketing, and the conversations on the Social Web itself that collectively wrap around and define the business. Figure 9.3 shows this layered view.

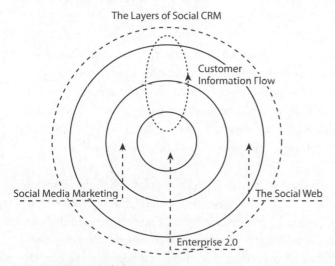

Figure 9.3 The Layers of a Social Business

It might be helpful to take a minute and understand why the adoption of Enterprise 2.0 practices—certainly not the only way to approach Social CRM but one that really brings a business and marketing focus to it—is so important. Consider traditional advertising and some of the eyeglass scratch-repair kits you may have seen advertised on TV, or many of the teeth whitening products that have been pushed your way online. Use Google to research these, and draw your own conclusions about how well they actually work: Fundamentally, most of them don't work, or at least not as claimed. Yet people still buy them, because traditional advertising is well-suited for creating demand. By contrast, when you search for these products on the (social) Web, you find the actual experiences of people who've tried them. In the case of the specific products mentioned, the actual experiences, ratings, and reviews drive considerably *less* demand.

The Social Web brings the power of collective experiences to the purchase process: When you use the Social Web to research teeth whiteners or eyeglass scratch-repair kits—or anything else—you benefit from the collective experience of anyone who has tried these products and written a review about the experience or its performance. This in turn drives the impact of social media on business and marketing, and in part gives rise to the adoption of social media as a part of a marketing program. Social CRM wraps this entire process, pulling the information contained in the reviews all the way back into the design of the products. Who knows: Maybe one day there will actually be a $50 teeth whitener that really works in an hour, or a $10 scratch repair kit that actually repairs your glasses. But don't hold your breath. Firms that will willingly lie to you, or who will create and run deliberately misleading advertisements, are least-of-all likely to seek customer input in the development of better products. Social technology is more likely—at least in the short term—to weed out these types of firms.

What Defines a Social CRM Program?

A typical social media program contains a listening component, an outreach component, and a participative component. It may include, for example, a social media analytics dashboard like those offered by Radian6 or Oxyme, a blogger outreach program powered by a tool like BuzzStream or Sysomos, and a participative presence, or brand outpost, in the form of a Facebook business page or Twitter presence where outbound messages are directed to fans and followers in response to specific questions, suggestion, or other comments.

Social CRM takes it one step further: Social CRM recognizes that conversations that occur on the Social Web—and in particular the conversations that marketers are *initially* interested in "controlling"—are in fact caused by experiences that result from processes *inside* the organization. By adding the ideation and support platforms, for example, to a social media program a direct connection is created between the business and its customers. This connection is the start down the path to social business, as it combines the collaborative underpinning of Web 2.0 technologies with the primary business inputs and processes that determine the outputs of that business or organization that show up in conversations on the Social Web.

Look back at Figure 9.2 for a refresher on this path from social media marketing to social business. It should be clear at this point that if the effort stops with social media *marketing*— if the social-media-based marketing programs are in place and working, and customers or constituents are actively providing input to the business— *without* connecting and enabling the organization internally that in fact a significant exposure to the business may be created.

Why? Consider the response when someone is asked for an opinion or review based on a prior experience with a product or service, and that opinion is subsequently *and overtly* ignored. The result is negative, ranging from mild disengagement to outright hostility. The same is true on the Social Web: Invite customers in, and then ignore them, and you can be sure that the next round of conversations will reflect this. Pulling customer conversations into your business through a Social CRM program helps avoid this kind of disconnect.

Enterprise 2.0 is the final element of your Social CRM program: Enterprise 2.0 is the internal connective tissue that enables, informs, and connects employees to customers, or staff to constituents. Consider the work of Bob Pearson at Dell: A large part of his work—and the business drivers for the formation of the Andy Sernovitz' Social Media Business Council that Bob now heads—reflect the significant work that is required to prepare an organization to implement social business practices in general and Social CRM in particular.

W. Edwards Deming and Social CRM

In the early 1950s, statistician William Edwards Deming offered a significantly different approach to the identification and handling of defects and the management of manufacturing processes associated with defect-sensitive inputs. In a parallel to social technologies, Deming noted— among other things—that failing to address the defects (or limits on variations) of inputs made the management of output quality difficult if not impossible.

In the same way, failing to address the internal processes ("upstream" in the language of Deming) that create customer experiences ("downstream") effectively removes any chance of managing the resultant conversations about a brand, product or service.

For more about W. Edwards Deming, see:

http://en.wikipedia.org/wiki/W._Edwards_Deming

http://www.britannica.com/EBchecked/topic/157093/W-Edwards-Deming

At this point it should be clear that there is an order to the integration of social technologies by businesses and organizations. There is also—as a direct parallel—a steady raising of the stakes at each step up. Traditional advertising is the easiest from a marketer's perspective because it cleanly separates marketing from operations and avoids the complications of customers who can "talk back." Likewise, traditionally structured businesses are able to operate in silos—and tap the efficiency associated with these industrial-age business process innovations—precisely because any defects or shortcomings can be addressed after the fact, after the traditional advertising messages and promotional tools have done their jobs.

Social technologies mess this up, in a major way: They literally turn siloed business processes on their heads, as customers are suddenly not only on an equal footing in terms of access to the information needed to make a smart choice, but are also equipped with this information before the purchase has occurred, effectively short-circuiting the traditional funnel. As you move from social-media-based marketing to social business, consider in detail the impact of this type of reorientation on your current business processes. Enterprise 2.0 can really help you in this regard.

Sun Microsystems: Web 2.0 in the Workplace

Sun Microsystems published a report on its own internal social platform, "The Estuary Effect," in 2008. The platform is featured in a related post titled "Relevance of Enterprise 2.0 for HR" published in 2010. You can read the post and download the original report here:

http://blogs.sun.com/vsehr/entry/relevance_of_enterprise_2_0

Firms such as Dell, Philips, and Sun Microsystems are using internal collaboration and knowledge-sharing applications to reduce innovation cycle times and respond more efficiently to customers. Sun Microsystems, for example, has created its own internal platform, SunSpace, that supports rich content types—video, photos, podcasts—and collaborative discussions between employees *and across divisions*. Not only does this speed the conveyance of information, it provides ready access to the employee-held knowledge that can facilitate the innovation process and customer/supplier/partner response programs.

Internal connectivity and knowledge sharing is particularly applicable when dealing with large numbers of customer suggestions: See Table 9.3 for some suggested starting points in creating an internal platform for collaboration around customer-generated ideas. Starbucks, for example, has received about 80,000 "ideas" from its My Starbucks Ideas platform since its launch in 2008. Based on these, about 200 innovations have been put into actual practice following internal discussion, as well as *external* reviews in full public view on the "My Starbucks Idea" site. Two hundred innovations between 2008 and 2010 works to an average of *two customer ideas implemented every week*. The business benefit is obvious: Starbucks stock price has recovered (and at a faster rate than other industry competitors). Microsoft has picked up on the same theme in its Windows 7 advertising, featuring testimonials wherein *customer* ideas that resulted in a specific software feature are highlighted to convey a sense of ownership for the product to Microsoft's *customers*. For a firm whose biggest celebrations were historically centered on "launch days"—which celebrate Microsoft *employees*— placing the *customer* at the center and making the customer the star is very smart.

▶ **Table 9.3** Representative Enterprise Collaboration Platforms

Platform Provider	Component Type	More Information
Jive Software	Internal collaborative communities	www.jivesoftware.com/
Lotus Notes Lotus Connections	Internal collaborative messaging and discussion applications	www.ibm.com/software/lotus/
Lithium Technologies	Support communities and Social CRM platforms	www.lithium.com
Oracle	Internal (employee) collaboration based on social and conversational data	www.oracle.com/socialcrm/
SharePoint	Collaboration, information management, and intranet-based collaboration	sharepoint.microsoft.com/
Socialtext	Connecting employees across the organization and specifically around social and conversational data	www.socialtext.com/

Review and Hands-On

Chapter 9 built on customer engagement and collaboration—the subject of Chapter 8— wrapping it around the business and then bringing it inside the organization. Collaboration is a key factor in creating the strong linkages that connect engaged customers and constituents with the organizations that create the product and service-related experiences that are the subject of the conversations on the Social Web.

Connecting these conversations with the organization—through the sequential process of listening, identifying influencers, distilling key issues, and soliciting ideas—is key to deriving business value: Social CRM—the connection of customer information though tools that operate internally using the same technological constructs as the Social Web—defines the connective tissue that enables customer-business collaboration.

Review of the Main Points

The key points covered in Chapter 9 are summarized below. Review these and develop your own vision and plan for a Social CRM program.

- Social CRM is less about a new form of CRM than it is a fusion of social technology—Web 2.0—and the business-centric analytical processes associated with CRM.

- Social CRM connects external conversations and ideas to internal functions and personnel who are able to act upon this information to improve the customer or constituent experience.

Going back to the purchase funnel plus feedback concept that powers social-media-based marketing, Social CRM is the primary set of technologies that draws this feedback—measurably—down into the business. It is through CRM that a planned, replicable program for managing the conversations that occur on the Social Web can be implemented.

Hands-On: Social Business Fundamentals

Review both of the following and apply these to your business or organization as you create your plan for integrating social technology into your fundamental processes.

1. Review the Sun Microsystems, SAS Institute, and IBM/Lotus products and associated case studies: While these are all large organizations, the principles of Social CRM are sufficiently well demonstrated that they can be applied to almost any business.

2. Review the general toolsets in the tables in this chapter, and take note of the order in which specific tools or technologies are applied. As with social-media-based marketing in general, the implementation process begins *not* with technology but rather with business objectives and strategy.

Hands-On: Apply What You've Learned

Apply what you've learned in this chapter through the following exercises:

1. If you haven't done so already, look at the social computing policy examples at the Altimeter site. In addition, visit the sites of firms or organizations like yours to see what they have done. Imitation—followed with an in-house legal review—is the sincerest form of … getting there faster!

2. Work with your IT or other applicable department to design a pilot program for internal collaboration. The exercise will challenge your organization, so choose a small project and recruit enthusiastic volunteers.

3. After completing the first two exercises, prepare and deliver a presentation to your colleagues (or customers, if you are a consulting firm or agency) on Social CRM.

Social Objects

10

Businesses wanting to tap the Social Web for marketing often face a crossroads in the design of the central strategy that guides their social media program. Do they join an existing community built around a point of interest relevant to their customer base, or build their own community around a specific brand, product, or service? This chapter explains how to accomplish either, and why ultimately your approach to social media and business needs to serve the interests of the participants involved to be successful.

Chapter Contents

What Is a Social Object?

A *social object* is something that is inherently talkworthy, something around which people will naturally congregate and converse. In the current context of social media—after all, social objects have existed since humans began socializing—a social object forms the link between participants at the center a conversation. Social objects anchor the online communities in which its conversations take place. Simply put, the social object is the "what" that people talk about.

Social objects include things that are as small or as granular as a blog post, a photo, or similar piece of content. People will certainly discuss any of these in a social setting. Think of Twitter and Flickr, for example, both of which are applications built around basic social objects such as short posts or photos, respectively. On Twitter, for example, one member posts something and then ten others talk about it. There are also larger social objects—the big things that people are interested in, such as the environment, politics, and art. These types of social objects can also sit at the center of community, drawing people together based on their shared interests in these kinds of topics or themes.

> *"Definition: A Social Object is some 'thing' we* share *with others as part of our social media experience on the social web."*

> GLENN ASSHETON-SMITH, 2009

What are some examples of the kinds of social objects that will pull large groups together? National pastimes and sports like baseball, cricket, NASCAR, and Formula 1 are just the sorts of activities that tens or hundreds of millions of people around the world will readily associate with and talk about. They'll form fantasy leagues—clearly a social construct—in order to extend their own level of participation. Fans gather around celebrity sites to share stories and feel a part of the excitement, while retirees readily join up with others in the same life stage in AARP's online community (www. aarp.org/online_community/) to talk about what the future may hold. Social objects extend to the more ordinary as well—a new mobile phone, a programming language, and a vacation destination can all be viewed as social objects. Oh, and did I mention pets and babies? They're both good candidates too!

More so than the granular elements—the posts and photos and videos—this chapter focuses on the larger social objects around which a community has been built, or could be built. This is because the larger social objects are generally more useful as the central elements that ultimately tie back to a cause, brand, product, or service.

Twitter, as an example, is built around short posts. This is great for individuals who want to share thoughts. So, Twitter is really useful as a place to participate and learn about what people are saying about your firm or organization, and to maintain a conversation with them. Twitter is great for building outreach, support, or information channels. Dell and Comcast are great examples of this. So are KinkFM (`@kinkfm`) and SomaFM (`@somafm`), my favorite radio stations: They use Twitter in part to push their playlists along with news and events to listeners.

As a business or cause-based organization, however, your business objectives are more likely rooted in connecting people and the passions that they have with the properties of your products and services that enable *them to excel*, to *fulfill their objectives*. This generally means that you'll be building or working around larger social objects—passions, lifestyles, and causes—and using them in ways that will facilitate engagement (collaboration) with your brand, product, or service. Compared with the example of Twitter as an outbound channel, it is much more likely that your community would be built around a passion like running than around the individual posts or photos that runners might actually share within that community.

Taken together, social objects are essential elements in the design of a social media marketing program built around a sense of community: Social objects are the anchor points for these efforts and as such are the "magnets" that attract participants and then hold a community together. While it may seem like so much semantics, when compared to the way in which people are connected or to whom they are connected, the social object provides the underlying rationale or motive for being connected at all. In short, without the social object, there is no "social."

Jyri Engeström

Sociologist, Jaiku cofounder, and now Google Product Manager, Jyri Engeström coined the term "social object" as a label for the things that people socialize around. Jyri provides a nice discussion of social objects in this video, on Vimeo:

`http://vimeo.com/4071624`

You can follow Jyri on Twitter (`@jyri`) and read his blog here:

`http://www.zengestrom.com/`

Take a look at the operational definition of "social object" at the start of this section again. What it really says is this: People will congregate around the things *they* are most interested in, and will talk about them with *others who share that interest*. This is what lies at the heart of the Social Web and applies directly to the use of larger social objects—a lifestyle, for example—as the starting point for a community program versus the granular objects like posts or photos. These small, shareable chunks of content need to be present; otherwise, what would actually be shared? For purposes here, though, the focus is on the larger objects: the objects that give rise to the interest in the community and the act of sharing itself.

By looking at the larger objects—human interests and pursuits such as quilting, being an entrepreneur, or looking for a job—it's easier to identify and build a social-media-based strategy that includes a community effort and helps the participants in that community be "better" at the things they are love or are interested in. People look to spend time with others like themselves, talking about the things in which they have a shared, common interest or purpose as an enrichment of their own existence. Your challenge is to connect those interests to the things you provide through your business or organization that facilitate their pursuit: Getting this right essentially ensures that the conversations which follow will help you grow your business over the long term.

Marketers, Beware!

The human tendency to form associations around interests is, ironically, both what powers traditional media and what leads people to avoid it. Virtually all traditional media marketing operates in the same basic way: On TV, a viewer's attention is interrupted so that a message may be inserted. Radio, print, direct mail, telemarketing, online advertising, Gmail's advertising sidebar, skywriting, and in-store sampling promotions are likewise all predicated on the underlying condition of someone paying attention to something that can be systematically interrupted. It even operates in day-to-day life; after all, as I often ask, *If you couldn't interrupt me, how would you reach me?* The answer, by the way, is via the Social Web, by participating in the same things as I am participating in.

People form associations around passions, lifestyles, and interests—watching an episode of "Lost" or shopping at a Whole Foods Market, for example—*because they enjoy doing these specific things*, and because they enjoy socializing as a part of the process. This kind of association and attention—shoppers at Whole Foods are actively engaged in the Whole Foods experience—creates the opportunity for an interruption, a relevant offer: "Would you care to try a bite of wild-caught Alaskan salmon?" The next thing you know, you're serving wild caught Alaskan salmon for dinner. To be sure, the Whole Foods Market experience flows from its associates who love their jobs, who have been specifically trained and motivated to deliver an exceptional experience. *Disclosure: My brother is the Store Team Leader in the Coral Springs, FL, Whole Foods Market.*

At the same time, the continuous barrage of interruptions—the oft-quoted but never sourced "3,000 messages per day" that come your way—also causes people to shy away when they see an interruption coming. When Jon Stewart says, "We'll be right back…" he means it, literally. He and his viewers (hence "we") are *all* going to disappear for a few minutes, maybe to grab a beverage, or maybe to search via Google for the background of the guest on that evening's *Daily Show*. Do anything, evidently, except watch the ads.

No More Interruptions

By repeatedly intruding into the personal attention streams of an audience, marketing has created a challenge for itself when it comes to social media. Unlike traditional media, where interruptions are part of the media stream's inherent properties, the opportunity and mechanism for an interruption is decidedly weaker on the Social Web. Interruptions are replaced by choice-based actions, under the control of the content consumer rather than the content provider. This makes the social object—the point around which social exchange occurs—fundamentally important. It also makes the way in which a marketer uses or participates in the context of that social object critical to success.

The shift in perspective—from the position of control to respect for the now-in-control participant—means that it is not always immediately obvious how to participate as a marketer in a social setting. Default behaviors—placing Facebook display ads like so many street postings scattered around a popular part of town—abound in the hopes that with so many people collected around Facebook activities that someone will notice the attendant advertising. Guess what? Some do. Facebook ads work, but they aren't (by themselves) social.

To be sure, this traditional approach to the Social Web can work in the same way that traditional advertising works on TV (through interruption and exposure), which is to say "can work pretty well." Display ads and similar traditional advertising efforts ported to the Web can be effective. Even better, they are measurable and can be tuned through established A/B testing efforts. So, display ads will likely be part of your overall program for the foreseeable future. But again, *display ads aren't social*, beyond the conversation that sometimes forms around the ad itself, for example as with Super Bowl spots.

The important aspect to understand here is that social media marketing is an extension, a complement (and sometimes the fundamental driver) of an overall marketing program. Getting the design of the social media marketing program right means tapping an additional and nonduplicative set of resources—social technologies and the social interactions and the connection points they enable. These *social* activities can help you sustain interest and activity around your business beyond the immediate awareness and point of sale advertising efforts: These social activities are ultimately built around one or more social objects.

This is why the social object—and your approach in creating, sustaining, or otherwise connecting the interest and actions that form around it to your brand, product, or service—is important. Because you can't easily interrupt people on the Social Web—at least not twice—you have to choose a social object that is inherently meaningful to some portion of your customer base and implement a *participative* strategy that naturally connects your business to your audience, through that social object. Figure 10.1 shows the Pampers Village community. The social object—babies, along with their parents' interest around all-things-baby, sits at the core. Pampers, as a product, is clearly relevant and connected but is otherwise removed from the central focus, as it should be. The focus is parenting and the social activities that happen around parenting.

Figure 10.1 The Pampers Community

Why Social Objects Matter

What is it about the Social Web and social media that engages people, and why do they congregate around specific activities or sites? There are actually two answers to this: First, people have in general—and now at least in some manner in most parts of the world—adopted social technologies as a means of keeping in touch. To be sure, it is only a minority of the global population that is involved, for a variety of reasons, but it is also steadily increasing. Sooner or later, the conversations in your markets will flow onto the Social Web. More likely, given that you are reading this, your market is already involved, whether through basic mobile services like SMS or always-on, always-with-you, broadband social applications.

Second, and especially in the United States and throughout the Americas and Europe along with many parts of India, China, and Russia, *the relationships created via the Social Web have become real* for the participants involved. This includes aspects of relationships like identity, reputation, trust, and participation. Do not underestimate this, as it strongly suggests the norms for your own online social conduct and it suggests how powerful the relationships you ultimately build online can actually become.

As a quick insight, when I first started working in India, I was immediately struck by the realization that I had two distinct sets of "physical"—or "3D friends" as my colleague Beth Harte would say—in the United States and India. As I traveled back and forth, I would simply switch between these two groups of friends and off I'd go. But I also had a third community, one that was always present, and one that never moved: Twitter. It surprised me the degree to which the "real" aspect of my Twitter community had snuck up on me, as my tweets had moved from pure business to a mix of business and personal. It seems so obvious, yet until I actually experienced it this had escaped me. If you haven't already, take the time to internalize the importance of the connections that people are making with each other through social technologies and especially through social networks. They're real.

The connection back to social objects is this: When you set out to build an audience around something that ultimately connects to your brand, product, or service, it's got to be something that connects people in the same way and for the same reasons as any other competing social activity when viewed *from their perspective*. Fish aren't interested in lures: fish are interested in eating. The online communities that people join and build relationships inside of are as real as any other social interaction; their rationale for joining and their evaluation of accrued personal benefits associated with membership and participation will be made in that same context. It sets a tough standard for your involvement, but meeting that standard is equally rewarding.

The combination of the increasingly "real world" aspect of social computing—participation in social networks and the engagement in personal and professional life in collaborative, online tasks—along with the emergence of meaningful social objects in that same context creates a social space where real interest flourishes. Creating these experiences and then connecting them to a business objective is an important factor in building a strong and durable social presence online.

Build on Existing Social Objects

When you begin formulating the plan for your use of social technology in your business, the perspective shifts to that of your customers and stakeholders (or employees, for internal social platforms). What are *they* interested in? What are the things that they are passionate about, or want to know more about? This will almost always raise the question of using an existing social object—something your customers are already collecting around—as a starting point in your own program. And well it should: Creating a social presence is more about participation in something larger than your own brand, and less about building yet another website and then expecting your customers to come to you.

Building around an existing social object provides immediate benefits, but at the same time presents a distinct challenge: On the plus side, those who find relevance in a specific social object will naturally congregate around it and talk about it. That's great, because it means you don't have to build that community—it already exists. Your first action—which you can accomplish with an effective listening program—is therefore to create an inventory of the communities and community activities that already exist, and around which your customers or constituents are already gathering. Also, because the social object has been established by the community members, the social object itself, along with the community around it, has a life if its own. This means that you don't have to keep it going, saving you the cost of maintaining the underlying interest in the community.

Of course, with an existing community or online interest group built around, for example, a lifestyle, passion, or cause-related social object comes a challenge: That challenge is connecting it to your brand, product, or service and building a visible, durable link between that object and your business or organization. It also raises the bar, so to speak, in terms of your obligation to remain relevant to the actions, interests, and standards of conduct of the preexisting community. Again, this means looking very specifically at the way in which whatever it is that you do or offer makes your customers' participation around the existing social object *better*, from *their* perspective.

This kind of reflection and planning leads right into successfully building a business presence around a social object: You (meaning, your professional self, your business, or your organization) become an actual, identifiable participant that is valued because of the enhanced experience your presence brings to the party. You may accomplish this through branded participation, or you may empower specific people, via your internal social media usage and conduct policies. However you participate, as you do you will come to be seen as a trusted resource and a part of the community, and you will have put in place a durable and relevant link to your customers, through the social object that you have *collectively* built around.

Build a Presence

Building a presence around an existing social object is a straightforward—but not necessarily simple—process. The following steps define the process: Each is explained in more detail.

1. Identify a suitable social object.
2. Create and plan your business connection alongside it.
3. Become a part of that community: give back, enrich other participants' lives, and build the community further.

Identify a Social Object

The first step in anchoring your brand, product, or service is sorting out where to actually connect to a preexisting community. The main questions to ask yourself (or your agency or work team, if the overall social strategy is in the hands of a distributed team) are the following:

- What is it that the people you want to participate with have in common with each other?

- Why are they participating in this activity?

- What do they like to do, and what is it about these activities that they find naturally talkworthy?

- How does your firm or organization fit into the previous points?

- Specifically, how can you improve the experience of the current participants as a result of your being there?

With the answers to the previous questions, you are ready to plan your own presence in that community, and you've got the beginnings of how this involvement can be tied to your own business objectives as you simultaneously become a genuine participant in this community.

What are some of the social objects that successful community participation has been built around? Table 10.1 provides a handful to get you started. More will be said about these in the sections that follow.

▶ **Table 10.1** Social Objects that Support Communities

Brand	Social Object	Participant/Brand Connection
Dell	Entrepreneurship	Entrepreneurs and small businesses use Dell hardware.
Pepsi	Women's Lives	Trop50 is a naturally healthy drink for you and your family.
Found Animals	Pets	Found Animals provides adoption services for that appeal to people.
Pampers	Babies	Babies and diapers…go together.
Red Bull	Action Sports	If two people are competing anywhere on the planet, one is wearing a Red Bull logo.

Looking at the brands and social objects in Table 10.1, the main take-away at this point is that each brand has identified for itself an existing social object around which to place itself in an existing social context. This is directly analogous to the process through which a brand is mapped to a core consumer value or articulated business purpose in traditional advertising: Where the advertising anchor points provide a context for communicating what a brand is or what it stands for, the social object provides the context for consumer and stakeholder participation in the activities that are related to the functional aspects of a brand, product, or service.

Create a Relevant Presence for Your Business

Once you've identified a viable social object, the next step is to connect to it. You've got choices in how you attach a particular business process to a social object: You may create a service that you offer, for example, that can itself become part of the way in which your audience pursues its involvement with the social object: Nike+ accomplishes this by connectors runners with its shoes through a service that connects runners...with other runners.

You may be thinking that the social object has to be large, or that larger brands—perhaps because they are perceived (not always correctly) to have "more resources" (they have profit and loss pressures, too)—have an easier time. Not true. Social objects come in all sizes, and you can generally find one that applies to just about any business audience segment of interest. Look again at Table 10.1: Being an entrepreneur or owning a small business, the care for abandoned animals, babies, action sports, and women's health are all built around powerful social objects. Not only is each of these a powerful social connector—you could easily throw a social event around any one of these topics—they are also perfect alignment points between customers and businesses that operate in these same consumer segments. This is what social objects are all about: They form the common-interest-based connection between your brand, product, or service and your customers, constituents, and employees.

Become Part of the Community

With your social objects identified and an activation program that connects your business into that activity built around it, attention turns to growing and supporting the community. Think about showing up at a friend's party: Unless specifically told otherwise, you'd likely bring a small gift to share: an appetizer or dessert, or maybe a bottle of wine if the setting is appropriate. The point is this: This sort of value exchange is recognition that a social gathering among friends is a collective activity, one that *is made better* as more participants contribute and share. Your business presence in a community or activity built around a social object works the same way: As but one of the participants—remember that the activity centers around the social object, and not you—your program will generally work better if you are an equal co-contributor to the general well-being of the community and its specific participants.

The result—looking back on the overall process—is that you have created a space for, or joined into, the interests, lifestyles, passions, and causes that matter to your customers and stakeholders. By practicing full disclosure and by taking care to contribute as much or more than you gain, you have successfully anchored your business in what matters to your customers, made things better for them, and created a durable supporting link that ties back to your business objectives.

Pets as Social Objects

Found Animals, based in Los Angeles, California (www.foundanimals.org), provides a great example of how a powerful social object—the love of pets and concern for their care—combined with a thought-out presence and community participation— come together to create a successful organization. Found Animals became an operating foundation in March 2008, hiring its first employee, Executive Director Aimee Gilbreath, at that same time. The foundation is committed to increasing the rate and quality of pet adoptions, thereby lowering pet euthanasia. To succeed, Found Animals provides financial and business-model support to the Los Angeles municipal animal care facilities with a focus on adoption, spay/neuter, microchipping, and licensing. Clearly, the love, care, and concern for animals—of any type, especially "companion animals"—is a natural, powerful social object around which a community can be created.

I spoke with Andrew Barrett, Director of Marketing for Found Animals, about how social media factored into the overall outreach and awareness programs.

> "We have several key messages intended for current and future animal adopters and we want our audience to trust us as their partner. These messages include: adopt your pet, rather than going to a store, spay/ neuter your pet to prevent pet overpopulation, microchip your pet so they can be returned if lost, and license your pet—it's the law. We are very active on Facebook and Twitter, and these channels have proven excellent tools for us to reach our intended audience and bring awareness to our programs and message in an efficient and popular method. To achieve this, we have an internal, full-time digital-media program coordinator responsible for the strategic and creative development and implementation of our social marketing across all digital channels."

Found Animals maintains an active Facebook presence in addition to its website: I asked Andrew about the experience with Facebook:

> "We have built a relationship with over 7,000 fans on Facebook. We engage them through traditional uses of Facebook and social media: polls, surveys, wall-post discussion, etc. Many times we use incentives to increase participation, like gift cards for pet-related spending. Currently, we are working to build on our social media success by developing metrics: comparing the amount of participation against the number of new adoptions or current adopters who rely upon us as a direct result of our social media program. We will also be measuring the impact of social media on our other initiatives; spay/neuter services, microchipping, and licensing."

Finally, I asked Andrew about the growth of Found Animals' Pet Club and its further plans to continue building its programs around the care and concern for animals.

> *"Let me preface this by saying in most cities once you adopt a pet and leave the animal care facility you're on your own. Your vet is available by appointment and for a fee. Your friends, family, and neighbors who have pet experience are available as well, when you can get their attention. Generally, there is no single, centralized resource with trusted information and a knowledge base built on personal experiences of thousands of pet owners. The goal of Found Animals and our Pet Club is to serve that need. Through social media, we've listened to our community and they have clearly expressed a desire for a tool like this that is not linked to an exclusive commercial product or line of products or a corporation with commercial goals. Our Pet Club will be a living, breathing and very personal online experience that will rely upon medical and professional experts, as well as the expertise of pet owners like you and me."*

What is particularly impressive about Found Animals is the way in which they have naturally integrated social-media-based marketing and community participation (both online and off) into the operational design and marketing of the foundation. Carrying this further, by listening carefully to their customers and community stakeholders, Found Animals has identified a clear need and a larger, more-valued service offering that it is now building into. That's social business, in action.

Identify Existing Social Objects

Existing social objects—the things that audiences are already organizing around—are generally centered on lifestyles, passions, and causes—the things that people think about frequently during the day or are involved with.

Lifestyles

Lifestyles make great social objects: People naturally tend to associate based on lifestyle choices—values, preferences, care, and concerns, and the ways in which these personal choices are made visible. Lifestyle is closely related to things like personal identity and culture: The Catalan culture in Spain, the Sikh traditions in India, the Cajun culture of Louisiana, the historical interests that power the Daughters of the American Revolution, or the surf lifestyle (complete with Dick Dale's Lebanese-inspired surf sound) of California...are all at the centers of powerful, compelling, and long-standing communities. Can your brand compete with these, or would it better to join into them and bring some unique benefits that connect the participants in communities like these to your business or organization?

Lifestyle-based social objects include action sports—skiing, kart racing, wakeboarding, and kite surfing—along with quilting, cooking, and online gaming. World of Warcraft, for example, is a great example of the kinds of activities that will spawn significant followings, literally. For small businesses—and the businesses and organizations that serve them—there is plenty of interest around the "small business ownership" lifestyle. Figure 10.2 shows the American Express "Open Forum," a business community that is built around the needs and interests of small businesses. Lifestyle associations are a great place to start when planning your Social Web presence: They provide natural places for you to participate and, assuming relevance, easy ways for your brand, product, or service to become a valued part of these communities.

Figure 10.2 American Express Small Business

Passions

Passions are another rich area when you're looking for existing social objects. Dell's "Take Your Own Path" and Pepsi's "Refresh" project are clear examples of the power of a natural alignment with the passions of customer segments that are important parts of these brands.

In the case of Dell's Take Your Own Path, the alignment occurs around the passion of being an entrepreneur or small business owner. In the case of Pepsi's Refresh project, the alignment is around social good: What are the solvable social issues, potentially better ways of addressing local or global problems, etc., that would be worthy of funding? The Refresh project is all about finding—and funding—them. Note that the social object at the center of Refresh isn't the problem or cause itself: It's a different group with different needs that signs up for ending hunger versus creating interest in sustainable energy, for example. The social object at the center of "Refresh" is the common thread between both: The *desire to make a difference,* and the desire to identify for one's self a specific cause around which to make that difference.

Look again at Dell's Take Your Own Path. Entrepreneurs and small/medium-sized business owners use computers and peripherals. By setting up a place for entrepreneurs to talk about funding, work/life balance, employee retention, or transition planning, Dell has created a place for its small and medium-sized business customers to talk about Dell products and the ways in which they use them in the pursuit of their businesses.

Shown in Figure 10.3, Red Bull University is a community built for enthusiasts interested in taking their passion for action sports to the next level. Beyond the program's entry point, student brand managers are connected to exchange best practices, tips, and generally assist each other in the development of a variety of promotional activities, in part by sharing information through the online social channels that form around action sports. How could you use a program like this in your organization? Could you actually *teach* your enthusiasts to become advocates? The real insight here is not so much having a "brand university"—although that's a pretty innovative step on its own. The big insight is in recognizing that for nearly any fan base, there is a thirst for getting closer to the action, for becoming part of the team. Fans don logowear for a reason: it's an act of *inclusion.* Be sure you consider this when planning your social media program, and more specifically, consider how you can *empower* your fans to become evangelists.

Causes

Right along with passions and lifestyles, *causes*—such as ending child hunger or advocating the humane treatment of animals—are natural social objects. Not only are causes easy to identify—after all, they generally form around issues that command attention—but the people involved are predisposed to talk about them, driven out of direct, personal interest. This makes cause-related social objects great vehicles for business programs as well as a natural focal point for cause-related organizations, for two reasons.

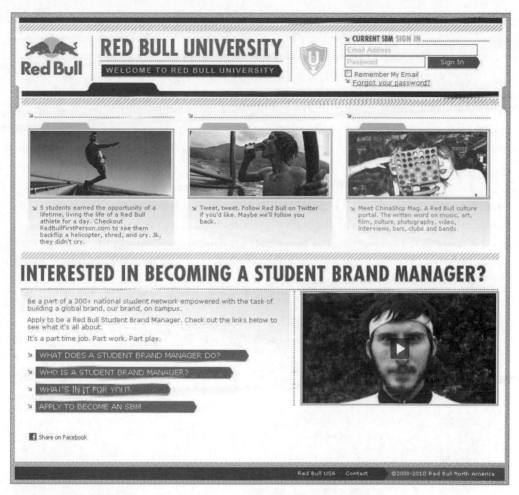

Figure 10.3 Red Bull University

Number one, by getting involved in a genuine and meaningful way, your business or organization brings more brains, muscle, and capital to the table. Your contributions, along with those of all others involved, make it that much more likely that the ultimate goal of the organization will be met, and that the participants around the effort will feel good about the process as a result.

Number two, you are able to create an additional and appreciated connection point between your brand, product, and service and the markets you serve. On this point, building a social presence around a cause-related social object is distinctly different than corporate social responsibility and similar philanthropic programs. Straight-up giving is absolutely appreciated—and vital—to many of the cause-based organizations that operate: corporate donations and in-kind contributions help them to deliver the services or benefits to society that they provide.

In comparison, by directly participating in the cause—by becoming involved in the community that has formed around it—your business or organization gains a new perspective on the cause itself. The issue-awareness created by association with cause-based organizations such as Habitat for Humanity or the Susan G. Komen Foundation within the businesses that support these organizations brings significant value to all involved.

At the same time, by being directly involved in a way that connects your business with a cause, you also create a new relevance and point of engagement with your customers and stakeholders. As they develop an appreciation for your participation—in however large or small a way you have chosen—you'll find yourself garnering favorable references on the Social Web and gaining new insights into how your existing business can better serve its markets.

Figure 10.4 shows the Tyson Foods "Hunger All-Stars" program, a cause-based effort that taps the company's unique capabilities across a number of social channels and additionally highlights the individual contributions of its Hunger All-Stars. This point is a big one: Highlighting the individual contributions—making the participants the stars rather than the brand—is an absolute "best practice" in social business.

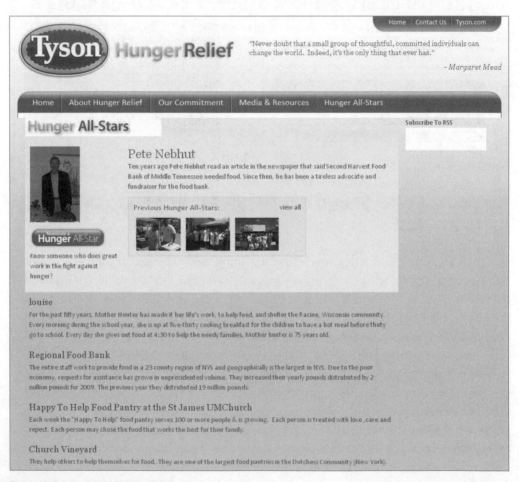

Figure 10.4 Tyson Foods' Hunger All-Stars

Figure 10.5 shows Aircel's efforts in raising awareness of the near-extinction of India's Bengal Tigers. The campaign goal, beyond awareness, is in its partnership with the World Wildlife Fund: The program is aimed at moving people to act in support of the protection of the Bengal Tiger. In both the Tyson and Aircel programs, the community-building goal is fundamentally around the cause and is intended to build on awareness and to move people to action. These programs—whether working in local hunger relief efforts or demanding that existing but overlooked laws regarding tiger poaching are actually upheld—tap the potential in the associated cause-related communities that exist around these social objects.

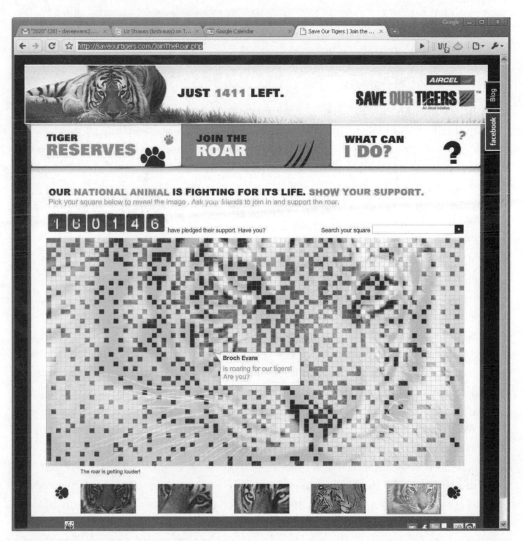

Figure 10.5 Aircel's "Save Our Tigers"

Worth noting in both of these examples is that they aren't so much examples of marketing alignments with popular issues as they are legitimate efforts to address worthy causes that are aligned with the values and missions of the companies involved and the people in the markets they serve. Tyson feeds families, and so feeding families that are sometimes unable to feed themselves is directly related to its own operations. Aircel describes itself as a "pioneer" and is clearly part of the next-generation of Indians. That this next generation should also be able to witness first-hand—and not in a zoo, or worse, an encyclopedia—the amazing presence of India's national symbol fits right into that.

Here's a great test that you can apply when thinking about building around a cause: Poll ten random employees in your business as to how some specific cause is connected to your business. If you get nine decent responses, you're onto something. If not, keep looking (for causes, not employees to quiz).

Create New Social Objects

There are times when a ready-made social object that fits your business objectives and strategy simply doesn't exist. Perhaps you can't find a relevant connection, or maybe your specific business objective really warrants its own purpose-built social space. While many brands, products and services aren't "big enough" to stand as the central object around which a *large* participant base will form (at least not for the right reasons!), defining a specific set of social activities for a particular subset may be a viable approach. In these cases, you may be well-served by building your social space—for example, by setting your brand, product, or service as the "social object" or as a direct enabler of it.

There is a distinct upside to building around your own business: The connection between the community you ultimately develop and your business is already in place and is obvious to the participants, since otherwise they wouldn't be there. At the same time, building your own social object will also present some unique challenges. Compared with social objects that are founded in a lifestyle, passion, or cause, a social object built around a brand, product, or service can be tougher to pull off, and equally challenging to sustain. This follows from the working definition of "social object" that the chapter opened with: something inherently talkworthy, around which people will naturally congregate and converse. You've got to get your brand, product, or service (up) to this level.

Why is this so tough? Working with TV or print to create a message with your brand at the center seems so easy that it can be hard to understand why taking the same tack on the Social Web doesn't work nearly as well. Part of the answer is that with traditional media the hard part—the creative work—is outsourced to an agency. Beyond reviewing it (and being held responsible for the consequences of bad creative work in addition to the glory of great work), the complexity of traditional media development is largely hidden. With social media, it's the implementation that is tough, and in particular it's the development and continued contributions to a blog or the ongoing duties of your in-house community managers that challenge most organizations.

The other part of the answer is a combination of issues common to any use of social media: When *you* talk about *your* products and services in a marketing context on the Social Web, there is an immediate credibility and trust issue. Compounding that, if you present your program in a social context *without* having made a provision for genuine social participation, the natural "multiplier effect" of the Social Web is stymied. So, your social strategy needs to establish the social role of your brand, product, or service, and it needs to provide a framework and purpose for real participation and collaboration.

Build Around Your Own Social Object

When building a social activity around your brand or other direct aspect of your business, the initial consideration is to think through how you will connect your audience to it. The key to a successful, branded community is ensuring that the connection between your audience and the community is very strong and easily understood by potential participants. You thinking that your own product is talkworthy is not enough: Your brand (or product, service, or organization) should not sit at the center but rather should act as a facilitation or expression related to the participant experience. If you are placing your interests at the center—and in particular if you find yourself in a conversation around "getting the creative" just right, so that it echoes your traditional media and static online presence, take this as a warning that you are heading into your social media program from a "we'll talk, you'll listen" perspective. In contrast to placing participants at the center, around an activity they find meaning in, an overly brand-centric approach rarely turns out well.

Here are the basic steps to follow:

1. Identify a talkworthy element: Select a starting point to build around, perhaps a unique aspect of your brand, product or service, for example, and set this as the social object.

2. Identify a social need or talking point from the perspective of your participants that is met by or through this aspect of your chosen social object.

3. Create a connection to these participants, and reinforce their place as the "center" of the activities that ensue.

Identify What Is Talkworthy

When you are creating a branded social object in the steps outlined above, the important questions to consider are the following:

- What aspect of what you do will your customers find remarkable?
- What is it about your brand, product, or service that is inherently talkworthy?
- What is it about the answers to both of these questions that your firm or organization's beliefs and mission tie directly into?

Touchpoint analysis is one of the most useful methods available to you when looking for a strong social object to build around. Touchpoint analysis helps you focus on the issues that matter to your customers, and it helps identify which among these you are doing "remarkably" well delivering. Anything you do well that is grounded in the values of your company, and that is talkworthy *of its own merit,* is a good candidate to build around. As an exercise, create a touchpoint map: you'll see directly where to start.

Note the emphasis on "of its own merit" with regard to candidate social objects: The implication is that the social object you select needs to be capable of driving its own conversation. If you have to spell it out, or have to entice people to actually talk about it, then keep looking and find a more naturally conversational social object.

Link to a Social Need

Next up is linking your candidate social objects to the needs of your customers or constituents. In the case of lifestyles, passions, and causes, the social need to talk already exists: People naturally engage in conversation around things that they find interesting. The same applies here: Your task is to identify a need or behavior among your potential participants that lends itself to social interaction around the talkworthy aspect of your brand, product, or service. Don't worry about finding a "big" social object in your product or service: as they say, "it's the little things that count." Samuel Adams, as an organization, is all about making a better beer for beer lovers, and a community will certainly form around *that*. Lesser Evil (http://www.lesserevil.com/)—a snacks company—has created a solid presence for itself around conversations and ideas related to "stopping bad snacking." Applying social objects in a B2B setting? Consider the following: A team of business analysts may be creating reporting tools for their own internal use on an analytical software platform that your company offers. As these analysts develop their own reporting extensions, you might create a community—perhaps built as a forum—that allows analysts across your customer base to share what they have built with each other. This is exactly what happens at SAS Institute, through ToolPool, an internal knowledge-sharing network created by SAS Chief Knowledge Officer Frank Leistner.

The same collective effort occurs around PGi's communications system API and its supporting external, PGiConnect community, and around open source efforts like WordPress, ExpressionEngine and Drupal with the development of themes, modules, and similar extensions to the core platforms. These languages and applications—the social object is indeed the product itself—have communities around them driven by the participant's own needs to be more productive, to build better solutions, and to gain personal recognition. On that last point—recognition—be sure to think through and plan your community's reputation system: It is a critical component in driving collaboration and, therefore, essential to the long-term success of your efforts.

Connect Your Audience

With your social object and the (participant) motive for social interaction planned out, the final step—once you've established your object(s)—is to make them available for sharing and to optimize the resulting work products of your participants for discovery via search.

The connection to your audience—making objects available—can be done through a combination of techniques. For social objects like photos, make sure they can be found: This means tying them to a URL of their own. Don't rely on the page or container for discovery and sharing. While it's true that many objects on the Web have a URL of some sort, make it easy to surface and share. If you are planning to use Flash or similar embedded content methods, pay special attention to this: If the only reference to a piece of content that someone would like to share is the top-level URL for the page, the ability to share what people would otherwise spread around may suffer.

Overt methods for sharing overcome this: "Send to a Friend" or "Share This" goes a long way in helping people start or engage in conversations. For discrete objects like photos, take the added step of optimizing them for discoverability by encouraging and providing examples of tags, titles, and descriptions for the objects that participants create. Rather than "Upload a photo" for example, your upload form should include a tag, title, and description field that are *required* to be populated for submission. It may seem like a burden, but this added information will actually help your community grow by making individual contributions more discoverable.

With the overall need established, and the tools that support social conversation and collaboration in place, tell your wider audience about it. Link to it, publicize it, and share it yourself. As your community begins to form, turn to your moderators to facilitate the growth of the community.

Types of Branded Communities

As you plan your community program, consider the type of community you want. Will this serve participants through the aspirations and values of the brand, or will it be more focused on specific products or similar aspects of the services you offer? As with a decision to build around an existing social object versus creating one of your own—and remember too that you can do both—think through the decision from the perspective of your customers and other expected participants. Does your brand represent a "near-lifestyle" aspiration? If so, consider building around that. Are your customers interested in sharing their knowledge around very specific applications of your products or services? You can build around that product or service, and then facilitate (and learn from) those conversations.

Brand Communities

Building a community around a brand implies that the brand itself is big enough—or has been made big enough—to anchor the social interactions of that community. For brands that are either sufficiently big themselves (such as GM) or sufficiently novel or talkworthy (such as Cannondale's commitment to cyclists or Tesla Motors with its electric automobiles), a brand-based community may well be viable. Tesla, GM, and Cannondale all connect to their customers in sufficient ways to support social interaction. Cannondale might build a discussion forum around terrain exploration and riding safety, while Tesla and GM might build around their own insight and innovation programs for future personal transportation using an ideation platform. For business-to-business applications, a company like EDS (now HP Enterprise Services) might build a community of suppliers and contractors, for example, who have a direct stake in the benefits of collaboration aimed at process improvement in the delivery of higher-valued IT services.

In each of these examples, the key is placing the community participant at the center, and encouraging interaction between participants that offer a dividend—like learning, insight, and a spreading of the brand presence—to the company or organization. If your strategic plan for a brand-based social community includes this specific provision you are on solid ground. Note the nuance here: The community (in this case) is built to emphasize a specific aspect of the brand. However, it is the participant, and not the brand, that is at the center of design and the activity that follows.

Product (or Service) Communities

By thinking about participants—rather than your brand, product, or service—as the central element you will avoid one of the biggest mistakes made when approaching social media marketing from a business perspective. That mistake is putting the brand, product, or service at the center of the social effort and then spending money—very often a lot of money—pulling people toward what amounts to a promotional program in the hopes that they will talk about it, and maybe even "make it go viral." This rarely if ever works over the long term, and even when it does it still fails to drive the sustainable social bonding and engagement behaviors that result in collaboration and ultimately advocacy. Be especially careful of this when implementing a community at the product or service level.

Figure 10.6 shows the Pepperidge Farm "Art of the Cookie" website, circa 2007. From nearly any traditional or online advertising perspective, the site itself was well done: It contained useful information and plenty of pictures of delicious cookies. As a social site—the actual objective of the program—it failed and was taken down. What went wrong? *The "Art of the Cookie" was not social.* It was built to promote the brand rather than encourage genuine social interaction between participants, and so was seen as a marketing ploy. Walmart's "The Hub," intended to be a MySpace-like social place for Walmart's (younger) customers to hang out and talk, failed in part for similar reasons. Sure, having a protected space for younger customers is certainly a reasonable objective, and it definitely fits with Walmart's adherence to its own culture with regard to family values. The problem is that these values are Walmart's and not necessarily the values or even the articulation of the values of Walmart's customers. Like "The Art of the Cookie", Walmart's "The Hub" has been discontinued.

Walmart's "The Hub" was on shaky ground from the start for another reason, also instructive as you consider your own efforts. "The Hub" was developed largely by people *outside* its target demographic. The lesson here is that when developing in "stealth mode," be sure that you've involved a solid sampling of your expected participants and their views as to what they find useful and relevant. Push back if someone tells you "we don't have time for that" or "we can't hand over that much control (to participants)." These types of objections are warning signs well heeded.

Figure 10.6 The Art of the Cookie

The "Art of the Cookie"—since replaced with a similarly nice looking but now purposely nonsocial product site—was representative of early community efforts for well-funded FMCG (fast-moving consumer goods, such as soft drinks and snack foods) and CPG (consumer package goods, such as washing powder and footwear) brands. It featured the product at the center and a handful of branded casual games or trivial interactions that could have been presented for *any* brand wrapped around it. If you are marketing packaged goods, and your "consumer" gut is telling you that "people are only going to talk about (this) product so much," then take stock and consider doing something else. By all means, build a casual game—people like them. Just don't confuse it with a "social presence." It's not.

To check your own ideas (or the pitches of others), here are three questions worth asking when designing a social experience:

- Why would consumers gather around this?
- What's in it for them if they do?
- Could you swap in some other product and *not* cause a change in the answers to the two questions above?

In both "The Art of the Cookie" and "The Hub," the failing wasn't the business objectives or the lack of a social object. There are plenty of social aspects to sharing cookies and the conversations that form around them—over tea, for example. Walmart's younger customers have plenty to talk about in regard to music, clothes, and school—all of which are directly related to what Walmart sells. These were not bad ideas—in fact, they were really good ideas that were executed poorly: The failing was that the participant experience was thin or contrived, and the conversation was controlled and oriented toward the brand or the products being sold. There is a big difference between participating in a branded, directed effort versus the more natural, casual conversation about topics that may well be present around a brand. It's a difference worth noting when building a product-based community.

Big note here: This is *not* a knock on Pepperidge Farm, which happens to be a brand that I love, nor is it a critique of Walmart. It's always good fun to poke fun at people for the way they look while dancing: It's another matter entirely to get out there and dance. Both firms deserve credit for trying. What is noteworthy about both examples is the importance—especially when working with a traditional agency—of not only getting the social object right (again, a Pepperidge Farm cookie *is a social object*) but also of ensuring that the opportunity for meaningful, participant (customer) driven social interaction exists. The really tough part of building a strong social site is ensuring that the participant—and not the brand or product—is at the center of the social interaction.

Compare "The Art of the Cookie" or "The Hub" with Pampers Village, or Pepsi's "The Juice", both built around the interests of *participants*. Themes like parenting, personal health, and well being act as the anchors for these programs, and it's the parents, the women, and their conversations that sit at the center of the action. Both afford plenty of opportunity for social interaction between participants, and plenty of relevant exposure and connection for the brands and products in the process.

Geolocation and Community Development

As mobile technology rapidly forces a shift in the access point for social interaction from the desktop or laptop to truly mobile devices like a netbook or smartphone, an additional class of social objects emerges: locations and location-based activities. Simply put, if my phone knows where I am, and a business application can be imagined to enhance both my personal and social presence at that location, then a social object built around that location probably exists.

As an example, consider Las Vegas. Clearly the idea of "Going to Vegas" is talkworthy. It's almost impossible to walk up to someone—anyone—and say, "I'm going to Vegas—any tips?" and *not* get a response. (The quality or accuracy of that response is, of course, another matter.) So, it makes sense that an organization like Wynn's—a popular destination resort and casino in Las Vegas—would build a community presence through simple-to-implement social tools like Twitter that naturally incorporate conversations about visiting Las Vegas. Through it participation on Twitter—used in part for social CRM, the topic of the prior chapter—Wynn's has created a social presence that makes it easy for its guests to share information and talk about their experiences with eath other and the hotel and casino. Creating the opportunity for conversation is nothing new for Wynn's. When Wynn's opened they invited every cab driver in town to enjoy the hotel for a night on the house. Their experiences are conveyed to visitors in countless cab rides, right along with the tweets and other social chatter. Las Vegas and Wynn's—as locations—are social objects.

Consider Whole Foods Market, where the store itself—the physical location—is the social object. Whole Foods Market—in its early days in Austin, Texas—had literally been "rescued" by the community around its original store. Following a flood that nearly spelled the end for the fledgling grocer, customers came together to protect it, clean it up, and put it back together. That gave Jon Lebkowsky, a colleague of mine at Social Web Strategies, an idea: Build Whole Foods Market's online presence around the physical community that supports each store. Whole Foods Market has built on this core idea, through both its online presence and its continued community actions such as its quarterly "5 percent days," during which it donates 5 percent of net sales to a local nonprofit.

Smaller, regional brands fit into the category as well. How many times have you visited an out-of-town friend, and heard "Hey, there's this place I've got to take you. They have the best _____." where your friend then fills in the blank with a place for music, shopping, food, people-watching...you get the idea. For these types of businesses and organizations, there is a ready-made social object that sits at the intersection of what they offer and the community in which they offer it. Here are some examples of food-related, location-based social objects:

If you find yourself in _____, then you must visit:

- Austin, TX: Black's, Iron Works, The Salt Lick or Cooper's for BBQ, or Péché, Austin's finest Absinthe bar
- Marshall, IA: Maid-rite, for a loose-meat sandwich
- Boston, MA: Woodman's, for fresh lobster and crab rolls
- Phoenix, AZ: Greasewood Flats, for music and entertainment
- Seattle, WA: Pike's Market, The Pacific Northwest Shop for Market Spice Tea
- The Basque region of Spain: To eat anything

Any one of these *locations* is an instant conversation-starter, and there are as many more as there are small towns or regional areas with something cool, delicious, or otherwise talkworthy to offer. Any one of them could be the center of a well-defined, passionate gathering that drives conversation about these specific businesses. Figure 10.7 shows a collection of the Facebook pages for some of these local brands: Facebook is a great place, by the way, to anchor a small-business presence. The larger social object—people hanging out together and sharing things—is already in place. All that's needed is a conversational brand, and if there ever was one, "The best ___ you've ever tasted!" is it. If you own a small business, think about Facebook: It's free, it's effective, it's easy and (your) customers are already there, waiting for you to do what you already do best: serve them.

The Workplace as a Social Object

Many organizations—and often those with a strong, well-defined internal culture (firms like Zappos, Progressive, SAS Institute, and Whole Foods Market)—are effectively tapping their own culture as a social object as they implement collaborative internal systems that drive external business success through their ability to outmaneuver and outperform competitors in terms of response and understanding of customer issues. SAS Institute CEO Jim Goodnight put it succinctly: "Our company culture is a competitive weapon." Tapping internal culture as a social object around which to unify employees is a powerful way to build a social business.

The organization itself—right along with the content its people produce—is thus a social object. Around these types of social objects, the culture of the company can be made tangible—through discussion, for example—and can be further strengthened through collaboration. Most importantly, "work" as a social object can form the basis for internal employee development and recognition programs, employee-to-customer collaborative efforts, and for the attraction of additional candidates to support the further growth and collective achievement of the organization.

The culture inside a company has always been a big deal: Plenty of organizational managers and HR professionals have spent countless hours trying to "get company culture right." Consider the firms referenced at the start of this section: Being known for their culture, they attract and retain the best people. Given the connected nature of consumers—and the ease with which they can and will share stories about experiences with employees—it's safe to say that at no time has business culture been a bigger deal than right now.

Figure 10.7 Local Cuisine as a Social Object

Use Social Objects in Business

Social objects exist as the connectors between participants. Remember, without a social object, there is no reason for a conversation to exist. Without a social network the conversation that might otherwise exist is hampered, but the (smaller) conversation still occurs. The two work together through a social application like Twitter or a support forum to facilitate participation and engagement.

Whether you've built around a lifestyle, passion, or cause, or you have more tightly defined your presence around a brand, product, or service; the payoff comes when you tie your business into it by being relevant rather than being loud. Recall that the Social Web is built around open and transparent participation. Leveraging a social object is best done by operating from the perspective of a genuine participant rather than assuming center stage as a contrived actor.

Drive Conversations and Connections

The most basic role of the social object is driving conversation. In the business applications discussed previously, the social object brings participants together based on a common interest around which a conversation occurs. It also provides a relevant context for a brand, product, or service. Pepsi's The Juice program built around its low calorie, all-natural Trop50 orange juice provides an example of the central role of the conversation in a social setting, and the role of the social object—women's health and well-being—while clearly tying the customer and product together.

This clear connection is important: Recall that a basic fact of social media is that in comparison with traditional media, it is harder to interrupt. This differentiator plays out in two ways: First, because it is harder to interrupt the activities of participants directly—like the way you can interrupt a TV program with an ad or an online page view with a pop-up—your activities with regard to your business objectives have to have an obvious relevance. Otherwise, you'll be ignored (best case) or asked to leave (worst case). The Social Web isn't a marketing venue, though it is a very powerful marketing platform.

Second, because it is harder to interrupt (if not impossible), your message, your value, and your contributions to the community must be delivered within the existing conversation. In an analogy to TV, think about the difference between product advertising on TV versus product placement within the TV program. In the case of product advertising, there is a clear distinction between the program and the ad: In the case of product placement, the product becomes part of the program.

Your participation in communities built with or around social objects is much closer to the product placement model. While you cannot "buy placement" on the Social Web, your participation needs to blend with its context in the same way that effective product placement does, to be part of the community rather than an interruption, or called out with a "brought to you by" message placed alongside it. Note here that "blend in" *does not* mean "hidden" and certainly does not mean "covert," but rather that as a transparent, disclosed participant, your message should be a natural element of the surrounding conversation.

Beyond building conversations, social objects and your business relationship to them provide the foundation of a strong connection to your audience in a branded community or to the participants in or around a lifestyle, passion, or cause-based effort. Again, consider a comparison to traditional media and the factors that drive advertising effectiveness. At GSD&M, we did a lot of work to quantitatively understand the relationship between what someone was watching and the types of advertising that would likely be of interest to that person. During adventure programming, for example, we'd place advertising for the Air Force that built on one's sense of accomplishment in overcoming challenges

The same relationships apply on the Social Web, and in particular in the communities that you build around or those you create yourself. Because there is a central theme (arising out of or facilitated by the social objects associated with the community), you have a direct path to a stronger connection within that community. Dell's "Digital Nomads" program relies on this aspect of community design to create a strong link to one segment of its customer base. By creating a place where tech-savvy individuals can talk about their own use of technology, Dell has a created a natural conversation around its own products. Note, however, that at no point does Dell interrupt or highjack the conversation for its own purposes: Instead, the community platform facilitates an engaged conversation that includes and references Dell products.

Get Found

With the social object in place, the next objective is building your audience. This means being "findable" through search Author Brian Solis, known for his work at the intersection of social media and Public Relations, has often stressed the importance of using the Social Web and social media as a part of your overall search optimization program. Because the photos, videos, blog posts, and similar content associated with social media can be tagged, described, and linked they can all be optimized for search. Don't make the mistake of dismissing this as a little more than a tip, trick, or technique to be implemented by search engine optimization (SEO) firms (although a good SEO specialist can really help you here). Instead, step back and consider the larger idea that Brian and others making this same point are conveying: People search for things, and they discover relevant content in this way. If great content—and the community that has been built around it—can't be found, then that content effectively does not exist: In that case, the community won't be found.

This much larger view of SEO makes clear that SEO applies to everything you do on the Social Web. Too often SEO is applied in a more narrowly focused application of page optimization or site optimization against a specific set of commerce-related keywords. This works, and it's better than nothing, but the real gain comes when each piece of social content is optimized in a way that promotes self-discovery and, therefore, discovery of the entire social community. As portals and branded starting pages give way to a search box or a running discussion, how people find things on the Web is changing dramatically. In the portal context, or the big, branded community, the assumption is that a preexisting awareness—perhaps driven by advertising—brings people to the content, after which specific items are discovered. For example, I may see a spot on TV that advertises the continuation of the story unfolding in the spot, and find at that site lots of interesting discussion around that spot and the associated product or service. More likely, however, people will find that community by searching for the content itself and discovering the community, working backward to the online version of the original TV spot, posted on YouTube.

It's really important to catch the significance of this. A common approach to promotion typically uses an ad of some type to drive people to a microsite or social presence point where the audience in turn discovers the content that ultimately encourages individuals to join, visit, or otherwise participate. This is not how the increasing use of search engines—everyplace, and increasingly on mobile devices—works. Instead, people search for specific things—often at a very granular level in searches for things like "wakeboard" rather than "action sports watercraft." With the emergence of ubiquitous search boxes, it is imperative that each single piece of content—each social object in the very narrow sense of the term—be optimized. By optimizing the individual social objects, you greatly increase the likelihood that the larger community will be discovered, since that community is the container for those objects. In the "Hands-On" section for this chapter, there is a specific exercise that shows you how important this is.

This all gets to the larger point of optimizing social media and social objects in particular. In a world with less interruption, in a medium that is literally driven by search and powered by direct personal interest along with sharing and recommendations, it is the *details* (the small items and pieces of content) that are the most desired and hence are the things most likely to searched for and the most likely to be appreciated, shared, and *talked about* upon discovery. Tags, titles, categories, and other forms of applicable metadata (for example, the *description* of your company video posted on YouTube) that apply to the content—to the social object—and not just the web page must be keyword rich, and must perform as well as "search attractors" as they do as "attention holders." Be aware here: It's quite common to focus (appropriately) on the content—good content matters, after all—and to completely ignore the tags, titles, and other meta information at the object level and instead focus SEO efforts at the website or page level only. Don't make this mistake: Work with your SEO team to optimize *everything*.

Review and Hands-On

Chapter 10 explored the social object in detail. While social objects are in general anything around which a conversation may form (a photo, a short post, or a lifestyle), Chapter 10 focused most on the larger social objects (lifestyles, passions, and causes) and the ways in which these larger objects can be used to encourage conversations around your business or organization.

Review of the Main Points

The main points covered in Chapter 10 are listed below. Review these and develop your own list of social objects around which to plan your social presence.

- Social objects are the center point of social activity. Without the social object, no meaningful conversation forms.

- Social objects are often built on lifestyles, passions, and causes because these are universal areas of commonality and discussion.

- Social objects include talkworthy aspects of your business or organization, or unique features of your product or service.

- Social objects, like any other type of online content, should be optimized for search and discoverability. Social objects are very much the connectors between a community and the people who enjoy or find value in being part of it.

Social objects are a building block of online social communities, and as such are an essential consideration in the development of your social business and social media marketing programs. Built around areas of shared interest, your participation in existing or purpose-built communities gives you a powerful connection point between your business or organization and the people with whom you'd like to build stronger relationships.

Hands-On: Social Objects

Review each of the following and connect them to your business.

1. Look at the work of Jyri Engeström, beginning with this video (http://vimeo .com/4071624) and his blog (www.zengestrom.com/blog).

2. Make a list of the social sites you are currently a member of (all of them). Connect each with the social object around which it is built, and then consider how your connection to this object drives (or fails to drive) your participation in that site.

3. Visit your own brand or organization website and brand outposts. Is a social object readily identifiable? Does this social object connect your audience to your business?

Hands-On: Apply What You've Learned

Apply what you've learned in this chapter through the following exercises:

1. Create an inventory of communities applicable to your brand, product, or service. Once you've compiled it, join a manageable set and understand the interest areas and social norms for each. Develop a plan for how you might integrate your own activities into these communities.

NOTE: *Always practice full disclosure, and refrain from "test driving" communities.*

2. Using Google, search for a lifestyle, passion, or cause that you are interested in. Note the documents that come back, and review a subset of them. Then do the same content search again but this time select only "image" results. Review the images and note the number of images that lead you to a social site of some type.

3. Visit Slideshare (http://slideshare.net) and search for "Gautam Ghosh Talent Communities." Gautam provides a nice overview of the ways in which social objects and communities can be used within the HR organization.

4. Define three core social objects for your business or organization around which you could build or enhance your social presence. Create a touchpoint map to help guide your selection.

The Social Graph

The social graph—nearly but not quite synonymous with "social network"—defines the way in which participants on the Social Web are connected and in the process suggests what they might be collectively engaged in at any given moment. The social graph—and your ability to traverse and explore it—is the basis for many of the social applications that exist on the Social Web. This chapter shows you why this is true and how to tap it.

11

Chapter Contents

What Is a Social Graph?

I've referenced three fundamental terms and associated concepts in the discussion of social business and the application of social technology to business. *Social objects,* covered in the prior chapter, range from small pieces of content—for example, photos or tweets—to larger things such as passions, lifestyles, and causes around which people will collect and form communities. *Social applications*—the tools that extend the general functionality of a social platform—were also mentioned briefly and will be covered in detail in the next chapter.

The third of the fundamental terms, *social graph,* is the subject of this chapter. The term itself is nearly synonymous with a related term—social network. In general discussion, the two are essentially interchangeable, and you may hear strong opinions and preferences for one over the other. So, a minute spent sorting this out is worthwhile.

The term *social graph* is rooted in the quantitative analysis of networks: It's the kind of term a mathematician or sociologist might use. The more general term is "social network"; so to avoid the tech babble that is often the cause of avoidable confusion when talking about social media, you can generally use "social network" instead of social graph and everyone will know what you mean.

The difference to be aware of is this: In conversation, "social network" generally refers to something like Facebook—the software, the apps, the people, the connections...all of it. By comparison, the term "social graph" refers specifically to the people who are members of a particular network (or graph) *as well as how those members within that network are connected*: The term "social graph" makes more explicit the fact that you are concerned with the details of the connections and relationships that make up a social network.

> *"Definition: The Social Graph is the representation of our relationships. In present day context, these graphs define our personal, family, or business communities on social networking websites."*

Jeremiah Owyang, 2007

Here's the important point: You can use either term, as long as everyone is clear on what is being talked about. For this chapter—and in fact throughout this book—the term *social network* refers to the collective object—to Facebook or Orkut or the Intel Developer's Network and everyone contained within it; the term *social graph* refers to the members of a social network and the details around the ways in which those members are connected. Figure 11.1 shows a simple social graph and the connections between specific members that make up a social network.

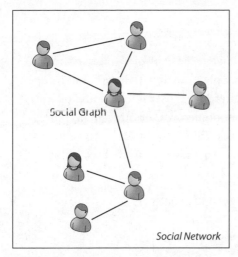

Social Graph

Social Network

Figure 11.1 A Simple Social Graph

Social Graph and Data Visualization

The *social graph* is the collection of links, interactions, and other connections that define the activities within a social network. Visualizing these links reveals relationships that offer insights into influence, who is connected to whom, the existence of expertise or interest groups within personal networks, and more. You can refer to this post at ReadWriteWeb for more on social graph visualization.

http://www.readwriteweb.com/archives/george_stephanopoulos_wolf_
blitzer_ana.php

With the definition of the social graph set aside, the importance of the social graph and its application in the business use of social media lies in its ability to simultaneously provide a framework for understanding the relationships that develop within a network (as well as between networks) *and* to provide an efficient description of the way in which the participants of a given social network are connected. The social graph and its application in business—for example, to help spot influencers or suggest opportunities for collaboration—is at the heart of using social networks to their fullest potential in driving engagement.

A Social Graph Primer

ReadWriteWeb author Alex Iskold published an article in 2007 that outlines the basic concepts underlying the social graph and its use in business. You'll find the post here:

http://www.readwriteweb.com/archives/social_graph_concepts_and_issues.php

Like-Mindedness Drives Association

Within a social network, the relationships that make up the social graph are often built—especially initially—between people who have some evident characteristic in common. Twellow, a Twitter utility that allows people to search Twitter based on specific physical locations or personal/professional interests, is useful for finding potential members to follow based on a common profession, hometown, or other shared interest. Search Twellow for "Austin, TX" and you'll find the Twitter profiles for Lance Armstrong and Whole Foods Market among other Austinites. A typical search of Twellow (for "Austin, TX") is shown in Figure 11.2.

Figure 11.2 Twellow: Twitter Members in Austin

Twellow provides an interesting insight into one of the primary "default" behaviors exhibited by members of social networks: This is the tendency for people of similar interests, background, locale, etc. to connect *more readily* than those with dissimilar interests. While it may seem obvious, this tendency actually has a significant impact on the way connections between members—and hence conversations—propagate. The tendency to associate based on interests can manifest itself in the formation of a social graph in distinct and important ways. It's worth understanding the tendency to preferentially connect with people sharing overt similarity when designing your social media and social business programs. For example, if you are after new ideas and are looking to a customer community to generate and discuss them, be sure that your participants haven't formed "cliques" and instead are making connections based on more than specific personal interest. Otherwise, instead of collaboration you're more likely to end up with competing factions.

Analyzing a Facebook Business Page

Using Gephi, Denmark-based Kristina Sedereviciute has produced a visualization and analysis of McKinsey's Facebook page, which she has posted to Posterous using the Gephi analytical software combined with Facebook's netvizz application. *If you are interested in applying tools like Gephi and netvizz in your work, this post provides a great tutorial.*

You can follow Kristina on Twitter (@kristtina) and read her analysis of McKinsey's page here:

http://kristtina.posterous.com/technical-network-analysis-case-mckinsey-and

Netvizz is a standard Facebook application. Search Facebook for "netvizz." You can learn more about Gephi and how to use it here:

http://gephi.org

One of the ways in which shared interests and the corresponding formation of relationships—referred to technically as "status homophily"—is the tendency of *similarly credentialed or titled individuals* to associate with each other. A CMO's group on Facebook or lawyers using Twellow to find other lawyers on Twitter are examples of relationships built on shared titles or occupations. Networks that encourage this type of relationship development include professional associations, skill-specific support forums—for example, a CIO discussion board or forum—and similar.

In contrast, *value homophily* is association based on shared interest, lifestyle, passion, or cause, without specific regard for status or title. An entire community—in real life—coming together to stack sandbags against a flooding river is an example of value homophily. Regardless of social status, the collective community shares in the immediate tasks required to protect itself. This plays out online in a social context when women across diverse walks of life come together to talk about common issues and challenges in places like the BlogHer Community. This sort of democratized social interaction is actually at the root of a lot of what happens on the Social Web.

The tendency for people to come together and organize around common issues given diversity is particularly important when designing a community application. When people are gathering around large social objects—lifestyles, passions, and causes—it is very likely that it is the shared values and purposes associated with these larger objects that are bringing together a variety of different people, in addition to the primary common interest itself (the specific passion, lifestyle, or cause that is shared). This in turn means that the shared outcomes, activities, and intellectual content produced within the community need to flow back in some form to *everyone,* regardless of who the actual contributor is: Otherwise, the individual interests will take over and the community will fragment.

Visualizing Partisanship

The tendency for like people to act together is nowhere more evident than in partisan politics. In this Ignite presentation, Andrew Odewahn visually presents the impact of coalitions in government by looking at the social graph that defines the United States Congress. You'll find the video presentation here:

http://radar.oreilly.com/2010/06/visualizing-the-senate-social.html

Starbucks' various online projects that focus effort on local physical communities—beginning with its association around the V2V (volunteer-to-volunteer) program in 2008, along with others like the Pepsi Refresh program that is active now—are examples of values-driven online social efforts, built around a collective interest in making a difference in one's local community.

The status community, by comparison, is very likely to be driven by the reputation management system within a community, forum, or other social application. The reputation management system provides many of the cues that alert members to their own status or that of others within that community. CTOs joining a C-level tech community know already that the title of "CTO" or its equivalent is a shared credential: What engages them in that community after that are the solutions, tips, referrals, and best practices that they can pick up and apply in their work. The reputation management system—which provides a visible indication of which members are most likely to have offered viable solutions, for example—will quickly sort out the relative *status* ranking—beyond title—within this type of community.

Reputation management plays a role in the development of values-based communities too: Status differentiation can and does occur as some contributors within a shared value-driven community will produce more and/or more useful content than other members. That's a natural condition, and members expect recognition for their efforts. What's important, though, is that the community as a whole does not lose sight of the overall values connection as some members are elevated as a result of varying contribution and participation.

Birds of a Feather Flock Together

Homophily—literally meaning "love of the same"—is a characteristic that has been generally observed in social networks. For more on this and the ways it expresses itself in a social context, see the following Wikipedia entry:

```
http://en.wikipedia.org/wiki/Homophily
```

Social Graphs Spread Information

Beyond linking people within a social network, the relationships that are present within a social graph play an important role in the spread of information throughout that social graph, and hence play a direct role in the sharing of content across a social network. Looked at another way, without sharing, a social network is a largely theoretical construct: *What difference do a thousand connections make if nothing of value is flowing between them?* Consider, for example, the value to you, personally, of a network that you may have joined without understanding why—except perhaps that everyone else was joining it—and as a result rarely find yourself using it: You have connections within this network, but of what use are they?

As an example, when I first joined Twitter I did not "get it." Half of my motivation for joining was "everyone else" I knew had already joined. I started using Twitter in 2007 at SXSW; I am member number 12,556,112. Given a bit of time, however, I started to develop actual relationships with people and began linking with people that I knew, or knew of, and with people interested in working on some of the same things I was interested in. That's when Twitter made sense—when I was able to utilize my social graph as it existed within Twitter in ways that benefited me and benefited the growing Twitter community around me. Again, the takeaway is that only with a meaningful social graph—only with connections between people with shared interests, common values, or aligned purposes, as examples—do the social networks that people may belong to become relevant.

The applications built around the direct use of the social graph are important: I spoke with Rapleaf's Michael Hsu—Michael is part of Rapleaf's marketing team—about applications that mine or otherwise tap the information exposed through the study of a particular social graph. Michael noted applications ranging from driving participation in online gaming— in one application, players with more than five friends in the game were significantly more engaged than those with four or less—to the observation that the spread of movie reviews is directly related to the respective graphs of the individuals who publish reviews. All of this suggests the value of knowing, through measurement, who is connected to whom, and how these connections can therefore be used to encourage additional connections.

In a specific example, Rapleaf worked with an online university to identify opportunities to increase engagement (more direct participation in classes) and encourage recommendations to friends for specific classes (new business growth). Using Rapleaf a program that identified the friends of prospective students who were already students themselves—all done with explicit permission—resulted in proof that a significant increase in likelihood of new student conversion (+320 percent) is associated with "having a friend who is also a student." This quantitative knowledge, gained through study of the social graph, resulted in the implementation of a "bring a friend to class" promotion (your friend gets to attend class with you for free, for one week), an online student center where prospective students can talk with current students, and a formal new student referral recognition program.

Rapleaf: Decoding the Social Graph

Rapleaf provides a tool set that enables understanding of how your customers are connected and what they are interested in. You can follow Michael Hsu, with Rapleaf's marketing team on Twitter (@mhsu) and learn more about the firm here:

```
http: //rapleaf.com
```

I asked Michael what he saw in the near-future as regards applications of social graph analytics and measurement tools:

> *"What's becoming clear is that an experience that is more 'social' and connected for people is an experience that is more rewarding and engaging. It's one where both customers and businesses win—for customers, this means more relevance, more fun, and more meaningful activity. For businesses, this means more activity, more repeated engagement, better retention, faster word of mouth and faster acquisition (through all the sharing).*

> *"What we're really going to see is a big push from consumer-facing companies to connect 'friends' into their offering. Movie/food review sites, shopping sites, media/newspaper sites, hotels, movie studios,*

restaurants, and more—everyone will start to integrate friendships and the social graph in creative ways in order to provide more relevance and to personalize content for the user."

It is the social graph—combined with tools that encourage or facilitate content creation and sharing—that literally powers a social network. Think back to the engagement process—consumption, curation, creation, and collaboration. The tools that support the sharing of information through the social graph drive the engagement process. Ultimately, collaboration is driven by relationships, and the relationships themselves are what form the social graph.

The Tools that Power a Social Graph

The tools that drive the formation of relationships and the engagement process itself range from essentially passive to highly active. During the design phase of your communities, ideation platforms, support forums, and similar, an important concept to remember is that *the more active the relationship encouragement is, the stronger in general the resulting social experiences that link participants will be.*

In a basic social-software platform—an entry level discussion or community platform, for example—deployed straight out of the box, participants are generally able to create basic profiles and engage in topic-oriented discussions. These basic social platforms may also include built-in support for photo uploading, creating profile pictures, writing individual blog posts, group formation and discussion, and so on. Note here that these are features that enable members to do things that relate primarily to consumption, curation, and creation: Members of a woodworking forum might be creating and publishing pictures of cabinets, tables, and other projects they have completed or a review of new table saw that has been recently purchased.

The exposure in these platforms is that there is often relatively little in the way of automated support for suggesting *relationships* ("Given your interest in these topics, you may be interested in these members.") or content suggestions ("You were interested in this topic, so you may also want to look at this."). Sorting out precisely who would be good to connect with is left to the participants.

As a result many discussion forums fail to move past the provision of a basic utility, providing quick one-off answers, for example, and so fail to become social sites that are visited frequently. *Note that this may be just fine with the participants at the outset:* If someone is looking for a tip on changing a fan belt in the family car or how to repair a canoe, the pure utility orientation of these basic forums and their member's *initial* interest in them starts with how quickly an answer can be found. But it doesn't—or needn't—end there. Communities grow based on the balanced interaction and contribution of *all* members: A robust social graph builds on the initial draw of basic utility—"Show me something cool I can do in this network…"—by connecting members into increasingly rich and relevant relationships with the other participants in that community to raise the overall experience to one that's more like "Show me something cool I can do with someone else that I have met through this network."

When you're creating a community, there's an additional reason to ensure a robust social graph: Purely practical value can be easily be copied into a competing network. Especially for the answers to common questions like auto repairs, minor health issues like the treatment of swimmer's ear, and DIY projects around the house, there is no shortage of sites that offer up *information*. The stickier sites, however, provide more: They add to the basic tools the experiences of more meaningful connections between members. The "stickier" the relationships are within the community, the stickier the community itself. As noted, *relationships* are what ultimately form the basis for *collaboration*, and it is collaboration that powers higher levels of *engagement*. It is, therefore, in your interest to implement or otherwise ensure that the tools within a candidate social platform strongly facilitate relationships. You buy these prebuilt in some platforms and build them on to many others. Either way, be sure that you understand what is required to implement the relationship-building activities that you'll need.

Because the development of meaningful relationships is central to the long-term value (the reason to return, again and again) of a social network, the tools that guide friendship development, social graph and content exploration, and similar actions that encourage participants to branch out are fundamentally important. As a best practice, spend some time in the design process—getting personally involved with your development team, agency, or design firm—as you plan and build social applications. Understand the capabilities and costs of the relationship-building tools and the rules that power them: The smarter and more active these tools, the more the participants will connect up, build relationships, and help each other move into the highest levels of the engagement process. This is what builds a strong community, online just as in real life.

In addition to the rules that power potential relationships (friending suggestions, for example) and engagement in the community, members need ways to find each other, to find people with whom a relationship might be beneficial. Twellow, the Twitter tool referenced earlier, is one such tool. At an even more basic level, Facebook's activity feed and Twitter's retweet capability—"RT" in Twitter parlance: the act of forwarding a tweet that you have received from someone you follow to all of your own followers— are themselves useful in discovering potential relationships.

The retweet in Twitter works to build one's social graph like this: Say Chris follows Pat, and that Pat posts something interesting that Chris sees. Chris retweets Pat's post—a lot like forwarding an email—and as a result *Chris's* followers (including those who may not have known of Pat) now see Pat's post. Chris's followers discover and follow Pat in this way—potentially increasing the size and reach of *Pat's* social graph, all because Chris thought Pat's post was interesting and simply passed it along.

In this example, it was Chris's social graph that acted as the conduit for Pat's post: The ability to easily retweet is what enabled Chris to share Pat's post, building Pat's social graph in the process. The process by which tweets propagate and drive expansion of the social graph within Twitter is shown in Figure 11.3. Pat's tweet, "something notable," is retweeted by Chris, one of whose followers sees it and decides to start following *Pat* as a result. Driving Twitter's success, among other factors, is the extreme ease with which one can grow a large social graph. As a result, Twitter gets sticky, fast.

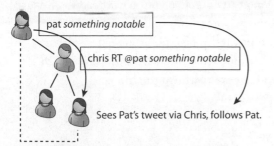

Figure 11.3 Growing the Social Graph

Beyond passing messages along, tools that enable searching, filtering, and aggregating content and sharing it between members serve to expand and refine personal social graphs. Facebook offers this capability through the combination of search and suggested friends (recommendations). Twitter introduced lists of specific members—a feature that built on and has since replaced Tweetdecks's popular groups—that people create and (optionally) share: Someone interested in horseback riding might build a list of riding coaches or professional equestrians to simply keep track of the posts from (just) these people. Twitter then provides the additional ability to share this entire list with others, making it very easy for others to further build their own social graph by following that entire list.

Use the Social Graph in Business

The social graph—and the navigation and investigation of it—are central to the use of social technology in business. Contained within the social graph are the relationships and structures that define influencers, the connections that that suggest shared interests and the pathways over which content, ratings, reviews, and a lot more move throughout a social network. So, the first step in creating a robust network or social application is to ensure that relationships form as members connect with each other and thereby enable social actions.

Make Sure People Connect

So how can you encourage participants in your social projects to connect? There are a few basics to consider, and you can always take a tip or two from the best practices used by other social networks in encouraging members' development of their own social graphs.

Recall the importance of *profile completion*. If members can't identify each other, they won't connect and build relationships. Think about it: Would you accept a LinkedIn connection request from "asdf ghjkl" in "anytown, usa"? (I actually received that request and promptly moved it to the trash.) If members are not completing profiles, add the tools that help them to do this, as is done on LinkedIn: LinkedIn shows you, as a member, the specific steps to take next to complete your social profile. Ensure that the networking platform you select supports something similar, either directly or which can be built. Many social applications offer a programming extension or an application programming interface (API), which itself offers a method by which extended capabilities can be easily added to the core platform functions.

Social Graph APIs

If you are interested in exploring the API—the programming extensions that can open up the social graph for your social applications—you may want to visit the Google and Facebook API reference sites. There are, of course, others but these will provide a useful starting point for those so inclined. You can always do more on your own!

http://code.google.com/apis/socialgraph/

http://developers.facebook.com/docs/api

Here's a tip: Figure out the capabilities you need in regards to how much you want to assist or suggest connections and similar friending activities, and then look for a pathway to implementing them *before* you select a platform. When you know what you want, it's lots easier to find it.

In addition to the tools that focus directly on social interactions and the things that facilitate them, consider contests, reputation and profile completion bonuses, and other incentives that encourage profile completion and social interaction. Relationships are possibly the single most important gating factor in the development of a strong community experience. Figure 11.4 shows LinkedIn's profile completeness indicator. As noted, relationships and the content sharing they enable are absolutely key to the progression toward engagement with your brand, product, or service.

Beyond the profile, what else can you do? The social profile—and its relative completeness—is certainly important in facilitating connections. But there are also active steps that can be taken to suggest friends, to recommend content (and hence content authors), and similar actions that help drive connections within a community. Facebook, for example, regularly recommends that friend requests be sent between members who are not currently friends, but have a number of mutual friends within the network. If Tom knows Jane, and Jane knows Mike, maybe Tom would have common interests with Mike as well. Note that this is not always the case: More than a few ill-advised "friend suggestions' have occurred as a result! But don't let that stop you: The underlying point is that through the analysis of how people are connected, reasonable suggestions can be made as to who else might benefit from also being connected. Offering that bit of helpful connection advice can make a big difference in how well your community applications develop over time.

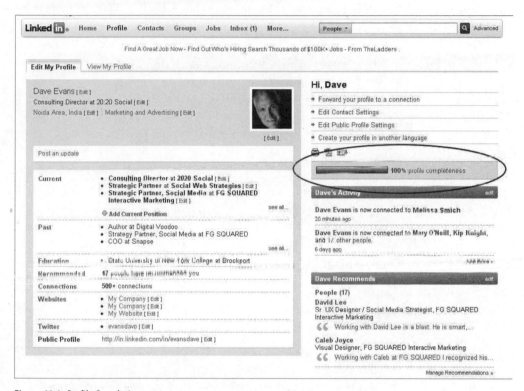

Figure 11.4 Profile Completion

In addition to recommending friends, Facebook also uses its awareness of its members' own social graphs to encourage engagement between current friends—for example, to keep "everyone involved in the party." Facebook community managers noticed that more than a few members had, as they described it, "dropped out." After an initial period of activity following their joining Facebook, the activity levels of some individuals declined to near zero.

To counter this decline in activity noted with some of its members, Facebook introduced its "reactivation" program, called "Reconnect," as an initiative to rekindle activity. However, rather than simply sending an email that said, "Hey, what's up? We haven't heard from you in a while...," Facebook turned to the social graphs of its members.

The "reconnect" initiative works like this: First, Facebook looks for people in your social graph that you haven't talked to in a while. Then, it prompts you to reach out and share something, for example, with them. After some growing pains—suggesting, for example, that someone reconnect with "an Ex-," the program effectively increased the overall member participation. With access to the social graph in the community networks that you create, and a bit of programming work, you can add this same capability to your own social efforts. Figure 11.5 shows Facebook's recommended activities, including a suggested friend and a suggestion to reach out to someone.

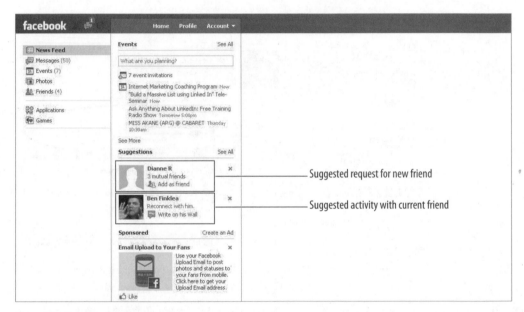

Figure 11.5 Suggested Activities

By the way, the Facebook managers noticed this—in a community of hundreds of millions—using the types of metrics covered in the final section of this chapter, "Measure the Social Graph." Don't jump there just yet, but rest assured that—as with all other aspects of social technology—the social graph is measurable.

An even simpler method of encouraging relationships and participation can be borrowed from Twitter and the way it encourages profile completion: Encourage the provision of data that will help members *find each other.* Look at the profile data that has been entered across *your* social network: Pay attention to what is required and what is optional and to the information you may *not be asking for* that is common in other networks. If people are accustomed to providing specific information in other networks, they may also be willing to provide it within yours. Take the time to find out: More information is generally better when it comes to encouraging relationships.

In particular, take steps to encourage members to responsibly provide *personally identifiable information.* You'll want to clearly explain why, and clearly disclose how it will be used and be sure this is reflected in your privacy policy. Likely too you'll need the underlying trust of your members. The big note here is that you are *not* doing this to share this information *directly* with others, but rather to provide others who already know this information from some other contact point with this member with an additional, easy way to discover friends. Got that? Here's an example: If you include an option for entering an email address in the profile—and keep it private, hidden from general view—it can still be used for *member discovery* by someone who knows that (person's) email address, providing an additional (and very efficient) method of finding friends already on Twitter. Figure 11.6 shows the email and similar data that can be used to help connect people on Twitter.

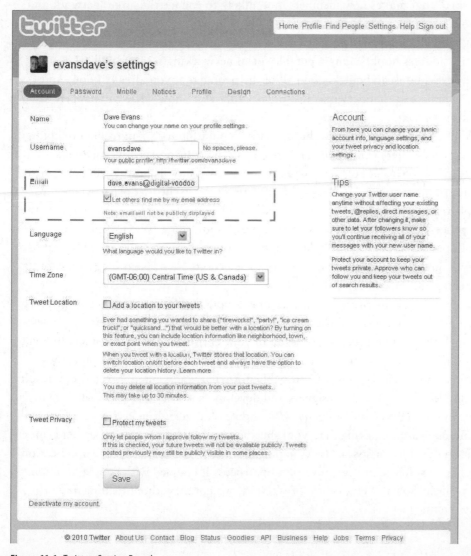

Figure 11.6 Twitter: Getting Found

Taking this one step further, by including an option for email addresses your social site—through built-in or built-on software extensions—can look into a new member's address book *with explicitly granted permission* and then suggest automatically friending or following any discovered "matches" between the new member's address book entries and the general network member's addresses.

This sort of automated "friend finding" provides a very easy way for a new member to quickly build a followers list and thereby "feel connected" to the community. Here's an example: When you join a new network, one of the sign-up steps will typically ask you for permission to access your address book, quickly locating people you already know who are also members of that network. Think of it as a social "jump start" that makes new members more likely to engage the larger network and its services.

While this can be handy, take care to *avoid* networks that immediately spam your entire address book! Many reputable social networking services will ask to look at your address book and quickly find all of the people that you already know, and who are members of that network. Just be sure that you know what will happen when you click "yes | next."

A quick note here: If you want to avoid a reputation for spam from developing around *a social network that you develop*, encourage your prospective members to *always* read the Terms of Service, and design your applications in ways that minimize the chance of inadvertent "spamming" from happening in the first place. Make it easy for people to understand the various "friending" options that are presented during the sign-up process rather than encouraging them to blindly click "Next, Next, Next." Above all, pay attention to your default sign-up options, since you already know most people will ignore the Terms of Service and click "Next, Next, Next" regardless of your warnings to the contrary.

Why does this matter? Consider as an example the dating site Jhoos. Jhoos has a sign-up process that includes friend discovery and automated invitations. A careless trip through the sign-up process will result in your entire address book—including your professional contacts—being sent invitations to join the dating site. This outcome—which comes under the heading of "probably not what you wanted"—is a direct result of a design decision by Jhoos' designers and developers. By automatically sending to *everyone* in your address book *by default*—rather than defaulting to the more conservative "no one" and requiring that (you) specifically choose—the dating site ends up taking it on the chin for spam. Use Google and search "Jhoos spam" for an indication of what happens when an aggressive sign-up process is coupled with people's *known* tendency on the Social Web to click "Yes, Next, Accept..." without reading *any* print, let alone the fine print.

Business in Social Networks

Social networks form according to a variety of primary applications—for example, for personal or cause-related activities (think Facebook, whose core appeal is for personal social interaction) or business use (as in Element 14's engineers' community where electrical designers review and purchase semiconductor components). Personal networks can attract large numbers of people who then engage in conversations and share purchase experiences, or to discuss and form groups around the interests and causes they support. Purpose-built business networks, such as Element 14's or the American Express Open Forum Small Business community, have clear business applications, built around the passions and lifestyles of the member professionals who use them.

For marketing purposes, having a business presence on personal and professional networks like LinkedIn, Facebook, or Twitter can also make sense, and in fact is now considered entry stakes for most businesses and organizations, in the same way that having a website is considered for most as a must-have. Stepping up from the basics, accessing and putting the respective social graphs to work is the basis for more substantive business applications built on or around these personal and professional networks.

Figure 11.7 shows an application of the LinkedIn social graph API, developed at 2020 Social in New Delhi. Using the combination of the LinkedIn display ads and the LinkedIn API, the application looks at the first-degree connections of the person exposed to the display ad in LinkedIn: If clicked, the landing page then lists the names of the employees of 2020 Social *who are also first-degree connections* of the LinkedIn member who saw and then clicked on the display ad: If you clicked it, you'd see the employees of 2020 Social that you knew. Taken together, the ability to examine the LinkedIn social graph and present relevant social data (first-degree connections who are also employees of 2020 Social) creates a very powerful landing page experience, and one that taps directly the value of the relationships contained in LinkedIn connections via the social graphs of its members.

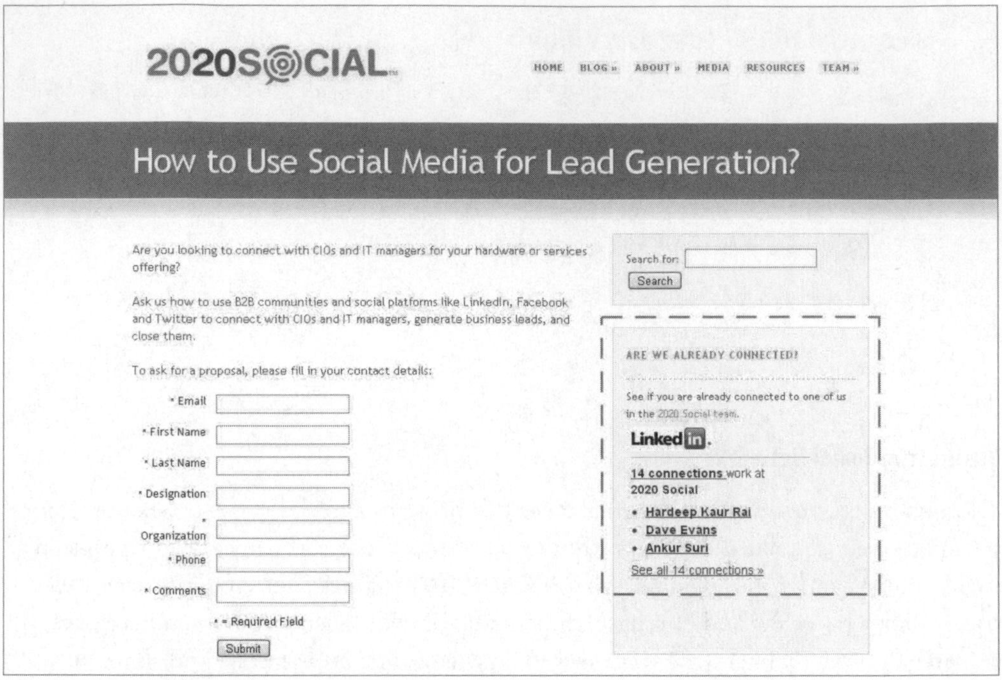

Figure 11.7 2020 Social's LinkedIn Landing Page

As another example of a practical business and organizational planning tool that leverages the social graph, Tungle.me—a shared meeting planning tool—wrapped its meetings organizer into the social graph of its users. Tungle added a publicly searchable directory that makes it easier for people to find each other: Rather than relying on two people with an existing need to schedule a meeting (and hence, giving rise to the need for use of the Tungle service between them), the Tungle Directory now opens up the service for use in quickly seeing who might be available for a meeting or other get-together.

Mapping Social Networks: LinkedIn and Gephi

LinkedIn Chief Scientist DJ Patil walks through his own LinkedIn profile using Gephi, a visual analysis tool that you can use to look at the connection patterns and other structural details within social networks. You can follow DJ Patil on Twitter (@dpatil) and watch his video presentation here:

http://gephi.org/2010/dj-patil-explaining-linkedin-social-graph-visualizations/

Malleable Social Networks

Blogger and technology evangelist Robert Scoble raised the idea of "malleable" social networks as a sort of "What's Next" or "What Should Be." Simply, a malleable social network is one that reconfigures itself dynamically, based on what a particular member is doing right now. In general, as currently implemented a member's social graph in Facebook, for example, is constant regardless of what that person is doing: Posting to your wall, or reading your news feed, for example, is *not* tied to the similar members sharing your current physical context—out of town, or at a party or conference, etc.— but rather to the larger set of members to whom you are (always) connected. Twitter and most other social networks are the same in this regard. When I am in New Delhi, my tweets go to everyone in the world who follows me, with no visibly evident context that would make these posts more relevant to the people who happen to be physically near me in New Delhi: It's up to them to make that connection, something that is not always easy. The same thing occurs when attendees gather at DrupalCon or Ad:Tech or Web 2.0 Expo. Twitter offers no mechanism—beyond the basic use of hashtags—to restrict or selectively push tweets to my followers *who are also at* the same event or are directly interested in it. On the one hand, this in some ways follows from the underlying value of sending conference information, as an example, out to people who aren't present: This practice shares the conference energy and teachings with a wider audience. On the other hand, it means that for two or three days *all* of my Twitter followers are going to get hit with posts that lack —at least in part—a proper context. A tweet like "Wow! I can't believe Chris Anderson really just said that! #adtechsf2010" is likely to elicit a wave of retweets among the conference attendees...and as many blank stares (along with a few unfollows) from my followers who are elsewhere or otherwise not interested.

The relatively fixed nature of the social graph as one moves around locally—the social graph of course still grows and shrinks over a longer time frame as friends are added or dropped—means that businesses wanting to tap into what people are doing *right now* miss out on the ability to provide the more finely nuanced offers that they could otherwise bring forth. Lacking the ability of a social graph to quickly reconfigure itself—having only the relatively crude vantage point of "one's entire graph" to act on—is akin to serving the mass rather than serving the individual. Checking in using a location-based service like Foursquare or Gowalla, for example, should immediately reconfigure my social graph on those services (and all others that have been enabled to receive this same check-in information) to focus on or otherwise highlight the activities, recommendations, and preferences of others who are nearby. At the same time, they might convey directly to one's larger following the current physical context of the individual, and so add value to the experiences of people not present (if only by alerting them that they can safely ignore the ensuing activity stream).

A business or cause-based organization could tap this directly. Running in real time against an API from a firm like Klout (see the sidebar and further description in the following "Measure the Social Graph" section), a retail establishment could quickly connect with influencers as they enter the store. A cause-related organization might reconfigure its own social graph, in real time, based on who checked in to an event. The organizers or ground staff at the event could quickly see how these people were related to other event attendees and then act on that (better) information to make the event more meaningful for these attendees. This is, in effect, what highly connected professionals do when they first walk into a networking event: They sort out quickly who is relevant to the achievement of the personal or professional objectives they have set for the event, and then create a path from the people they know to the people who can help them achieve those goals. A malleable social graph can do the same thing, but with the power of a network that is orders of magnitude larger.

The connection to business is this: In real life, most people have a few dozen "connections" and an address book with a few hundred people in it. The value of these connections is context-specific. The best known real-life connections are probably personal, family and friends while the address book is dominated by business contacts. People manage their connections within these contexts. On the Social Web, having hundreds or thousands of connections—links, friends, and followers—is common. Social business applications that present (only) the relevant portions of someone's social graph given the immediate context—think Twitter Lists—allow for easier (and therefore more frequent) use of that business application. Social applications like Foursquare and Gowalla that show which of one's friends are (also) nearby based on one's current location are beginning to make inroads into the business applications that extract from a larger social graph only those connections that are immediately relevant.

Spot Influencers

Within any community or social construct—the kind of social space that is defined by the existence of a social graph—some participants are more influential or more valuable than others in any given situation. Reputation management—touched on earlier and in Chapter 4, "The Social Business Ecosystem"—governs the *visible* aspects, the signals or markers, if you will, that identify the influencers, the leaders, and the experts within a social network, generally based on content contribution and the ratings or recommendations of other participants within that community.

Examining a particular member's social graph on its own provides a potentially different—and not always consistent—view of influence within a social network. The social graph provides an insight into influence and reputation through a study of how participants are connected. Somewhat esoteric terms like "adjacency" (the relative connectedness of individuals in a network) or "centrality" (the relative importance of an individual in a network) can also be used to determine "who matters, to whom, and why" within a social network. If you could walk into a party and see this kind of information in your augmented reality browser (neatly displayed behind your sunglasses), how much more effective could you be as a networker? The same principle applies—in much more realistic terms—to your business or organizational use of social graph analysis and visualization tools today.

As understanding of "who matters" is great information for a wide range of social applications. However, there is one broad class of applications in particular where this type of information is absolutely critical: support networks. In a support network, participants depend on each other for solutions, and the consequences of bad information can be much worse than, say, getting bad advice on a movie or a meal out. In a support forums, spotting, elevating, and otherwise ensuring that the experts remain engaged is essential to the long-term success of that support platform.

When the social graph is examined and compared to the reputation management system outputs, the experts can be located, groomed, and specifically catered to, thus ensuring that they a) have what they need to consistently deliver the best answers as they support the community at large, and b) feel that their time is distinctly noted and valued. On the former, when expert candidates are identified—for example, by high centrality—having a relatively high number of followers, the managers of that community might invite those people to attend a special training event or to become a part of an "insiders" program to ensure that they continue to have access to the information needed to deliver quality solutions within the support community. *Adjacency* (who is connected to whom) is equally important. Think about how LinkedIn adds value by showing its members the direct or potential path(s) from the people they know to the people they want to know. Indeed, a deeper study or observation of the social graph of your customers and constituents can be very beneficial.

If you haven't already, take a look at the video referenced in the "Mapping Social Networks: LinkedIn and Gephi" sidebar. Consider the usefulness of understanding—at a mass scale—the social graph detail that is exposed through the use of visual mapping tools. Being able to see clusters of customers, for example, built around specific concerns or organized into specific subgroups within your larger social business application is very useful when developing specific activation strategies for important customer segments.

Spread Content Further

In addition to connecting people (members and participants) outright, the social graph is also useful as a conduit in spreading content—thoughts, ideas, words, pictures, and videos—across social networks. In the earlier Twitter example, I referenced Pat's tweet and showed how Chris picked it up and retweeted it, expanding Pat's social graph and spreading Pat's content beyond Pat's own immediate social graph in the process. Not only was Pat's social graph expanded in the process, Pat's content was spread further when Pat's and Chris's individual social graphs were momentarily merged through Chris's retweet of Pat's content.

In this way, the social graphs of members can be used to spread content further, to and between members across distinct social networks whose social graphs intersect. What does it mean to say that two social networks—or the individual social graphs contained within them—*intersect*? Simply, it means that two members, each with their own social graph, have someone (generally, another person) in common. Looked at a different way, if Marcia is a member of both Facebook and Twitter, then Marcia's personal social graph actually spans two networks, and you could describe Marcia as a *point of intersection* between these distinct graphs.

Going further into the larger graphs that span social networks, Facebook introduced "Open Graph"—a set of tools built around its API that makes it easy to connect content (and hence, participants) in social networks or content sites *outside* of Facebook with its members *inside* of Facebook. It works like this: Using a small code block that can be automatically generated on the Facebook Developer's pages (see sidebar), content developers on almost any network can introduce Facebook's "Like" function to their content that is outside the Facebook social network. When someone clicks a Like button associated with a specific piece of content that is *outside* of Facebook, a status update is published *inside* Facebook, alerting others who are themselves Facebook members that this content exists and that someone they know "likes" it. As people inside (and outside) of Facebook see these notices, and as a result click the Like button that is associated with that same content, the "like" rating of that content goes up, furthering its spread.

Managing Your Social Graph

Minggl is a browser-based plug-in that connects your social graphs across the major social networks: Using Minggl you can centrally manage your Facebook, LinkedIn, Twitter, and MySpace profiles and friends lists. Disclosure: I am a cofounder and shareholder in Minggl.

`http://www.minggl.com`

The kinds of connections and content visibility offered via Facebook's Like plugin can be a very powerful way to increase the visibility of content outside of Facebook—say, content in your branded community—that is also conveyed into Facebook; for example, by connecting to your Facebook business page. This capability drives social graph growth (through content spreading) as much as it is driven by the social graph itself (through member-initiated friending, for example): New friends can be suggested, for example, based on the common "likes" of specific content or other objects, and can likewise be introduced to "suggested friends" who also happen to like this same content. This extends as well to recommendations and other forms of content that can also be personalized as they are shared, adding an additional element of clutter-cutting credibility to the entire process.

By extension, what works for published content—across networks—also works for content served into networks—content like ads, for example. Using the social graph, content that is being syndicated or published into a social network can be optimized based on the likes and dislikes of those in a particular member's social graph. Going a step further, advertisements that leverage the social graph can actually display the fact that others within a particular person's social graph happen to "like" this advertised product or service. It's a sort of 2.0 version of "All your friends are doing it, so perhaps you'd like to try it as well."

KickApps, purveyors of a white-label (they provide the core application, and you brand it) social networking platform and toolset aimed at publishers, has built this exact capability into their platform. Called the KickApps Social Graph Engine, the functional value is the optimization of incoming advertising according to the collective likes and dislikes of the member's friends, expressed through an individual's social graph.

KickApps: Social Graph Engine

KickApps offers a companion suite of social graph plug-ins and tools that work with Facebook and other social and content publishing tools. You can review the KickApps platform here:

http://www.kickapps.com/applications/the-kickapps-platform

Connect Communities

As a final point in the application of the social graph, consider the imminent rise of the "universal social graph" and its potential impact on business and cause-based organizations. While the Social Web is certainly about connecting and sharing—and to a much greater degree than websites, whether business or personal, ever were—there is still an element of "one winner must emerge." What was once AOL and then Friendster, then MySpace followed by Facebook and Twitter, and... will continue to morph.

Off in the distance lies the universal social graph—the single-location collection of your various profiles and personas. Think of personas as tuned personal profiles, sort of like your accountant (one persona) who takes to the highway on a Harley-Davidson Softail every other weekend (a different persona, related to the same underlying individual, or profile). The universal social graph approaches the challenge of maintaining multiple profiles, friends lists, and activity feeds by collecting it all around an individual and then plugging an appropriate identity into specific social applications as needed.

Of more-than-trivial consequence, the fact that most social networks require individual participants to create an entire, complete profile for use exclusively inside that specific social network actually limits cross-network participation. As a practical matter, how many profiles do you really want to maintain? This is a question that more and more social networking participants are beginning to ask, and eventually you will have to address this in the design of your social business applications.

As an alternative to the network-centric profiles of Facebook and similar networks, consider Ning. Ning members create a single identity, and then use that as the basis for membership across the various Ning communities that they choose to join. A Ning member may be associated with one or more sports communities, a professional group, a college alumni network and one or more lifestyle- or cause-based Ning communities. Regardless, it's the same individual that is linked in all of these. This is similar to the approach of Looppa (referenced earlier in Chapter 4) in the development of its connected communities, wherein members of specific communities are able to create and share content across linked communities rather than only within one community.

Very important here—and a key in understanding the differences in potential implementations between a Ning-based presence versus Facebook, for example—is that Ning is not simply a "single sign on" protocol applied to a collection of individual networks. Instead, Ning is an example of an approach to social networking that begins with the personal profile, and then attaches that profile to the various social applications that have relevance to the individual represented by that profile. This is definitely a trend to watch as it is yet another push in the movement away from centralized social hubs and "websites-as-islands" and toward a social experience that is defined first by the identity of the participants (via the profile) and then second by the context (specific social applications) in which they participate.

The take-away from this discussion is this: As you set out and plan your social technology, consider how (and if) members of your support forum, for example, will join it and share content as appropriate outside of that network—for example, in another community where they may be advocating the use of your products for which they are (also) seeking support through your support forum. Whether through a mechanism like Facebook's Open Graph, Ning's approach of "one identity, multiple communities," or the use of OpenSocial (a social networking toolset developed by Google, MySpace, and others), you will want to make it easy for your participants to share experiences and move content across social networks just as they do within a single network. As business applications involving social technology develop further, the ability to easily traverse intersecting social graphs will gain in importance.

Measure the Social Graph

In the process of building a community or support forum or similar program the need for measurement obviously arises. Aside from basic measures such as page views, bounce rate, and the other standard web analytics that are often reported within social communities—these are after all still web applications, at some level—there is a richer set of measurable quantities that get directly at the behaviors of most interest.

Participation, influence, and the spread (growth) of the social graph can all be observed and measured. Importantly, by tracking the types of social activities that are direct indicators of social behaviors, a community, for example, can be "tuned" according to the preferences of its members and thereby become more useful, more likely to be embraced and shared, and more likely to survive and thrive as a result.

Participation

Measuring member participation is a great starting point for understanding how likely a social network is to grow. Participation is a direct indication of how useful the community or forum is considered *by its members* to be. Measuring participation is straightforward: Because there are obvious external indicators such as "number of members" or the degree to which profiles are complete (unlike "bounce rate" or "time spent on a page," which require analytics tools and conjecture as to meaning), the social behaviors can be monitored easily. Big Note: This also means that members of the social network can see them. If the measures "aren't good," then this will be visible to everyone.

Table 11.1 presents a set of metrics that can be used as indicators of participation. These are measures of *individual* rather than group (shared) behaviors. For example, week-over-week growth rate among members (as well as among for-pay versus freemium membership, etc.), the number of profiles that are complete, and the number of groups formed or active (if applicable) or similar associations (new forum topics, and participation within them, for example) are all great (and easy to obtain) measures that can be tracked and used to guide the growth of the social network.

▶ Table 11.1 Suggested Measures of Participation

Metric	What It Means
Registered Members	Overall membership level: Indicates how many people are *potentially* interested in participating in this application. It's "potentially" because *joining* a network and *using it* are two different things.
Profiles with Photo	Number of members who have taken this significant step in profile completion: Building on "registered members," the various elements associated with profile completeness give a better indication of actual interest in the social application.

Metric	What It Means
Profiles by Completeness	Tiered profile completion: Looking at the trends and overall completion curve can provide insight as to how to encourage higher levels of completeness. High levels of profile completeness drive friending and similar relationship development.
Active Groups, Number of Open Topics	Activity levels around specific topics, interest areas. Along with profile completeness, the relative tendency for participants to form or participate in groups is a direct indication of usefulness and interest in the social application.
Average Members per Group	The degree to which groups are broadly attractive versus tuned to niche interests provides insights in ways in which the social application can be extended.

Beyond the metrics in Table 11.1, participation can be measured externally by tracking publishing events outside the network (through the Facebook Open Graph events, for example), as well as through social analytics and similar tools that are able to report on the end-products of activities within the community—things like content, ratings, reviews, and other social actions.

Influence

Like participation, *influence* can also be measured. Influence can be measured inside the social network using the visible indicators described in Table 11.2 and using network-specific tools such as netvizz (a Facebook application). The analytical tools they provide within Facebook can be used to measure the quality of interactions and activity data overall that is associated with business pages. Influence can also be measured through the use of external tools.

Additional measures of behavior—for example, behaviors that connect what is happening on one particular network with the larger discussions happening elsewhere on the Social Web—include influencer analysis through the use of tools like BuzzStream. Tools designed to spot influencers as they act *inside* the community are also valuable. Lithium Technologies offers a particularly robust set of "expert identification" tools that are very helpful in spotting and supporting the "experts" that emerge (naturally) in a support or similar type of community. Klout (see sidebar) offers an interesting, for-pay service in addition to its free service. Interested individuals can visit Klout and calculate the influence score for their own social presence. On top of that, Klout offers—via its own API—a for-pay service that allows anyone to calculate the relative influence scores for participants in their own social networks.

▶ **Table 11.2** Measures of Influence

Metric	What It Means
Average Number of Friends	The degree to which people are connecting to others is useful in understanding the ease with which relationships form. If this is low relative to expectations, look at the mechanism for friending or consider adding automated suggestions for relationships.
"Top 10" by Friend Count	Who are the most connected, and does this change over time? This will help you identify your community leaders.
Popular Group or Topic Themes	What are the big interest areas? Knowing this is fundamental to encouraging the development of new applications.
Most popular brands, products, services	What are the common interests, focused on marketing and business? What are people talking about that is important (business-wise) to you?
Most viewed events, members, etc.	What are the popular activities? Combined with popular groups and conversational themes, this information provides specific guidance in ongoing activity development.

Spread

One final measure that may be of interest: Referring back to the discussion of homophily—the tendency for like-minded individuals to link together in a social network—there are ways to measure the degree to which this is happening. This is useful to know because it suggests, for example, the degree to which a particular site is bringing individuals together as a rate that is different from what would happen by chance.

In other words, by studying the effects of homophily in a social setting, the degree to which the social network itself is successfully driving friendships or other relationships over and above what would be expected, provides an indication as to the value and performance of the relationship tools—the ability to search and discover interesting connections, for example—and hence a measure of how likely the community is to grow, and the degree to which it is adding social (versus purely functional) value to its members.

314

Review and Hands-On

Chapter 11 provided a deeper look into the social graph and the role that it plays in connecting individuals, in driving new relationships, and in spreading content. Chapter 11 drew a subtle distinction between two other nearly interchangeable terms: a *social network*—an interconnected set of people, relationships, and activities built around a common theme or platform—and the *social graph*—as defined here to be the actual links between members and the ways in which those members are connected.

Review of the Main Points

The key points covered in Chapter 11 are summarized below. How might you incorporate these points into the design or use of the social applications you are planning for your business or organization?

- The social graph is key to the sharing of content and the spreading of shared experiences across social networks.

- The social graph can be used in business, both as an indicator of who is connected to whom, and as an indicator of who might like to meet whom or where specific content should be pushed.

- The behavioral aspects of the social graph can be measured and used to monitor and tune the larger social network.

The social graph—while not as immediately obvious or as visible as shared content or the direct use of a social application—is an absolute key in developing and maintaining a vibrant social experience for the benefit of the participants in that shared experience. The role of the moderators, the design of the interaction points, and the degree to which participants can discover potentially valuable relationships are all driven by the existence and makeup of a participant's social graph(s).

Hands-On: Review These Resources

Review each of the following, and then take note of what you learn and insights you gain. How can you apply (or specify the use of) these items in your own projects and the further development of your understanding of social technology?

Facebook Open Graph Plug-ins for use in social-media-based marketing:

http://developers.facebook.com/plugins

Open Social and its applications in business: (See: "Get Started")

http://wiki.opensocial.org

The use of the XFN Protocol in business:

http://gmpg.org/xfn/

Tools, papers, and resources available through membership in the INSNA and the larger discussion of social network analysis:

http://www.insna.org/

Hands-On: Apply What You've Learned

Apply what you've learned in this chapter through the following exercises:

1. Draw out your first-degree network in your office, and then do the same in some personal aspect of your life, a civic organization for example. Who is in both networks? What content is shared between these networks as a result?

2. Look at your friends in some of the social networks you belong to: How many of these friends or people you follow are people you knew prior to joining versus the number you met after joining? How were those you met after joining referred or suggested?

3. Develop a set of specific metrics for your social business applications that involve the social graph. Create a regular report, and track these measures over time.

Social Applications

Social applications combine the attraction of social objects, the power of the social graph, and the natural tendency for people to gather and converse. Because social applications connect, enable, and coordinate the interactions of participants within and across communities and other social networks to which they belong, they offer a straightforward way to realize a powerful business presence on the Social Web. This chapter wraps up Part III with a look at how to define and implement successful social applications.

Chapter Contents

What Is a Social Application?

Social applications, simply, are software components that facilitate interaction between members of a social network. Social applications are built around social objects—lifestyles, passions, and causes, along with myriad talkworthy smaller objects such as short posts (tweets, for example), photos, videos, and more. Social applications are driven by the connections embodied in the individual social graphs of participants, and as such act as efficient conduits for the spread of information within the network.

While the distinction between "social network" and "social application" may be debated elsewhere, as used here the terms are defined specifically. ReadWriteWeb offers a particularly succinct definition of *social application* in the context of the business use of social technology:

> *"Social Application: Software that coordinates group interaction that is important to running your business or organization."*

Here's an example: Facebook, in general conversation, would most typically be referred to as a social network. Friends are connected to each other within Facebook's social network through the individual social graphs of respective members. SocialVibe's charitable giving application, shown in Figure 12.1, is one of the thousands of applications available within Facebook. SocialVibe is a social application: It allows Facebook members to turn views of their own profile pages into cash donations that benefit a charitable cause that they themselves have selected. Note too that while SocialVibe was cited in the example of a social application, social applications aren't limited to these kinds of discrete applications. Facebook —when talking about its software and the native functions it provides to its members—is itself a social application.

As established in prior chapters, the definitions actually matter less than being consistent about what is meant by terms like social networks, social graphs, and social applications. Throughout this chapter, the term *social application* refers to social software and embedded or installed applications within a social context that facilitate social interactions between participants with that network.

The central idea that a social application combines group interaction and capabilities "important to running your business or organization" is related to the focus of this book: the business use of social technology. Suffice it to say that if a particular social activity is not relevant to your business, it's probably not a good candidate for your social media and social business programs.

A second point to consider with regard to social applications is that they typically play a role in elevation of or otherwise depend on the presence of an *identity*, typically expressed through the profiles that define the "nodes" within a social graph. Recall the discussion around identity and the work of J. D. Lasica in Chapter 4,

"The Social Business Ecosystem." Without *identity* in at least a general or contextual sense—and with the exception of specific applications that for a variety of reasons appropriately allow anonymity—sharing and collaboration are *much less* likely to occur, if they occur at all. For typical business applications of social technology, sharing and collaboration are among the primary goals: Identity—and details like profile completeness—really matter. On Facebook and Twitter, for example, there are no guarantees ("verified" accounts aside) of claimed identity: However, with friends or followers in common across participants, it is fairly simple to assure yourself that at least the basic elements of most profiles are in fact authentic.

Figure 12.1 A Social Application

What kinds of social applications appropriately relax their identity requirements? Think about a nonprofit, for example, that might encourage participants to share stories about cancer survival, corporate noncompliance, or physical abuse. As well, a sporting goods company or one of its retailers may want submissions of experiences using its gear, but may provide the option of not publishing the names of those submitting these stories. Social apps come in a variety of forms, and not all of them require that a full personal identity be provided. How much needs to be included in order that your social application encourages participation by and among members is for you to decide. One way to answer this is to ask participants how much they are willing to share, taking care to explain the benefits of providing such information as well as exactly how it will be used.

What this all comes down to is the realization that it is the combination of both *identity* and *functionality* that support high degrees of social interaction within a social application. Profile completeness and reputation management are important aspects in the design of social applications, right along with specific functional tools including those that support content uploading, friending, sharing, rating, tagging, and more. If participants don't know with whom they are sharing—or can't curate or share content easily—they are less likely to share at all, shutting down the higher levels of engagement like content creation and collaboration that are central to realizing value through the business applications of social technology.

Taken together, it's the combination of the above that is important to your business or organization. Consider this within the context of a social network that involves identifiable participants (again, as appropriate) and in so doing create the opportunity for highly specialized social applications that enable collaboration and content sharing. This is the overall approach that defines the successful social application in the business context.

Social Applications Drive Engagement

Examples of social applications that drive higher levels of engagement include SocialVibe's charitable giving application (mentioned in the opening of the chapter), Starbucks' use of Foursquare (a location-based social application), the Foursquare "mayors" program that rewards frequent visitors, and Dell's use of Twitter as one of its many brand outposts. In Europe, Opel|Vauxhall have created a customer service built on Twitter using its basic accounts, @opelblog and @vauxhall along with the hashtags #OpelService and #VauxhallService, allowing customers to easily connect, ask questions, and make other inquiries relating to these automobiles. Twitter is a social application with obvious business development and customer care applications: Twitter enables two-way interaction between a business and its customers (and between customer themselves). Dell's Small Business group, Comcast's customer service team, and Australian telecom firm Telstra all use Twitter as a conduit for information that connects their respective business programs with their customers. The majority of the cases and examples presented in this book have been, in some form or another, a type or instance of a social application.

Given the encompassing nature of social applications, how then does one segregate the various functions and uses of these tools for planning and design purposes? Clearly, lumping together Dell's "IdeaStorm," SocialVibe's charitable giving application, and Foursquare's "Mayor's" designations as used by Starbucks and saying "I want one of those" isn't likely to produce a successful outcome. What's needed is a way to categorize the various types of social applications so that they can be connected with business objectives. Business objectives, after all, drive the specification and development of social applications.

I Love You More Than My Dog

As an aside, read the book *I Love You More Than My Dog* (Portfolio Hardcover, 2009). Author Jeanne Bliss goes into detail in the processes that create amazing customer experiences: Not only are these are the kinds of insights gained through collaborative social applications, they also point up the degree that Operations and Marketing must work together to build long-term customer loyalty. You can follow Jeanne on Twitter (@jeannebliss) and read more about Jeanne and her work here:

http://customerbliss.com/

Important to note here is what is meant by a "successful outcome." Josh Gordon, President of Selling 2.0, published a whitepaper in *Social Media Today* entitled "The Coming Change in Social Media Business Applications: Separating the Biz from the Buzz." Josh points out the roughly 60/40 split between the use of social technology in business for branding (about 60 percent) versus *collaborative* applications (about 40 percent). While lots of businesses and organizations are using social media—recent CMO surveys have put adoption at something north of 80 percent—the majority of these uses are still rooted in a traditional approach to marketing. Given the numbers of people who collect around social sites, the appeal of marketing programs that are intended to push a message into these sites is understandable, but it misses the larger gains in engagement that come about through social applications that support content creation, sharing, and collaboration. Using social applications for *awareness* can provide a starting point, but there is more that can be done.

For social-media-based marketing, the beneficial impact to branding efforts, increased lead generation, and "more buzz" are all success-oriented objectives. To be sure, however, these applications barely scratch the surface of social technology. What is of interest here—and what defines "success"—is the degree to which *collaboration* as a result of the implementation of social technology is achieved. The degree to which collaboration between participants is achieved is, therefore, one of the primary indicators of a "successful outcome," again with the note that this is always measured within the context of the underlying business objectives.

The take-away from the discussion around defining successful outcomes and the use of social technology is this: Social technology deployed in a business context drives higher levels of engagement (content creation and collaboration). Social applications serve as connectors between participants, as extensions of built-in social network functionality, as crowdsourcing and content publishing tools, and more within the communities they define or the social structures in which they are implemented. Sure, social technology can be used to drive awareness, but so can a dozen other channels. What social technology and social applications in particular are uniquely great at is driving participation—sharing, creating, and collaborating around content rooted in lifestyles, passions, and causes.

As an example of social applications driving engagement at higher levels like creation and collaboration, consider New Belgium Beer, makers of Fat Tire amber ale and other beers. The team at New Belgium laid out its business objectives:

- Engage New Belgium's existing fan base on Facebook and reach out to their friends.

- Pick up on the style, vernacular, and creative assets already used on the New Belgium website, and then reflect through the fans' voices.

- Create contests and similar engagement applications that fit the brand image and appeal to the underlying passions and interests of the fans.

- Ultimately, further grow New Belgium's Facebook fan count by attracting *true* fans, not just those looking for the next brand giveaway.

Working with Friend2Friend, based in Palo Alto and Barcelona, an engagement program was put in place that connected New Belgium fans with the brand ethos by building around the passions and interests of those fans. *Disclosure: I am an advisor to Friend2Friend.*

I talked with Friend2Friend CEO Roger Katz about the New Belgium engagement program. When I asked about the origin of the program, Roger described it like this:

"New Belgium wanted to increase the number of fans on its Facebook Fan Page through entertaining, social activities while staying true to the brand image. They also wanted to preferentially attract authentic New Belgium fans—real beer drinkers who enjoyed fine beer. The program team includes Backbone Media (Agency of Record for New Belgium) and Friend2Friend."

I then asked Roger about the Friend2Friend social application and what it was intended to do. Roger explained:

"Friend2Friend picked up on the vernacular of the New Belgium website and created 'What's Your Folly?', a contest where Facebook members can become a fan and describe their folly—their passion or interest—and thereby enter a weekly drawing for a limited edition New Belgium cruiser bike: The bicycle is also a part of the New Belgium brand ethos."

As fans read of others' follies (content consumption) and then declared their own personal follies (content creation), the interest in the contest grew, spreading through Facebook via the Friend2Friend social application. Roger added:

"The resulting Folly Gallery of over 6,000 follies gives New Belgium a base of branded user-generated content to jump-start their next promotional programs."

Simply put, New Belgium's customers are, as a result, collaborating with the company and its agency to design the next round of engagement campaigns.

Now for the hard question: "What happened, and how was it measured?" Roger's response:

"In a five week period, almost 7,000 users downloaded the social application and submitted personal follies, generating over 1 million social impressions through news-feeds, wall posts, and Fan Page visits. New Belgium gained 10,000 new fans. Contest participants spent an average of four minutes creating their entries and reviewing those of others."

Compared with a 30-second spot, that's a big gain in attention.

In summary, New Belgium built its engagement campaign around Facebook, using an existing social application (Friend2Friend) that was customized for this particular use. Higher levels of engagement were clearly seen, and the results were measured and successfully tied back to the original underlying business objectives.

As you look for ways to use social applications in your business, consider the specific type of applications that you can choose from: The New Belgium example of contest-driven engagement and fan recruitment is but one of the choices available to you. Following are the primary buckets into which social applications can be organized to simplify the process of creating a strategy that links your business objectives with the many types of social applications that are available or which can be built.

Social Graph Applications

Social applications connect people: That much is obvious. It's what happens beyond the basic connection that matters, and especially in business applications of social technology. Consider Twitter: It's possible—but rarely recommended—to buy followers (literally, for money). Prices run a hundred dollars, give or take, for a few thousand followers. The question is why—beyond *looking* popular—would you want to do this? I sure don't have the answer.

Instead of buying followers, what generally makes more sense is to introduce into a social network the tools that make following happen naturally and spontaneously. Think back to touchpoint analysis: What is it about your brand, product, or service that makes it talkworthy? Now apply this same thinking to your social presence: What about it would make someone want to follow your brand on Twitter, join your business page on Facebook, or offer up their own ideas through an ideation application? Combining the answers to these questions with specific tools or applications that make it easy for the participants in your social application to connect will grow a stronger network than will buying one.

Facebook and Twitter, for example, both have functionality built into the platforms that suggests friends or recommends interaction between friends, both of which drive additional connections. LinkedIn offers an overt "profile completeness" indicator: A higher percentage of relatively more-complete profiles encourages more connections between social network participants. When planning and building a social application (or joining into one, as a business), it's a best practice to include explicit indications of profile completion—for example, indicating the current completeness level *and* advising members as to what else needs to be done to fully complete individual profiles.

Twitter Marketing: An Hour a Day

If you're interested in learning more about how Twitter can be applied to business, take a look at *Twitter Marketing: An Hour a Day* (Sybex, 2010) by Hollis Thomases. You can follow Hollis (@hollisthomases) on Twitter as well.

In addition to the basic connection and automation tools that encourage additional connections based on specific personal factors—content interests or other current friends—consider a social application like Slide's "Top Friends" Facebook application. Top Friends has about 8 million people actively using it: Top Friends facilitates the creation of a secondary social graph within Facebook based on your closest friends or must trusted advisors. Why the interest in Top Friends? Read on.

Within Facebook, someone may have 300 friends overall: That's a lot of people to keep track of. Through the Top Friends application—which you can find on Facebook by searching for "Top Friends"—this same person can designate an "inner circle," so to speak, that is limited to a much smaller group. This use of the Top Friends social application results in increased value to the specific members involved as it allows them to reconfigure their respective social graphs in ways that better reflect their own social needs and relationships within the larger (and less personal) context of Facebook as a whole.

How might "Top Friends" be adapted as a business-oriented social application? Jive Software includes modules that indicate the top participants and most popular content, for example, both of which can be used to focus participant attention on the members (and content) getting the most play. As you plan your social application, give plenty of forethought to exactly how it is that participants will manage the friends and members that collect around that person with that application.

Why This Matters in Business

Whether you choose to create a social application of your own or join one that is already in place, the extent to which connections are *actively encouraged* and can be *efficiently managed* are important considerations. Look for tools, functions, and processes—along with the ability to build on them or modify them in ways that make it more likely that participants will create connections between themselves. Not only will this result in increased use and "stickiness" of the community or larger social application, it will also help participants create richer social graphs that facilitate content sharing and the general spread of ideas between people.

As you look at the ways in which you can encourage connections, consider adopting and trending specific metrics and KPIs (Key Performance Indicators) that reflect the degree to which connections and two-way relationships are being created. These KPIs can help you evaluate the effects of connections-oriented tools that you may use, create, or add later on. In addition, insisting on a focus on measurement right from the start puts your social business program on a solid base.

Social Network Extensions

When building a social network, whether from scratch or through a ready-to-use "software as a service" (SaaS) or proprietary platform, or instead building onto an existing social networking platform like Orkut or MySpace, there will be a set selection of prebuilt components and functions that you'll use to define your core participant interactions. Typical of these prebuilt functions are content ratings, member reputation, content uploading, blogging or posting, and similar functions. While these will likely cover the majority of what you'd like participants to be able to do within that application—creating a profile, friending, uploading content, etc.—there will also be a set of more specific activities driven by your business objectives that may not be immediately available. You'll have to specify and implement these features yourself.

The starting point when building (or specifying) custom social applications and components that extend the base functionality is your stated business objective. For example, when Dell built "Take Your Own Path," its entrepreneur community, the objective was creating a connection *outside of the brand* that was attractive to an important segment of its small business and entrepreneurial customer base. Using this connection, those participants are able to learn more about how other similar business owners and technology managers are using the kinds of hardware that Dell provides.

In the "Take Your Own Path" example, connecting with customers was the business objective. When Indian mobile operator Aircel wanted to simultaneously differentiate its brand—its business objective as a newer telecom firm being development of market share and awareness—it chose an application that gave current customers an identifiable reason to talk with friends and family about Aircel and its unique (within the Indian market) and highly simplified approach to pricing and marketing its Internet (versus voice) services: Aircel created a voicemail application *inside* Facebook, where Aircel knew that a significant number of its mobile customers spent time. By creating a voicemail application within Facebook, Aircel effectively said to its customer base, "We understand that you like to socialize and stay in touch with each other *online*: Having to check your voice mail is a distraction from these activities. So, we've integrated the conversations that happen on *our* network into *your* network, where you and your friends already spend time."

Beyond creating a community or implementing an extension of the available functionality within a social network, how else can you use social technology to extend your own social points of presence—your blog or your website, for example? If your business objectives include expanding your presence, spreading awareness of your business or organization, or similar objectives built around visibility and participation, then one approach might be to *link* your current online content and popular presence points that are relevant to your customers or stakeholders. For example, using the Like plug-in, you can connect your website or blog content directly into Facebook: When someone visits your (external) web page or blog and clicks the embedded Like button, that person is simultaneously (assuming this person is a member of Facebook) sharing this content with friends in Facebook. In Figure 12.2 you can see how this works: When I visit my colleague Gaurav Mishra's blog, my clicking the Like button results in a posting to my wall in Facebook that my friends see, exposing them to Gaurav's post.

How else might you connect to a wider audience via the social graph and social applications that are built on it? Pandora uses Facebook's social graph applications to connect members who are also friends around shared interests in music: one member will be prompted to listen to a particular artist because the *friends* of this person are also listening to that artist. Whether or not this seems a bit "Big Brother-ish" is secondary (unless that aspect of these kinds of social applications directly conflict with your brand values). What matters more is that it's becoming an acceptable way to spread content. As much as we all pride ourselves on being individuals, a lot of what we do (and therefore purchase) is driven by what we see others like ourselves doing.

Figure 12.2 Facebook's Like Button

Facebook Marketing: An Hour a Day

If you're interested in learning more about how you can use YouTube in business, check out the newest edition of Chris Treadaway and Mari Smith's *Facebook Marketing: An Hour a Day* (Sybex, 2010). You can follow Chris (@ctreada) and Mari (@marismith) on Twitter as well.

Finally, through the basic best practice of ensuring that everything you produce is easy to share, be sure to include links to the obvious: Twitter, Digg, and similar sharing services can make a big difference in the visibility of the content created by participants within your social applications. Include links to these services in everything you do, and by extension to everything that is created in your applications. Be sure as well that you create your own presence, where appropriate, in existing social networks, especially if your customers or stakeholders spend time there. Known as *brand outposts*, these networks are an easy way to extend your presence into the places where your customers spend time.

Why This Matters in Business

In the previous examples, the firm's business objectives (being more relevant to more customers to drive more sales) and social technology strategy (being more relevant in the places where customers are already spending time) are what lead to the implementation of the respective applications. Extending the functionality of an existing social network in which you create an outpost, or creating new functionality for a white-label or SaaS social application that you are building around can be an important aspect of a business or cause-related effort to both *build* (awareness) and *activate* (collaboration) customers and stakeholders.

Importantly, as you review and consider the examples presented throughout this book, do so with your own business objectives and the behaviors of your own audience in mind. Unless a specific example or social technology application was called out as something to avoid, you can assume that if it's in this book (or being talked about elsewhere on the Web) that it is or was a "good idea" *for someone*. However, don't be led into the trap of chasing others' good ideas: Instead, link the applications you see here and elsewhere with the underlying business objectives that gave rise to them and then see if *your* business objectives (and the behaviors and capabilities of your audience) line up with them. If so, you've got a potential match: If not, note the idea for possible future review (perhaps creating an entry for it on your internal "future ideas" application) and then move on.

Content Publishing and Sharing

In addition to outright social networks and the more tightly defined extensions and functional tools that enable participants to accomplish very specific goals, social applications include more generalized software services around which some form of social interaction takes place. Examples of these types of social applications include YouTube for general media sharing, along with services like Scribd, Google Docs, and Slideshare. Scribd and Google Docs, for example, both support publishing and *sharing* nearly any type of document; Slideshare is specific to—and therefore particularly good at—sharing slide presentations. Slideshare and Scribd are excellent places to publish thought-leadership content that your business or organization creates: You'll benefit from the social interaction (commenting and reviewing) and increased visibility (sharing) that these social sites provide.

YouTube offers the immediate usefulness of posting content (rather than hosting it yourself) and sharing it from that point both within YouTube and by embedding that video content elsewhere. YouTube is an ideal place to post content that is then shared through your other points of social presence (making content easier to manage, since you don't have copies floating about). YouTube also provides the built-in benefits of sharing and exposure in its own social contexts: YouTube offers branded business channels, for example, something you can use to organize and share sequences of related content.

What else can you with YouTube? A lot, as it turns out. Conduct interviews with customers and employees, and then post them: In Chapter 3, "Build a Social Business," Freescale's use of YouTube for employment videos and product announcements was noted. You can show customers using your products, offer testimonials, and provide coverage of your own presentations as a part of your outreach and thought leadership efforts. Figure 12.3 shows a video of a presentation with Intuit CEO Brad Smith, as he talks about what Intuit has learned as it embraces social technology as a business. You can find the video on YouTube by searching for its title, "User Generated Unemployment at Intuit." This video is definitely worth watching: Brad describes his firm's coming to grips with some of the very challenges that any organization implementing social technology is likely to face.

34 Ways to Use YouTube for Business

B2B social media professional Meryl Evans (no relation) offers this list of some of the many ways that YouTube can be used as a part of a social media program in business.

http://webworkerdaily.com/2009/07/28/34-ways-to-use-youtube-for-business/

Figure 12.3 Intuit CEO Brad Smith's Interview on YouTube

While the benefits of sharing content through social applications like Twitter and YouTube are largely self-evident, there are additional applications for content-sharing social sites. If your business objectives include establishing a position as a thought leader, or if you are looking for collaborative input around early ideas that are appropriate for sharing publicly, consider using applications like Scribd, Google Docs, and Slideshare. If you've hosted a webinar, or developed a research paper around a topic of general interest, consider publishing it on these sites.

Slideshare and Scribd are particularly useful for small businesses, consultants, and anyone else regardless of the organization size or vertical specialty interested in thought leadership. Combined with a corporate blog, for example, Slideshare can be used as a sharable publishing point for past presentations as well as presentations created specifically for Slideshare to explain the use of a software service or impact a legislative debate. Figure 12.4 shows the use of Scribd in sharing the owner's manual for a Sony Ericsson mobile phone, along with a Slideshare-based presentation on healthcare, authored by Dan Roam and C. Anthony Jones, M.D. This presentation won Slideshare's World's Best Presentation of 2009 contest: It has been viewed more than 200,000 times, and it has been embedded in more than 600 other online locations.

Figure 12.4 Scribd and Slideshare: Document Sharing

Why This Matters in Business

Social applications like YouTube, Slideshare, and Scribd offer simple ways to extend the reach of your existing content, and they provide a ready-for-sharing platform for your ideas, presentations, whitepapers, and similar content. YouTube, Slideshare, and Scribd support *embedding*—meaning *others* can place your presentation into *their* online site, with full credit automatically extended to you—and as such are excellent vehicles for a component of a thought leadership or similar program in addition to simply getting the word out about your brand, product, or service.

As you set out to plan and implement social applications, make note of the ways in which content publishing sites like YouTube can be used. You don't have to reinvent content uploading, video storage, and streaming, nor do you have to build your own community to distribute thought-leadership materials. Take advantage of existing social applications like YouTube, Scribd, and Slideshare. Save your money (and time) for creating the very specific social applications—such as Aircel's Facebook-based voicemail application or Penn State's "Outreach" employee collaboration and knowledge-sharing platform. And if you haven't already done so, develop and implement your social computing policies. Instead of reinventing what already exists, build off of it and use your resources to fill in the gaps or bring unique value to your customers and stakeholders.

Curation and Reputation Management

So far, the social applications and tools covered have centered on extending the functionality of social networks, facilitating member connections within them, and using these platforms to publish and share content. In a simplified view, these applications have involved or enabled (further) content consumption, setting up the content-sharing process that leads to collaboration. The next sections cover the applications that you can use, build, or subscribe to in order to move site participants to these higher levels of engagement, to contribute their own thoughts and ideas, and to facilitate collaboration between participants themselves and with your business.

The previously mentioned Facebook Like button is a simple implementation of a more sophisticated class of social applications that support curation, the basic act of voting something (or someone) up or down, of rating, reviewing, etc. *For nearly any type of content, in nearly any application, one of the "new realities" of the Social Web is that people generally expect to able to rate it, to review it, or to otherwise share it and indicate their own relative assessment of its worth in the process.* This is a subtle but very important insight: Where not too many years ago a web page or online advertisement was largely assumed to be a one-way message, the expectation now exists for the *option* to participate. Posting an article without providing an easy way to rate it or comment on it effectively screams to your audience, "We'll talk, you'll listen."

Curation applies to social interactions—liking someone's Wall post, for example—and to content itself. For these types of applications, there are as many choices for plug-ins and curation tools as there are platforms. In the general application of ratings and reviews as applied to *commerce* (the items being placed into a shopping basket), the near universal choice among online/offline retailers (for example, physical retailers with an online presence) is Bazaarvoice, and for good reason. Not only does Bazaarvoice offer a proven, easy-to-implement platform, they also provide a rich set of metrics that help their customers tune their online and offline commerce programs. In June of 2010, Bazaarvoice introduced SocialConnect, a platform capability that integrates customer's comments between social networks like Facebook and the brand's own websites. SocialConnect supports the Facebook "Like" functionality as well, all of which adds up to enhanced engagement, potential gains in sales, and importantly a reduction in product returns. Best of all, it's measurable.

Ratings and Reviews Made Easy

From the SaaS-based offering of Bazaarvoice to the DIY/Plug-in components of Js-Kit/Echo, Disqus, and Intense Debate, adding ratings and comments to your social sites is literally a click way.

http://www.bazaarvoice.com

http://aboutecho.com/

http://disqus.com/

http://www.intensedebate.com/

If your business objectives call for adding ratings and reviews to a noncommerce site (a thought leadership blog, for example), look in particular at the ready-to-use components from providers like JS-Kit/Echo, Disqus, Intense Debate, and others. Social technology providers offer plug-in modules for use in almost any application, as well as specific components for use with DIY favorites including Wordpress, ExpressionEngine, Drupal, Joomla, and other social software platforms. For nearly any online social platform, there is an associated curation solution: If the platform you are using does not support curation (again, most do), consider strongly moving to one that does.

Why This Matters in Business

Absent the ability to curate, the progression to higher forms of engagement is effectively stopped. In nearly any act of sharing, for example, there is at least an implied sense of rating: "If (I) didn't think some particular piece of content was worth (your) time then (I) would not have shared it with you." Beyond the polar "share/don't share" as a surrogate for curation, more finely grained ratings and reviews, testimonials and other forms of direct, overt curation provide participants in social business applications with a direct pathway to collaboration. Providing the ability for customers and stakeholders to publicly comment and share opinions is essential in drawing people into your social applications and thereby moving participants ultimately toward collaborative involvement in your business or organization.

Crowdsourcing

Crowdsourcing—turning to the Social Web and its participants en masse for input to specific challenges or needs—is a social activity that directly drives collaboration: Like ideation, covered separately in the next section, crowdsourcing not only makes "everyone a participant" but does so in a way that provides public credit for this participation. In doing so, crowdsourcing *encourages future participation* and build "stickiness" with regard to that social application.

That crowdsourcing applications have the ability to grow and develop an audience over time is a significant plus: Crowdsourcing applications can be used as a part of a larger social business program to not only pull participants in, but also to keep them involved over the longer term. This is especially helpful when your objectives include both the need to solve a problem or challenge that is suitable for crowdsourcing and also to simultaneously build and sustain a community or similar social structure in the context of your business.

In business applications, crowdsourcing often takes the basic form of publicly asking for ideas or suggestions against a specific business objective. Building on consumption and curation, crowdsourcing is a viable method for accomplishing specific types of tasks that *appropriately* involve your customers or stakeholders. The development of confidential or proprietary processes, for example, is clearly an internal matter, so in these cases consider an internal crowdsourcing application: Dell's "EmployeeStorm," or Ford's use of the Covisint ideation and collaboration platform across its suppliers network are solid examples.

What is suitable for crowdsourcing? Designing a logo, supporting a cause, providing answers to a question, and similar challenges where a diversity of ideas or talents contributing to the solution are all possibilities. Building on a *wiki*—a collaborative document framework that is itself an example of crowdsourcing—Anjali Ramachandran has compiled a list (see sidebar) of business-related crowdsourcing examples. Robert Scoble offers a similar list: Search the Web for "crowdsourcing examples"—and you'll find plenty more, ranging from design challenges to lawn mowing services to the top apps for mobile phones.

As an additional practical example of crowdsourcing, consider the Dachis Group's Social Software Wiki, shown in Figure 12.5 and referenced earlier in Chapter 4. The social software wiki is a dynamic list of social tool and platform providers that is maintained by people inside *and outside* of Dachis Group. The Dachis Group's Social Software Wiki is a "go to" place for businesses interested in learning more about the types of tools available. The collateral benefit—accruing to Dachis Group—is the combination of thought leadership and lead generation.

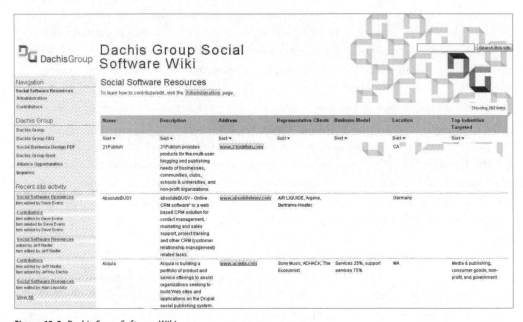

Figure 12.5 Dachis Group Software Wiki

Pepsi's "Refresh" project, referenced in detail in Chapter 7, "Five Essential Tips," along with Coke's "Fannovation," referenced in Chapter 4, are likewise examples of crowdsourcing. In both cases, the brands involved are appealing directly to those participating in these social applications to direct the efforts of the brands according to the business objectives as they relate the respective programs. In the case of Fannovation, the objective is the association of Coke with NCAA sports, accomplished by linking the brand with the crowdsourcing application built around the NCAA fan experience. In the case of Refresh, the business objective is linking the brand—Pepsi—with the causes of its participants through a corporate social responsibility program directed not through an internal committee but directly and transparently through a crowdsourcing application.

Why This Matters in Business

Directly involving customers, stakeholders, potential customers, and others in appropriate collaborative activities conveys to these participants a sense of ownership and control—a stake in the brand, so to speak—that is not possible in a read-only context. Not only does crowdsourcing offer the potential of better outcomes— as defined by those who *participate* in such programs—but also further moves these same participants "up" the engagement ladder, ultimately toward brand advocacy.

Ideation

Ideation—a derivative of crowdsourcing built around generating, organizing, and applying fresh ideas to a specific set of business or organizational challenges—is a form of collaboration that warrants special attention. Unlike the marketing-oriented applications of social technology, ideation often drives directly at the operations side of the business.

Ideation platforms are a powerful class of social applications that lend themselves to both business management (for example, process, product, or service innovation) and the quantitative assessment of outcomes. Customer-driven ideation—the specific practice of pulling customers into the business-design process—is important on at least two fronts. First, as noted it is a source of innovation and competitive differentiation. When you've been making the same thing for years and years, certain established practices begin to shape every decision. Getting some fresh eyes—and in particular the eyes of the people buying your product or service—applied to rethinking these accepted processes can be really beneficial.

Second, by opening up at least part of the responsibility for collective thinking outside of the current thought leaders, the entire pool of ideas is expanded, driving not only product and service-level change but also process change. Along with better "things" come better ways to make those things. These are exactly the results noted by Starbucks, Dell, Germany's Tchibo, and Intuit's Small Business community, all of whom are using the ideation platforms as ways to improve their respective businesses by forging collaborative relationships with their customers.

What really makes an ideation platform work is not the "idea solicitation" per se. After all, how many people really believe that anything actually happens as a result of an anonymous note dropped in a suggestion box? The problem with the classic suggestion box—anonymous or not—is that the suggestion *acceptance* process and any actual outcomes are not visible to the person making the suggestion. In other words, there is a lack of transparency, a lack of accountability (on both sides), and therefore a lack of significance. "Why bother?" is the most common response, and the opportunity to gather real feedback is lost.

Note that this loss of feedback happens inside and outside the business. In India, more so than any other place I've been, following nearly any service delivery in a restaurant, pub, airline flight, etc., I am offered a comment and feedback card. What happens with the data collected is not always clear, though this much I do know: I have received *personal* responses from Kingfisher Airlines following comments and suggestions that I have made using the in-flight comment cards—shown in Figure 12.6—that are *always* offered onboard Kingfisher flights. The result is that, at least when flying on Kingfisher, I *always* fill out the comment card and add a personal note if I have something additional to offer.

Figure 12.6 Kingfisher Airlines In-flight Survey Card

The Kingfisher example provides a key insight into the requirements for socially linking a business, its customers, and its employees: visibility and accountability. The ideation platforms, more than anything else, bring total transparency to the suggestion and feedback processes. Ideas are publicly submitted where they are visible to everyone (content creation and consumption). Next, they are voted up or down by participants at large (curation). Finally, the business stakeholders—a Product Manager, for example—selects from the highest ranked items and offers various versions for implementation, *which are then reviewed again by the participant community* (collaboration). The resulting innovations become additional bonding points for customers as credit is given back to them. The entire process is visible, and the outcome—the actual disposition of any given suggestion—is clear to everyone.

Note that ideation comes in many forms: In addition to purpose-built ideation platforms, small groups of personally invited participants can be very effective: As an example, consider the specifically invited LEGO fans who helped design LEGO Mindstorms, or impromptu feedback sessions with larger groups as a part of existing industry events. Ideation, while it is the formal name given to this new-style transparent suggestion process, does not itself have to be formal.

Why This Matters in Business

The result of extreme transparency around ideation and innovation, combined with a clear process that steps through the engagement ladder—consumption, curation, creation, collaboration—is that rough ideas are readily provided and turned into solid product and service enhancements with credit flowing right back to customers. *That is a powerful loop.* Check out the My Starbucks Idea site, or even better visit a store and look for "Inspired by You" No-Splash sticks, or reusable Via cups, or the recycling program piloted in the Seattle market, or my favorite—One-Click Wi-Fi—and see for yourself how the brand is reconnecting itself with its customers by listening and implementing the ideas they gain as a result.

In addition to the benefits of new ideas, there's also the practical reality of customers being *less likely* to complain when their own ideas are put into practice, something that extends beyond the idea itself. Because they see their own ideas reflected in the brand (or, equivalently, other ideas from the Ideation community to which they belong), actual credit is bestowed on these individuals and/or the community groups that drove the innovations.

Finally, when customers are also collaborators in the brand, product, or service, they are more likely to recommend it and defend it. They have ownership for the innovation, and they act accordingly. As they take "ownership" of the brand, instead of complaining they join *with* the brand and go to work on making their own experience better. See the Forrester Reports sidebar "Building Competitive Advantage" for more on how ideation combined with touchpoint analysis can be used to drive competitive wins.

Building Competitive Advantage

Tapping Social Web conversations can lead to an understanding of the places where your customers—or those of your competitors—feel shortchanged. Combining this information with touchpoint analysis can lead to insights into building long-term competitive advantage, or as Dr. Natalie Petouhoff put it in her Forrester Research report, "Businesses that understand and execute on the competitive potential of technology to innovate customer experiences can easily blow away their competition." For more, you can follow Natalie on Twitter (@drnatalie) and read her blog here:

http://drnatnews.com

Support Communities

If ideation is the "fresh thinking" business application built around the practice of crowdsourcing that delivers ideas into business and organizations, then support communities—again, these are social applications—are the analogous tools that deliver needed information and solutions back to customers, based on the combined principles of crowdsourcing and direct customer empowerment.

When Dell set out to rebuild its customer service program, Dell's internal teams noticed something: In its existing online (and offline) support environment, there existed *customers* who really wanted to see Dell succeed, customers who often had some of the answers that were needed in the course of fielding support issues. Inside Dell, something clicked: If there were customers who had specific knowledge that could benefit other customers, and if these same customers were also Dell advocates, could they be directly tapped to help Dell improve and scale its customer service program?

This is the thinking that in part gave rise to the now rebuilt Dell support communities, and it uncovered a basic fact that is common across many industries: Customers are often experts—at least as regards their use of a product or service—and as such are in collective possession of a sizeable body of knowledge. *Properly applied, this collective body of knowledge can radically change their experience as customers.* The problem is that this knowledge is largely unstructured, and it's distributed in ways that make actual bits of knowledge hard to spot when they are really needed.

Enter the support forum: Organized by topic, and driven by the allure of brand support and the elevation in personal status (a form of "social capital") for providing correct answers—in public, to other customers—support forums make it easy for customers to tap the larger collective, to self-serve and quickly solve their own problems. Customers can subscribe (typically via RSS) to specific topics—mobile applications or service issues for their particular laptop or TV set—and ask questions and/or offer answers as they are so moved. Over time, that extensive body of knowledge contained in the minds of customers is reexpressed in the support forum discussions where it is curated ("this solution works/this solution doesn't"), organized, and tagged so that it can be found and applied by those in need.

GetSatisfaction.com

GetSatisfaction is social application built for use by consumers and stakeholders as they share the problems and challenges they encounter with products and services so that they can collaboratively discover and spread solutions. As a business, GetSatisfaction.com can provide a social component to your overall customer support program.

http://getsatisfaction.com

Why This Matters in Business

Participant-driven support forums provide the possibility of both improved service and the actual determination of ROI. Service may be improved, for example, because the support forum is available 24x7, including all day on gift-giving holidays when the need for support typically spikes, and because the larger body of participants will often have more answers for more issues. Because customers themselves often possess a deep body of collective knowledge about how to fix, extend—think LEGO Mindstorms here, where enthusiasts hack the internal control programs and publish their findings for use by the Mindstorm community—and in general get more out the products and services they purchase, support forums become central to the redefined, collaborative customer experience.

Finally, an answer too on the ROI question: Support calls have a known cost. Support incidents that are fully resolved in a support forum represent a call-center cost *avoided*, leading directly to formal ROI measures and standards to which even the CFO will give two thumbs up.

Workplace Collaboration

What's been discussed so far has been done so largely from the perspective of a customer or external participant-facing social applications. In addition to externally-facing social applications, every one of the previous points can be applied internally, to encourage the same collaboration *inside* the workplace that customers exhibit *outside* the workplace. In other words, businesses and organizations can adopt social technologies for use internally—citing the same expected benefits—as their customers, suppliers, and business partners who operate on the outside of the business.

To this point, social media consultant and community manager Heidi Miller (see sidebar) noted in a recent blogpost:

> *"Research from McKinsey & Company and the Association for Information and Image Management (AIIM) shows that companies are seeing measurable benefits from the use of Enterprise 2.0 applications and technologies. Specific benefits include an increased ability to share ideas, more rapid access to knowledge experts, and a reduction in travel, operations, and communications costs."*

By "Enterprise 2.0" what is meant is the same types of collaboration inducing, information-sharing tools that define the Social Web. In Chapter 2, "The New Role of the Customer," and Chapter 3 I referenced Socialtext and similar Enterprise 2.0 workplace solutions. Enterprise 2.0 puts on every employee's desktop the basic social tools and applications that are in use across the Social Web: a profile, the ability to "friend" and "follow" colleagues and other employees, a set of wiki pages and similar collaborative tools, communications streams similar to Twitter (but built for secure use inside the business or organization), and more. What it all adds up to is an internal structure that is built around collaborative teams, whose members are able to quickly find and share the information they need to get their jobs done, including the (new) tasks of directly responding to and collaborating with customers, suppliers, partners, and stakeholders.

Heidi Miller

Social Media Manager at Spoken Communications and GotVoice, Heidi Miller is a consultant and community manager working with businesses and nonprofits interested in building and running communities and social applications. You can follow Heidi on Twitter (@heidimiller) and read more about her and her "Diary of a Shameless Self-Promoter" podcast here:

http://www.heidi-miller.com/

Enterprise 2.0 tools facilitate connections, inside and outside the organization, to channel the discovered conversations, support requests and collaborative input via workflow processes to the teams that are best able and most qualified to respond. These teams may well be virtual, which is to say that the sorts of teams supported by Enterprise 2.0 applications are very likely to be cross-functional rather than traditionally aligned. That is a powerful idea: If, as you've been reading this book, you've been wondering in the back of your mind how an organization actually *responds* to collaborative overtures from its customers, now you know: It does so by organizing itself in the same way as they would, using many of the same tools as its customers would use.

Yammer, as an example, is a popular tool, used *inside* over 70,000 businesses and organizations including AMD, Nationwide Insurance, Cisco, and social "coupon" service Groupon. Yammer is essentially a "private network" counterpart to Twitter. Employee collaboration tools like Socialcast, deployed on Sharepoint, or collaborative platforms like Socialtext and Lotus Connections from IBM are examples of the ready-to-use tools that you can apply *inside* your organization to keep pace with what is happening *outside*.

Again, Dell is an example of this exact process: Externally, Dell's IdeaStorm collects customer's ideas around specific topics. Inside Dell, EmployeeStorm provides employees with the same basic toolset to create and manage their own "idea storms" as they see process changes and similar structural or organizational tweaks that would improve Dell's overall ability to service its customers. Combined with its overall commitment to Enterprise 2.0 tools and practices, the result is an organization that is able to respond to and collaborate with its customers.

Why This Matters in Business

Ultimately, running a social business is about organizing around your customers and stakeholders, and involving them directly in your business in the evolution of your brand, product, or service. Very often, the most challenging aspect of this is getting your own organization to cooperate in a way that facilitates working *collaboratively* with your customers, and with other employees. Take a look at the Enterprise 2.0 tools that match your needs, budget, and current IT infrastructure. Align your organization internally to support the demands for collaboration, self-service, and faster response times by your customers. The motivating factor for pulling marketing and operations (and everyone else) together in support of your customers and what you are learning from them and about them on the Social Web is, after all, long-term growth and financial security.

Get Started: Plan a Social Application

Active, participative engagement means that your customers and stakeholders are "buying in" to your business or organization in ways that transcend any actual purchase or transaction. They are aligning around values—established, perhaps, through advertising but then proven out through social applications like "The Good Guide" and "My Ideas." In addition, your customers are offering their contributions freely as to how your brand, product, or service can evolve beyond the satisfaction of basic needs and wants, and further align with their personal values, passions, and causes.

Closing the loop, the higher levels of engagement possible through social applications can be tapped as drivers of your business objectives. (If not, what's the point of any of this?) What's required is a planning methodology that at once recognizes the connection between business objectives, customer or stakeholder desires and behaviors, and the cross-functional nature of your internal collaborative teams to whom the task of delivering talkworthy experiences will fall.

> ## Branded!
>
> Interested in the application of social technology to retail business? Pick up a copy of *Branded!* (Wiley, 2010) by Lori Shafer and Bernie Brennan. *Branded!* provides in-depth case studies of Starbucks, Zappos, Wet Seal, Macy's, 1-800-Flowers.com, JCPenney, Pizza Hut, and Best Buy. If you're all about retail, this book is all about you.

The Planning Process

The planning process leading to the successful deployment of a social application necessarily begins with business objectives. Along with them, it defines acts in service of customer and stakeholder behaviors. The planning process uses these same factors to shape the *organizational preparations* that precede the implementation of a social business effort.

> *Caveat: This book is focused on the application of social technologies in the support of business objectives. As such, the viewpoint is decidedly "external" to the firm or organization. Recognize that more advanced applications of social technology in business will often require significant attention and change with regard to internal processes that may exist. The short discussions of "workplace collaboration" and references throughout the book to Enterprise 2.0 and internal collaboration are intended to provide an entry point for your further study of this critical aspect of social business.*

This caveat is not as limiting as it may first seem: Beginning with social-media-based *marketing*—the use of Twitter and Facebook as "outbound" channels for example, or the implementation of a corporate blog and similar outreach activities—the required tools and skills can all be managed to great effect solely within the marketing and communications departments of nearly any organization. Social applications—and the *collaborative* processes associated with the higher forms of engagement—require a more developed strategy for customer involvement, and as a result an elevated response capability, and in general an organization that is able to act *holistically* rather than along functional lines (aka, silos).

> ## If This Seems Difficult...
>
> ...it's because it is. Where creating and managing a basic social presence requires deciding how and where you'll participate, implementing social technology in your business can force efforts "up to and including rebuilding your entire business." Articulating perfectly why social technology is becoming an imperative, Gartner's Michael Maoz put it this way: "It is more difficult to build a business case based on community participation, satisfaction, and loyalty metrics than on efficiency metrics, but loyalty and satisfaction are what drive revenue growth." For more from Gartner, see
>
> http://www.gartner.com
>
> or follow Gartner on Twitter (@gartner_inc).

This does not, however, mean that massive organizational change is required to make effective use of social applications. What it does mean is that you need to pay specific attention to the portions of the planning process shown in Figure 12.7, wherein your larger working teams are defined. Simply put, when customers begin talking to you, you need to be ready to respond. Among other things, this will directly raise implementation decisions as to how to best use an agency or other intermediary as a blogging or response partner: Customers expect a timely, genuine response and one way or another you'll need to staff for that.

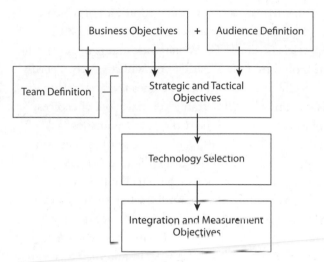

Figure 12.7 Planning Process

Business Objectives and Audience Definition

The application of social technology is best anchored in business objectives, for several reasons:

- Throughout your firm or organization, while people may not agree on the virtues of social media and collaborative technology applied in business, they do agree on business objectives. If not, you have larger challenges that need to be addressed prior to implementing social technology: If you've ever witnessed a family feud in a restaurant, you've got a good idea of what a business that doesn't know why it's in business looks like on the Social Web.

- By tying to business objectives, the likelihood is far greater that any social technology implementation will produce measurable, beneficial results. Experiments are fine—but then call them that and tie them to a business objective like "being seen by customers as innovative." Identifying an objective like the one in this example isn't a trick—it's a *start* down the "best practices" pathway of *always* tying to business objectives.

- Understanding your business objectives and organizing your social technology planning process around them ensures that your approach is "business challenge and expected contribution first, choice of technology second." Note that his bullet item has an ROI of its own. If you doubt it, add up the costs in your own organization of technology implementations that failed because the chosen technology never matched the business. Cost avoidance—in this case, not making that mistake with social technology—has a knowable and legitimate ROI.

On this last point, in the 12 chapters of this book there have been references to a large number of technology platforms, partners, and solution options, all of which do basically the same thing: They support the development of conversations and ultimately encourage collaboration between participants in a defined network that is important to your business. Starting with business objectives ensures that you will correctly identify the technology *best suited* to your specific situation. When it comes to social technology, given all of the unknowns, there is one thing that is certain: You have lots of choices.

Right along with business objectives, consider next the participants (or lack thereof) that you expect to interact with or learn from. While the use of ratings and reviews is nearly a given across *all* age groups within the United States, Canada, and Europe, this is not always the case in developing markets where technology adoption itself has a pronounced "age" factor. In India, for example, while there is a very important (and large) component of the marketplace that *is using social media* in substantially the same way as any other marketplace, the difference between those connected and those *not* connected to the Social Web is significant and therefore must be considered. When Godrej (a respected Indian manufacturer of a wide range of consumer goods) announced its plans for its online community called GoJiyo (meaning "Go Live"), Godrej patriarch Adi Godrej described the effort at a conference I spoke at in Bangalore as being intended to *reconnect* Godrej with the emerging Indian youth culture. The insight is this: Godrej has a much larger marketing effort supporting its entire marketplace. GoJiyo is *one component*, tied to a specific business objective and created for a specific (and growing) customer segment. That is smart thinking at Godrej, and it's the right approach anywhere.

Internal Readiness: Workflow and Your Response Plan

Coincident with your external social technology plan, begin early the process of identifying and recruiting colleagues across business units for the development of your cross-functional social technology team. Need help getting started? Go back to the identified business objectives: Who has profit responsibility associated with those objectives? Those are good people to start with. Add representatives from your legal team: They can help you create effective social media policies that are consistent with the culture of your firm or organization. HR and Finance/Compliance are part of this too: Sarbanes-Oxley, in the United States, and the unfettered employee use of social technology—including by employees when *outside* the workplace—can be a troublesome mix, to say the least. Customer Support is as well a great potential partner in your social technology planning process.

Workflow is an important factor in your implementation, so look for intelligence tools (for example, social media listening and analytics platforms) that offer robust workflow support. Refer back to the flowchart (see Chapter 1, "Social Media and Customer Engagement") developed by the U.S. Air Force for systematizing your response efforts. In particular, consider who will actually respond, and create estimates for the amount of time a response to a tweet or blog post will require and then build this into your cost and effort plan for the upcoming period. Attention to details like this will pay huge dividends as you ramp up collaborative social media programs.

Social Web Presence

With your business objectives and audience(s) defined, and a thought-through plan for how you'll manage conversations directly involving customers and stakeholders—for example, responding to tweets, managing and participating in comments on your blog, or keeping a Facebook business page updated—you can complete a basic specification for the kinds of activities you'd like to engage in.

Listening is always a great starting point (See Chapter 6, "Social Analytics, Metrics, and Measurement" and Chapter 7), especially for inputs to your planning process. You can estimate the workload associated with your response efforts by studying what is being said about your brand, product, or service in current social channels. Add to this your basic outreach channels—a business presence on Facebook, Twitter, YouTube, or Linked In—and then ask the bigger question: Given your business objectives, audience, and current social media programs, what needs to happen to move customers and stakeholders to higher levels of engagement, and what is it that you specifically want to accomplish as a result?

The higher forms of engagement—content creation and collaboration—are essential elements of contemporary marketing. Business objectives relating to the development of brand ambassadors and advocates, enhancing the value proposition of your product or service, inspiring and guiding innovation, and the improvement of brand image are parts of this planning process. Comcast used Twitter not only to address its critics' negative posts with regards to the firm's perceived lack of visible care for its customers, but also to call attention to its own positive adoption of social technology and improved response capability in a public forum so that (offsetting) credit would rightly flow to the brand as it worked to reestablish itself in the eyes of its customers.

Initiate Your Plan

There are some surprisingly easy-to-use tools that can help you get started building beyond social media marketing and head deeper into the realization of a socially connected business. Table 12.1 connects the broad classes of social applications to common tactical business objectives.

▶ **Table 12.1** Social Applications and Tactical Objectives

Social Application	Tactical Objective
Listening	Learning, conversation analysis, source (influencer) identification
Publishing and Sharing	Conversation initiation, knowledge transfer, content creation (engagement).
Support	Problem identification, product and service enhancements (innovation)
Ideation	Collaboration, innovation, competitive differentiation, brand loyalty
Community	Advocacy, brand loyalty, development of sustained conversations
Internal Applications (Enterprise 2.0)	Internal knowledge transfer, collaboration, response facilitation

Building on the basic planning process, and with your internal workflow and response programs defined, this first step up from social media marketing—toward the higher levels of customer engagement like content creation and collaboration—centers on connecting your online presence socially, into the communities and social activities of your customers and stakeholders. If you've taken—or are ready to take—the relatively hard steps of preparing your internal operations for the collaborative involvement of your customers, suppliers, partners, and stakeholders, you'll find that implementing and thereby benefiting from social tools is relatively easy by comparison.

Review and Hands-On

Chapter 12 tied together the concepts of higher-level forms of engagement—content creation and collaboration for the purpose of driving advocacy—with the basic best practices around the use of social objects and the social graph. The discussion of social applications centered around enabling the kinds of activities that lead to conversation, new ideas and innovations, and suggestions guiding your continuous improvement programs.

Review of the Main Points

Review the main points covered in Chapter 12, listed below. Consider these as you begin to develop your overall plan for the integration of social technology in your business or organization.

- Social applications tie social objects and social graphs together. Simply put, people connect with other people around the things that interest them in order to accomplish tasks that improve their lives.

- Internal readiness—the capability to respond and to address business challenges holistically rather than functionally—is an element of your social technology implementation effort.

- Social technology begins with business objectives. Don't let the technology guide your implementation, but instead let your objectives guide the technology selection.

In summary, unless you are ready to tackle Enterprise 2.0 (or you are working in an organization that is already doing this), the starting point in applying social technology to business is in *connecting your customers and stakeholders through collaborative processes* that link business objectives with the higher levels of engagement. You can speed this process within your own functional area with the assistance of informal cross-functional teams. Take the time to build support in other parts of your business, and you'll find the entire process significantly easier. The typical starting point—after the implementation of a listening program—is generally connecting your business presence into the existing social spaces where customers spend time, setting up an effective listen-understand-respond process. That is then followed by the implementation—as driven by your business objectives—of collaborative tools such as support and ideation platforms to drive a basic business norm of "Listen, Understand, Evolve."

Hands-On: Review These Resources

Review each of the following, and then take note of what you've learned or gained insight into: How can you apply (or specify the use of) these items in your own projects?

- Visit the tutorials* and resource pages for the APIs and social plug-ins associated with Facebook, MySpace, Twitter, Foursquare, Layar, and similar platforms. Gain an appropriate understanding of the intended uses of each, and then look at the examples of how they have been used to create differentiated social technology solutions.

  *If you are not a programmer, read the summaries and cases associated with each. The objective here is to obtain ideas on how these services and tools might be used.

- Visit the websites of Jive Software, Lithium Technologies, GetSatisfaction, Microsoft Sharepoint, Lotus Connections, SAS Institute, Socialcast, and Socialtext. Gain an appropriate understanding of the intended uses of each, and then look at the examples of how they have been used to create branded social applications.

- Visit Slideshare and search for presentations on "Social Applications." You'll find great resources for almost any type of business.

  http://www.slideshare.com

- Using Twitter, follow the conversations around global applications of social CRM. You'll find the conversations organized for you under the "#globalscrm" hashtag.

  http://twitter.com/#globalscrm

Hands-On: Apply What You've Learned

Apply what you've learned in this chapter through the following exercises:

1. Articulate your business objectives, and define your audience.

2. Given the discussion of social applications, develop an idea for a social application that serves your business objectives and fits with your audience behaviors. Write a complete brief around its deployment. Include within this your development efforts supporting a cross-functional internal team.

3. Tie this plan to your existing marketing and business efforts, and to your accepted business metrics. Define your guiding KPIs, and if appropriate the basis for establishing ROI.

Appendices

The appendices include definitions of key terms, lists of resources, and a summary of the hands-on material presented in the book.

Appendix A: **Terms and Definitions**
Appendix B: **Online References**
Appendix C: **Hands-On Exercises**

NOTE: You will find copies—including updates—as well as printable (PDF) versions of appendices at ReadThis.com.

Terms and Definitions

In any sufficiently precise study—and the application of social technology is certainly no exception—the need will arise for specific terms that enable concepts to be translated into actions. The definitions of many of the terms that are core to social technology are still evolving; however, within this book the following have been adopted and used consistently. More important than agreeing on specific terms—at a general level some of these are nearly interchangeable—is understanding the meaning of the following terms and then applying these meanings as you develop your social technology and business programs. Appendix A presents the key definitions used in this book, in the order in which they build on each other.

Chapter Contents

Social Object

> *Definition:* A Social Object *is some "thing" we* share *with others as part of our social media experience on the Social Web.*

GLENN ASSHETON-SMITH, 2009

What It Means and Why It Matters

A *social object* is something that is inherently talkworthy, something around which people will naturally congregate and converse. Social objects are an essential element in the implementation of social technology: Social objects are the anchor points for these efforts and as such are the "magnets" that hold a community together.

While it may seem like so much semantics, when viewed in the context of the way in which people are connected or to whom they are connected the social object provides the underlying rationale or motive for being connected at all. In short, without the social object, there is no "social."

Social Application

> *Definition:* A Social Application *is software that coordinates* group interaction *that is important to running your business.*

JOHN MILAN, ReadWriteWeb, October 12, 2006

What It Means and Why It Matters

The term *social application*—expressed in this definition in a decidedly business context—refers to the specific tools or functions available to participants in a social network—that is, the tools and functions that allow those participants to perform specific social tasks such as friending, connecting, sharing, and similar. The social application includes larger software components as well, up to and including entire social networks.

In this sense, it's the social application that "allows social activity to happen" in a distributed (e.g., virtual or online) context. In real life, the social application is the living room sofa, where conversation is facilitated, or the postal system, through which party invitations and RSVPs are exchanged. In online communities, this same type of social exchange is facilitated through software applications.

Social Graph

Definition: The Social Graph *is the* representation of our relationships. *In present day context, these graphs define our personal, family, or business communities on social networking websites.*

JEREMIAH OWYANG, 2007

What It Means and Why It Matters

The term *social graph* refers to the relationships between members of a social network and the details around the ways in which those members are connected. The social graph of an individual may extend beyond a single network, in which case this individual forms a link between adjacent networks.

The social graph is important in business applications. By understanding the ways in which participants in a social network are connected, it is possible to predict how information will be transmitted through that network, and therefore the social graph forms the basis for optimizing business participation in social networks.

Social Network

A social network *is a social structure made up of individuals (or organizations) which are tied (connected) by one or more specific types of interdependency, such as friendship, kinship, common interest, financial exchange, dislike, sexual relationships, or relationships of beliefs, knowledge, or prestige.*

WIKIPEDIA

What It Means and Why It Matters

The term *social network* refers to the collective facility—to Facebook or Orkut or the Intel Developer's Network and everyone contained within it.

In this sense, the term social network is a noun: it refers to a *place* (however virtual it may be) where social interactions—aka "social networking"—occurs.

Social CRM

"Social CRM is the company's response to the customer's control of the conversation."

PAUL GREENBERG, 2009

What It Means and Why It Matters

Social CRM is a key business concept. It combines the traditional practice of paying attention to customer data; however, it operates in the social rather than transactional context. Social CRM connects the conversations that circulate on the Social Web with the internal decisions and business processes that gave rise to those conversations.

If you are interested (highly recommended), Paul provides a more in-depth version of this same definition along with his logic here:

http://the56group.typepad.com/pgreenblog/2009/07/time-to-put-a-stake-in-the-ground-on-social-crm.html

You can find this quickly by searching for "paul greenberg definition of social crm" using Google.

Online References

B

The following resources are great starting points as you extend the material contained in this book to the current and still-evolving best practices and emerging thought leaders who are defining social business.

Thought Leaders and Best Practices

The following people—listed alphabetically—are noted within the book and are collected here to provide a convenient reference to their ongoing work and thinking. Take the time to check them out: Consider following them on Twitter and subscribing to their blogs and podcasts.

Susan Abbott

President and senior consultant and researcher at Abbott Research, Susan helps clients discover insights and develop response strategies that support their business. You can follow Susan on Twitter (@SusanAbbott) and read her blog here:

> http://www.customercrossroads.com/customercrossroads/

Glenn Assheton-Smith

Glenn describes himself as "very curious." That alone makes his work worth reading: He has an excellent set of blog posts on applying social media to business. You can follow Glenn on Twitter (@GlennAssh) and do read the set of posts he has created, beginning here:

> http://glennas.wordpress.com/2009/11/12/defining-requirements-for-social-web-site-design-part-1-overview/

Rohit Bhargava

Rohit is a founding member of Ogilvy's 360 Digital Influence and the author of *Personality Not Included* (McGraw-Hill, 2008). Rohit blogs actively and also teaches marketing at Georgetown University. You can follow Rohit on Twitter (@rohitbhargava) and read his blog here:

> http://rohitbhargava.typepad.com/

Jeanne Bliss

Author Jeanne Bliss (*I Love You More Than My Dog*, Portfolio Hardcover, 2009) is passionate about the processes that create amazing customer experiences. You can follow Jeanne on Twitter (@jeannebliss) and read more about Jeanne and her work here:

> http://customerbliss.com/

Krishna De

Dublin, Ireland based Krishna De blogs about social media and its application in business. You can follow Krishna on Twitter (@krishnade) and read more about Krishna and her work here:

> http://www.krishnade.com/blog/

Jyri Engeström

Sociologist, Jaiku cofounder, and now Google Product Manager, Jyri coined the term "social object" as a label for the things that people socialize around. You can follow Jyri on Twitter (@jyri) and read his blog here:

> http://www.zengestrom.com/blog

Gautam Ghosh

Gautam Ghosh is an HR professional with a passion for internal collaboration: You can follow Gautam on Twitter (@gautamghosh) and read his blog here:

> http://www.gautamblogs.com/

Nathan Gilliatt

Nathan Gilliatt, Principal, Social Target, provides thinking and services supporting the implementation of active listening and business strategy. You can follow Nathan on Twitter (@gilliat) and read Nathan's blog here:

> http://net-savvy.com/executive/

Paul Greenberg

Paul Greenberg is a recognized thought leader in Social CRM. You can follow Paul on Twitter (@pgreenbe) and read more from Paul here:

> http://the56group.typepad.com/

Rachel Happe and Jim Storer

Rachel Happe and Jim Storer are behind "The Community Roundtable," a great resource for community managers. You can follow Community Report principals Rachel Happe (@rhappe) and Jim Storer (@jstorer) on Twitter, and read more about their work here:

> http://community-roundtable.com/2010/01/the-value-of-community-management/

Jeff Jarvis

Well known partly for his work involving Dell, Jeff is a recognized leader in the application of social technology in business and customer service. You can follow Jeff on Twitter (@jeffjarvis) and read his blog here:

> http://www.buzzmachine.com/

Avinash Kaushik

Avinash is the author of *Web Analytics: An Hour a Day* (Sybex, 2007) and *Web Analytics 2.0* (Wiley, 2009). Avinash Kaushik publishes the blog "Occam's Razor." You can follow Avinash on Twitter (@avinashkaushik) and read his blog here:

> http://www.kaushik.net/

Peter Kim

Peter works with Austin's Dachis Group. Formerly with Forrester Research, Peter focuses on social technology and its impact on business. You can follow Peter on Twitter (@peterkim) and read his blog here:

http://www.beingpeterkim.com/

Esteban Kolsky

Esteban's work focuses on Social CRM and the application of social technology and the development of social business strategy. You can follow Esteban on Twitter (@ekolsky) and read his blog here:

http://www.estebankolsky.com/

J. D. Lasica

Writer J. D Lasica offers his views on social technology, cloud computing, and more. You can follow J. D. Lasica on Twitter (@jdlasica) and read his blog here:

http://www.socialmedia.biz/2009/05/08/free-ebook-identity-in-the-age-of-cloud-computing/

Frank Leistner

Frank Leistner, author of *Mastering Organizational Knowledge Flow* (Wiley, 2010) is SAS Institutes' Chief Knowledge Officer. You can follow Frank on Twitter (@kmjuggler).

Brent Leary

Brent Leary is co-founder and partner of CRM Essentials LLC, a CRM consulting/advisory firm focused on small and mid-size enterprises. You can follow Brent on Twitter (@BrentLeary) and read his blog here:

http://BrentLeary.com

Charlene Li

Charlene is the author of Open Leadership and coauthor of Groundswell; she is the founder of Altimeter Group and a former analyst with Forrester Research. You can follow Charlene on Twitter (@charleneli) and read her blog here:

http://www.charleneli.com/blog/

Ross Mayfield

Ross Mayfield is the founder and Chairman of Socialtext. You can follow Ross on Twitter (@ross) and read his blog here:

http://ross.typepad.com/

Heidi Miller

Social Media Manager at Spoken Communications and GotVoice, Heidi is a consultant and community manager working with businesses and nonprofits interested in building and running communities and social applications. You can follow Heidi on Twitter (@heidimiller) and read more about Heidi and her "Diary of a Shameless Self-Promoter" podcast here:

http://www.heidi-miller.com/

Gaurav Mishra

Gaurav Mishra is the CEO of 2020 Social, the firm I work with in India. You can follow Gaurav on Twitter (@Gauravonomics) and read more from him at his blog:

http://www.gauravonomics.com

Kate Niederhoffer

Dachis Group principal Kate Niederhoffer offers her perspective on social technology and its measurement. You can follow Kate on Twitter (@katenieder) and read her blog here:

http://socialabacus.blogspot.com/

Nick O'Neill

Writer and Industry Analyst Nick O'Neill publishes "Social Times," a collection of reviews and commentary on a variety of social media topics including the use of analytics. You can follow Social Times on Twitter (@allnick) and you'll find the Social Times online site here:

http://www.socialtimes.com/about/

Jeremiah Owyang

Altimeter's Jeremiah Owyang is a recognized expert in the tools, technologies, and techniques that are essential when applying social concepts to business. You can follow Jeremiah on Twitter (@jowyang) and read his blog here:

http://www.web-strategist.com/blog/

K. D. Paine

Tired of hearing "The problem with social media is that you can't measure it?" Encourage people within your organization to look at K. D. Paine's "PR Measurement Blog." You can follow Katie on Twitter (@kdpaine) and read more from her here:

http://kdpaine.blogs.com/

DJ Patil

DJ Patil is Chief Scientist at LinkedIn. You can follow DJ on Twitter (@dpatil), where he often references topics and concepts related to the social graph.

Dr. Natalie Petouhoff

Consultant and Speaker Dr. Natalie Petouhoff offers her views on the potential of social technology applied to business. You can follow Natalie on Twitter (@drnatalie) and read her blog here:

> http://drnatnews.com

Kaushal Sarda

Kaushal Sarda leads the enterprise applications and products practice at 2020Social in New Delhi. You can follow Kaushal on Twitter (@ksarda) and read his blog here:

> http://kaushalsarda.com

Susan Scrupski

Susan Scrupski is the founder of "The 2.0 Adoption Council," a professional organization for large enterprise organizations interested in learning about and sharing best practices around the use of social technologies. You can follow Susan on Twitter (@itsinsider) and read more from Susan and the The 2.0 Adoption Council here:

> http://itsinsider.com/
> http://www.20adoptioncouncil.com/

Kristina Sedereviciute

Currently a Master's student at Århus Universitet in Denmark, Kristina is a former project manager. You can follow Kristina on Twitter (@kristtina).

Filberto Selvas

Filberto Selvas is the Product Director at Crowdfactory, a provider of social networking tools. You can follow Filberto on Twitter (@filbertosilvas) and read his Social CRM blog here:

> http://www.socialcrm.net/

Shashi Tharoor

If you are looking for an example of the value of social media in advancing intellectual points of view that impact business and government, take a look at the works of Shashi Tharoor, a former Indian Minister of State for External Affairs. You can follow Shashi Tharoor on Twitter (@shashitharoor) and learn more about him here:

> http://en.wikipedia.org/wiki/Shashi_Tharoor

Ted Shelton

Ted Shelton is CEO of The Conversation Group, a social media and technology firm. You can follow Ted on Twitter (@tshelton) and read his blog here:

tedshelton.blogspot.com/

Social Business Resources

Presented in the following section—more or less in the order that you will encounter or need these resources if you're working through the social business planning process for the first time—are a set of resources that will help shape your thinking around the application of social technology to your business.

Reading and Planning

Before beginning, scan these resources. There's no sense stumbling where someone else has already tripped up, and was then thoughtful enough to reflect on it and write up a better practice. Move faster and get further by learning from those who have been through this already. As you gain your own experiences, consider sharing them within the social business community.

Social Capital

Author and thought leader Brian Solis offers a clear, concise view on "social capital" and its importance in business. You can follow Brian on Twitter (@briansolis) and read his post on social capital here:

http://www.briansolis.com/2010/03/social-capital-the-currency-of-digital-citizens/

A Social Graph Primer

ReadWriteWeb author Alex Iskold published a nice article in 2007 that outlines the basic concepts underlying the social graph and its use in business. You'll find the post here:

http://www.readwriteweb.com/archives/social_graph_concepts_and_issues.php

Social CRM Use Cases

Altimeter's Ray Wang (@rwang0) and Jeremiah Owyang have produced a useful summary and "next steps" guide that is very helpful when sorting out your Social CRM strategy. The guide is useful as a both a learning document for your team and as a guide to choosing Social CRM solution paths. You will find the guide here:

http://bit.ly/socialcrmpaper/

Social Networking for Business

For more on the direct application of social networking and social computing for business, consider reading Rawn Shah's *Social Networking for Business* (Wharton, 2010). Follow Rawn on Twitter: @Rawn.

> http://www.onlinecommunityreport.com/archives/599-Online-Community-Expert-Interview-Rawn-Shaw,-IBM.html

Social Computing Policies

IBM offers its social computing policies for review. Some time spent with these is highly recommended.

> http://www.ibm.com/blogs/zz/en/guidelines.html

Social Computing Policy: Ready-Made Examples

Altimeter has compiled a representative listing of social computing policies, including large and small businesses as well as nonprofit and service organizations. You will find the listing by searching "social computing policy examples" or by visiting the following URL:

> http://wiki.altimetergroup.com/page/Social+Media+Policies

Choosing a Social Object

Altimeter's Jeremiah Owyang offers a handy reference when considering various social objects, including social objects built around brands, and products or services. You'll find the chart here:

> http://www.web-strategist.com/blog/2010/04/08/matrix-how-to-choose-social-media-programs-by-brand-lifestyle-product-or-location/

Knowledge Assimilation

Ross Mayfield, founder and CEO of Socialtext, talks in detail about the use of collaborative tools inside businesses: You can review his post here:

> http://ross.typepad.com/blog/2009/08/crm-iceberg.html

Implementing Social Technology

As you begin to plan and implement your social business programs, the following resources will prove valuable.

Social Media Today

A highly recommended resource for marketers and similar business professionals interested in B2B application of social media and social technology is "Social Media Today," cofounded by Jerry Bowles and Robin Carey. Social Media Today includes contributions by literally hundreds of the best social media/ B2B thinkers and practitioners.

http://socialmediatoday.com/

Social Source Commons: Nonprofit Resources

A current listing of collaboration tools—with a particular relevance for nonprofit organizations—is maintained at the Social Source Commons:

http://socialsourcecommons.org/tag/collaboration

The Dachis Group's Software Service Wiki

Headquartered in Austin, TX, the Dachis Group maintains a wiki-based listing of social software. It's a great resource. You'll find it here:

http://softwarewiki.dachisgroup.com/

Responding to Social Media Mentions

Wondering how to handle a negative mention? The United States Air Force and Altimeter developed a flow chart that shows you what to do. You'll find the chart here:

http://www.web-strategist.com/blog/2008/12/31/diagram-how-the-air-force-response-to-blogs/

Measuring Relative Participation

Bud Caddell's insightful measurement technique for assessing the degree to which a community is influenced versus peer led is a great thought-starter. You can follow Bud on Twitter (@Bud_Caddell) and read about his measurement techniques here:

http://www.seomoz.org/ugc/measuring-participation-inequality-in-social-networks

International Network for Social Network Analysis

The International Network for Social Network Analysis (INSNA) offers resources for researchers interested in social network planning and performance. INSNA hosts the annual Sunbelt conference, centered on social network use and analysis.

http://www.insna.org/

Ratings and Reviews Made Easy

From the SaaS-based offering of Bazaarvoice to the DIY/Plug-in components of Js-Kit/Echo, Disqus, and Intense Debate, adding ratings and comments to your social sites is literally a click way.

http://www.bazaarvoice.com

http://aboutecho.com/

http://disqus.com/

http://www.intensedebate.com/

34 Ways to Use YouTube for Business

B2B social media professional Meryl Evans (no relation) offers this list of some of the many ways that YouTube can be used as a part of a social media program in business.

http://webworkerdaily.com/2009/07/28/34-ways-to-use-youtube-for-business/

Facebook Marketing: An Hour a Day

If you're interested in learning more about how you can use Facebook in business, check out the newest edition of Chris Treadaway and Mari Smith's *Facebook Marketing: An Hour a Day* (Sybex, 2010). You can follow Chris (@ctreada) and Mari (@marismith) on Twitter as well.

Community Moderation: Best Practices

Jake McKee, Chief Strategy Officer at Ant's Eye View (as well as the technical editor for this book) offers a great interview on moderation "Best Practices." You can follow Jake on Twitter (@jakemckee)

http://www.communityguy.com/

In addition to Jake's blog, The Community Roundtable is a great resource for community managers: You can follow Community Report principals Rachel Happe (@rhappe) and Jim Storer (@jstorer) on Twitter and read the Community Roundtable blog here:

http://community-roundtable.com/blog/

Technical Resources

Finally, if you want to roll up your sleeves and try some of this yourself, the following will get you started. You'll actually be amazed at how easy it is to add basic social capabilities to nearly any existing site. It makes you wonder why *everyone* isn't doing this already.

Social Graph APIs

If you are interested in exploring the API (the programming extensions that can "open up" the social graph for your social applications), you may want to visit the Google and Facebook API reference sites. There are others, of course, but these will provide a useful starting point for those so inclined.

http://code.google.com/apis/socialgraph/
http://developers.facebook.com/docs/api

Facebook: Open Graph

Facebook offers easy access to tools that connect content across social networks with the members of Facebook. For more on these tools, and to quickly generate the code required to connect your own content into the Facebook social network, see the Facebook Developer's page:

http://developers.facebook.com/plugins

Social CRM and the Social Web "Bill of Rights"

Joseph Smarr, Marc Cantor, Michael Arrington, and Robert Scoble offered a point-of-view on the use of personal data—not just identity, but also their activity streams ("Bob just uploaded a photo...") and the relationships they form (part of their personal social graph). The Social Web Bill of Rights is worth reviewing as you think through your Social CRM strategy. You can read more about the Social Web Bill of Rights here:

http://opensocialweb.org/2007/09/05/bill-of-rights/

The Social Web Bill of Privacy Rights

Beginning with the right to make an informed choice, the Electronic Frontier Foundation has suggested starting a Bill of Privacy Rights for people using social networking services.

http://www.eff.org/deeplinks/2010/05/bill-privacy-rights-social-network-users

Hands-On Exercises

As my college physics professor often declared, "You won't learn if you don't do the homework." Appendix C contains all of the review and applied exercises recommended throughout the book.

Note: You will find a printable (PDF) version of Appendix C at ReadThis.com.

Chapter 1: Social Media and Customer Engagement

Review each of the following and connect them with the objectives of your business or organization:

- Starbucks' "My Starbucks Idea" ideation application:

  http://mystarbucksidea.com/

- The blog of Gaurav Mishra, on the topic of social business:

  http://www.gauravonomics.com

- The blog of Peter Kim, on the topic of social business:

  http://www.beingpeterkim.com/

Apply what you've learned through the following exercises:

1. Define the basic properties, objectives, and outcomes of a collaborative application that connects your customers to your business and to your employees.
2. Define an internal application that connects employees and enables efficient resolution of customer-generated ideas.
3. Map out your own customer engagement process and compare it with the engagement process defined in this chapter.

Chapter 2: The New Role of the Customer

Review each of the following and connect them with the objectives of your business or organization:

Paul Greenberg's "Social CRM Comes of Age"

http://www.oracle.com/ocom/groups/public/@ocompublic/documents/
webcontent/036062.pdf

Jeremiah Owyang's listing of Social CRM tools

http://www.web-strategist.com/blog/2009/12/08/list-of-companies-providing-
social-crm/

The 2009 Edelman Trust Barometer

http://www.edelman.com/trust/2009/

Apply what you've learned through the following exercises:

1. Define your ideal Social CRM platform: What are your business objectives, and who are you looking to create relationships with? How would your current customers fit into this, and how might they participate in your business or organization?

2. Integrate step 1 into your current CRM and product design programs. Who will participate in the various initiatives that define your plan? What is the role that you see customers playing?

3. Identify the key stakeholders in the departments you will need to work with in order to implement the *broad types* of issues you are likely to encounter.

Chapter 3: Build a Social Business

Review each of the following and connect them with the objectives of your business or organization:

- Arrange a meeting with your CIO or IT leadership to review the social capabilities of your current intranet or similar internal information sharing tools.

- Create an inventory of your current social media programs. List out home bases, outposts, and passports (see sidebar earlier in this chapter for definitions of each) and then define the metrics and success measures for each.

- Meet with the leadership of your customer service and product design teams, and meet with legal and HR to review the requirements or concerns with regard to connecting employees in a more collaborative manner, or engaging more fully on the Social Web.

Apply what you've learned through the following exercises:

1. Define the basic properties, objectives, and outcomes of a collaborative application that connects your customers to your business and to your employees.

2. Explore the available internal (enterprise) applications that connect employees with each other and with customers and thereby enable efficient response and resolution with regard to customer-generated ideas or challenges.

3. Draw a map of how external information about a selected product or service currently flows through your business or organization and how it might (better) flow if internal collaboration were the norm or more fully developed and practiced.

Chapter 4: The Social Business Ecosystem

Review each of the following and connect them with the objectives of your business or organization:

- Brand outposts like Coca-Cola's Facebook page are viable alternatives to one-off microsites and branded communities:

  http://www.facebook.com/cocacola

- Atari's Tweet in Klingon is an example of a social application:

  http://tweetinklingon.com/

- Clearly articulated policies create a strong platform for collaboration and the adoption of social computing:

  http://www.ibm.com/blogs/zz/en/guidelines.html

Apply what you've learned through the following exercises:

1. If you use Twitter or Linked In, bring your personal profile up to 100 percent completion.

2. If your office or organization has a profile-driven knowledge-sharing application, repeat exercise 1 for your profile.

3. List your favorite social communities, and describe an application that your business or organization might offer within that community. *Connect it to your business objectives.*

Chapter 5: Social Technology and Business Decisions

Review each of the following and connect them with the objectives of your business or organization:

- Spend time reading Esteban Kolsky's blog (http://www.estebankolsky.com/), and in particular search for and read the entries on "analytics engines." As a hands-on exercise, create a plan for integrating social analytics into your *operational* (not marketing) processes.

- Review Kaushal Sarda's 2010 InterOp Mumbai presentation on slideshare. The easiest way to find this is to visit slideshare (http://www.slideshare.com) and search for "Kaushal Sarda." In the InterOp presentation, look at the product innovation cycle and map this onto your business and identify the specific areas or functions within your business that contribute to innovation. Think about the Bengaluru International Airport example as you do this. How can you "design in" the experiences you want your customers or stakeholders to talk about?

- Visit Socialtext (http://www.socialtext.com) and watch the short videos that show you how this product is used inside an organization. As a hands-on exercise, use that information combined with visits to additional collaboration tools to create and present to your team a survey of enterprise collaboration tools, tying them to your business.

Apply what you've learned through the following exercises:

- Visit with the IT, Marketing, or Operations teams that use your existing CRM data. Explore ways of incorporating social data into these processes, and connecting that information to your business or organization.

- Building on your exercises in Chapter 1, define one or more internal collaboration points based on what you discovered in exercise 1, above.
- Building on your exercises in Chapters 2 and 3, create a workflow path for social data (e.g., conversations) that carries this information to the points inside your organization that can act on it. Include a method for tracking results.

Chapter 6: Social Analytics, Metrics, and Measurement

Review each of the following and connect them with the objectives of your business or organization:

Avinash Kaushik's blog, "Occam's Razor"

http://www.kaushik.net/

Nick O'Neill's "Social Times"

http://www.socialtimes.com/about/

The Dachis Group's Kate Niedehoffer

http://www.dachisgroup.com/author/kate/

Apply what you've learned through the following exercises:

1. Identify the primary social, web, and business analytics that matter to you.
2. Run a correlation analysis on them, and then investigate why certain metrics are correlated and how this correlation might be used to further your understanding of how the Social Web is impacting your business or organization.
3. Develop a basic dashboard or incorporate one or two new business fundamentals that you identify through the above into your current business scorecard.

Chapter 7: Five Essential Tips

Review each of the following and connect them with the objectives of your business or organization:

Threadless

http://www.threadless.com

Foursquare (You will need a Foursquare and a GPS-capable phone or similar hand-held device for this.)

http://foursquare.com

HARO

http://www.helpareporter.com

Apply what you've learned through the following exercises:

1. Prepare a short presentation using Threadless or Dell's Digital Nomad project as the subject, or any other collaborative business design application that you choose. Talk to your team about what makes the application work and how social technology has been built into the business.

2. Looking at your own firm or organization, list three ways that your customers could collaborate directly with each other to improve some aspect of your product or service.

3. Develop an outline for a business plan based on exercise 2 that involves multiple departments or functions to implement. Win the support of those people.

Chapter 8: Engagement on the Social Web

Review each of the following and connect them with the objectives of your business or organization:

- The "Engagement db" report from Altimeter (use Google to search for "engagement db"). Try the self-ranking; where does your firm or organization fit?

  http://engagementdb.com

- The whitepapers in Jive Software's resources library, in particular "Social Business Software Adoption Strategies." Look for the similar resources offered by other social business software firms, and begin building a library.

  http://www.jivesoftware.com/resources

Apply what you've learned through the following exercises:

1. Make a note of every recommendation you give or receive over the next week. Rank them according to the degree of enthusiasm on the part of the recommender.

2. Review your own engagement programs, and carefully examine how you are measuring or evaluating engagement, and from whose perspective you are defining "engagement."

3. Assuming that you have an appropriate social media policy for employee use in place, design a plan for an ideation, support, or discussion platform that will actively solicit customer-led conversations about your firm or organization, or about your brand, product, or service.

   NOTE: *If you do not have a social media and technology use policy in place, now would be an excellent time to create and implement one.*

Chapter 9: Social CRM

Apply what you've learned through the following exercises:

1. Review the Sun Microsystems, SAS Institute, and IBM/Lotus products and associated case studies: While these are all large organizations, the principles of Social CRM are sufficiently well demonstrated that they can be applied to almost any business.

2. Review the general toolsets in the tables in this chapter, and take note of the order in which specific tools or technologies are applied. As with social-media-based marketing in general, the implementation process begins *not* with technology but rather with business objectives and strategy.

Apply what you've learned through the following exercises:

1. If you haven't done so already, look at the social computing policy examples at the Altimeter site. In addition, visit the sites of firms or organizations like yours to see what they have done. Imitation—followed with an in-house legal review—is the sincerest form of...getting there faster!

2. Work with your IT or other applicable department to design a pilot program for internal collaboration. The exercise will challenge your organization, so choose a small project and recruit enthusiastic volunteers.

3. After completing the first two exercises, prepare and deliver a presentation to your colleagues (or customers, if you are a consulting firm or agency) on Social CRM.

Chapter 10: Social Objects

Review each of the following and connect them with the objectives of your business or organization:

1. Look at the work of Jyri Engeström, beginning with this video (http://vimeo.com/4071624) and his blog (www.zengestrom.com/blog).

2. Make a list of the social sites you are currently a member of (all of them). Connect each with the social object around which it is built, and then consider how your connection to this object drives (or fails to drive) your participation in that site.

3. Visit your own brand or organization website and brand outposts. Is a social object readily identifiable? Does this social object connect your audience to your business?

Apply what you've learned through the following exercises:

1. Create an inventory of communities applicable to your brand, product, or service. Once you've compiled it, join a manageable set and understand the interest areas and social norms for each. Develop a plan for how you might integrate your own activities into these communities.

    NOTE: Always practice full disclosure, and refrain from "test driving" communities.

2. Using Google, search for a lifestyle, passion, or cause that you are interested in. Note the documents that come back, and review a subset of them. Then do the same content search again but this time select only "image" results. Click into the images, and note the number of images that lead you to a social site of some type.

3. Visit slideshare (`http://slideshare.net`) and search for "Gautam Ghosh Talent Communities." Gautam provides a nice overview of the ways in which social objects and communities can be used within the HR organization.

4. Define three core social objects for your business or organization around which you could build or enhance your social presence. Create a touchpoint map to help guide your selection.

Chapter 11: The Social Graph

Review each of the following and connect them with the objectives of your business or organization:

-   Facebook Open Graph Plug-ins for use in social-media-based marketing:
    `http://developers.facebook.com/plugins`

-   Open Social and its applications in business: (See: "Get Started")
    `http://wiki.opensocial.org`

-   The use of the XFN Protocol in business:
    `http://gmpg.org/xfn/`

-   Tools, papers, and resources available through membership in the INSNA and the larger discussion of social network analysis:
    `http://www.insna.org/`

Apply what you've learned through the following exercises:

1. Draw out your first-degree network in your office, and then do the same in some personal aspect of your life, a civic organization for example. Who is in both networks? What content is shared between these networks?

2. Look at your friends in some of the social networks you belong to: How many of these friends or people you follow are people you knew prior to joining versus

the number you met after joining. How were those you met after joining referred or suggested?

3. Develop a set of specific metrics for your social business applications that involve the social graph. Create a regular report, and track these measures over time.

Chapter 12: Social Applications

Review each of the following and connect them with the objectives of your business or organization:

- Visit the tutorials* and resource pages for the APIs and social plug-ins associated with Facebook, MySpace, Twitter, Foursquare, Layar, and similar platforms. Gain an appropriate understanding of the intended uses of each, and then look at the examples of how they have been used to create differentiated social technology solutions.

  *If you are not a programmer, read the summaries and cases associated with each. The objective here is to obtain ideas on how these services and tools might be used.

- Visit the websites of Jive Software, Lithium Technologies, GetSatisfaction, Microsoft Sharepoint, Lotus Connections, SAS Institute, Socialcast, and Socialtext. Gain an appropriate understanding of the intended uses of each, and then look at the examples of how they have been used to create branded social applications.

- Visit slideshare and search for presentations on "Social Applications." You'll find great resources for almost any type of business.

  http://www.slideshare.com

- Using Twitter, follow the conversations around global applications of social CRM. You'll find the conversations organized for you under the "#globalscrm" hashtag.

  http://twitter.com/#globalscrm

Apply what you've learned through the following exercises:

1. Articulate your business objectives, and define your audience.

2. Given the discussion of social applications, develop an idea for a social application that serves your business objectives and fits with your audience behaviors. Write a complete brief around its deployment. Include within this your development efforts supporting a cross-functional internal team.

3. Tie this plan to your existing marketing and business efforts, and to your accepted business metrics. Define your guiding KPIs, and if appropriate the basis for establishing ROI.

Index